Companion to the European Union

Companion to the European Union provides information and analysis on the key developments and policies of the EU. Divided into five sections, particular features include:

- An overview that sets out the context of European integration
- A detailed section on all the Institutions of the EU, from the European Commission and the European Parliament to the European Ombudsman and European Central Bank
- Analysis of the major policies of the EU, from Economic and Monetary Union to Trade Policy
- An extensive glossary which is aided by the provision of a synoptic index and cross referencing
- A detailed chronology which reviews the major stages in the formation of the EU

The book also includes features such as biographies of key personalities, maps, a detailed guide to further reading, and 35 tables that provide accessible information relating to the EU. The *Companion to the European Union* provides a comprehensive and timely guide to the European Union since 1945 and is essential reading for students of European and International Politics.

Alasdair Blair is Jean Monnet Professor of International Relations at Coventry University. His research interests are focused on British foreign policy and European integration. Recent publications include *The European Union since 1945* (Longman, 2005), *Saving the Pound? Britain's Road to Monetary Union* (Prentice Hall, 2002) and, co-authored with Anthony Forster, *The Making of Britain's European Foreign Policy* (Longman, 2002).

Politics/Current Affairs

Companion to the European Union

Alasdair Blair

Routledge
Taylor & Francis Group

LONDON AND NEW YORK

First published 2006
by Routledge
2 Park Square, Milton Park, Abingdon, Oxon OX14 4RN

Simultaneously published in the USA and Canada by Routledge 270
Madison Avenue, New York, NY 10016, USA

Routledge is an imprint of the Taylor & Francis Group
© 2006 Alasdair Blair

Typeset in Garamond by
Prepress Projects Ltd, Perth, UK
Printed and bound in Great Britain by
TJ International, Padstow, Cornwall

British Library Cataloguing in Publication Data
A catalogue record for this book is available from the British Library

Library of Congress Cataloging in Publication Data
A catalog record for this book has been requested

ISBN 10: 0–415–35896–5 (hbk)
ISBN 10: 0–415–35897–3 (pbk)
ISBN 10: 0–203–56744–7 (ebk)

ISBN 13: 978–0–415–35896–5 (hbk)
ISBN 13: 978–0–415–35897–2 (pbk)
ISBN 13: 978–0–203–56744–9 (ebk)

For my brother

Contents

Illustrations

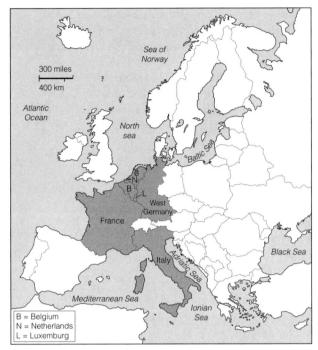

Map 1 The Six member states (1957)

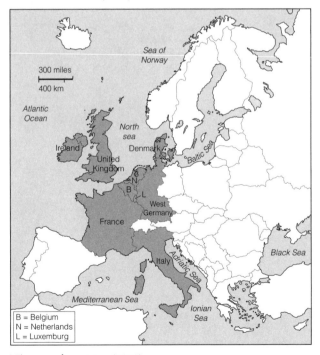

Map 2 The Nine member states (1973)

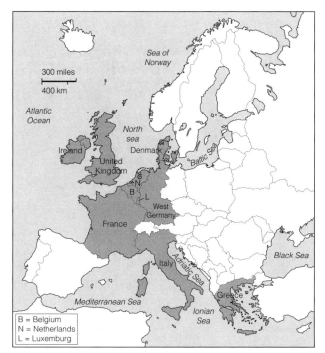

Map 3 The Ten member states (1981)

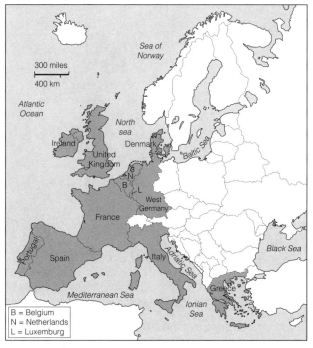

Map 4 The Twelve member states (1986)

Map 5 The Fifteen member states (1995)

Map 6 The Twenty-Five member states and applicant countries (2004)

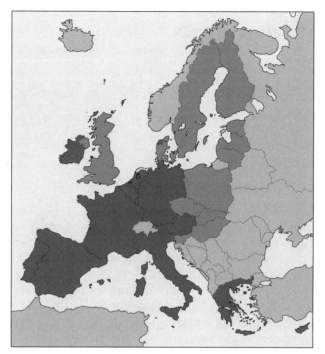

Map 7 The 12 member states of the eurozone

Acknowledgements

This *Companion* is intended to provide, in a concise and accessible format, the essential facts on European integration. A publication such as this one draws heavily on the work of others and the considerable expansion in the range of materials available to study the EU has eased my task in completing this book. In my writing of this book a great many friends and colleagues have shared their thoughts with me and in one way or the other have had an impact on the outcome. I would like to record my gratitude to the support that I have received from colleagues at Coventry University, namely Steven Curtis, Jacques Gallagher, Neil Forbes, Brian Hocking, Alex Kazamias, Ken Matthews, Caroline Page and Alex Thomson. On the production side, I must express my thanks to the editorial staff at Routledge, and in particular to Craig Fowlie for commissioning this book. Finally, and not least, my thanks and love to Katherine for her support, and to our son William, who managed to put everything into perspective.

Alasdair Blair, Thornton, December 2005

Abbreviations

ACP	African, Caribbean and Pacific
ACUSE	Action Committee for the United States of Europe
AFSJ	Area of Freedom, Security and Justice
ASEAN	Association of South East Asian Nations
Benelux	Benelux Economic Union (Belgium, the Netherlands and Luxembourg)
BIS	Bank for International Settlements
BLEU	Belgo-Luxembourg Economic Union
CAP	Common Agricultural Policy
CBI	Confederation of British Industry
CDU	Christian Democratic Union
CEES	central and eastern European states
CEN	European Committee for Standardization
Cenelec	European Committee for Electrotechnical Standardization
CERN	European Organization for Nuclear Research
CFSP	Common Foreign and Security Policy
CJTF	Combined Joint Task Force
CMEA	Council for Mutual Economic Assistance
COMETT	Community Action Programme for Education and Training for Technology: EU high technology cooperation
CoE	Council of Europe
CoR	Committee of the Regions
Coreper	Committee of Permanent Representatives: member states' ambassadors to the EC: Coreper I consists of Deputy Permanent Representatives, while Coreper II consists of Permanent Representatives
COREU	Telex Network among EPC 'correspondents Européens' (European correspondents)
COST	Committee on European Cooperation in the Field of Scientific and Technical Research

CSCE	Conference on Security and Cooperation in Europe (now OSCE)
DG	Directorate General: name for departments within the Commission
EAGGF	European Agricultural Guidance and Guarantee Fund
EBRD	European Bank for Reconstruction and Development
ECB	European Central Bank
ECHO	European Community Humanitarian Office
ECHR	European Court of Human Rights
ECIP	European Community Investment Partners
ECJ	European Court of Justice
Ecofin	Council of Economic and Financial Ministers
ECSC	European Coal and Steel Community
ECU	European Currency Unit
EDC	European Defence Community
EEA	European Economic Area
EES	European Economic Space: original term for EU–EFTA negotiations
EFTA	European Free Trade Association
EIB	European Investment Bank
EIF	European Investment Fund
EMC	European Military Committee
EMCF	European Monetary Co-operation Fund
EMI	European Monetary Institute
EMS	European Monetary System
EMU	Economic and Monetary Union
EMUA	European Monetary Unit of Account
EPC	European Political Cooperation
Erasmus	European Community Action Scheme for the Mobility of University Students
ERDF	European Regional Development Fund
ERM	Exchange Rate Mechanism
ERP	European Recovery Programme (Marshall Plan)
ESC	Economic and Social Committee
ESCB	European System of Central Banks
ESDI	European Security and Defence Identity
ESDP	European Security and Defence Policy
ESF	European Social Fund
ESPRIT	European Strategic Programme for Research and Development in Information Technology
ETUC	European Trade Union Confederation
EUA	European Unit of Account, the forerunner of the ECU
EUI	European University Institute
Euratom	European Atomic Energy Community
Eureka	European Research Co-ordination Agency

Europol	European Police Office
Eurostat	Statistical Office of the European Communities
GATT	General Agreement on Tariffs and Trade
GDP	gross domestic product
GDR	German Democratic Republic
GNP	gross national product
IBRD	International Bank for Reconstruction and Development (World Bank)
IEA	International Energy Authority
IGC	intergovernmental conference
IMF	International Monetary Fund
JHA	Justice and Home Affairs
MCAs	Monetary Compensatory Amounts
MEP	Member of the European Parliament
NACC	North Atlantic Cooperation Council
NAFTA	North American Free Trade Area
NGO	non-governmental organization
NTA	New Transatlantic Agenda
OECD	Organisation for Economic Co-operation and Development
OEEC	Organisation for European Economic Co-operation
OPEC	Organization of Petroleum Exporting Countries
OSCE	Organization for Security and Cooperation in Europe
PHARE	Poland and Hungary Assistance for Economic Reconstruction Programme (subsequently applied to all of eastern and central Europe)
PR	proportional representation
PSC	Political and Security Committee
QMV	qualified majority voting
SEA	Single European Act
SHAPE	Supreme Headquarters Allied Powers Europe
SIS	Schengen Information System
TACIS	Technical Assistance to the Commonwealth of Independent States and Georgia
TEMPUS	Trans-European Mobility Programme for University Studies
TEN	trans-European network
TEU	Treaty on European Union (Maastricht Treaty)
Trevi	Intergovernmental group on international crime
UNICE	Union of Industrial and Employers' Confederations of Europe
WEU	Western European Union
WMD	weapons of mass destruction
WTO	World Trade Organization

1 Overview

The context of European integration

When one examines the process of European integration, it is evident that since the early beginnings of the European Coal and Steel Community (ECSC) the nature of cooperation has changed dramatically. First, there has occurred a widening of membership, from the six states of the ECSC to 15 member states in 1995 and to 25 member states in 2004. Second, there has also occurred a broadening of policy competence at the European Union (EU) level as the work of the Community has spread from economic to political integration. Over time, this has resulted in many areas of policy being covered by the EU, from consumer affairs to international trade policy. The growth in the number of these policies has in turn led to them becoming routine aspects of the EU. One product of these developments has been to make the study of the EU a more complicated process. The expansion in the number of policies dealt with at the EU level has, for instance, raised concerns over the ability of all member states to adopt EU policies at the same speed. Considerable attention has therefore been attached to flexible models of integration that allow the EU to progress as a whole while at the same time taking account of specific national interests.

This distinction between the national and supranational viewpoint has been reflected in the focus that has been attached to intergovernmental and supranational models of integration. Intergovernmental interpretations highlight the fact that key decisions continue to be taken by member states, particularly those relating to the type of powers exercised by EU institutions and the extent to which the decision-making capacity of member states should be pooled. Advocates of the intergovernmental method adopt a state-centric approach. Such an approach has in recent years paid specific attention to the key intergovernmental conference negotiations that have dominated much of the EU's agenda and which have produced landmark changes to the EU, including the Single European Act (SEA), the Treaty on European Union (TEU), the Amsterdam Treaty and the Nice Treaty.

The supranational viewpoint is, by contrast, based on the premise that the key dynamic of integration is determined by EU organizations and not as a result of the decisions taken by member states. Supranational models of EU integration inevitably map the policy outcomes of such EU institutions as the European Commission and the European Court of Justice (ECJ). The European Commission (which acts as the central bureaucracy and executive body) has responsibility for upholding EU laws, monitoring patterns of implementing legislation, preserving the integrity of the single market, managing the annual budget of the EU and administering such policies as the Common Agricultural Policy (CAP).

Somewhat inevitably, not every EU government or every individual within a member state has welcomed the possibility of binding decisions being made beyond the realm of individual nation state sovereignty. This state of affairs has led to the emergence of the phenomenon of Euroscepticism in all EU countries, being particularly apparent in Denmark and the United Kingdom (UK). It is a situation that has been influenced by Eurosceptic concerns that member states have experienced erosion in their capacity to administer policies at the national level. This inability to exercise independent authority is commonly viewed as a loss of sovereignty. A second and very much related concern is the perception that, while there has been a transfer of authority to the European level, the citizens of Europe are basically powerless to influence EU decision-making. This view of remoteness from EU decision-making has in turn been mirrored in a general decline in voter turnout at European Parliamentary elections. Indeed, the average level of voting fell for the sixth time running at the 2004 elections (see Table 2.5). A direct impact of this reduction in the percentage of the electorate voting in European Parliamentary elections is that it has raised further concerns over how democratic is the nature of the EU.

Those who subscribe to the Eurosceptic position draw on the argument that, prior to joining the EU, member states were able to make their own decisions. While this view might hold particular resonance in many countries, including the UK, it is equally important to point out that nation states do not operate in a vacuum. For instance, the internationalization of financial affairs has meant that it is virtually impossible to talk of national sovereignty with regard to economic issues. EU membership consequently needs to be set within the context of a general trend towards increased levels of interdependence that affect all countries.

It is certainly the case that the activities of all member states have been constrained by EU membership. But, while it is true that governments are bound by a whole plethora of rules and regulations, it is also true that European integration has offered a great deal of opportunities to governments. To take an example, the single market programme required member states to accept the setting of new EU standards and the ability of the European Commission to monitor a member state's progress in implementing the necessary EU legislation. Despite these constraints, the single market offered, among other benefits, new opportunities in cross-border trade as a result of the abolition of border controls for goods.

Apart from these direct developments, the single market acted as a catalyst for promoting further advances in European integration, including the promotion of a social dimension and the eventual creation of a single currency. And, although many Eurosceptics question the value of participation in a single European currency (because it represents an unacceptable erosion of national sovereignty), many states are nonetheless attracted to the single currency because (among other factors) it offers a formal degree of influence over the setting of a European monetary policy which previously had been largely determined by the German Bundesbank. For some countries, such as Italy and Greece, a single European currency has also been welcomed because the Italian lira and the Greek drachma had been relatively unstable currencies. Thus, in answering the question why sovereign states have been prepared to abandon their national currencies in favour of the euro, we have to appreciate the fact that the single currency has offered a number of different advantages for member states.

A balance of power

A significant amount of the debate that has taken place within the EU has focused on determining which policies should be subject to decision-making at a EU level and which should be retained solely as the preserve of the member states. There has also been a significant amount of discussion as to which policies to be discussed at an EU level should be subject to full agreement among member states (unanimity) and which policies should be decided on a basis of qualified majority voting (thereby providing the opportunity for an individual state to be outvoted) (see Table 2.11).

But, despite differences as to the methods to be used when taking decisions, and the commonplace perception that member states have somehow relinquished national power, the key EU decision-making body is in fact composed of member states (the Council of Ministers). Thus, while the European Commission has the ability to propose new EU laws and policies, the formal authority for acceptance rests with the Council of Ministers. Acceptance does, however, take place after the Council has debated the policy with the European Parliament. In recent years the European Parliament's powers have certainly increased as a response to criticisms that, despite being the only democratically elected EU institution, its powers were of a limited nature. The European Parliament's influence now extends to being a co-legislator (co-decision procedure) with the Council of Ministers over a majority of issues. In addition, the European Parliament possesses a number of supervisory powers over such matters as the appointment of the Commission, and has other legislative powers that include the setting of the EU budget. (But, while these changes have gone some way in rectifying concerns about the presence of a democratic deficit within the EU, somewhat less attention has been given to the role of national parliaments, which in some countries only have a limited ability to scrutinize national decision-makers.) It is these institutions – the European Commission, the Council of Ministers and the European Parliament – that represent the key decision-making institutional triangle of the EU. The Court of Justice is also of considerable importance in determining the limits and impact of European integration. Of lesser importance are the Committee of the Regions and the Economic and Social Committee, both of which are able to offer advice and can be consulted by the Commission and the Council.

We can therefore see that, although the EU is characterized as a supranational organization, it comprises a number of institutions that reflect supranational as well as intergovernmental structures. Chief among the supranational institutions is the European Commission, which includes Commissioners (nominated by national governments) who are assisted by an administrative staff that are divided into directorates general which cover a range of EU policies. This structure is similar to that found in the government departments of member states. Other supranational institutions include the Court of Justice and European Parliament, while there are in addition a number of more specialized institutions such as the European Central Bank (which sets interest rate levels for those countries using the euro – the so called 'eurozone') and Court of Auditors (which audits the accounts of the EU institutions). Sat against these institutions, the Council of Ministers acts as the main beacon of intergovernmentalism in the EU through its role as the key decision-making body. But, while decisions are taken by member states, the main method of agreement is qualified majority voting (where the votes of a member state are weighted partly to account for differences in the size of its population) which permits the possibility of a proposal being accepted if it receives the necessary number of votes and similarly being rejected if a sufficiently large number of states vote against it (commonly referred to as the blocking minority).

Explaining integration

It is apparent that the EU comprises a mix of intergovernmental and supranational procedures, and this outcome is very much a product of the negotiating preferences of member states. In the postwar period

many member states were willing to engage in new forms of cooperation and to create supranational structures to administer common policies purely because they considered that individual governments were
not able to deal adequately with the challenges that western Europe
faced. In examining the factors that motivated states to engage in such
a process of integration, it has been emphasized that the creation of
the ECSC represented a desire to satisfy French national interests by
ensuring the continued economic recovery of France. This focus on
the national interest has led to the argument that European integration
only took place when it was demanded by nation states and that supranational institutions were established for specific purposes and not as a
means of eclipsing the nation state.

In contrast to this viewpoint, others have argued that the process
of European integration will ultimately result in the creation of a new
supranational state and thereby the demise of the nation state. This
view is somewhat harder to sustain, not least because the national interest was a key factor that propelled the strategies of nation states.
For instance, Germany was keen to participate in the ECSC because it
provided a means of rehabilitation (as did Italy), while the smaller nations of Belgium, Luxembourg and the Netherlands realized that they
could not economically afford to distance themselves from the markets
of France and Germany.

Just as some countries considered participation in the ECSC to be
central to their national interest, there were at the same time others
who had no interest in joining. This was particularly true for the UK.
Because it had a dominant share of western Europe's foreign trade, the
economic arguments in favour of participating in the ECSC were sim-
ply not as convincing for it as they were for other member states. At
the same time, the UK's reluctance to join the ECSC was influenced
by its rejection of the belief that individual nation states should share
their sovereignty in such areas as commerce, trade and agriculture in
the hope of economic benefits. Britain therefore did not participate in
the ECSC and the 1957 Treaty of Rome because of a belief that such
ventures did not serve its national interests. This was a view held by
other states, including Denmark.

It can be seen that the national interest has been a key factor in
determining the strategies adopted by individual governments. The
UK's decision to apply for Community membership as early as 1961
(only four years after the formation of the EC) was motivated by a
realization that the economic benefits to be obtained from being a
member of the Community far outweighed the costs of relinquishing
some power to the new supranational organization. In a slightly different vein, France's hostility towards plans to extend the number of
policy areas that could be subject to majority voting at the European
level resulted in the French government boycotting the Community

between July and December 1965 (a period referred to as the empty chair crisis). To resolve this dispute, the Luxembourg compromise of January 1966 stipulated that 'when very important issues are at stake, discussions must be continued until unanimous agreement is reached'. This outcome established the importance of member states within the EU and initially limited the ability of the supranational Commission to propel integration further forward.

Such was the significance of the Luxembourg compromise in defending the interests of member states that it was not until the 1987 Single European Act (SEA) that the majority of member states concluded that the future progress of the Community would be severely hampered if national governments continued to effectively exercise a veto on areas of policy that happened to be sensitive to their national interests. Even the British government of Margaret Thatcher realized that majority voting on certain policies, such as the single European market, was essential. This was because a continuing reliance on unanimity for decision-making ensured that individual policies could be hijacked by the preferences of any member state that was prepared to veto a proposal because it did not reflect its own interest.

Moves towards the taking of decisions at a European level and the transfer of power away from member states have been partly the result of the pragmatic decisions of member states. And even in those areas of decision-making that member states explicitly established on an intergovernmental basis, the practical experience of operating such policies has often resulted in the need to move away from intergovernmental procedures. To take an example, while the 1993 Treaty on European Union established a Common Foreign and Security Policy (CFSP) on intergovernmental grounds, the weaknesses and limitations of this area of policy-making became evident throughout the 1990s as the EU attempted to grapple with the outbreak of unrest in the former Yugoslavia. To overcome an absence of a central coordinating structure, member states committed themselves in the Amsterdam Treaty of 1997 to establish centralized planning units to administer the CFSP and to appoint a 'High Representative' to coordinate policy. More recently, the Constitutional Treaty included the provision for the creation of the post of EU Minister for Foreign Affairs.

The examples that have been outlined in this introductory chapter may lead some observers to consider that the present-day structure of the EU is the result of a series of bargains negotiated by member states. To be sure, it is the case that the various intergovernmental conference (IGC) negotiations that have become commonplace in the EU's calendar have been subject to agreement by member states. But, at the same time, the institutions of the EU have provided a significant amount of the momentum behind European integration. This has been particularly true in the case of the European Commission and the European

Court of Justice. To this end, the conflict between supranationalism and the ability of national governments to exercise their own decision-making remains a key feature of the process of European integration and is a recurring theme in the information that is presented in this companion.

2 Institutions

European Commission

The European Commission plays an important role in the integration process because in most areas of EU policy-making it carries the sole responsibility for new legislation. This has provided the European Commission with an important role in framing the agenda and shaping the evolution of the EU. It has also meant that it has become a target for national governments, organized interests and the European Parliament.

Structure

Based in Brussels, the European Commission consists of, at the upper level, 25 Commissioners (one from each member state) who are appointed for five years (which is renewable) on the recommendation of national governments with the responsibility to be independent of all external influences. Commissioners are not, or should not be, open to influence or direct orders from their national governments as they represent the European ideals of the European project. For the most part, the Commissioners have tended to be politicians who have occupied senior office in their respective member state, although some Commissioners have been businessmen, trade union leaders and senior administrators. Meetings of European Commissioners take place once a week. Whereas the President of the European Commission (Table 2.1) is chosen by Heads of State or Government after consultation with the European Parliament, other members are solely nominated by member states. The European Commission has to be approved by the European Parliament before members can take office. If a vote of censure is made by the European Parliament, then the European Commission is required to resign en bloc.

In support of the Commissioners is a multinational civil service of approximately 17,000, of which one-third work in translating and interpreting the 20 official languages of the EU. The European Com-

Table 2.1 Presidents of the European Commission

Period in office	President	Nationality	Party affiliation	Members of the Commission
1958–67	Walter Hallstein	West Germany	Christian Democratic Union (CDU)	9
1967–70	Jean Rey	Belgium	Liberal Reformist Party (PRL)	9
1970–72	Franco Maria Malfatti Resigned	Italy	Christian Democracy (DC)	9
1972–73	Sicco Mansholt	Netherlands	Labour Party (PvdA)	9
1973–77	Francois-Xavier Ortoli	France	Gaullist	13
1977–81	Roy Jenkins	UK	Labour Party	13
1981–85	Gaston Thorn	Luxembourg	Democratic Party	14
1985–95	Jacques Delors	France	Socialist Party	17 (14 members in 1985, 17 after 1986 enlargement)
1995–99	Jacques Santer	Luxembourg	Christian Socialist People's Party (CSV)	20
March 1999– September 1999	Manuel Marin (Interim Presidency)	Spain	Spanish Socialist Workers' Party (PSOE)	20
1999–2004	Romano Prodi	Italy	Olive Tree	20
2004–	José Manuel Barroso	Portugal	Social Democratic Party (PSD)	25

mission is divided into 36 departments and directorates general (DGs). A DG is headed by a director-general, who in turn reports to an individual European Commissioner responsible for that area of work (see Table 2.2). Each is served by a group of officials known as a Cabinet, whose purpose is to provide advice on policy initiatives, of which a large proportion are citizens of the nation that the Commissioner is from. Heads of Cabinet meet every week with the primary purpose of clearing issues prior to, or after, meetings of the European Commission.

Table 2.2 European Commission Directorates general

Policies
Agriculture and Rural Development
Competition
Economic and Financial Affairs
Education and Culture
Employment, Social Affairs and Equal Opportunities
Enterprise and Industry
Environment
Fisheries and Maritime Affairs
Health and Consumer Protection
Information, Society and Media
Internal Market and Services
Joint Research Centre
Justice, Freedom and Security
Regional Policy
Research
Taxation and Customs Union
Transport and Energy

External Relations
Development
Enlargement
EuropeAid Cooperation Office
External Relations
Humanitarian Aid Office – ECHO
Trade

General Services
European Anti-Fraud Office
Eurostat
Press and Communication
Publications Office
Secretariat General

Internal Services
Budget
Group of Policy Advisers
Informatics
Infrastructures and Logistics
Internal Audit Service
Interpretation
Legal Service
Personnel and Administration
Translation

Political effectiveness

The political effectiveness of the Commission depends upon the influence of the Commission President (Table 2.1). The President of the Commission is the one who holds the Commission together on two counts. First, the President has a major influence in terms of how the Commissioners work together given that the President is seen as the 'first among equals' and is responsible for directing the work of the Commission. Second, much depends upon on how the President relates to the member states of the Union from the outset. In recent years the political effectiveness of the Commission has been hampered by the difficulties that it has encountered in the period after Jacques Delors's Presidency. In part, this was the result of a desire of the member states and other institutions to reassert their influence, but it was also because of problems relating to inefficiencies, scandals and financial mismanagement. This was highlighted in the 1999 resignation of the Santer Commission. A direct impact of these issues is that in recent Treaty reforms the Commission has lost out to the Council and Council of Ministers as heads of government have sought to ensure that they had a greater role within the EU.

Initiation powers

The European Commission plays a primary legislative role as the Council of Ministers and the European Parliament need a proposal from it before they can pass legislation. It has often been remarked that 'the Commission proposes and the Council disposes'. EU law cannot be made without a European Commission proposal, at which stage it is often targeted by interest groups (including national governments, industry, trade unions, special interest groups and technical experts) so that the motion will hopefully represent their views. In this context, the European Commission attempts to reflect what is best for the EU as a whole, rather than specific interests. After a legislative proposal has been made to the Council and the European Parliament, it is important that full cooperation take place among these three bodies to ensure a smooth law-making process. The European Commission often provides the impulse towards wider integration, including the launching of the strategy which resulted in the completion of the single market and the drive towards Economic and Monetary Union (EMU) as evidenced by the 1985 White Paper on completing the single market and the 1989 Delors Report on monetary union. Individual European Commissioners are crucial to this process, providing political leadership to direct policy initiatives. As they have often served in national governments they bring added experience to their posts.

General powers

Apart from its powers of initiation, the European Commission plays a significant part in upholding EU laws, sustaining and managing agricultural and regional development policies, and preserving the integrity of the single market. It also plays a major role in furthering research and technological development initiatives, while it is of importance to initiating development cooperation with the countries of central and eastern Europe, Africa, the Caribbean and Pacific. Broader responsibilities include ensuring compliance among member states by monitoring the implementation of legislation. If obligations are broken then the European Commission can take legal proceedings at the Court of Justice. Scrutiny of national governments also covers central government subsidies to industry and types of state aid. Individual firms can be fined for violating Treaty law (although they have the right to appeal to the Court of Justice). A crucial task is managing the annual budget of the Union, dominated by spending on agricultural policy and structural funds. The latter are designed to eliminate disparities between rich and poor areas. As the central executive of the Union, the European Commission plays an important part in international negotiations, particularly those relating to trade through the General Agreement on Tariffs and Trade (GATT). Over 100 countries have agreements with the Union, of which the countries that were covered by the Lomé Convention have since 2000 been covered by the Cotonou Agreement.

Accountability

Accountability has for a long time been an important concern with regard to the workings of the Commission. The Commissioners are nominated by national governments, and in this sense they are 'unelected' despite the fact that their appointment is subject to the approval of the European Parliament. This is not to say that the Commission is unaccountable. The Commission cannot operate in a political vacuum and that vacuum is filled by the Council of Ministers and the European Parliament. Indeed, the strengthening in the powers of the Commission throughout the 1980s, together with more general concerns about the democratic deficit with the then Community, led to growing concerns about the democratic credentials of the Commissioners and the President of the Commission. The most immediate response was a redefinition of the European Parliament's powers of supervision vis-à-vis the Commission.

European Parliament

The European Parliament is the institution that represents the citizens of the EU and is the successor to the Parliamentary Assembly of the

European Coal and Steel Community (ECSC). The foundation of the EEC under the Treaty of Rome (1957) gave the Parliamentary Assembly no codified legal rights or powers but did allow the Assembly the relatively powerless right of issuing a non-binding Opinion on matters of legislative interest – Opinions which the Council of Ministers could happily ignore if it chose, and for most of the period from 1957 onwards the Council did choose to ignore the Assembly. In effect the Assembly (or Parliament as it was to become) was only able to debate issues which it considered of interest, and to issue Opinions, but its debates were essentially pointless because the Assembly (or Parliament) was rarely able to change legislation through either debate or amendment. The end result was that until the 1980s the history of the European Parliament was one of an institution with little or no power, with it attempting to persuade both the Commission and the Council to hear its Opinions on matters of legislation and to adopt its suggested amendments.

Location

The European Parliament conducts its work in Brussels, Luxembourg and Strasbourg. Meetings of the whole Parliament (plenary sessions) take place in Brussels and Strasbourg, Committee meetings take place in Brussels, and the administrative offices (General Secretariat) are based in Luxembourg.

Functions

The European Parliament has three main functions: (1) it considers the policy proposals put forward by the European Commission and is involved in the legislative process with the Council of Ministers which increasingly is on a co-legislator basis as a result of the co-decision procedure; (2) it plays an important role in confirming the appointment of the European Commission and additionally has the power to censure the Commission; (3) it is involved in debates on the budget and shares power in this policy area with the Council of Ministers in terms of voting on the annual budget. Outside these key areas, the European Parliament appoints an Ombudsman who has the task of investigating complaints from EU citizens, and has the ability to establish temporary committees of inquiry.

The European Parliament provides democratic legitimacy to the EU, having been given greater powers in the SEA through the cooperation procedure and in the Treaty on European Union through the co-decision procedure and having had these granted to a wider policy area in the Treaty of Amsterdam, Treaty of Nice and Constitutional Treaty (Table 2.3). It is fully involved in adopting Community legislation and

Table 2.3 Treaty changes to the European Parliament's powers

Year	Development	Impact on the European Parliament
1987	Single European Act entered into force	Cooperation procedure introduced
1993	Treaty on European Union entered into force	Co-decision procedure introduced. Nomination of European Commission is subject to approval by the European Parliament
1999	Treaty of Amsterdam entered into force	Extension in the use of the co-decision procedure. European Parliament was given the power to confirm or refuse a nominated president of the European Commission
2003	Treaty of Nice entered into force	Extension in the use of the co-decision procedure

the budget, supervising the activities of the European Commission and the Council, while MEPs represent interests of the citizen via the Committee on Petitions and by appointing the European Ombudsman. It has the power of veto over agreements made between the EU and other countries and over the enlargement of the EU. It has to be consulted by the European Commission and the Council of Ministers on most proposals and policy initiatives. The European Parliament adopts the Union's budget each year (usually in December) with the signature of the President bringing it into effect, and it exercises democratic supervision over all Community activities and can set up committees of inquiry. The European Parliament meets every month for a plenary session in Strasbourg, the agenda of which is drawn up by a bureau comprising the president and 12 vice-presidents. In addition to plenary sessions, working sessions or Committee meetings are held in Brussels.

Legislative role

There has been a gradual expansion in the European Parliament's legislative role since the Treaty of Rome gave the European Commission the ability to propose and the Council to decide after having consulted the Parliament. If the obligation to consult is not met then a Community law becomes null and void. The European Parliament now shares the power of co-decision equally with the Council in a large number of areas, while it can request the European Commission to take a particular initiative that it views to be important. The European Parliament additionally examines the European Commission's annual work programme.

Relations with other institutions

In terms of its relations with other EU institutions, the Treaty on European Union provided the European Parliament with an important role in appointing the President and members of the European Commission, with the latter having to be approved by the Parliament in a vote of investiture. This is in addition to the European Parliament's ability to censure the European Commission, with a 'motion of censure' forcing it to resign. MEPs can put written or oral questions to the European Commission, while members of the European Commission take part in parliamentary committee meetings. The European Parliament's influence over the Council expanded with the introduction of the co-decision procedure in the Treaty on European Union, thereby providing a legislative balance. Each Council president-in-office presents the work programme of that member state to the European Parliament at the beginning of each Presidency, and the fruits of that programme are discussed at the end. Council Ministers also attend the plenary sessions of the Parliament, while MEPs can put oral or written questions to them.

Elections to the European Parliament

In the 1970s it was decided that the European Parliamentary Assembly should become a directly elected Parliament, with the Parliament being directly elected for the first time in 1979 (Table 2.4). MEPs are largely distributed among (and within) member states on the basis of population (Table 2.5). Although this has resulted in Germany being at one end of the spectrum with 99 MEPs and Malta at the other with five MEPs, the situation is reversed when the number of electors per MEP is taken into consideration. Thus, whereas there are approxi-

Table 2.4 Growth of the European Parliament

Year	No. of MEPs	Number of member states	Nature of MEPs	Nature of body
1952	78	6	Nominated	ECSC Common Assembly
1958	142	6	Nominated	EC Common Assembly
1973	198	9	Nominated	European Parliament
1979	410	9	Elected	European Parliament
1981	434	10	Elected	European Parliament
1986	518	12	Elected	European Parliament
1994	567	12	Elected	European Parliament
1995	626	15	Elected	European Parliament
2004	732	25	Elected	European Parliament

Table 2.5 European Parliament elections, 2004

Member state	Joined EU	Number of seats in the Parliament	Voting method
Austria	1995	18	PR, national lists
Belgium	1957	24	PR, regional lists
Cyprus	2004	6	PR, national lists
Czech Republic	2004	24	PR, national lists
Denmark	1973	14	PR, national lists
Estonia	2004	6	PR, national lists
Finland	1995	14	PR, national lists
France	1957	78	PR, national lists
Germany	1957	99	PR, regional lists
Greece	1981	24	PR, national lists
Hungary	2004	24	PR, national lists
Ireland	1973	13	PR, single transferable vote
Italy	1957	78	PR, national lists
Latvia	2004	9	PR, national lists
Lithuania	2004	13	PR, national lists
Luxembourg	1957	6	PR, national lists
Malta	2004	5	PR, national lists
Netherlands	1957	27	PR, national lists
Poland	2004	54	PR, regional lists
Portugal	1986	24	PR, national lists
Slovakia	2004	14	PR, national lists
Slovenia	2004	7	PR, national lists
Spain	1986	54	PR, national lists
Sweden	1995	19	PR, national lists
UK	1973	78	PR, regional lists (of which 3 MEPs in Northern Ireland were elected by PR, single transferable vote).

mately 60,000 voters per MEP in Malta, there are some 640,000 voters per MEP in Germany. In other words, Malta has more MEPs per head of population, a state of affairs that further emphasizes the lack of uniformity in elections to the European Parliament. The elections are themselves held every five years, with the Parliament that was elected in 2004 having 732 MEPs.

The expansion in the size of the European Parliament and the growth in its powers have, however, not had a dramatic impact on voter turnout in elections to the European Parliament. At the last elections in 2004 the average level of voting fell for the sixth time running (Table 2.6). That is not to say that voting turnout is similar among all member states, because there is in fact a wide divergence of voting patterns

Table 2.6 Voter turnout in European Parliament elections

State	1979	1981	1984	1987	1989	1994	1995	1996	1999	2004
Belgium	91.4		92.2		90.7	90.7			91	90.81
France	60.7		56.7		48.7	52.7			46.8	42.76
Germany	65.7		56.8		62.3	60.0			45.2	43
Italy	84.9		83.4		81.5	74.8			70.8	73.1
Luxembourg	88.9		88.8		87.4	88.5			87.3	89
Netherlands	57.8		50.6		47.2	35.6			30	39.3
Denmark	47.8		52.4		46.2	52.9			50.5	47.9
Ireland	63.6		47.6		68.3	44.0			50.2	58.8
UK	32.2		32.6		36.2	36.4			24.0	38.83
Greece		78.6	77.2		79.9	71.2			75.3	63.22
Portugal				72.4	51.2	35.5			40	38.6
Spain				68.9	54.6	59.1			63	45.1
Austria								67.7	49.9	42.43
Finland								60.3	31.4	39.4
Sweden							41.6		38.8	37.8
Cyprus										71.19
Czech Republic										28.32
Estonia										26.38
Hungary										38.5
Latvia										41.34
Lithuania										48.38
Malta										82.37
Poland										20.87
Slovakia										16.96
Slovenia										28.3
EU	63		61		58.5	56.8			49.8	45.7

Source: Extracted from website: http://www.elections2004.eu.int

among the member states. The UK has traditionally had the lowest turnout. By contrast, other member states have experienced a higher voter turnout, particularly Belgium, Italy and Luxembourg. There are some clear reasons for these differences. Nations such as Belgium and Luxembourg generally have a high degree of support for the EU. This is not surprising as both countries receive large financial injections from having EU institutions based there and accordingly concepts of public apathy and discontent are less relevant. The high turnout in Italian elections can be explained from a public desire to support a democratic European Parliament in the face of domestic corruption. However, it is very important to note that voting is compulsory in Belgium, Greece and Luxembourg and, while not so in Italy, it is still regarded to be a public duty. Where turnout is declining, it is worth considering that voting apathy is influenced by the perceived need to participate in other domestic elections, such as local and regional, which are often held at the same time as European elections. Irrespective of the turnout within each member state, European elections face the additional problem of being used as a sounding board for national policies, especially when the European election falls within a government's term of office.

Political groups

MEPs do not sit in national delegations, but instead form cross-national political groups that represent the various political tendencies within the European Parliament, from the Eurosceptic to the pro-federalist. After the 2004 European Parliament elections there were seven groups, with a further 29 MEPs choosing to remain non-affiliated (Table 2.7).

Table 2.7 Distribution of Political Groups within the European Parliament (June 2005)

European People's Party (Christian Democrats) (EPP)	268
Party of European Socialists (PES)	201
Alliance of Liberals and Democrats for Europe (ALDE)	88
Greens/European Free Alliance (EFA)	42
European United Left/Nordic Green Left Group (EUL/NGL)	41
Independence/Democracy Group (IND/DEM)	36
Union for a Europe of Nations (UEN)	27
Independents (non-affiliated) (NI)	29
Total	**732**

Table 2.8 Presidents of the Common Assembly of the ECSC (1952–58)

1952–54	Paul Henri Spaak
1954	Alcide de Gasperi
1954–56	Giuseppe Pella
1956–58	Hans Furler

Table 2.9 Presidents of the European Parliament (1958–79)

1958–60	Robert Schuman
1960–62	Hans Furler
1962–64	Gaetano Martino
1964–65	Jean Duvieusart
1965–66	Victor Leemans
1966–69	Alain Poher
1969–71	Mario Scelba
1971–73	Walter Behrendt
1973–75	Cornelis Berkhouwer
1975–77	Georges Spénale
1977–79	Emilio Colombo

Table 2.10 Presidents of the European Parliament since 1979 (direct elections)

1979–82	Simone Veil
1982–84	Piet Dankert
1984–87	Pierre Pflimlin
1987–89	Sir Henry Plumb
1989–92	Enrique Baron Crespo
1992–94	Egon Klepsch
1994–97	Klaus Hänsch
1997–99	José María Gil Robles
1999–2002	Nicole Fontaine
2002–4	Pat Cox
2004–	Josep Borrell Fontelles

Council of Ministers

Based in Brussels in the Justus Lipsius building (and since 1993 officially known as the Council of the European Union), it is one of the most important EU institutions. The Council of Ministers is the primary body for representing the interests of the member states and is viewed as being one of the most intergovernmental EU institutions. It is where the member states legislate for the EU, set its political objectives, coordinate national policies and resolve differences between themselves and other institutions. The Council comprises national government ministers that take part in technical Councils that are organized on sectoral lines, such as agriculture, finance, internal market and transport. Meetings generally take place every month (August is a holiday month), while some, such as Transport, Environment and Industry, meet two to four times a year. The most important Council meeting is the General Affairs and External Relations Council, which is composed of EU Foreign Ministers and meets on a monthly basis, as do the Council of Agriculture Ministers and the Council of Economics and Finance Ministers (Ecofin) as a result of the sheer amount of work that they have to cover. Meetings usually take place in Brussels, except in April, June and October when all Council meetings take place in Luxembourg. Additional meetings take place within the nation that chairs the Council Presidency. Over the years the number of Councils has grown so as to keep pace with the expansion of the activities of the EU, and most meetings only last for one or two days.

Decision-making

The Council of Ministers importance stems from its role in the taking of decisions and increasingly these decisions are the production of a co-decision procedure with the European Parliament. This has made the Council of Ministers and the European Parliament 'co-legislatures'. Thus, after the European Commission has put forward a new law or policy, it is the task of the Council of Ministers and the European Parliament to discuss and make changes to the law or policy. Proposals that are of a particularly complex nature will have initially gone from the Commission to a specialist working party of the Council that will highlight areas of both agreement and disagreement as well as respond to the European Parliament's suggestions. Thereafter, the proposal will progress to the Committee of Permanent Representatives (Coreper), which, after having resolved as many issues as it can, will forward the proposal to the ministerial level of the Council for a decision to be taken. Within the Council, ministers have three main options for a vote:

- Unanimity. Although in theory this provides each member state with a power of veto, the Treaty of Amsterdam created the option of a 'constructive abstention' that enables a member state to abstain in a Council vote that would otherwise have unanimous support. The constructive abstention therefore allows an opportunity for member to states to pursue an option other than a veto in those policy areas where they would otherwise find it difficult to support the policy.
- Simple majority. This method of voting has declined in use as more policy areas have required the use of qualified majority voting.
- Qualified majority voting (QMV). This method of voting is used for virtually all areas of policy where ministers have been unable to obtain a consensus. In this situation, ministers are provided with votes that are approximately in proportion to the population of the member state that they represent (Table 2.11). For a proposal to succeed, it must achieve 232 votes from a possible 321 votes (72.3 per cent of votes), while at the same time a majority of states must also support the proposal and the overall votes supporting the proposal have to reflect at least 62 per cent of the total EU

population. Just as a proposal needs to pass these hurdles, it can also be stopped by a blocking minority comprising at least four member states that represent a minimum of 35 per cent of the population. Finally, the new Constitutional Treaty slightly alters the method of QMV, whereby a proposal can succeed if it obtains 232 votes with support from 55 per cent of the member states and 65 per cent of the population.

Table 2.11 Weighting of votes in the Council of Ministers

Member state	Weighted votes
Germany	29
France	29
Italy	29
UK	29
Poland	27
Spain	27
Netherlands	13
Greece	12
Czech Republic	12
Belgium	12
Hungary	12
Portugal	12
Austria	10
Sweden	10
Denmark	7
Finland	7
Ireland	7
Lithuania	7
Slovakia	7
Cyprus	4
Estonia	4
Latvia	4
Luxembourg	4
Slovenia	4
Malta	3
Total EU-25	321
Romania	14
Bulgaria	10
Total EU-27	345

Legislation

All of the legislation made by the Community and common positions dispatched by the Council to the European Parliament are published in the official languages of the EU in the Official Journal. Greater efforts have additionally been made by the Council to make its work more accessible to citizens. This process of transparency has meant that all legislative votes are automatically made public, journalists have been provided with wider briefings and background notes and detailed press releases are assembled by the Press Service after Council meetings. The actual adoption of legislation by the Council (or by the Council and the Parliament through the co-decision procedure) takes various forms:

1   regulations, which are applied directly with no need for national measures in the implementation process;
2   directives, binding member states to the achievement of objectives, but giving national authorities the ability to choose the method and form to be used;
3   decisions, acting as binding measures to those which they are addressed, which can be served to all or any member state, to individuals or to undertakings;
4   recommendations and opinions, which are not binding.

Permanent representatives

Much of the preparation for the Council meetings is done by member states' permanent representations to the EU, which comprise a mix of diplomats and officials from government departments whose work is heavily shaped by the EU, such as agriculture, industry, employment and social affairs. These permanent representations are headed by Permanent Representatives who are usually senior diplomats. As a group they constitute the Committee of Permanent Representatives (Coreper) that forms a vital link between the activities of the EU in Brussels and national governments.

The Presidency

Each member state has held the Presidency of the Council of Ministers on a six-monthly rotating basis, the purpose of which has been to give direction to the work of the Council (Table 2.12). The government that holds the Presidency is responsible for creating compromises and brokering packages among member states, setting the agenda of the Council of Ministers and the European Council, chairing meetings of the Council of Ministers and the European Council, promoting cooperation between member states, and overseeing EU foreign policy. In addition, the Presidency has also been responsible for representing the EU on an international basis, including the annual G8 meetings, and taking part in meetings with non-EU heads of state and government, such as the President of the United States. A significant addition to these tasks has been the increased number of meetings between the Presidency and the European Parliament, whereby the latter is kept fully informed of developments. There has been a marked increase in the number of visits by the Presidency to the European Parliament, with the former no longer just presenting a 'report' at the start of its six-month term of office, but rather being subjected to a more rigorous questioning and examination by the Parliament throughout the Presidency. In practical terms, this has been reflected, particularly since the 1997 Treaty of Amsterdam, in each Presidency spending more time with the Parliament than the previous Presidency did.

Although these range of duties attaches prominence to the member state (and leader) holding the Presidency and gives prestige to small member states, the rotating basis of the position has nonetheless been subject to criticism. The workload of the Presidency is a considerable strain on the resources of most national governments, with this being true for small member states. Moreover, the six-monthly change has not always helped to promote continuity of EU policies, especially those with an international dimension.

In response to these developments, the EU Constitutional Treaty has proposed three new developments. First, the abolition of the ro-

Table 2.12 Rotating Presidency of the Council of Ministers

Year	January–June	July–December
1991	Luxembourg	Netherlands
1992	Portugal	United Kingdom
1993	Denmark	Belgium
1994	Greece	Germany
1995	France	Spain
1996	Italy	Ireland
1997	Netherlands	Luxembourg
1998	United Kingdom	Austria
1999	Germany	Finland
2000	Portugal	France
2001	Sweden	Belgium
2002	Spain	Denmark
2003	Greece	Italy
2004	Ireland	Netherlands
2005	Luxembourg	United Kingdom
2006	Austria	Finland

tating basis of the Presidency, and instead for the European Council to elect an individual for a term of 2½ years whose job will be to run the activities of the Council. It is an argument that was supported by many of the large member states, including France, Germany and the UK, who all stressed the benefits of having one individual that can offer stability and represent the interests of the member states on an international basis. Second, the Constitutional Treaty provided for a 'Team Presidency' of three member states of 18 months to replace the existing six-monthly rotating Presidency (Table 2.13). The practical reality of such a proposal is that one member state would preside over all the Council meetings for six months, with support provided by the other member states in the Team. Third, the Constitutional Treaty established a new post of EU Minister for Foreign Affairs, with there being a merger of the existing roles of the European Commissioner for External Relations and the High Representative for Common Foreign and Security Policy (CFSP). The intention of such a merger is that the Foreign Minister would be able to ensure that there was greater consistency to the foreign policy of the EU.

Table 2.13 Proposed 'Team Presidency' under the Constitutional Treaty

January 2007–June 2008	Germany Portugal Slovenia
July 2008–December 2009	France Czech Republic Sweden
January 2010–June 2011	Spain Belgium Hungary
July 2011–December 2012	Poland Denmark Cyprus
January 2013–June 2014	Ireland Lithuania Greece
July 2014–December 2015	Italy Latvia Luxembourg
January 2016–June 2017	Netherlands Slovakia Malta
July 2017–December 2018	United Kingdom Estonia Bulgaria
January 2019–June 2020	Austria Romania Finland

European Council

At the Paris summit of December 1974 the then nine EC member states formally recognized the important role that summits had come to play in the Community's progress and confirmed that heads of government would meet three times a year in the form of the European Council. The value of such 'summit' meetings had been evident since President Georges Pompidou of France had called for a special meeting of the six member states to be held at the Hague in December 1969 in order to 'relaunch' the Community. Although in the period after 1969 several occasional summits took place, such as in Paris in 1972, the first formal European Council took place in Dublin in March 1975. Since that first Dublin meeting, the European Council has played an important role in the development of European integration through giving political direction, establishing priorities and resolving disputes (Box 2.1). This has become particularly apparent in recent years as the European Council has met three or four times a year despite the fact that a decision was taken in December 1985 to limit the meetings to twice a year. For instance, in 1990 two additional European Council meetings were held in April and October to deal with, respectively, the issue of German unification and the forthcoming intergovernmental conference negotiations that resulted in the Maastricht Treaty on European Union.

Role

The very need for more than just two European Council meetings was demonstrative of the fact that many key issues relating to European integration need to be dealt with at the highest level of political office. The combination of the informal nature of these meetings (which generally take place over a weekend), the seniority of the individuals concerned and the fact that decisions are taken in secret (summarized in communiqués) has provided the European Council with a relatively free hand in shaping the direction of European integration. But, while the informal nature of the meetings has been an important advantage in creating solutions to problems, the fact that many of the decisions that emanate from the meetings are of a political and not a legal nature has ensured that the governments of the member states have not always interpreted the resulting communiqués in a similar manner.

Just as with the Council of Ministers, the European Council is led by the country holding the Presidency, and so the opportunity for problems to resolved and new developments to emerge greatly depends on that country. Much is also influenced by external economic and political events taking place at the global level.

The European Council's influence has been reflective of a broader trend relating to the role played by member states in shaping the direction of Europe, which in many ways has been at the expense of the traditional role played by the European Commission. The evidence to support such an argument rests in over three decades of European Council meetings that have helped to give future guidance to European integration or managed to resolve key disputes. Crucial European Council meetings have included the decision to launch the European Monetary System (EMS) at Bremen in 1978 and the resolution of the British budget problem at Fontainebleau in 1984. The signing of the agreement on a Single European Act in 1985 (which gave legal recognition to the European Council) and the subsequent negotiations that led to the Treaty on European Union, Treaty of Amsterdam, Treaty of Nice and Constitutional Treaty (subject to ratification) have brought further prominence to the European Council.

These recent Treaty reforms have also conferred additional powers on the European Council. The three pillar temple model established in the Treaty on European Union established the European Council as the 'roof' over the 'temple' with it being responsible for setting general political guidelines and providing annual state of the Union reports to the European Parliament. The Council was also entrusted with key responsibilities in the area of the Common Foreign and Security Policy (CFSP) and has taken the final decision on whether countries are ready to participate in Economic and Monetary Union (EMU) as well as appointing members of the European Central Bank (ECB). It can therefore be seen that the influence of the European Council has grown in recent decades. Many of the decisions taken by the European Council have also played a crucial role in deepening European integration, which in itself is somewhat of an irony given that the European Council is an intergovernmental institution.

Box 2.1 Key meetings of the European Council

The Hague, 1–2 December 1969

In an effort to 'relaunch' the Community, agreement was reached on the question of enlargement (France had blocked the UK's applications in 1963 and 1967) and on deepening the EC's activities by means of extending cooperation in the economic and political fields. The premier of Luxembourg, Pierre Werner, was given the responsibility for leading a committee to examine the case for monetary union, while the future Belgian European Commissioner, Etienne Davignon, led the committee which investigated the possibility of closer political integration.

Paris, 19–20 October 1972

As part of an effort to map out the future path of European integration, agreement was reached on the commitment to achieve the goal of monetary union by 1980 (as had been set out in the Werner Report) and the need to establish a common external trade policy towards the Soviet Union and Eastern Europe. A key development that came out of the meeting was the agreement to establish a European Regional Development Fund (ERDF).

Paris, 9–10 December 1974

In recognizing the important role that summits had come to play in the progress of the Community, member states agreed that these summits would in future take the form of a European Council. The Paris meeting also established the exact size of the ERDF, noted the principle of direct elections to the European Parliament, and took the decision to commission the Belgian Prime Minister, Leo Tindemans, to provide a report on European union.

Dublin, 10–11 March 1975

The first formal meeting of the European Council resulted in agreement on the outstanding issues of the UK's renegotiations.

Rome, 1–2 December 1975

Agreement was reached on the European passport and the holding of European elections.

Rome, 1–2 December 1975

Conclusion of the UK's renegotiation of its terms of membership.

Brussels, 12–13 July 1976

Agreement was reached on the total number of seats in the European Parliament and the exact distribution of these seats among the member states in relation to size of population.

Brussels, 5–6 December 1977

Agreement was reached on the introduction of the European Unit of Account from 1 January 1978.

Brussels, 4–5 December 1978

Resolution that the EMS would be established from 1 January 1979. The appointment of 'Three Wise Men' to produce a report on possible revisions to the institutional structure of the Community (Edmund Dell, Barend Biesheuvel and Robert Marjolin).

Dublin, 29–30 November 1979

UK claims for a reduction in its budget contribution to the Community were first raised at the fifteenth meeting of the European Council.

Venice, 12–13 June 1980

Agreement was reached on the Venice Declaration with regard to the Middle East.

London, 26–27 November 1981

The European Council focused on the Genscher–Colombo proposals for political union.

Stuttgart, 17–19 June 1983

Adoption of the 'Solemn Declaration on European Union' which outlined possibilities for increased cooperation and development within and between the Council, European Parliament, European Commission and Court of Justice.

Fontainebleau, 25–26 June 1984

Agreement on a 1984 budgetary rebate for the UK, thereby ensuring that focus could be switched to other Community policy areas. This included a decision to establish an *ad hoc* committee on institutional affairs to make suggestions to improve the functioning of European cooperation within the Community.

Brussels, 29–20 March 1985

Agreement was reached on the Integrated Mediterranean Programmes which provided special help to the southern regions of the Community.

Milan, 28–29 June 1985

The six original members of the Community, plus Ireland, voted in favour of an intergovernmental conference on institutional reform. Denmark, Greece and the UK opposed the vote, but agreed to attend the conference which was scheduled to commence on 9 September 1995. The meeting also endorsed the Cockfield White Paper on completing the single market.

Luxembourg, 2–3 December 1985

Agreement on a document to revise the Treaty of Rome, although subject to further approval by Foreign Ministers on 16 December 1985. This concluded the intergovernmental conference negotiations that had commenced on 9 September 1985. The areas of reform included the setting of a deadline of 31 December 1992 for the establishment of a single market; the further development of economic and social cohesion; the introduction of the cooperation procedure within for the decision-making of the European Parliament; the improvement of policy areas within the social field, including the working environment regarding the health and safety of workers.

Hanover, 27–28 June 1988

Member states confirmed the objective of progressive realization of EMU and decided to examine at the June 1989 Madrid European Council the means to achieve it. A committee chaired by the President of the European Commission, Jacques Delors, was entrusted with the task of examining and proposing stages towards EMU. Member states agreed that their central bank governors would participate in the committee in a personal capacity, while it would also include a further member of the European Commission and three specialists.

Madrid, 26–27 June 1989

Having examined the Delors Report on EMU, agreement was reached that the first stage of EMU would commence on 1 July 1990.

Strasbourg, 8–9 December 1989

A majority of member states (not the UK) called for the convening of an intergovernmental conference to examine EMU. The UK was also opposed to the agreement by the then 11 other member states to adopt the Social Charter.

Dublin, 28 April 1990

Agreement that the Community would establish an EMU and that the intergovernmental conference would open in December 1990. The European Council additionally agreed to a declaration on German reunification.

Dublin, 25–26 June 1990

The meeting noted that the first stage of EMU (which was to commence on 1 July 1990) should be used as a means of ensuring convergence in member states' economic performance, to propel cohesion and to further the use of the ECU. The meeting also agreed to establish a second intergovernmental conference that would examine political union and run in parallel to the negotiations on EMU.

Rome, 14–15 December 1990

The European Council established a broad framework for the negotiations on the parallel IGC's on EMU and political union, which were formally opened by the Council on 15 December.

Maastricht, 9–10 December 1991

Agreement on the Draft Treaty on European Union based on the texts concerning political union and economic and monetary union. The UK obtained an opt-out from the third stage of EMU, which established a deadline of 1999 for the introduction of a single currency. The Treaty also provided for intergovernmental co-operation in the fields of common foreign and security policy and justice and home affairs. A further development was the granting of increased powers to the European Parliament through the co-decision procedure.

Edinburgh, 11–12 December 1992

The European Council solved the Treaty on European Union rat-ification crisis which had begun with the 'no' vote in the Danish referendum of June 1992. Member states approved a clear defini-tion of subsidiarity whereby 'it aims at decisions within the Eu-ropean Union being taken as closely as possible to the citizen'. Denmark was granted exemption from citizenship of the Union, the introduction of a single currency, defence policy coopera-tion, and cooperation on justice and home affairs. The European Council also produced agreement on the future financing of the Community, known as the 'Delors package'. A major part of this was an agreement to increase support to southern members of the Community, a development particularly advocated by Spain.

Copenhagen, 21–22 June 1993

Member states agreed on a set of enlargement criteria (Copenha-gen criteria) for the countries of central and eastern Europe. The meeting also discussed the European Commission's White Paper on growth, competitiveness and employment.

Brussels, 10–11 November 1993

Agreement was reached on an action plan on employment in re-sponse to the European Commission's White Paper on growth, competitiveness and employment.

Corfu, 24–25 June 1994

Despite the fact that the European Council was dominated by the failure of member states to agree on the appointment of the President of the European Commission, agreement was nonetheless reached to establish a reflection group to prepare for a forthcoming intergovernmental conference in 1996.

Essen, 9–10 December 1994

The Essen European Council set out a pre-accession strategy to prepare the countries that had signed an Association Agreement for membership of the EU.

Madrid, 15–16 December 1995

The Commission presented an interim report that emphasized the benefits of enlargement with respect to peace, security and the economic growth of Europe. It also emphasized that the adoption of the Community acquis commmunitaire was a prerequisite for accession.

Florence, 21–22 June 1996

A compromise was reached on the BSE crisis and brought to and end the UK policy of non-cooperation which had commenced in May 1996 after the EU implemented a ban on UK beef exports. Over a four-week period the UK had used its veto on more than 70 occasions.

Amsterdam, 16–17 June 1997

The conclusion of the intergovernmental conference negotiations that had commenced in March 1996 resulted in agreement on a Treaty of Amsterdam.

Luxembourg, 12–13 December 1997

Member states reached agreement that enlargement negotiations with the countries of central and eastern Europe would commence in March 1998.

London, 2–3 May 1998

A decision was taken on the third stage of EMU.

Berlin, 24–26 March 1999

The European Council reached an overall agreement on Agenda 2000 and to appoint Romano Prodi President of the European Commission. With respect to enlargement, agreement was also reached on the creation of two pre-accession instruments: a structural instrument (ISPA) and an agricultural instrument (SAPARD). Member states also agreed to double pre-accession aid from 2000.

Cologne, 3–4 June 1999

Agreement was reached on the appointment of Javier Solana as the High Representative for CFSP, and member states also noted that an IGC on institutional reform would take place in 2000.

Tampere, 16–17 October 1999

Member states agreed to establish a committee to draft a Charter of Fundamental Rights.

Helsinki, 10–11 December 1999

A decision was taken to create a European Security and Defence Policy (ESDP) based on the establishment of a multinational corps of 60,000 by 2003.

Lisbon, 23–24 March 2000

Member states came to an agreement that the EU should become 'the most competitive and dynamic knowledge-based economy in the world'.

Feira, 19–20 June 2000

In addition to reviewing the ESDP, agreement was reached on a Mediterranean strategy.

Nice, 7–9 December 2000

Member states agreed on a new Treaty of Nice that sought to prepare the EU for further enlargement, and endorsed the Charter of Fundamental Rights.

Laeken, 14–15 December 2001

Adoption of the Laeken Declaration on the Future of Europe which identified the need for the EU to improve its internal workings and ensure that it was capable of playing a full and active role in world affairs.

Copenhagen, 12–13 December 2002

The European Council meeting formally concluded the enlargement negotiations for Cyprus, the Czech Republic, Estonia, Hungary, Latvia, Lithuania, Malta, Poland, Slovakia and Slovenia.

Brussels, 18 June 2004

Agreement on a new Constitutional Treaty that consolidated all the previous treaties into one single document to provide the EU with a simpler and more accessible set of rules.

Court of Justice

Based in Luxembourg, the Court of Justice comprises 25 judges (one per member state) and eight Advocates General who help the Court by making preliminary recommendations that are almost invariably followed. The judges and Advocates General are appointed by member states for a renewable six-year term of office. One of the judges is selected to be President of the Court for a renewable term of three years, with the task of the President being to direct the work of the Court. Until 1 September 1989 the Court of Justice worked alone. Thereafter a Court of First Instance was attached to it with the aim of dealing with most of the actions brought by individuals and companies against decisions of the EU institutions (judgments can be liable to an appeal taken before the Court of Justice, but only on a point of law). Thus, the Court of Justice has concentrated its activities on its fundamental task of ensuring a uniform interpretation of EU law, that is deciding on cases brought by member states, EU institutions, individuals and companies. It accordingly interprets the Treaties or secondary EU legislation when disputes arise, but does not have any jurisdiction over the courts and laws of member states. The rulings that the Court makes are directly applicable to all member states concerned, though an appeal may be brought to the Court of Justice. The decisions of the Court decisions have made EU law a reality for the citizens of Europe, resulting in important constitutional and economic consequences.

Organization

Members of both Courts are appointed by common accord of the governments of member states for a renewable six-year term. The President of the Court of Justice is elected from and by the judges for a three-year term, during which he/she is responsible for directing the work of the Court and presiding over hearings and deliberations. The President of the Court of First Instance is elected in a similar manner; there are no Advocates General. The Court of Justice may sit as a full Court, in a Grand Chamber (13 judges) or in chambers of three or five judges. It sits in plenary session when it so decides or if requested by a member state or an EU institution which is a party to the proceedings. For its part the Court of First Instance sits in chambers of three or five judges, and may sit in plenary session for certain important cases.

Role

The Court of Justice is a particularly important EU institution as its decisions are binding on the parties concerned. These decisions can be on disputes over Treaty provisions or on secondary legislation such as directives and regulations. In the area of social policy the Court has been particularly active. The need for the Court of Justice to exist is a practical one based on the fact that, as the EU is a legal body, there is a real necessity for an institution to act as an interpreter of the extent to which the legislation has been put in place by a member state. Many rulings of the Court have been of a contentious nature and it has been criticized for having a general tendency to favour solutions to policies that have been of an integrationist nature. In this context the Court has done much to further the integration of the EU. Many governments have been critical of this sort of policy enaction by the Court because it has been at the expense of their own national sovereignty.

In terms of importance, the Court of Justice has the ultimate authority for interpreting EU law. It can hear cases that are taken by EU institutions, member states and citizens of the EU. In terms of its role, the Court of Justice is responsible for maintaining a balance between the respective powers of the EU institutions, the powers transferred to the EU and those retained by member states. An important contribution of the Court has been establishing the direct effect of EU law in member states and the primacy of EU law over national law. This has ensured that European citizens are able to challenge a national law if it is contrary to EU law. Thus, the principle of EU law has become a reality, a factor particularly important to the free movement of goods, creation of a common market and removal of barriers protecting national markets. In this context, the 1979 Cassis de Dijon judgment ensured it was possible for European consumers to purchase in their own country any food product from another European country through a policy of mutual recognition. This was a particularly important case as it provided a pathway towards the single market programme.

Of the rulings to emerge from the Court of Justice, one of the main beneficiaries has been the European Parliament. Over a number of judgments it has given decisions that have increased the powers of the European Parliament. Otherwise, the Court has also had an impact on the general nature of EU law whereby it has made rulings that have advanced EU law further than member states would have liked. A classic example is the 1990 Factortame judgment, which concerned fishing rights. In this case Spanish fishermen had purchased UK fishing vessels and with them the quotas that were attributable to the UK. Thus, Spanish fishermen were using UK quotas to land fish that they had caught in Spain. In response to this state of affairs, the UK government passed the 1988 Merchant Shipping Act which required 75 per cent of the shareholders and directors of a company to be British so as to allow the company to be able to register itself as British. The Spanish fishermen claimed that this was a breach of their rights to be given equal status as EC citizens. In the end the Court ruled that the 1988 Merchant Shipping Act was a breach of EC law on the ground of equal treatment of citizens and the ruling consequently overturned the Merchant Shipping Act. The UK government was obviously extremely upset by this decision, but it provides a classic example of the Court overturning an Act of Parliament and thereby demonstrating the supremacy of EU law over domestic law.

Cases

In general terms the cases that can be brought before the Court of Justice can be divided into: disputes between member states; disputes between the EU and the member states; disputes between the institutions; disputes between individuals, or corporate bodies, and the EU; opinions on international agreements; and preliminary rulings on cases referred by national courts.

The growing significance of the Court of Justice has been evidenced by its increased workload, with the number of new cases brought before the Court having increased from four in 1953 to 527 in 2004.

Over that period, a total of 13,493 cases have been brought before the Court, with the majority of these cases being since 1980. In 1954 the Court of Justice issued two judgments. In 1984 the Court issued 165 judgments, and in 2004 the Court issued 375 judgments. In total, from 1952 to 2004 the Court issued 6,465 judgments. The vast majority of these judgments have been made since the entry into force of the Single European Act (SEA) in 1987, which vastly expanded the competences of the Community. Thus, whereas the Court of Justice made 2,292 judgments from 1952 until 1986, it made 4,173 judgments from 1987 until 2004. A discrepancy between the number of cases and judgments made is in part a cost of this increased workload, with a case often taking up to two years to be dealt with.

Court of Auditors

Based in Luxembourg and established on 22 July 1975, the Court of Auditors aims to check whether the accounts of all EU institutions are in accordance with current legislation and jurisdiction. Its creation coincided with the extension of the European Parliament's powers in the field of budgetary control and the financing of the EU budget through own resources. It was therefore vital to create an independent organization to audit the Community's finances, which became a reality when the Court became operational in October 1977. Its authority was subsequently strengthened when it was promoted to the rank of an institution on 1 November 1993 with the entry into force of the Treaty on European Union.

Organization

The Court of Auditors is composed of 25 members (one from each member state) who are appointed by a unanimous decision of the Council of Ministers, after consulting the European Parliament, for a (renewable) term of six years. Members come from those who belong or have belonged to external audit bodies in their respective member states, or who are particularly qualified to carry out the duties of office. The President of the European Court of Auditors is elected by colleagues for a three-year term (with the possibility of re-election), his or her role being to ensure the smooth running of the Court's departments and the pursuit of correct procedures.

Role

Every year, the Court of Auditors examines whether revenue has been received and expenditure incurred in a legal and correct manner and whether financial management has been sound. The Court is essentially therefore a guarantor that certain administrative and accounting principles are adhered to in the Union, with its reports serving as a means of applying pressure on institutions to ensure proper management takes place, thereby reassuring public opinion that money is being responsibly spent. This has meant that all bodies and institutions which have access to EU finances are scrutinized by the Court of Auditors. It specifically audits the general budget of the Union, Community loans and borrowings, the revenue and expenditure of the European Development Funds, the Euratom Supply Agency, the European Centre for the Development of Vocational Training, the European Foundation for the Improvement of Living and Working Conditions, the Joint European Torus research undertaking, the European Schools and other bodies including the new satellite agencies. Because approximately 80–85 per cent of the EU's budget is used by the member states themselves and is administered by national authorities, an important part of the Court's controls takes place in the member states, in cooperation with national audit authorities and other relevant bodies.

When discrepancies are identified by the Court it then highlights the action to be taken by the pertinent administrations and other bodies, while equally illustrating those points which have allowed problems to occur. The Court can make its views known at any time by issuing reports on specific areas of budget management, which are published in the Official Journal. In this context it carries out its control and consultative functions autonomously and independently. Views are published in its annual report, as well as correspondence from the particular institution concerned. This is adopted annually in November, having been subjected to examination by the European Parliament on a recommendation of the Council when it is considering whether or not to give a discharge to the European Commission for its management of the budget.

Economic and Social Committee

The Economic and Social Committee was established in 1957 by the Treaties of Rome with the aim of involving economic and social interest groups in the establishment of the common market. Based in Brussels, its primary purpose is to advise the European Commission and the Council of Ministers on social and economic matters. It comprises 317 members, representing employers and employees as well as other groups such as consumers and farmers, who are distributed among member states on the basis of population (Table 2.14). Members are nominated by national governments and appointed by the Council and serve a four-year term of office which is renewable. The main task of the members is to issue opinions on matters referred by the European

Table 2.14 Distribution of members of the Economic and Social Committee and the Committee of the Regions

Member state	Number of members of each committee
France	24
Germany	24
Italy	24
United Kingdom	24
Poland	21
Spain	21
Austria	12
Belgium	12
Czech Republic	12
Greece	12
Hungary	12
Netherlands	12
Portugal	12
Sweden	12
Denmark	9
Finland	9
Ireland	9
Lithuania	9
Slovakia	9
Estonia	7
Latvia	7
Slovenia	7
Cyprus	6
Luxembourg	6
Malta	5
Total	317

Commission and the Council to the Economic and Social Committee (ESC). In certain cases it is mandatory for the European Commission and the Council to consult the ESC, being optional in others, while it may also adopt opinions on its own initiative. These roles were reinforced by the Single European Act and the Treaty on European Union, especially new policies such as environment and regional policy. This process was continued by the Treaty of Amsterdam providing for the ESC to be consulted by the European Parliament. The Treaty of Nice made a slight change to the description of ESC members, noting that the Committee should comprise 'representatives of the various economic and social components of organized civil society'. The Treaty of

Nice also stressed that, in an enlarged EU, the total number of members should not exceed 350.

Committee of the Regions

Based in Brussels, the Committee of the Regions (CoR) was established by the Maastricht Treaty on European Union to take account of the views of regional and local government in European decision-making, thereby reflecting the interests of those elected closest to the citizen and taking into consideration the principle of subsidiarity. Although it must be consulted by the Council of Ministers, European Commission and European Parliament before the adoption of decisions that affect regional interests, it can also deliver opinions on its own initiative.

Organization

The Committee of the Regions comprises 317 members (plus 317 alternates) who are appointed by the Council for a four-year period, having been nominated by the member states (see Table 2.14). The President and First Vice-President are elected from among the members for a two-year term. There is in addition one Vice-President per member state. Members of the CoR are represented in national delegations and political groupings (European People's Party, Party of European Socialists, Alliance of Liberals and Democrats for Europe, and Union for Europe of the Nations – European Alliance). As with the Economic and Social Committee Membership of the CoR is proportionally distributed among the member states.

Role

The influence of the CoR has grown since its first plenary session in March 1994. Its remit was initially limited to five areas where there was obligatory consultation: economic and social cohesion; trans-European networks in the field of transport, energy and communications; public health; education and youth; and culture. The Treaty of Amsterdam widened the number of policies that the CoR has to be consulted on to include: environment policy; social policy; environment policy; vocational training; and transport. Outside these policy areas the Council, European Commission and European Parliament can request an opinion from the CoR where they consider it appropriate. The CoR may also decide to prepare an opinion when the Economic and Social Committee has been consulted and where as a result particular regional interests are involved. Finally, if it considers it appropriate, the CoR may choose to prepare an opinion on its own.

The Constitutional Treaty which was signed by the member state governments in Rome in October 2004 (subject to ratification) provided the CoR with a key responsibility for overseeing the principle of subsidiarity. It also gave the Committee the right to launch proceedings at the Court of Justice if it was of the opinion that a EU law had been enacted without taking into consideration the powers of local and regional authorities.

European Investment Bank

Based in Luxembourg, the European Investment Bank (EIB) is a non-profit development bank with the primary aim of promoting long-term loans and guarantees for investment in industry and infrastructure projects in priority areas. These include less developed regions, industrial modernization and joint industrial projects. The activities of the EIB have expanded beyond the EU and now embrace the 78 African, Caribbean and Pacific (ACP) nations and other countries which have association agreements with the EU. The Bank's operations are financed by borrowing on both the international and EU capital markets.

Funding of regional development projects by the EIB often takes place in tandem with grants from the EU's structural funds and Cohesion Fund, a process which ensures the need for a close collaboration with the European Commission to establish complementarity. The EIB has been particularly active in providing finance for trans-European networks (TENs) in transport and telecommunications and energy, projects which require large amounts of investment. To provide guarantees for TENs as well as for small and medium-sized enterprises, the EIB, in collaboration with the European Commission and the banking sector, established the European Investment Fund (EIF).

In addition to funding projects within the borders of the Union, the EIB has also granted loans to projects undertaken outside the Union, including:

1 central and eastern European states;
2 fostering cross-border infrastructure and environmental projects as well as developing the productive private sector in Mediterranean non-member countries;
3 assisting the Middle East peace process, notably in Lebanon, Gaza and the West Bank;
4 the signatories to the Lomé Convention, and the Republic of South Africa;
5 financing projects of mutual interest, including technology transfer, joint ventures and environmental protection in Asian and Latin American countries which have signed cooperation agreements with the EU.

European Ombudsman

The office of the European Ombudsman was established by the Maastricht Treaty on European Union as part of the citizenship of the EU. It is essentially the guardian of good administration within the EU. As such, the Ombudsman investigates complaints about maladministration (including administrative irregularities, discrimination and abuse of power) by institutions and bodies of the EU, with the exception of the Court of Justice and Court of First Instance when acting in their judicial role. It is also not able to deal with complaints regarding national, regional or local administrations of the member states.

The institution, which is generally known as the Ombudsman, has grown in importance from just a two-person team that was based in Strasbourg in 1995. During that period the cases that the Ombudsman has dealt with has grown considerably. In 2004 the Ombudsman received 3,726 new complaints and dealt with a total of 4,048 cases. This number of new complaints represented a 53 per cent increase compared to 2003, and of this 53 per cent some 51 per cent were accountable to complaints from the 10 new member states that joined the EU in 2004. In terms of the geographical distribution of complaints, it is evident from Table 2.15 that, although Spain made the greatest number of complaints, when the ratio of complaints to population is taken into consideration, Malta had the highest rate while the UK had the lowest rate. Where a country has a rate of submission that is greater than 1, then this rate is higher than would be expected in terms of the size of its population.

European Central Bank

Based in Frankfurt, the European Central Bank (ECB) was established in 1998 under the Maastricht Treaty on European Union. The ECB is the successor to the European Monetary Institute (EMI), which came into operation in January 1994. The main primary purpose of the ECB is to manage the euro (the EU's single currency) and to establish the EU's economic and monetary policy. These tasks are carried out in conjunction with the European System of Central Banks (ESCB) which embraces all 25 member states of the EU.

The main decision-making body of the ECB is the Governing Council. This consists of the six members of the Executive Board, which includes the President of the ECB, the Vice-President and four additional members that are appointed by the heads of government of the countries participating in the single currency (euro area). Although the Executive Board members are appointed for eight years (non-renewable), Wim Duisenberg's tenure as the first President of the ECB ended in 2003 when he was replaced in November by Jean-Claude Trichet.

Table 2.15 Geographical origin of complaints to the European Ombudsman in 2004

Country	Number of complaints	% of complaints	% of EU population	Rate
Malta	38	1.0	0.1	11.7
Luxembourg	40	1.1	0.1	10.9
Cyprus	59	1.6	0.2	10.0
Belgium	268	7.2	2.3	3.2
Slovenia	38	1.0	0.4	2.3
Finland	73	2.0	1.1	1.7
Ireland	53	1.4	0.9	1.6
Greece	129	3.5	2.4	1.4
Spain	482	129.0	9.2	1.4
Portugal	116	3.1	2.3	1.4
Slovakia	52	1.4	1.2	1.2
Czech Republic	98	2.6	2.2	1.2
Sweden	84	2.3	2.0	1.2
Austria	69	1.9	1.8	1.1
Poland	285	7.6	8.3	0.9
Denmark	32	0.9	1.2	0.7
Germany	464	12.4	18.0	0.7
Netherlands	88	2.4	3.5	0.7
Hungary	53	1.4	2.2	0.6
Lithuania	18	0.5	0.8	0.6
Estonia	7	0.2	0.3	0.6
France	303	8.1	13.5	0.6
Italy	269	7.2	12.6	0.6
Latvia	9	0.2	0.5	0.5
United Kingdom	195	5.2	13.0	0.4
Others	404	10.9		

Source: European Ombudsman, *Annual Report 2004.* http://www.euro-ombudsman.eu.int/report/en/default.htm

Note
The figure of the rate was arrived at by means of a division of complaints by the percentage of the population.

The Governing Council comprises the six members of the Executive Board and the central bank governors of the twelve member states participating in the single currency.

A key task of the ECB is the maintenance of price stability within the euro area and therefore ensuring that inflation is kept under control. One of the main ways to achieve this objective is by controlling the money supply through the setting of interest rates throughout the euro area. In this sense, reductions in the level of interest rates help to stimulate consumer demand while increases in the level of interest rate help to dampen down consumer spending and thereby reduce inflationary pressures.

3 Policies

The European Union's Budget

Overview

Despite the budget of the EU being over 100 thousand million euro, it is a small amount in terms of the total wealth of the member states and represents just over 1 per cent of their combined gross domestic product (GDP). The actual size of the budget has increased in tandem with the enlargement of the EU and the expansion in the number of policy areas that the EU embraces. The budget is a contentious issue and has sparked many conflicts within the EU. The budget is proposed every year by the European Commission (which also has the responsibility for its implementation), but has to be adopted by the Council of Ministers and ultimately the European Parliament.

For historical reasons, the single largest element of expenditure is the Common Agricultural Policy (CAP), which has tended to represent half of all spending (42.3 per cent in 2005). Of the remaining expenditure, the biggest component has been regional aid. One outcome of this has been that the budget has had an uneven impact across the EU, as poorer member states with a large agricultural sector have been the main beneficiaries. Member states such as Greece, Ireland, Portugal and Spain have all received significant benefits, obtaining from the EU more than twice what they have paid in. By contrast, Germany has been the biggest total net contributor to the budget, although the Netherlands is the largest per capita contributor. Small rich countries, such as Austria and Sweden, have also made significant contributions. Of other member states, France and Italy have both received significant levels of subsidies for their large agricultural sectors, and the UK's position as a net contributor has been offset by its budget rebate. Over the years there have been a number of efforts to reform the budget and in particular the CAP, not least because of the May 2004 enlargement of the EU to include poorer central and eastern European states. The latter further highlighted the funding discrepancies associated with the CAP.

History

The initial budget of the Community, as established by the Treaties of Rome, was wholly dependent upon contributions from the member states. This state of affairs quickly proved to be inadequate as the costs of a number of the Community policies (particularly the CAP) meant that there was a need for the Community to have an independent financial basis. In the mid-1960s the attempt by the President of the European Commission, Walter Hallstein, to provide the Community with a stronger financial basis for the CAP was rebuffed by the French president Charles de Gaulle, and proved to be a contributing factor behind the empty chair crisis of 1965. National contributions were eventually abolished in April 1970, with the Community's revenues to be obtained by a system of own resources (Table 3.1). These 'own resources' were designed to ensure the Community had sufficient income to satisfy all the policies that the Commission administered. This funding would be achieved through a combination of:

- agricultural levies charged on the importation of agricultural products from third countries;
- customs duties levied on industrial products imported into the Community;
- a small amount of funding that would not exceed 1 per cent of the revenues a member state obtained from value added tax.

In practical terms, this funding agreement meant that those countries – such as Germany – which imported large quantities of agricultural produce and industrial goods would account for a greater proportion of the contributions to the Community's budget than a country that had fewer imports. It also meant that Britain faced a requirement on its accession to the Community of having to pay significant sums into the

Table 3.1 Financing the EU's Budget (own resources)

Agricultural levies. Levies are charged on less expensive agricultural products which emanate from non-member countries to ensure that the more expensive agricultural goods produced within the EU remain competitive

Customs duties. These are duties obtained from tariffs that are imposed on non-agricultural goods imported into the EU

VAT resources. The EU collects a percentage of all VAT revenues from all member states

GNP resources. The EU obtains income from each member state which varies in relation to the member state's GNP

Community budget, and because it had an efficient agricultural sector it would receive little back in the way of CAP funding.

All in all, this funding arrangement proved to be insufficient to cope with the expansion in the Community's policies (including the CAP) and provided the basis for the British budget problem. As a result, subsequent years were dominated by the need to make a number of reforms to the budget:

- The 1984 Fontainebleau European Council resolved the British budget problem.
- The 1988 Delors I package provided an increase in the overall budget so as to cope with the additional policies that had been introduced in the Single European Act (SEA). The 1988–92 budget was increased by 7.6 per cent, but in return the size of the EU budget was limited to 1.15 per cent of EU GNP.
- The 1992 Delors II package increased the 1999 budget by 22 per cent and also increased the limit on the size of the EU budget to 1.2 per cent of EU GNP.
- The 1999 inter-institutional agreement increased the 2000–6 budget by 15.9 per cent and increased the limit on the size of the EU budget to 1.27 per cent of EU GNP.
- In 2005 agreement was reached on the EU budget for the 2007–13 period, including a commitment by the UK to forgo a percentage of the rebate that it received from the budget and at the same time a commitment by some member states, such as France, to increase their contributions to the budget in line with UK payments. The 2007–13 budget represents 1.045 per cent of the EU GNP of 25 member states.

Disputes

Debates over the funding of the budget have often proved to be the most contentious in the EU, with member state government often unwilling to give ground because of their concern over the possible backlash from their domestic electorate. In the late 1970s and early 1980s the UK was, for instance, adamant about the need for a rebate on its contributions to the budget. At the same time, France has constantly objected to budget reform that will impact on the CAP, for which France has been the largest beneficiary. Consequently, the interlinking of these two issues – CAP spending and the budget – has meant that the attainment of an agreement among member states has often proved to be a complex task. It is a situation that is acerbated by the need for member states to agree on a budget deal by unanimity, which is clearly harder to achieve in an EU of 25 member states. Indeed, in agreeing on the 2007–13 budget at the December 2005 Brussels European Council, member states were unable to fully resolve the issue of CAP funding, with it having been decided that a review of CAP funding would take place in 2008. And although the total budget sum is relatively small (just over 1 per cent of EU GDP), the fact that budget debates are often protracted means that member state governments are regularly distracted from the real issues that are of relevance to European integration. This includes, for instance, the need to complete the Single Market.

Revenue

The budget is primarily financed via the EU's four own resources.

An additional limited contribution to the EU budget is made from other revenue, including bank interest and tax and deductions from staff remuneration.

Spending priorities

Of the areas which make up the budget, the CAP has witnessed a decline in its proportion of total EU spending, having declined from 68 per cent in 1985 to just over 42 per cent today (although still being a dominant share). The decline in the importance of agriculture has, however, been matched by an increase in the proportion of the budget allocated to the structural funds which finance regional and social policies designed to raise employment levels and reduce wealth disparities between EU regions (Table 3.2). At present the structural funds constitute approximately one-third of the budget, compared to one-sixth in 1988, and is accordingly the second most important spending category. Other important spending priorities include research and external action, while just over 5 per cent of the budget is spent on the administrative running costs of EU institutions and bodies.

Table 3.2 EU Budget spending priorities in 2005 (%)

Agriculture	42.3
Structural measures	36.4
Internal policies	7.8
Administration	5.4
External action	4.5
Pre-accession strategy	1.8
Compensations	1.1
Reserves	0.4

Scrutiny

Each year the budget is audited by the Court of Auditors to ensure money is spent for its designated purpose, thereby guaranteeing financial accountability. This scrutiny extends to all the institutions of the EU, while local, regional and national administrations that manage EU funds also have to satisfy the objectives of the Court, which therefore plays an important role in reducing fraud.

Economic and Monetary Union

Overview

On 1 January 2002 12 EU member states started the process of replacing their distinct national currencies with euro banknotes and coins. The introduction of the euro marked one of the most significant developments in the history of European integration since the end of the Second World War. One of the most obvious implications of the euro is that it is easier to travel and do business within the so-called 'eurozone' countries by reducing the need for currency conversion. Acceptance of the euro is, however, not without its potential costs, particularly the impact on national sovereignty. The key question that all member states face is whether it is better to retain control over their national currency or greater benefits are to be obtained from participation in a single currency.

History

The Treaty of Rome made no direct reference to the coordination of monetary policy or the creation of a single currency. Developments changed with the February 1969 Barre Report which stressed that economic policies should be coordinated among member states. A few months later in December 1969, the Hague Summit noted that Economic and Monetary Union (EMU) was to be recognized as an official goal of European integration. This in turn led to a study on monetary union that was chaired by the then Luxembourg premier, Pierre Werner. His report, which was published in October 1970, set out a possible route for the attainment of monetary union by 1980. This included plans to harmonize economic policies and included the provision for member states to coordinate their exchange rates through the creation of the 'snake in the tunnel' system which aimed to reduce currency fluctuations by restricting movement within a set band.

It was an ambitious plan and required member states to enter into a greater degree of commitment to European integration than they were willing to. This was not least because of the impact of the 1974 oil crisis which was a major factor behind the economic turmoil that beset much of the 1970s. As member states were preoccupied with dealing with the impact of oil price rises and high levels of unemployment they showed little or no interest in progressing to the goal of monetary union by 1980, as had been set out in the 1970 Werner Report.

In the wake of the Werner Report, the impetus towards monetary integration was revived in the late 1970s by the then President of the European Commission, Roy Jenkins. A product of his efforts was the commitment by member states to establish a European Monetary System (EMS) which came into existence in 1979 and contained two elements: first, a European Currency Unit (ECU) that could act as a parallel currency; second, an Exchange Rate Mechanism (ERM) that sought to reduce exchange rate instability by fixing the exchange rates of the participating currencies. In light of the experience of the 'snake', member states did not hold out a great deal of expectation for the ERM to be successful. And while instability dogged the ERM in its early years, the ERM managed to provide a more stable framework by the mid-1980s. The combination of this stability and the Single European Act's (SEA) commitment to create a single market led to a renewed interest in the objective of EMU.

Treaty on European Union

These developments led to a further study on monetary union that was chaired by the President of the European Commission, Jacques Delors, and which published its findings in April 1989. The Delors Report advocated a three-stage route to monetary union and stressed that EMU was necessary to achieve effective economic integration through the further development of the single market. A central aspect of this argument was the view that the maintenance of distinct national currencies and fluctuations in exchange rates impacted on business competitiveness. It was an argument that was shared by other member states and directly led to the establishment of an intergovernmental conference (IGC) to fully investigate and provide a routemap for the establishment of EMU. The end product of this was the Maastricht Treaty on European Union that set out a three-stage route to EMU:

- Stage 1 was concerned with efforts to promote economic convergence and commenced on 1 July 1990.
- Stage 2, which commenced on 1 January 1994, involved the creation of institutions to administer EMU, notably the European Monetary Institute (EMI).
- Stage 3, which commenced on 1 January 1999, involved the irrevocable locking of exchange rates, the replacement of national currencies with a single currency and the establishment

of the European Central Bank (replacing the EMI) with it being responsible for monetary policy.

To ensure that progression to monetary union was based on sound economic principles, the Treaty on European Union established four convergence criteria. These were a high degree of price stability, with an average rate of inflation of not more than 1.5 per cent higher than that of the three best performing member states; a sustainable financial position, including a budget deficit of not more than 3 per cent of GDP and a public debt ratio not exceeding 60 per cent of GDP; currency stability, with participation in the narrow bands of the ERM for two years without severe tension or devaluation; and interest rate convergence, of which member states should have an average nominal long-term interest rate not more than 2 per cent higher than that of the three best performers. The Treaty therefore provided some flexibility in deciding which member states met the criteria. The European Council would take the final decision over which member states would meet the criteria.

Stability and Growth Pact

Although the Treaty on European Union included a provision that EMU could commence in 1997 if a majority of member states had met the criteria, this objective proved too difficult to meet. In response to this situation and a concern about the economic costs of committing to the single currency, the less developed member states of Greece, Ireland, Portugal and Spain obtained extra financial support via the Cohesion Fund to ensure that they could meet the requirements of the convergence criteria. At the same time, to ensure that member states participating in the single currency would maintain a stable level of economic progress (and therefore not jeopardize the single currency), the December 1996 Dublin European Council set out the conditions of a Stability and Growth Pact that required member states to adhere to detailed fiscal and budgetary measures to avoid excessive deficits. The pact, which was adopted in 1997, stressed that member states should respect two key annual criteria:

- an annual budgetary deficit below 3 per cent of GDP;
- an annual public debt lower than 60 per cent of GDP.

While the pact stressed that if a member state were to breach these limits then sanctions could be imposed, it was nonetheless subject to criticism because it was viewed as being too inflexible and the criteria needed to be applied over the economic cycle rather than just one year. Moreover, the imposition of sanctions on member states has proved to be impossible. For instance, France and Germany (both of which championed the creation of the stability pact) have in recent years run excessive deficits for which sanctions have not been applied against them. The combination of these factors led member states to reach an agreement at the EU summit of 22–23 March 2005 to relax the rules of the pact.

Launching the single currency

In deciding which member states were eligible to progress towards the single currency, the European Commission recommended in March 1998 that 11 of the 15 member states had met the convergence criteria as set out in the Treaty on European Union. The 11 countries were Austria, Belgium, Finland, France, Germany, Ireland, Italy, Luxembourg, the Netherlands, Portugal and Spain. Although Denmark, Sweden and the UK had basically met the criteria (Sweden also needed to ensure the independence of its central bank), all three states had taken the political decision not to participate in the single currency. By contrast, Greece had failed to meet the criteria. The end result of these developments was that the European Council accepted the Commission's recommendations in May 1998 and the 11 member states therefore joined the single currency on 1 January 1999. They were joined two years later by Greece in January 2001. The May meeting of the European Council also appointed Wim Duisenberg as the first president of the European Central Bank which was charged with the responsibility for managing the single currency (the 'euro'). On 1 January 2002 euro notes and coins were introduced in the member states and by 28 February 2002 they had replaced national currencies after a short period of 'dual circulation'.

Implications of the single currency

The adoption of the euro severely limits the ability of a national government to exercise freedom over its economic policy. This is a factor that is further highlighted by presence of a common interest rate for all 'eurozone' countries. Interest rates cannot be varied according to particular national concern. But, in addition to these concerns over the conduct of macroeconomic policy, opponents of monetary integration equally point to the conversion costs associated with participation in the single currency, such as the reprogramming of shop tills. Against these points, advocates of the single currency tend to set the concern about a loss of sovereignty within a wider context whereby the forces of globalization mean that national economic policy is affected by a variety of factors that a government is essentially powerless to control. Supporters of the single currency point to the transaction benefits of not having different currencies. A more strategic argument is that participation in the single currency helps to preserve (and enhance) the influence that a member state has within the EU, and consequently non-participation could result in diminished influence.

Concern over the appropriateness of membership of the single currency has, however, not just been the preserve of those countries that are yet to join. To this end, the restrictions that the single currency places on the governments of the member states which have chosen to adopt it has also resulted in significant disquiet in those countries. For instance, while economic difficulties in France and Germany have in recent years resulted in swollen budget deficits because of a combination of increased social security payments and reductions in taxation revenue, it is a situation that has nonetheless produced criticism from the European Commission. It highlights the reality of life in the eurozone: member states have given up control over the setting of interest rates to the European Central Bank and are therefore subject to policy decisions that reflect the priorities of the eurozone, yet at the same time the very national governments nonetheless often have to pursue localized economic policies that are in contradistinction to the objectives of the single currency. Such issues raise questions as to the appropriateness of the 'one size fits all' nature of the eurozone and whether it is possible to establish a single monetary and fiscal policy that best represents the interests of all those participating in it.

Single market

Overview

The single market emerged from the publication of the European Commission's White Paper on completing the internal market in 1985, under the authorship of UK Commissioner Lord Cockfield. The paper listed nearly 300 items that would be necessary to achieve the removal of all internal barriers within the Community to enable the free movement of people, services, capital and goods by 1992. The single market allows EU citizens to live, work and study in another member state, while partnerships and alliances have been created not just between companies across national borders, but also between universities. The direct benefit to companies of the single market is that they are able to obtain lower transport costs through the abolition of formalities on the free movement of goods at national border crossings. Such benefits extend beyond the areas covered by the harmonization of national laws as the principle of mutual recognition ensures that member states have to recognize each other's national rules and regulations. The single market programme also prompted an examination of areas of other areas of European integration that had hitherto rested with member state governments. This included the question of monetary union and the establishment of common policies dealing with social affairs.

History

The promotion of free trade was a cornerstone of the Treaty of Rome, which noted in Article 2 that 'the Community shall have as its aim, by establishing a common market and progressively approximating the economic policies of member states, to promote throughout the Community a harmonious development of economic activities, a continuous and balanced expansion, an increase in stability, an accelerated raising of the standard of living and closer relations between its member states'. A direct result of this was that member states agreed to a number of common practices and standards that centred on eliminating the distinctions – and borders – between the different national markets. This included the total abolition of tariffs and restrictive practices, such as price fixing and the dumping of products. In addition to these internal policies, member states also agreed to the creation of a common external tariff to ensure that non-Community countries were presented with a common tariff irrespective of which member state they traded with. In the end, a full customs union was established by 1 July 1968.

In the period after 1968 the objective of creating a 'common market' did, however, become bogged down as member states – in the face of domestic economic difficulties – adopted inward-looking policies that were prompted by a desire to protect domestic jobs from foreign competition. The reality of this state of affairs was that, while member states had become more closely integrated, there were nevertheless barriers that hindered the Community's competitiveness. In other words, the concept of a common market based on the free movement of workers, goods and the mutual recognition of products had not been realized. This situation was emphasized in the Court of Justice's (ECJ) 1979 Cassis de Dijon ruling which tackled a German ban on the importation of alcoholic beverages from other member states that did not meet minimum German alcohol contents, with the Court's decision emphasizing the principle of mutual recognition. This decision, however, did not result in a dramatic change of fortunes, as national governments continued with the practice of using non-tariff barriers to trade to protect their domestic markets.

Yet the use of non-tariff barriers by member states to protect domestic employment levels had a direct impact on the competitiveness of the EC as a whole because the use of subsidies helped to sustain high-cost production as companies were sheltered from wider market competition. Such a course of action arguably represented a retreat from, rather than advance towards, a common market; there continued to exist a number of barriers that hindered the concept of the free movement of goods, peoples or services among the member states. This state of affairs was moreover reflected in a slowdown in the growth of intra-European trade. At the same time the Community was faced with increasing levels of imports from the United States and Japan, while the poor competitiveness of the Community limited its number of exports. The ability to tackle these issues at the Community level in the early 1980s was hindered by the fact that the energies of the institutions and member states was focused on resolving the British budget dispute. That dispute was settled at the 1984 Fontainebleau and resulted in attention being focused on the creation of a genuine common market.

Single Market White Paper

At the same time as these developments, there was pressure both from business groups and member states for the removal of the so-called non-tariff barriers. This view was championed by Jacques Delors, who assumed the position of President of the European Commission in 1985. This directly led to member states requesting the European Commission at the March 1985 Brussels European Council to establish a plan that would result in the creation of a genuine 'single market'. The task was entrusted to the UK Internal Market Commissioner, Lord Arthur Cockfield, and resulted in the publication of a White Paper entitled 'Completing the Internal Market'. It established some 300 actions that would have to be achieved for a single market to be created by 1992, and in particular for the removal of all the internal barriers within the Community to enable the free movement of people, services, capital and goods.

In advancing the case for the single market, the Commission argued that the progress of the Community was hindered by the presence of physical, fiscal and technical barriers.

- Physical barriers concerned the presence of custom and immigration controls. It was argued that they should be abolished because they placed a burden on business competitiveness.
- Fiscal barriers related to the different levels of value added tax (VAT) that existed among member states. Although the European Commission did not advocate a total harmonization of VAT rates, it nonetheless proposed that VAT rates should be harmonized into two bands of 14–20 per cent and 4–9 per cent.
- Technical barriers concerned the technical regulations and standards that differed in each of the member states, which therefore meant that it was possible for a product that met the requirements of one member state to be unacceptable to another. In response to this situation, the European Commission advocated that a process of mutual recognition of national standards should be established.

Table 3.3 Transposition by member states of Internal Market rules into national law (as at 15 November 2004)

Country	Percentage deficit	Number of directives not notified
Czech Republic	9.6	151
Latvia	7.0	110
Slovakia	6.3	99
Malta	6.0	95
Greece	5.1	80
Estonia	5.0	79
Italy	4.5	71
Cyprus	4.4	69
Luxembourg	4.2	67
Belgium	3.4	54
Portugal	3.2	51
Slovenia	3.2	51
France	3.2	50
Poland	2.9	46
UK	2.5	40
Germany	2.5	40
Ireland	2.4	38
Finland	2.3	37
Denmark	2.3	36
Austria	2.1	33
Sweden	2.0	32
Hungary	2.0	32
Netherlands	2.0	31
Spain	1.3	21
Lithuania	1.0	15
EU average	3.6%	

Source: European Commission

Extracted from website: http://europa.eu.int/comm/internal_market/en/update/strategy/2nd-impl-report_en.pdf

Single European Act and Cecchini Report

In reflecting on the ambitious legislative proposals that were set out in the Cockfield White Paper, member states concluded that a new treaty should be negotiated in an intergovernmental conference (IGC) to ensure that the institutional and decision-making structure of the Community reflected the challenges that had been set. This particularly applied to the need to apply the method of qualified majority voting (QMV) to the decision-making process to ensure that policies relating to the single market could not be stopped by the views of individual member states.

In an attempt to demonstrate the likely economic benefits of the single market, the European Commission appointed Paolo Cecchini to lead a committee to examine the 'costs on non-Europe'. The report, which was published in 1988, set out the costs to firms of maintaining customs controls and the opportunity costs of lost trade. It specifically stressed that significant economic benefits would accrue to the Community as the remaining barriers to the free movement of goods, capital, labour and services were removed.

The single market and beyond

Despite the perceived benefits of the single market, its implementation has not always been a quick process. Indeed the single market is still not complete today, with member states not having implemented all of the internal market directives. The European Commission's November 2004 report on completing the internal market highlighted that only two member states had met the 1.5 per cent transposition deficit that had been set by successive European Councils (Table 3.3).

Agricultural policy

Overview

The Common Agricultural Policy (CAP) is a system of subsidized agriculture that represented 42.3 per cent of the EU's budget in 2005. In basic terms, the operation of the CAP is based on three principles: first, the direct payment of subsidies for crops; second, the application of import tariffs on certain goods that are imported into the EU so as to ensure that the world market price for these goods is equivalent to the EU price – in other words, EU farm production protected from cheaper production outside the EU; third, the setting of an intervention price whereby, if the price of a good falls below a desired level, then the EU will intervene by purchasing goods to increase the price of the good. These strategies were influenced by the desire to ensure agricultural production in the early years of the Community. The CAP has been subject to considerable criticism because it accounts for such a significant share of the EU budget. In terms of institutional dynamics, the European Commission is responsible for formulating and initiating policy proposals and the Council of Ministers is the decision-making body and establishes the primary policy guidelines for the CAP.

History

The general orientations of the CAP were introduced in January 1962, being based upon the principles of market unity, Community preference and financial solidarity. Article 39 of the Treaty of Rome stressed that the CAP had five objectives, each of which recognized the need to take account of the structural and natural disparities between agricultural regions:

1   to increase agricultural productivity;
2   to ensure a fair standard of living for the agricultural community;
3   to stabilize markets;
4   to assure food supplies;
5   to provide consumers with food at reasonable prices.

The CAP was established as a means of rectifying the deficit in food production within Europe through supporting internal prices and incomes. This policy was conducted via intervention and border protection and proved to be an important development for the Community for both economic and political reasons: in 1955 it accounted for a significant percentage of the share of the labour force and made a notable contribution to national GDP. The respective figures were: France 25.9 per cent of the labour force and 12.3 per cent of GDP, Italy 39.5 per cent and 21.6 per cent, Germany 18.9 per cent and 8.5 per cent, Luxembourg 25 per cent and 9 per cent, the Netherlands 13.7 per cent and 12 per cent, and Belgium 9.3 per cent and 8.1 per cent.

Cooperation on agricultural policy also demonstrated the willingness of the member states to establish a common policy that brought together distinct national systems of agricultural support, the work of which would be taken over by supranational organizations. The first regulations on agricultural matters were introduced in January 1962 and by 1968 a fully effective agricultural policy was in existence. To achieve its goal of plentiful production, the CAP established a rather complex system that provided farmers with subsidies and price guarantees, being administered by a European Agricultural Guidance and Guarantee Fund (EAGGF). As its name suggests, the EAGGF consists of two parts. The guidance element of the fund accounts for less than 10 per cent of the total EAGGF expenditure, is one of the structural funds and provides help to assist with the reform of the farm structures and the development of rural areas. By contrast, the guarantee section supports agricultural production through the maintenance of farm income and accounts for by far the greater part of EAGGF expenditure.

Problems of the CAP

While there is much truth in the assessment that the CAP was a success story because of its effects in forging closer integration, the CAP has nonetheless been subject to a significant amount of criticism. First, to encourage agricultural production, the CAP provided farmers with a guaranteed price for their products that essentially meant that producers inside the Community were more favourably placed than overseas competitors. Moreover, to place its own market at an advantage, the Community established a system of tariffs and customs duties that protected farmers from lower cost imports. Such a system encouraged efficient farmers to maximize output and consequently led to significant variance in the level of support provided, whereby large farms benefited over small farms. Apart from putting a question mark over the 'common' nature of the CAP, the structural design of the system encouraged the production of surpluses that the European Commission purchased to protect prices and guarantee farm income. Indeed, the agricultural production of the Community increased by 2 per cent per annum between 1973 and 1988, while internal consumption increased by only 0.5 per cent per annum. A consequence was the creation of large surpluses within certain product areas, creating so called 'wine lakes' and 'butter mountains'.

Second, the very success of the CAP caused tension with the Community's trading partners as surpluses of certain products were 'dumped' in other countries (many of which were underdeveloped) at reduced prices (thereby undercutting national producers in those countries). Third, the desire to produce more food brought with it environmental damage to certain regions. Fourth, criticism of the CAP's emphasis on production also extended to a concern that the prices of agricultural products within the EU were often higher than world market prices. Finally, the fact that some EU member states have larger agricultural sectors than others (particularly France, Portugal and Spain) has meant that they have traditionally received more money under the CAP, while other member states, such as the UK, have traditionally received less from the CAP. The reality of this state of affairs was the basis upon which the UK secured a rebate from its contribution to the EU budget.

As a consequence of these factors a particular criticism of the CAP is that significant portions of the EU budget are devoted to keeping inefficient farming sectors in some member states in business. To this end, questions relating to the operation of the EU budget have for the most part been intrinsically linked to the CAP.

Reform

Concern over the problems associated with the CAP and the fact that it was a costly drain on EU finances (approximately 50 per cent of the budget was spent on the CAP) has resulted in various attempts at reform. This was apparent as early as 1968 with the publication of the Mansholt Plan, which emphasized the need to reduce the number of people directly employed in agriculture and creation of larger and more cost-effective farms. Subsequent reforms included those advanced in

1992 by the Irish Commissioner responsible for the CAP, Ray Mac-Sharry, which were largely driven by the need to limit the potential for the CAP to be criticized by the EU's external trading partners during the Uruguay round of the General Agreement on Tariffs and Trade (GATT) negotiations. At the heart of Ray MacSharry's proposals was a reduction in guaranteed farm prices, whereby the levels of support were reduced by 29 per cent for cereals and 15 per cent for beef. Other measures included encouraging 'set-aside', whereby land was withdrawn from production, the promotion of forestation, and the payment of incentives to encourage early retirement.

The prospect of enlargement to central and eastern European states focused the minds of decision-makers who were conscious that the accession of countries with large agricultural sectors necessitated further reform. This, in conjunction with criticism about large-scale production of food and concern over food safety, evidenced by the beef crisis in the 1990s, has meant that greater attention has been attached to food safety, environmental objectives and the promotion of sustainable agricultural production. As a result, in 2003 a decision was taken to basically decouple the payment of subsidies from specific crops, with the focus instead being on 'single farm' payments that reflect a broader set of priorities which take into consideration issues relating to the environment and the quality of agricultural production. It can therefore be seen that there has been a move away from EU support being linked to agricultural production; instead it is now targeted at rural development strategies and providing aid directly to farmers.

Despite these efforts, the CAP has nonetheless been a difficult policy to reform and today it continues to account for in excess of 40 per cent of the EU budget. This has principally been because of the entrenched interests of the farming community that the CAP favoured (particularly within France). It has proved to be not only particularly difficult to reform but impossible to remove from the Community agenda. This is despite the fact that, in contrast to its dominant position in the postwar economy, agriculture no longer accounts for a significant percentage of the national labour force or makes a major contribution to the GDP of member states.

Fisheries policy

Overview

The Common Fisheries Policy (CFP) was established to manage fish stocks within the EU. This is achieved through setting limits on the amount of fish that can be caught. The policy has, however, been subject to severe criticism from fishermen and scientists studying fishing stocks. Scientists have often complained that the policy has not fully addressed the need to tackle dwindling fish stocks, while fishermen have complained that attempts to conserve fishing stocks have threatened their livelihoods. The relevance of the latter point has been enhanced by the fact that, although the fishing industry constitutes a very small percentage of the EU workforce, it is an industry that is concentrated in particular locations and as a result has an important role in the local economy.

History

Although the rationale for a CFP rests on the fact that the creation of rules and regulations regarding the fishing industry is the only way to ensure the conservation of fishing stocks, there was little requirement for a CFP in the early years of the Community. It was in fact only in 1971 that a CFP was implemented, with emphasis being attached to the removal of barriers so as to allow access to permit each member state to access each other's fishing waters and the provision of financial assistance to fishing economies. Somewhat significantly, this policy – which contained no reference to the conservation of fishing stocks – was also agreed just as the Community was about to enlarge to include Denmark, Ireland and the UK, all of which had significant fishing industries. Concern in those member states over the CFP resulted in the removal of the provision of access to each other's fishing waters, which was replaced with the new member states being granted fishing exclusion zones. Such was the anxiety among member states about the distribution of fishing stocks that little progress was made with regard to the CFP for much of the 1970s.

The 1980s brought with it a change in this state of affairs. This was the result of a desire to establish some form of regulations because of the impending accession of Portugal and Spain (both of which had sizeable fishing fleets). The end product was an agreement on a second CFP in 1983, at the heart of which was the principle of open access to allow the national fishing industries of each member state access to all EU waters, the conservation of fishing stocks, the provision of financial assistance to fishing economies, and the establishment of agreements with third countries.

Operation

A central feature of the CFP is the total allowable catch, which stipulates the amount of particular species of fish that can be caught. This is reflected in member states being given an individual quota which takes into consideration both the overall total allowable catch as well as the amount of the catch that the member state has historically been entitled to. Inevitably, this has favoured existing member states and has therefore been criticized by new member states. The actual limits of the allowable catch are determined by the Council of Ministers on an annual basis, with the decision being influenced by the views of scientific advisers regarding the status of fishing stocks. But, while the overall nature of the policy is set at the EU level, the actual enforcement of the total allowable catch is for the most part left to member states to police their individual quota.

As the purpose of the total allowable catch is to conserve fishing stocks, regulations may determine that particular areas are to be closed for fishing, while other regulations may stipulate the fishing gear that can be used so as to ensure that specific sizes of fish cannot be landed to enable the replenishment of stocks. In reality, however, the operation of the policy often means that, as fishermen are given quotas on the species of fish to be caught, they regularly have to discard those species for which the quota has already been met (basically through the dumping of the catch at sea). To many observers this is itself a wasteful system and is one of the elements that has led to criticism of the CFP.

Social policy

Overview

EU employment policy is promoted through the European Social Fund (ESF), which is one of the four structural funds. Action priorities have included attempts to combat labour market exclusion and long-term unemployment, while emphasis on education and training has been especially directed towards youth unemployment. Social policy covers a myriad of topics, including social security and welfare issues, collective bargaining and industrial relations, and individual rights of workers. Recent emphasis on social policy can be traced to the period after the Single European Act (SEA) when there was considerable concern that the single market should not worsen social disparities, while the concern of some countries about the prospect of 'social dumping' increased support for labour market regulation. But, while member states attempted to make further progress on social policy in the Treaty on European Union, opposition from the UK resulted in it having an opt-out from what was known as the Social Chapter. This opt-out was subsequently overturned in the Treaty of Amsterdam. By that time the focus on social policy had started to shift from regulating social conditions to creating employment strategies. Moreover, the co-decision procedure has become the main mechanism for the taking of decisions on social policy.

History

Social responsibility initially arose in the provisions of the Treaty of Rome, but these were limited in practice. While the Treaty considered social policy to be a mechanism for correcting market distortions (free movement of workers), it also set up the ESF. By 1972 political support for the extension of Community social policy led to the first in a series of Social Action Programmes intended to provide a coherent plan of action for a four-year period. Nevertheless, limited progress took place in the 1970s (extension of the ESF and action on sex discrimination). This was changed when the SEA extended social policy, promoting labour–management dialogue between 'social partners'. Article 118A of the SEA provided for qualified majority voting (QMV) on proposals to encourage improvements in the working environment, health and safety of workers and the harmonization of conditions in these areas. Article 118B stressed the normalization of a corporatist policy network, whereby the 'dialogue between management and labour at the European level could, if the two sides consider it desirable, lead to relations based on agreement'.

The European Commission and some member states looked towards a 'social dimension' of the single market, culminating in the Social Charter at the December 1989 Strasbourg European Council. This was a non-binding 'solemn declaration' covering 12 categories of fundamental social rights of workers, namely freedom of movement; employment and remuneration; social protection; improvement of living and working conditions; freedom of association and collective bargaining; worker information, consultation and participation; vocational training; equal treatment for men and women; health and safety protection at the workplace; elderly people – upon retirement everyone is entitled to a pension that will provide a decent standard of living; disabled people – to improve social integration people with disabilities are to be helped, especially with regard to housing, mobility and employment; protection of children and adolescents. However, the UK did not sign, with the government's position reflecting an ideological rift between liberal capitalism and free market versus social welfare and intervention. The President of the European Commission, Jacques Delors, was of the latter school and championed a social dimension to the Community. The majority of member states shared this vision, which was followed by a Social Action Programme of 47 measures (27 of which were in the form of directives or other binding measures). Delays took place in the implementation of some measures, such as the UK derogation on the working time directive, and action on 'atypical' (part-time and temporary) workers stalled.

The Treaty on European Union created a confused situation after 11 member states (not the UK) signed the Social Protocol and Agreement on Social Policy (Social Chapter). This allowed them to implement measures using EC procedures, but crucially outside the *acquis communitaire*. Under the Social Chapter some areas were subject to QMV vote, excluding the UK, namely health and safety of workers, working conditions, information/consultation, sex equality, and integration of persons excluded from the labour market. Other topics were subject to unanimity, excluding the UK, including social security/social protection of workers, protection of workers after termination of employment, representation and co-determination, employment conditions of non-EC nationals and subsidies for job creation. Those areas which were excluded from the Agreement included wages, right of association and the right to strike/lockout.

The Treaty on European Union also formalized dialogue with 'social partners' whereby consultation with management and labour, and opinions or recommendations from the two sides, are required before proposals are submitted to the Council. The first EU directive to pass under the new procedures established by the Treaty on European Union was the European Works Council Directive adopted by the Council in September 1994. It required works councils to be established in companies employing in excess of 1,000 people with establishments in at least two member states. In a similar development, the Social Affairs Council adopted on 29 March 1996 the directive on parental leave via the same procedures. Its significance, however, was that it was the first time legislation had been adopted by Ministers on the basis of a collective agreement proposed by the social partners to the Council. The victory for the Labour Party in the May 1997 UK general election witnessed a change in UK social policy when the government accepted the Social Chapter at the June 1997 Amsterdam European Council and as result it was incorporated into EU policy-making proper.

The Amsterdam Treaty also included a new Employment Chapter that promised a coordinated social policy strategy that was closer to the priorities of the UK than France. This in turn led to an agreement at the Luxembourg European Council of November 1997 on a European Employment Strategy, which had emerged out of a growing concern about the high levels of unemployment within the EU and in many ways was a furtherance of strategies set out in the 1993 White Paper on growth, competitiveness and employment and 1994 Social Policy White Paper. Both of these White Papers marked new focus on balancing high levels of social protection with European competitiveness. The 1993 White Paper acknowledged that high rates of unemployment on the continent were partly due to labour market rigidities which were not present in nations such as Japan and the United States. It proposed a 'social pact' where productivity gains produced by a limited deregulation of the labour market are used to fund job creation and training opportunities. This emphasis on job creation, flexibility, reduced non-wage labour costs, structural reforms of social security and taxation systems signalled a decline in Community activism, with attention directed towards consolidation rather than new initiatives. As a consequence there has therefore taken place a gradual move away from traditional social welfarism to the dual goals of protection and flexibility.

Regional policy

Overview

Although the EU contains some of the wealthiest nations in the world, there are nonetheless economic and social disparities between its member states and among its regions. It is a situation that has, for the most part, been accentuated by the process of enlargement, with the 1973 accession of Denmark, Ireland and the UK to the Community proving to be the catalyst for the development of a regional policy. Before that point regional policy was not a specific objective of the work of the Community. To this end, the Treaty of Rome only referred to regional policy within the context of the preamble, which stressed the need 'to strengthen the unity of their economies and to ensure their harmonious development by reducing the differences existing among the various regions and the backwardness of the less-favoured regions'.

History

In the early years of the Community, efforts to improve economic and social cohesion were primarily channelled through the European Social Fund (ESF) and the European Agricultural Guidance and Guarantee Fund (EAGGF), both of which were set up in 1958. The situation changed with the 1973 enlargement of the Community to include Denmark, Ireland and the UK. This was because the enlargement not only brought into the Community economically underdeveloped countries (Ireland), and countries with significant economic and social disparities (UK), but also meant that the nature of the UK economy would mean that it would receive little in the way of financial assistance from the Common Agricultural Policy (CAP). Moreover, the UK also was faced with the prospect of being a significant contributor to the Community's budget. A combination of these factors resulted in the member states agreeing to establish a European Regional Development Fund (ERDF) in 1975 with the purpose of redistributing financial assistance to the poorest regions of the EU.

The accession of the Mediterranean states of Greece, Portugal and Spain to the Community in the 1980s, and the need for all member states to progress towards a single market, resulted in the Single European Act (SEA) establishing the basis of a cohesion policy to support the less favoured regions of the Community, and in particular the southern countries. Thereafter the Treaty on European Union attached further emphasis to cohesion policy through the creation of a Cohesion Fund to support environment and transport projects in the least prosperous member states. By the mid-1990s one-third of the EU's budget was devoted to cohesion policy. In 1993 the Financial Instrument for Fisheries Guidance (FIFG) was established to assist with the modernization of fishing fleets and to support a diversification of employment in areas traditionally dependent on fishing. In the late 1990s the planned expansion of the Community to countries of central and eastern Europe resulted in the EU providing dedicated pre-accession aid so as to assist in improving the economic and social conditions in those countries. Of the 10 countries that received aid, eight became members in 2004 (Czech Republic, Estonia, Hungary, Latvia, Lithuania, Poland, Slovakia and Slovenia), while Bulgaria and Romania (which are scheduled to join the EU in 2007) continue to receive aid. Such aid is required because a direct impact of the 2004 enlargement of the EU is that there has been a widening in the social and economic disparities among the member states, while there has also been a decline in the average GDP of the EU (Figure 3.1).

Structural funds

In tackling the disparity between the member states, the EU's efforts are channelled through the structural funds, which are made up of four elements:

1   the European Regional Development Fund (ERDF) that was established to provide infrastructure support for businesses and local development projects;
2   the European Social Fund (ESF) that was created to assist the return of unemployed and disadvantaged sections of society to the workforce;

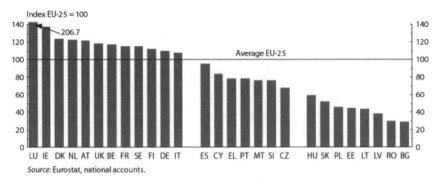

Figure 3.1 GDP per head, 2002. Source: http://europa.eu.int/COMM/regional_policy/intro/ working3_en.htm

3 the European Agricultural Guidance and Guarantee Fund (EAGGF) that was set up to finance the CAP;
4 the Financial Instrument for Fisheries Guidance (FIFG) was created to assist with the modernization of the fishing industry.

The March 1999 Berlin European Council made some reforms to the structural funds, so that for the 2000–6 period some 94 per cent of the structural funding was concentrated on three objectives:

1 to assist regions where economic development is not progressing at an appropriate pace;
2 to support economic and social conversion in those areas that face difficulties;
3 to promote employment through the modernization of training.

Cohesion fund

In addition to the funding provided by the Structural Funds, a Cohesion Fund was created in 1993 with the purpose of tackling the need for improvements in infrastructure projects (energy, telecommunications and transport) in the poorest member states. Such a project was essential to ensure that the budgetary restraints imposed on member states in participating in a single currency would not hinder efforts to reduce the economic and social diversity among the member states. The financing provided by the Cohesion Fund initially applied to Greece, Ireland, Portugal and Spain, although improvements in Ireland's economy meant that it only received funding until 2003. The accession of 10 new member states in 2004 has meant that significant resources have been targeted at those countries (one-third of all funding between 2004 and 2006), in addition to the continued funding given to Greece, Portugal and Spain.

Environment policy

Overview

Despite the fact that the Treaty of Rome did not contain any legal provision for a European environmental policy, it is nevertheless the case that issues relating to the environment have become an increasingly important concern of the EU. The lack of initial consideration given to an environmental policy was, of course, a reflection of the general lack of interest in matters relating to the environment in the early years of the Community's development. It is a situation that has altered because of the growing awareness of issues relating to climate change and the fact that, in the face of these, individual member states need to offer a common viewpoint that represents the interests of the EU. Today the EU plays an important role in matters relating to the environment throughout Europe and indeed the world by participating in global negotiations on the environment, including the Kyoto Protocol on Climate Change.

History

Since the EU's environmental policy was established in 1972 there has developed a substantial body of environmental law to protect against pollution (water, air, noise) as well as to impose controls on certain industries (chemical, biotechnology and nuclear). The Single European Act (SEA) was a major development in terms of environmental policy as the Community was granted an explicit statutory/legal mandate in the field of environmental policy for the first time. The SEA declared the Community's aims were:

1 preserving, protecting and improving the quality of the environment;
2 protecting human health;
3 prudent and rational utilization of natural resources.

The Maastricht Treaty on European Union added to the Union's role with regards to environmental policy by providing an additional objective of promoting measures at the international level to deal with regional or worldwide environmental problems. The Treaty also committed the EU to aim for a high level of environmental protection, taking into account regional diversity and that environmental protection had to be integrated with other policy areas. In terms of decision-making, the Treaty on European Union also provided for greater use of qualified majority voting (QMV) on most environmental issues. Further developments included the promotion of the concept of sustainable development in the Treaty of Amsterdam.

The growing importance of Community environmental policy over the past three decades can be attributed to a number of factors, including the 'green' movement that developed from the 1970s and the recognized need for cross-border cooperation on environmental issues given that 'pollution knows no borders'. Nevertheless, an effective EU environmental policy has been hampered by a number of factors:

1 There has been a wide variation with regard to environmental standards within the EU, with some member states such as Austria, Denmark, the Netherlands, Finland, Sweden and Germany having traditionally employed higher environmental standards than other member states, such as Greece, Portugal and Spain.

2 Environment policy has proved difficult to enforce and police, with few of the member states fully applying EU environmental policy to national legislation.
3 There has sometimes been a lack of a clear division between EU and national competence with regards to environmental policy. While matters relating to the environment have a localized impact within member states (such as road building programmes), other matters impact on the EU as a whole and the wider world (such as acid rain and chlorofluorocarbon gases (CFCs)).
4 Some member states have been concerned about the impact of environmental protection on the international competitiveness of their economies.

European Environmental Agency

In 1993 a European Environmental Agency was set up to monitor the European environment. The agency currently comprises 31 member countries and was the first EU body to welcome the applicant nations from central and eastern Europe. The 31 countries of the agency are:

- the 25 member states of the EU;
- the three EU candidate countries: Bulgaria, Romania and Turkey;
- Iceland, Liechtenstein and Norway (all members of the European Economic Area).

Foreign and Security Policy

Overview

Matters relating to foreign and security policy touch on some of the most sensitive nerves of member states because it relates to the extent that European integration should encroach on those areas of policy that have tended to be dealt with at the national level. For this reason, member state governments have been keen to maintain control over aspects relating to foreign and security policy. Thus, European Political Cooperation (EPC) provided really no more than a framework for coordination among member states. And although the Treaty on European Union established a Common Foreign and Security Policy (CFSP), it was designed on intergovernmental lines with member states in control. This picture of national control has, however, been challenged by subsequent events where the EU has not always been able to respond in as coordinated or as effective a manner as it would like to. As a result, there has been a hardening and to some extent a deepening of cooperation on foreign and security policy, whereby structures and procedures have been created within the EU institutions to deal with this policy.

History

One of the enduring factors of European integration has been the re-peated interest that has been shown towards defence and foreign poli-cy. Such initiatives took place even before the foundation stone of the EU was laid in the 1957 Treaty of Rome. In 1950 the French Prime Minister, René Pléven, put forward a plan for an integrated European army that directly led to the European Defence Community (EDC) Treaty of 1952. But, because of concerns in France of possible German dominance, the French National Assembly rejected the Treaty in Au-gust 1954. In response to the failure of the EDC, Britain advanced the less federal Western European Union (WEU) in 1954 as an alternative security organization. But, while the WEU offered a collective security identity for western Europe, it was a far weaker organization than the 1949 North Atlantic Treaty Organisation (NATO) and was moreover not directly linked to the EEC.

Throughout the 1960s France called for closer political cooperation within the field of foreign and defence policy. Such views were outlined in the November 1961 Fouchet Plan (named after the French foreign minister) but, because of a lack of agreement among member states, negotiations on the Fouchet Plan collapsed in 1962. By the late 1960s EEC member states were once again considering options for closer for-eign policy cooperation, and in 1970 agreement was reached on EPC. It served as a vehicle for foreign policy consultation among member states until the Treaty on European Union, a period in excess of 20 years. The EPC process was based on intergovernmental cooperation and there was little room for the supranational institutions of the Eu-ropean Community, such as the European Commission.

By the mid-1980s EC member states did, however, display an appetite for a stronger mechanism for coordinating foreign policy cooperation. Of the factors that influenced this viewpoint, external developments such as the collapse of Communism in eastern Europe, the fragmenta-tion of the Soviet Union and German reunification were important. These developments pressurized EC member states to reassess the political nature of the Community in an intergovernmental conference (IGC) that commenced in December 1990. The reassessment was fi-nalized at the Maastricht European Council of December 1991.

The outcome of those negotiations was that the EC (to be renamed the EU) established a CFSP. While cooperation continued to be based on an intergovernmental method, with member states being the domi-nant force, the agreement did allow for the now EU to express common positions on foreign policy. They were specifically aimed at ensuring that the member states acted as a cohesive whole. Moreover, the Treaty also specifically noted that the WEU would become the defence arm of the EU, though to pacify Britain, Denmark, the Netherlands, Portugal, and the USA the Treaty emphasized that NATO would remain the dominant vehicle for coordinating European foreign and security policy.

Developing a Common Foreign Policy

At the same time that the Treaty on European Union was being negotiated, member states were also faced with the disintegration of the former Yugoslavia from the summer of 1991 onwards. Of all the crises that EU member states had to respond to in the post-Maastricht period, the Balkans proved to be the most testing. It demonstrated the weaknesses of cooperation within the EU and the limitations of the CFSP to be able to respond in an effective manner.

The Maastricht agreement did, however, include a commitment to further review the CFSP provisions (and the other aspects of the Treaty) by 1996. The question of how to increase the effectiveness of the CFSP was accordingly a core aspect of the IGC negotiations that commenced in March 1996, reaching their conclusion at the Amsterdam European Council of June 1997. The outcome of those negotiations was a Treaty of Amsterdam that, among other aspects, further developed the EU's capabilities in the field of foreign and security policy. This specifically included the creation of a new position of a CFSP High Representative, while the European Council would be able to appoint 'a special representative' to focus on specific issues. This development reflected strongly on the practice of using such representatives in the course of the Bosnian conflict, including Lord Carrington, David Owen and Carl Bildt. In bolstering the support network that dealt with the CFSP, the Amsterdam Treaty also established a new policy-planning unit to advise the High Representative.

Towards a Common Defence Policy

In the wake of the Amsterdam Treaty, EU member states were faced with a further crisis in the Balkans, which this time concerned Kosovo. Despite the recent commitments to bolster the CFSP, and irrespective of the learning experience of the EU's response to the former Yugoslavia some years before, the EU was still to be found wanting in its dealings with the conflict in Kosovo. Yet at the same time there was a narrowing of differences among European governments as to both the objectives and the means of a European defence identity. The end product of this was agreement at the June 1999 Cologne European Council to provide the EU with a defence capacity by means of transferring the majority of the WEU's functions to it. The Cologne meeting committed member states to a common policy on security and defence to provide the EU with 'the capacity for autonomous action backed up by credible military forces, the means to decide to use them, and a readiness to do so, in order to respond to international crises without prejudice to NATO'. The second development concerned the appointment of Javier Solana, the former NATO Secretary General, as the first EU High Representative for foreign and security policy.

Thereafter, at the December 1999 Helsinki European Council, member states reached a commitment to establish a multinational corps of 50,000 to 60,000 forces with the capability of mounting an autonomous European mission if NATO declined to get involved in a crisis situation. In terms of institutional dynamics, agreement was also reached at Helsinki on the establishment of three military and political bodies that would be responsible to the Council of Ministers:

- A standing Political and Security Committee (PSC), meeting once a week, consisting of senior national officials having responsibility for all areas of the CFSP, including a European Security and Defence Policy (ESDP). The PSC will essentially have political control of military operations in a crisis situation.
- A European Military Committee (EMC) comprising national Chiefs of Defence to be represented by appointed military delegates, with Chiefs of Defence meetings taking place as and when required. The EMC offers military advice to the PSC, whilst also giving directions to the European Military Staff.
- A European Military Staff as part of the structures of the Council so as to give military support to the ESDP. The Staff has responsibility for providing situation assessments, early warning and strategic planning for the Petersberg tasks.

These developments represented a substantial achievement and highlighted the progress that discussions had made to what was now called the European Security and Defence Policy (ESDP). The institutional structures confirmed that defence questions would be subject to intergovernmental methods of decision-making, with there being no direct input for the European Parliament and Commission.

The Constitutional Treaty that was agreed to by member states in 2004 made further changes to the CFSP. Concern over the EU's international identity led to the creation of a new EU Minister for Foreign Affairs that will combine the existing positions of the Council's High Representative for foreign policy and the European Commissioner for external relations. The reasoning behind this strategy was that the new post would ensure that there would be a single spokesperson able to provide clear coordination of EU foreign policy At the same time, the Constitutional Treaty strengthened EU defence policy by permitting a core group of countries to enhance their cooperation on military matters if such a move is approved in the Council by majority vote. Thus, those member states that are more willing (and more able) will take a stronger role in EU military operations.

Justice and home affairs

Overview

It is only in recent years that the EU has become involved in matters relating to justice and home affairs (JHA). The Maastricht Treaty on European Union established a pillar structure that included a specific role for JHA in pillar 3, albeit based on intergovernmental cooperation. The reasoning for establishing cooperation on JHA issues was that there was a need for stronger cooperation between interior and justice ministries with the removal of internal borders between states. When this was combined with the collapse of communism in central and eastern Europe, there was an acknowledgement on the part of member states and the EU institutions of the need for closer cooperation on such matters as asylum policy.

History

Although the Treaty of Rome made reference to the free movement of persons, no attention was given to aspects directly relating to this provision. Thus, it did not refer to such matters as border crossings or visa policy. This state of affairs continued for a number of decades, and it was only in the 1970s that member states commenced a process of trying to establish some form of cooperation on police and judicial issues. Such cooperation was becoming ever more important because of a growing awareness of the need to combat such threats as organized crime and drug trafficking. Yet, where cooperation did take place, it was of an informal nature and outside the legal framework of the Community. To this end in 1975 the Trevi group was established with the purpose of creating informal cooperation among EU ministers to tackle drug trafficking and international terrorism. Thereafter the Single European Act's (SEA) commitment to establish a single market further raised awareness about the need to respond to issues relating to asylum and immigration policies, for instance. This was of relevance because of the four freedoms that were at the heart of the single market, namely the free movement of goods, capital, services and persons.

Such cooperation that did take place was nonetheless outside the framework of the Community and was devoid of dynamism. A direct consequence of this was the creation of the Schengen Agreement in 1985 by France, Germany, Belgium, Luxembourg and the Netherlands. Although the agreement sought to remove border controls between the participating nations, it also sought to establish common procedures relating to asylum, police and judicial cooperation as well as improving controls at external borders.

Treaty on European Union

The major change relating to JHA came in the Treaty on European Union and was a direct consequence of the need to develop stronger cooperation among police and judicial ministries in the aftermath of the end of communist rule in eastern Europe. The Treaty on European Union was concerned with asylum policy; rules governing the crossing of the external borders of the member states; immigration policy; combating drugs; combating international fraud; judicial cooperation in civil and criminal matters; customs cooperation; and police cooperation. Decision-making was, however, based on an intergovernmental design (as with the CFSP), and as such the EU institutions were not directly involved in the process.

Reform

In response to some of the criticisms that had been levied at the operation of JHA under the institutional design of the Treaty on European Union, the Treaty of Amsterdam offered a more precise view of cooperation. This included an agreement to establish an area of freedom, security and justice, and resulted in a number of aspects of the JHA provisions of the third pillar being incorporated in the regular first pillar provisions of the EU. This specifically applied to those matters that related to the free movement of people, including matters relating to asylum, immigration and visas. The Schengen agreement on the free movement of persons between member states was also incorporated into the first pillar provisions of the EU. The effect of these changes was that the third pillar was renamed 'Police and Judicial Cooperation in Criminal Matters'. This emphasis on the need for common action in police and judicial cooperation among member states was the product of the growing threats posed to member states from organized crime, including illegal immigration and money laundering. Terrorist threats were additionally an important factor, particularly in the wake of the 11 September 2001 terrorist attacks on the United States. Further reforms were included in the Treaty of Nice, including the extension of the use of qualified majority voting to those areas that had been brought within the Community framework. This included the free movement of persons. Those issues that have remained in the third pillar continue to be governed by unanimity.

Trade policy

Overview

Trade is one of the most fundamental activities of the EU. In the history of European integration, some member states have argued that the EU should primarily be an organization that facilitates free trade rather than a political body which impacts on the sovereignty of national governments. Despite such differences of views, it is nonetheless the case that, although the 25 member states of the EU represent 7 per cent of the world's population, they account for in excess of 20 per cent of all global imports and exports and the EU is the largest trading bloc in the world. The combined economic strength of the member states means that the EU is able to play an important role in matters relating to trade. Indeed, to ensure that the influence of the 25 member states is maximized, EU negotiations on trade policy are conducted by the European Commissioner responsible for trade rather than by individual member states. As such, EU negotiations in the General Agreement on Tariffs and Trade (GATT) and its successor the World Trade Organization (WTO) were led by the European Commission.

Tariff barriers

A central tenet of trade policy is the removal of tariff barriers so as to allow trade to take place by means of market policy. This was a key objective of the Treaty of Rome, whereby the removal of tariff barriers among the initial six member states so as to enable free trade within the then Community was achieved by 1968 (18 months earlier than scheduled). This removal of internal tariff barriers continued with the accession of new member states, while at the same time a common external tariff was established so as to ensure that all trade entering the Community was subject to the same conditions no matter the member state that it gained access to. Within the EU, measures to reduce trading barriers did, however, fail to tackle all trade barriers between member states and it was not until the SEA that these matters were addressed in the creation of a single market.

Criticism

Inevitably, because trade policy centres on access to markets with other countries and the operation of a 'level playing field', there have often been disagreements between the EU and other countries on matters relating to market access and the use of subsidies. This has included the Common Agricultural Policy (CAP), where criticism has been levied at the subsidies that the EU essentially pays to its farmers. Some trade disputes have been between the EU and specific countries. This has included the US, where there have been disputes over the financial assistance that the EU has provided to Airbus, which the US has claimed has impacted on the ability of Boeing to compete. At the same time, some non-EU countries have, for instance, complained about the preferential access that African, Caribbean and Pacific (ACP) countries have to EU markets, which in the 1990s sparked a trade dispute between the USA and the EU over bananas. In the face of such criticism, the EU has argued that it is important to bring the ACP countries into the world economy, as highlighted in the February 2000 Cotonou Agreement. In March 2001 the EU launched the 'Everything but Arms' initiative, whereby the world's 50 least developed countries were provided with access to EU markets without the imposition of any duties.

4   Glossary

A

À la carte Europe

A concept of **differentiated integration** whereby member states are able to select policies as if they were a menu and, while they would be fully committed to that policy, the overall progress of European integration would not be uniform as states would not be moving towards the same goal. Nevertheless, there would still remain a minimum number of common objectives. This process creates a danger of erosion of the *acquis communitaire* because it permits an **opt-out** and a permanent **derogation**, thereby undermining solidarity and the institutional framework.

Abatement

At the Fontainebleau **European Council** of June 1984 the UK obtained a rebate on its contribution to the EU budget as a solution to the **British budget problem**. Although the rebate is generally known as the **Fontainebleau agreement**, it is technically referred to as the abatement.

Abstention

It is possible for a member state to abstain from a vote in the **Council of Ministers**.

Accession

Refers to the act of joining the EU. The treaties which cover the conclusion of the negotiations between applicant countries and EU member states are known as 'Treaties of Accession'. In June 1993, the

Table 4.1 From application to accession

Country	Date of application	Accession
Denmark	August 1961	January 1973
Ireland	October 1961	January 1973
United Kingdom	August 1961	January 1973
Greece	June 1975	January 1981
Portugal	March 1977	January 1986
Spain	July 1977	January 1986
Turkey	April 1987	
Austria	July 1989	January 1995
Cyprus	July1990	May 2004
Malta	July1990	May 2004
Sweden	July 1991	January 1995
Finland	March 1992	January 1995
Hungary	March 1994	May 2004
Poland	April 1994	May 2004
Latvia	October 1994	May 2004
Romania	June 1995	
Slovakia	June 1995	May 2004
Estonia	November 1995	May 2004
Lithuania	December 1995	May 2004
Bulgaria	December 1995	
Czech Republic	January 1996	May 2004
Slovenia	June 1996	May 2004
Croatia	February 2003	

Copenhagen European Council set out a series of criteria for the accession of **central and eastern European states** to the EU (**Copenhagen criteria**). Countries that join the EU are often granted periods of adjustment to permit their economies to be able to fully implement EU policies which might otherwise cause some difficulty (see **association agreement** and **enlargement**).

Accountability

Since the 1990s the question of accountability has been a key concern of the EU because of an increasing perception that the EU institutions are remote from the European population. Despite the fact that the **European Parliament** is directly elected, surveys commissioned by **Eurobarometer** regularly report that EU citizens consider decision-makers in Brussels to be unaccountable. As a response to this state of affairs, the EU has attempted to promote greater **transparency** and openness.

Acquis communitaire

This French term refers to the body of legislation and guarantees between member states as a result of the Treaty obligations, regulations and laws since the **Treaties of Rome** establishing the **European Economic Community** (EEC) entered into force in 1958. All prospective members of the EU have to accept the *acquis* before they can enter. Subsequent **intergovernmental conference** (IGC) negotiations that resulted in the **Single European Act** (1987), the Maastricht **Treaty on European Union** (1993), the **Treaty of Amsterdam** (1999), and the **Treaty of Nice** (2003) have attempted to reform the *acquis communitaire* by making changes to the existing Treaties of the European Union. The most recent reform was the **Constitutional Treaty** that was signed by member states in June 2004 and will enter into force once it has been ratified at a domestic level by individual member states.

Action Committee for the United States of Europe (ACUSE)

A small pressure group formed by **Jean Monnet** in October 1955 after his resignation as president of the **European Coal and Steel Community** (ECSC). It campaigned for greater European integration and played an influential role in the creation of the **European Economic Community** (EEC). The group, which included representatives from political parties and trade unions, was disbanded by Monnet in 1975.

Acts of the Community Institutions

The acts which are adopted by the **Council of Ministers** and the **European Commission** are divided into four categories: (1) **regulations** that have direct force of law in all member states; (2) **directives** that require member states to adopt appropriate rules, although they are left with a choice of how to achieve the objectives; (3) **decisions** which have direct effect in law – they refer to specific individual cases that can be addressed to firms, individuals or a member state; (4) non-binding recommendations and opinions.

Additionality

The principle that EU funds for specific projects (primarily from the **structural funds**) are in addition to, rather than instead of, funding from member state governments. The additionality rule was introduced in 1988 at the time of a reform of the structural funds and reflected the desire to tackle the temptation of member states to permit EU funding to replace national funding. Compliance with this rule is monitored by the **European Commission**.

Adenauer, Konrad (1876–1967)

First Chancellor of the Federal Republic of Germany from 1949 until his resignation in 1963, having been re-elected in 1953 and 1957. Between 1951 and 1955 he also held the office of Foreign Minister. He negotiated German entry into the **Council of Europe, North Atlantic Treaty Organisation** (NATO) and European Communities. In 1955 he established diplomatic relations with the USSR, which included an agreement by the Soviet Union to return German prisoners of war. His foreign policy was known as a 'policy of strength' and had two main objectives: the rehabilitation and reunification of Germany. Adenauer resolved the dispute with France over the Saarland and went on to develop a close relationship with the French president, **Charles de Gaulle**. This produced the 1963 **Treaty of Friendship** between the two nations and served as the basis for the Franco-German axis that shaped the development of the **European Community**. Earlier in his career he was president of the Prussian State Council between 1920 and 1933 and served as mayor of Cologne from 1917–33, but was then removed by the Nazis. During the Weimar Republic he was a key member of the Catholic Centre Party and subsequently founded the Christian Democratic Union in 1945. He led the German delegation to the Congress of Europe at The Hague in 1948.

Adonnino Committee see Committee for a People's Europe

Adoption

The forming of a measure that has legal effect.

Advocate general

An officer of the **Court of Justice**, whose job is to submit a 'reasoned opinion' in open court based on the information submitted by all the parties. This opinion serves to provide a recommendation on the judgment to be taken by the Court. In the majority of cases the judges follow the recommendations of the **advocate general**.

AETR judgment

In 1971 the **Court of Justice** ruled that where the European Communities had an explicit internal competence they also had a parallel external competence. The significance of this ruling was that it stressed that in those areas where the EC had competence then the member states were unable to take action that was independent of the EC.

African, Caribbean and Pacific States (ACP)

The term given to the developing countries that have an **association agreement** with the EU (Table 4.2). Whereas the original provisions were directed towards the former colonies of **the Six**, and documented by the 1963 and 1969 **Yaoundé Convention**, the **enlargement** of the Community has brought new members into the agreement which, although initially covered by the 1975 **Lomé Convention**, have since 2000 been covered by the **Cotonou Agreement**. A majority of the 78 ACP states, which comprise a total population of approximately 650 million people, are extremely poor and underdeveloped countries. All ACP states are able to obtain funds from the **European Investment Bank** (EIB) and the **European Development Fund**.

Agenda

The **European Parliament** adopts its plenary agenda at the start of each part-session, having already consulted members of the various political groups about its contents. By contrast, the **Council of Ministers**

Table 4.2 African, Caribbean and Pacific States

Angola	The Gambia	Rwanda
Antigua and Barbuda	Ghana	St Kitts and Nevis
Bahamas	Grenada	St Lucia
Barbados	Guinea	St Vincent and the
Belize	Guinea Bissau	Grenadines
Benin	Guyana	Samoa
Botswana	Haiti	Sao Tomé and Principe
Burkina Faso	Jamaica	Senegal
Burundi	Kenya	Seychelles
Cameroon	Kiribati	Sierra Leone
Cape Verde	Lesotho	Solomon Islands
Central African Republic	Liberia	Somalia
Chad	Madagascar	South Africa
Comoros	Malawi	Sudan
Congo-Brazzaville	Mali	Surinam
Congo-Kinshasa (Zaire)	Marshall Islands	Swaziland
Cook Islands	Mauritania	Tanzania
Côte d'Ivoire	Mauritius	Togo
Djibouti	Micronesia	Tonga
Dominica	Mozambique	Trinidad and Tobago
Dominican Republic	Namibia	Tuvalu
East Timor	Nauru	Uganda
Equatorial Guinea	Niger	Vanuatu
Eritrea	Nigeria	Zambia
Ethiopia	Niue	Zimbabwe
Fiji	Palau	
Gabon	Papua New Guinea	

agenda is principally established by the member state which holds the **Council Presidency**, though it is equally subject to consultation with other interested parties.

Agenda 2000

Jacques Santer, the President of the **European Commission**, presented Agenda 2000 to the **European Parliament** in Strasbourg on 16 July 1997. The 1300-page package of plans covered EU **enlargement**, the **budget** and the future of the **Common Agricultural Policy** (CAP). The Agenda 2000 report contained:

- a Commission Opinion on each of the 10 eastern European states asking for membership of the European Union with the recommendation that membership negotiations be opened with the five leading candidate states (the Czech Republic, Poland, Hungary, Estonia, Slovenia) plus Cyprus – the 5 + 1 states;
- analysis of EU policies and recommendations on how to strengthen those policy areas so that they could deal with the strains of enlargement;
- proposals on how to finance enlargement.

The Agenda 2000 report has shaped and directed the debate and decision-making on the question of EU enlargement since its publication. Agenda 2000 also established a financial framework for supporting the pre-accession process in the applicant countries. This has taken the form of the **PHARE** programme, aid for agricultural development, and structural aid to help applicant countries comply with EU infrastructure standards in the transport and environmental sectors.

Agenda setting

Refers to the means by which an issue appears on the **agenda** and is framed for a later debate.

Agricultural levies

A duty charged on farm products imported into the EU from non-member countries which offsets differences between price levels inside the Community and externally lower world market prices. In this context, the actual rates change according to world market prices. The effect of this process is that EU farmers are guaranteed high prices while providing finance for the EU (see **Common Agricultural Policy**).

Airbus

This air industry project originally began in 1965 as an Anglo-French proposal, with Airbus Industrie being founded in 1990 as a European economic interest grouping. It is now one of the most widely known collaborative projects within the EU. The most significant members of the project are France, Germany and the UK, while Belgium, the Netherlands and Spain make smaller contributions. The main assembly plant is in Toulouse, with the UK's contribution being primarily the design and manufacture of the wings. The success of Airbus and the development since 2000 of the superjumbo Airbus A380 (which is able to carry 555 passengers) has led to tension with United States (US) aircraft manufacturers, in particular Boeing. This is because US manufacturers consider that Airbus has benefited from a competitive advantage in the form of subsidies from EU member states, a situation which contravenes the rules of the **World Trade Organization** (WTO).

Amendment of the Treaties

Proposals to amend the Treaties may be submitted by any member state to the Council. The Council can call an **intergovernmental conference** of the member states after having consulted the **European Parliament** and the **European Commission**. An amendment has to be ratified by all member states.

Amsterdam Treaty see *Treaty of Amsterdam*

Andean Community of Nations

Formerly the Andean Pact, this customs union comprises Bolivia, Colombia, Ecuador, Peru and Venezuela. It has formal ties with the EU.

Annual work programme

At the end of each year the **European Commission** publishes an annual work programme which both highlights the progress achieved in the past year and establishes priorities for the forthcoming year.

Antici group

An informal group of assistants to member states' **Committee of Permanent Representatives** (Coreper) that acts as a forum where a **Council Presidency** can coordinate work programmes. At **European Council** meetings the Antici group acts as a liaison between national delegations and Heads of State or Government. The Antici group was named after the Italian Deputy Permanent Representative to the Community, Paulo Antici, who was its first chairman in 1975.

Anti-dumping

Anti-dumping duties are imposed on goods that are imported into the EU at lower prices than those in the exporter's home market. As a result of the EU's **Common Commercial Policy**, the **European Commission** has the responsibility to examine cases of dumping and, if needed, to impose duties on goods that are concluded to have been 'dumped'. The Commission does, however, have to be careful in its application of anti-dumping duties because of the potential to create claims of a **Fortress Europe**.

Anti-Fraud Office (OLAF)

Based within the **European Commission**, it is an independent office that since its establishment in 1999 has been responsible for combating fraud against the EU budget as well as more general fraud or illegal action that is counter to the **budget** and broader aspects of organized international crime.

Anti-poverty programme

This was highlighted as one of the primary tasks of the 1974 Social Action Programme and was adopted by the **Council of Ministers** in 1975.

Anti-trust

To ensure free and fair competition, EU rules forbid companies which have a strong position in the market to abuse that position, and prohibit agreements that restrict competition, such as those that could result in increased prices of goods. Companies that are found guilty of anti-competitive procedures can be fined by the **European Commission**. In December 2005 the European Commission issued formal charges against Microsoft for having broken EU competition rules through abusing its dominant market position with regard to computer operating systems.

Applicant country

When a country makes an application to join the EU it is referred to as an 'applicant country'. Once the application has been officially accepted, it becomes a **candidate country**.

Approximation

Approximation was the term that was initially used in the Treaty of Rome to refer to the process that is today known as **harmonization**.

Area of Freedom, Security and Justice (AFSJ)

The **Treaty of Amsterdam** further developed cooperation in the fields of **justice and home affairs** that had been initially set out in the Maastricht **Treaty on European Union**. This initiative was borne out of a desire to promote greater freedom of movement for individuals within the EU and at the same time to provide the means for more effective coordination to combat crime. As a result, the AFSJ has incorporated the **Schengen agreement** and provided for the abolition of frontier controls, the free movement of people, and cooperation between judicial and police authorities to combat cross-border crime.

Article

A clause or unit of a Treaty that can be divided into paragraphs.

Arusha Convention

Refers to an aid and trade agreement that was signed in 1969 between **the six** and Kenya, Tanzania and Uganda. Although it took effect in January 1971, the Arusha Convention was succeeded in 1975 by the **Lomé Convention**.

ASEAN see Association of South East Asian Nations

Assembly

Previous name of the **European Parliament**.

Assent procedure

The assent procedure was introduced in the **Single European Act** (SEA) and ensured that the assent of the **European Parliament** (by means of an absolute majority of its members) was necessary before certain important decisions can be adopted. In other words if the European Parliament did not provide its assent then the decision could not adopted. The procedure provided the European Parliament with an ability to accept or reject a proposal, but not to amend it. The procedure is applicable to decisions on the accession of new member states, the conclusion of certain international agreements, specific tasks of the

European Central Bank (ECB), amendments to the statute of the **European System of Central Banks** (ESCB) and of the ECB, the **structural funds** and **Cohesion Funds**, the uniform procedure for elections to the European Parliament, and the appointment of the **European Commission**. The **Treaty of Amsterdam** extended this remit so that the European Parliament's assent has been necessary where sanctions are imposed on a member state when there has been a breach of fundamental rights. However, as a result of the attempt to simplify EU legislative procedures, the **Constitutional Treaty** has brought assent procedure under the heading of 'special legislative procedures', stipulating that, while the term 'assent' should no longer be used, the procedure would nonetheless be used under the term 'approval procedure' for European laws and framework laws.

Assizes

Describes consultative meetings of representatives from **national parliaments** who seek to support the process of European integration.

Association agreement

Refers to the original means for establishing agreements between candidate member states and the EC, of which the first was signed in 1961 with Greece. Subsequent agreements have included Malta (1970), Cyprus (1972), Turkey (1973), Poland and Hungary (1991) Bulgaria, the

Table 4.3 From association agreement to EU membership

Country	Association agreement signed on	Accession application submitted on	Joined the EU on
Bulgaria	1/3/1993	14/12/1995	
Croatia	29/10/2001	21/2/2003	
Cyprus	19/12/1972	3/07/1990	1/5/2004
Czech Republic	6/10/1993	17/1/1996	1/5/2004
Estonia	12/6/1995	24/11/1995	1/5/2004
Hungary	16/12/1991	31/3/1994	1/5/2004
Latvia	12/6/1995	13/10/1995	1/5/2004
Lithuania	12/6/1995	8/12/1995	1/5/2004
Malta	5/12/1970	3/7/1990	1/5/2004
Poland	16/12/1991	5/4/1994	1/5/2004
Romania	8/12/1993	22/6/1995	
Slovakia	6/10/1993	27/6/1995	1/5/2004
Slovenia	10/6/1996	10/6/1996	1/5/2004
Turkey	12/9/1973	14/4/1987	

Czech Republic, Romania and Slovakia (1993), Estonia, Latvia and Lithuania (1995), Slovenia (1996) and Croatia (2001). The ending of the **Cold War** brought forth a new type of **Europe Agreements** for **central and eastern European states** that sought membership of the Community (see **Accession** and **Enlargement**).

Association of South East Asian Nations (ASEAN)

The Association of South East Asian Nations was established on 8 August 1967. Since then the original group of five member countries – Indonesia, Malaysia, Philippines, Singapore and Thailand – has expanded to 10: Brunei Darussalam (1984), Vietnam (1995), Laos, Myanmar (both 1997) and Cambodia (1999). With a combined population of 500 million people, ASEAN is an important partner for the EU (and vice versa). In 1972 the **European Economic Community** was the first organization to establish informal relations with ASEAN and since 1978 there has been a political cooperation agreement between the Community/EU and ASEAN. This has resulted in a biennial conference of EU and ASEAN foreign ministers, while a permanent bureau (ASEAN Brussels Committee) ensures that continuous contact is achieved. Cooperation between ASEAN and the EU has intensified since the 1990s, with the EU recognizing in 1994 that ASEAN would continue to the central linchpin in the EU's dialogue with Asia. The first Asia–Europe Meeting (ASEM) took place in March 1996 in Bangkok. The importance of the EU–ASEAN relationship is emphasized by the fact that the EU is ASEAN's second largest export market, while EU foreign direct investment in the ASEAN countries has increased significantly in recent years.

Asylum

Although all EU member states subscribe to the principle of asylum it was not until 1990 that the EU finally responded to this issue in a formal manner through the Dublin Asylum Convention, which entered into force only in 1997. Until then, the commitment of EU member states to recognizing asylum was based on Article 14 of the 1948 Universal Declaration of Human Rights ('everyone has the right to seek and to enjoy in other countries asylum from persecution') and Article 1A of the Geneva Convention which was further strengthened by a 1967 Protocol on the Status of Refugees. In recent years the question of asylum policy has become increasingly important for the EU because of the instability that has been a common feature in world politics since the end of the **Cold War**. A significant proportion of this tension has been near the EU's own borders, in **central and eastern European states** and the Balkans. Further afield there have been conflicts in Afghanistan, Iraq, elsewhere in Asia and in Africa. As a result the EU has witnessed a considerable increase in the number of individuals who have sought asylum. However, the responsibility for granting asylum rests with individual member states. Within member states the issue of asylum has increasingly become an important domestic political issue as citizens question the ability of nation states to absorb asylum seekers. This has in turn fed into debates on European integration and is partly linked to a rise in **Euroscepticism** and extreme national parties, such as the National Front.

Atlantic Alliance

A common name for the **North Atlantic Treaty Organisation** (NATO).

Atypical worker

An individual who does not operate in full-time permanent employment, such as a part-time, fixed term or temporary employee.

Audit board

Established by the **Treaties of** Rome to examine the revenue and expenditure of the Community, it was replaced by the more dynamic **Court of Auditors** in 1977.

Austria

Population: 8.14m (2005)
Capital: Vienna
The Republic of Austria was founded in 1919 and re-established in May 1955 after the Second World War. Although Austria was a founding member of the **European Free Trade Association** (EFTA) it nevertheless pursued from the outset the prospect of becoming a member of the **European Community**. Austria was, however, not initially successful, not being able to achieve an **Association Agreement** with the Community as a result of negotiations from 1965 to 1967. Other members of EFTA were more successful with their hope of becoming a Community member (Denmark, Ireland and the UK joined in 1973). By 1977 Austria was, along with other EFTA members, able to benefit from a **free trade agreement** with the Community. Although this gave some comfort to its desire to gain access to the Community market, the further advances in European integration in the 1980s that were signified by the single market programme prompted Austria to review the issue of joining the Community. This resulted in it submitting a formal application for membership on 17 July 1989.

As a developed and prosperous nation, Austria was faced with few difficulties in joining the Community as it would become a net contributor to the Community budget. The only area of concern was that its neutral status conflicted with the aim of creating a **Common Foreign and Security Policy** (CFSP) that had been set out in the **Treaty on European Union**. In the end Austria joined the EU on 1 January 1995 along with Finland and Sweden and has been an active member. It joined the **Exchange Rate Mechanism** (ERM) on 9 January 1995 and four months later became the tenth member state to sign the **Schengen agreement** on 28 April 1995 (implementation from 1 April 1998). In March 1998 it was one of 11 member states to be named by the **European Commission** as having met the **convergence criteria** for **Economic and Monetary Union** (EMU) and it adopted the **single currency** from 1 January 1999. But, while Austria found the task of adapting to the EU to be a relatively straightforward task in terms of implementing policies and procedures, it nevertheless experienced a period of diplomatic isolation in 2000 as a result of Jörg Haider's far-right Freedom Party taking part in a coalition government.

Avis

Opinions issued by the **European Commission** on the suitability of an application by a country for EU membership are referred to by the term avis.

B

Balance of payments

Refers to the external transactions of a country over a certain period of time. A surplus occurs in the balance of payments when the total amount of exports of goods and services (plus capital investment in the country from other nations) exceeds the total amount of imports of goods and services (plus the total amount of investment overseas by nations of the state).

Balladur memorandum

The name given to the French government's report on the reform of the **European Monetary System** (EMS) with respect to the completion of the internal market which was presented by the then Finance Minister, Edouard Balladur, in January 1998. It advocated that all member states should join the **Exchange Rate Mechanism** (ERM) in the context of the 'rapid pursuit of the monetary construction of Europe'. It was influential in providing momentum towards **Economic and Monetary Union** (EMU).

Baltic states

In July 1994 the three Baltic states of Estonia, Latvia and Lithuania each signed a free trade agreement with the EU. Ten years later, in May 2004, they became EU member states.

Bananas

Throughout the 1990s bananas were the source of a trade dispute between the EU and the USA. This was because the EU allowed former British and French colonies from the **African, Caribbean and Pacific** (ACP) States to have preferential access to EU markets and as a result restricted access for US companies such as Chiquita and Dole. The US in turn appealed to the **World Trade Organization** (WTO) disputes settlement panel, which in noting the discrimination required the EU to reassess its policy on bananas. However, pressure from France and the UK to defend the preferential treatment for ACP states ensured that a resolution could not be reached and in response in 1999 the US imposed significant tariffs on a number of British and French products that entered the US market. This trade conflict was finally resolved in April 2001 when the EU and the US reached an agreement that by 2006 bananas would be the subject of a tariff-only system.

Bank for International Settlements (BIS)

Founded on 17 May 1930, the BIS is the oldest international financial organization in the world. Based in Basel (Switzerland), its role is to assist cooperation between central banks and ease international financial operations.

Banking sector

The banking sector plays a central role in the introduction of the **euro** as the **single currency**. Although the **European Central Bank** issues euro notes and coins, banks facilitate the increasing amount of automated transactions, including loans, securities and payment by cheque and bank card. Because many national currencies have been replaced by the euro, banks have to ensure that all transactions can operate in euros.

Barber Protocol

This protocol, which was introduced in the Maastricht **Treaty on European Union**, stressed that employers could offer unequal pensions for men and women for work performed prior to 17 May 1990, when the **Court of Justice** ruled in the case of *Barber* v. *Guardian Royal Exchange* that pension was part of pay and that men and women should be paid the same for equal amounts of work. Consequently, it judged that allowing women to retire on full pension at the age of 60 was unfair to men.

Barcelona declaration

EU member states agreed to the Barcelona declaration with 12 adjoining Mediterranean states at a conference in November 1995, the aim of which was to guarantee security in the Mediterranean region. In so doing, three pillars were established. The first pillar provided for a political and security partnership, guaranteeing human rights and basic political freedoms. The second pillar had the aim of establishing a Euro-Mediterranean free trade area by 2010. The third pillar dealt with cultural and social issues, including a mutual respect for culture and religion.

Barre Plan

In the wake of the 1968 monetary crisis the Vice-President of the **European Commission** with responsibility for economic and social affairs, Raymond Barre, submitted a memorandum on 12 February 1969 that proposed closer economic and monetary cooperation. This included the provision for medium-term financial assistance and short-term monetary assistance. The plan, which was adopted by the Council on 17 July 1969, had been put forward in the wake of the 1968–69 monetary crisis which had resulted in the devaluation of the French franc and the revaluation of the German Deutschmark.

Barroso, José Manuel (b. 1956)

President of the **European Commission** since 1 November 2004 (five-year term of office), having taken over from **Romano Prodi**. An academic by training (law, political science and international relations), Barroso was a successful Portuguese politician, having previously held various position including Prime Minister (2002–4) and Foreign Minister. As Prime Minister and Foreign Minister he was actively involved in **European Council** meetings. As President of the Commission, Barroso has the important task of providing a strong sense of direction in the Commission, which in recent years has not enjoyed the influence that it did under the Presidency of **Jacques Delors**. One of Barroso's important tasks is overseeing the largest **enlargement** in the history of European integration (10 countries joined on 1 May 2004), and providing a framework for the future development of the EU. The latter has been complicated by the difficulties that surrounded the ratification of the **Constitutional Treaty**.

Barriers to trade

The **single market** aimed to remove barriers to trade such as tariffs and quotas.

Basket of currencies

This term referred to the currencies of the countries that determined the value of the **ECU** (European Currency Unit). Currencies within the basket were given different weights which reflected the Gross National Product (GNP) of the particular country. The ECU was a component of the **European Monetary System** (EMS) and was succeeded by the **euro** in 1999.

Beef crisis

On 20 March 1996 UK authorities announced that there could be a link between bovine spongiform encephalopathy (BSE) found in cattle and the fatal disease found in humans known as Creutzfeldt–Jakob disease. On 25 March the EU veterinary committee voted by 14 to 1 to recommend a total ban of UK beef exports (the only dissenter being the UK). This was immediately implemented on the export of beef and beef products from the UK. As a response to this ban the UK government of **John Major** adopted on 21 May 1996 a policy of non-cooperation with the EU until a timetable to lift the ban on the export of beef was settled. At the Florence **European Council** of June 1996 the UK government agreed to end its policy of non-cooperation in return for agreement on a phased lifting of the ban on beef exports. Although the policy of non-cooperation was short-lived, it inflicted considerable political damage to the UK's position within the EU and only served to isolate it among the other member states.

Belgium

Population: 10.31m (2005)
Capital: Brussels
Belgium has traditionally been perceived to be a strong supporter of European integration. The Belgian prime minister **Paul-Henri Spaak** helped establish **Benelux**, the 1948 **Hague Congress** and the **Council of Europe** (where he was the first President of the Consultative Assembly), and proved to be a key figure in the 1955 **Messina conference**

that led to the 1957 **Treaties of Rome**. Some years later, Prime Minister **Leo Tindemans** was the author of the 1975 **Tindemans Report** that aimed to propel the Community out of a period of slow growth. Belgium's advocacy of deeper European integration (and a strengthening of the EU's institutions) was reflected in its negotiating position during **intergovernmental conference** (IGC) negotiations, such as the **Treaty on European Union**. Belgium has, for instance, consistently argued for a stronger European defence identity. This support for European integration is reflected in the overall view of the population and by indicators such as a high turnout at **European elections**. To some extent this is not surprising as Belgium obtains considerable financial benefits from having so many of the EU institutions located in Brussels. That is not to mention the headquarters of other international organizations, such as the **North Atlantic Treaty Organisation** (NATO).

Belgo-Luxembourg Economic Union (BLEU)

A **customs union** between Belgium and Luxembourg which was created in 1921 and subsequently expanded in 1944 with the creation of **Benelux**. The presence of the BLEU resulted in financial statistics for Belgium and Luxembourg being jointly documented.

Benchmarking

This is the method by which the performance of a member state or business is measured against a similar competitor.

Benelux

The **customs union** of Belgium, the Netherlands and Luxembourg, which was agreed to by treaty in February 1958 and came into effect on 1 November 1960. All three countries were original members of the European Communities and have for the most part been advocates of closer European integration. Many individuals from Benelux have occupied influential positions in European institutions. This has included **Paul-Henri Spaak, Jean Rey, Jacques Santer** and **Gaston Thorn**. The aim of Benelux is to coordinate the macroeconomic and budgetary policies of the member countries with a view to promoting economic stability. It is governed by a Committee of Ministers assisted by an institutional structure comprising a secretariat, court of justice, economic and social committee and interparliamentary council.

Berlaymont

The name of the building which housed the **European Commission** from 1969 until renovations commenced in 1992 when staff were temporarily moved to the Breydel building. The word 'Berlaymont' did, however, remain synonymous with the European Commission.

Berlin blockade

In June 1948 the USSR closed road, rail and inland waterway access to West Berlin from the western zones of occupied Germany. These actions were prompted by initiatives being taken by the Western occupied powers (France, UK and the USA) to promote the founding of a West German state and to introduce a new and more stable currency in their zones. The USSR opposed these initiatives and sought to gain control and influence over them in return for access to necessities such as food and fuel. The blockade was, however, broken by the Berlin airlift, whereby the basic necessities were flown into West Berlin. The success of this initiative resulted in the blockade being lifted in May 1949, with the conclusion of the airlift in September 1949.

Berlin Wall

In August 1961 a wall was erected by the German Democratic Republic (GDR) to control the movement of individuals from West Berlin to East Berlin, after a period in which there was significant migration into West Germany via Berlin. The wall, which was made of concrete, was surrounded by a cleared area in the East Berlin side that was mined, floodlit and patrolled. It came to signify the division between the USSR led Eastern bloc and the US led Western bloc and was a key image of the **Cold War**. The lessening of the Soviet imposed controls on the Eastern bloc in the late 1980s resulted in the eventual collapse of the East German regime and the demolition of the Berlin Wall.

Beyen Plan

On 4 April 1955 the Netherlands foreign minister, Johan Willem Beyen, proposed in a memorandum the establishment of a customs union among **the Six** members of the **European Coal and Steel Community** (ECSC). In the period after the failure to create a **European Defence Community** (EDC) in 1954, Beyen's proposal was an important initiative in further advancing the cause of European integration by leading to the **Messina conference** which resulted in the **Treaties of Rome** that established the **European Economic Community** (EEC).

Bilaterals

Terminology for negotiations between two sides, such as meetings between member states or a member state and the **European Commission**.

Bipolarity

A situation in international relations when two states are in competition for dominance over the other. During the **Cold War** the competition between the United States and the Soviet Union was regarded as a bipolar relationship.

Black Monday

This refers to the meeting of EU Foreign Ministers that took place on 30 September 1991 to discuss the political union dimension of the **intergovernmental conference** (IGC) negotiations that were charged with the task of drafting the **Treaty on European Union**. At that meeting EU Foreign Ministers rejected an ambitious draft treaty on European Political Union that was put forward by the Netherlands government, which at that time occupied the position of **Council Presidency**. The text, which advocated the goal of deeper integration (including plans to give the Community control of defence, foreign policy and immigration matters as well as conferring greater powers on the **European Parliament**), was considered too integrationist. A direct consequence of this was that the negotiations thereafter focused on a proposal from the Luxembourg government to structure European political cooperation within a pillar framework, whereby cooperation on **common foreign and security policy** (CFSP) and **justice and home affairs** (JHA) would be based on **intergovernmental cooperation**.

Black Wednesday

This is the term commonly used to describe the UK's exit from the **Exchange Rate Mechanism** (ERM) on 16 September 1992. On that day sterling came under a great deal of pressure from currency speculators who considered that it was too weak to stay in the ERM. The ERM had, in fact, been unstable for much of the summer after Denmark rejected the Maastricht **Treaty on European Union** in a June **referendum**. On the fateful 16 September the British government desperately tried to support sterling by increasing interest rates from 10 per cent to 12 per cent and then subsequently to 15 per cent. The Bank of England also used nearly £3,000m of official reserves to support sterling. This had little effect, with the result that Britain withdrew from the ERM.

Blair, Anthony (b. 1953)

UK prime minister since the May 1997 general election and leader of
the Labour government that was re-elected in the general elections of
2001 and 2005. Blair entered parliament in 1983 and was elected to the
shadow cabinet in 1988. A committed pro-European, he has attempted
to raise the UK's profile in Europe and has been particularly active
in developing a stronger **European Security and Defence Policy.** At
the June 1997 Amsterdam **European Council** he agreed that the UK
would subscribe to the **Social Chapter** and thereby ended the **opt-out**
that had been negotiated by **John Major** in the Maastricht **Treaty on
European Union.** Blair also played an important role in the discussions that resulted in the **Treaty of Nice** and the **Constitutional Treaty.** But, despite these pro-European credentials, Blair's commitment
to the EU has not extended to the UK participating in **Economic and
Monetary Union** (EMU), which is as much a result of political as of
economic considerations. Nevertheless, it has been notable that in the
period since 1997 the UK economy has enjoyed a stronger economic
performance than many of the **eurozone** countries, which it has been
argued is a result of the UK not being constrained by the decisions of
the **European Central Bank** (ECB), although another important factor has been the increased labour market flexibility and less state regulation on industry within the UK. Blair's style of government has been
regarded as somewhat presidential, whereby he has tended to delegate
much to individual ministers, although at the same time preferring to
intervene in key debates. His decision to support the United States
in the **Iraq conflict** to topple Saddam Hussein caused deep divisions
within the EU and within the Labour Party, not least because of the
absence of weapons of mass destruction (WMD) in Iraq which Blair
had emphasized as being one of the main reasons for the conflict.

Blue Flag

Every year the EU recognizes beaches that reach certain standards of
water quality with the award of a Blue Flag.

Border controls

A **single market** initiative for member states to align their national
rules through **mutual recognition** to ensure border controls could
be got rid of by 1 January 1993. While this was achieved for traffic
in goods, controls on individuals were not dismantled until 26 March
1995, though only covering those countries which had signed the
Schengen agreement.

Bosman case

On 15 December 1995 the **Court of Justice** ruled that the imposition of transfer fees by football clubs on football players was incompatible with the right of free movement of individuals. This important decision permitted football players to transfer to another club for 'free' if they were outwith their contract. The ruling had arisen because in 1990 a Belgian footballer, Jean-Marc Bosman, had refused to renew his contract and as a consequence he was placed on the transfer list of his club, RC Liège. However, in accord with the practices which then governed transfers between football clubs, RC Liège advocated that a transfer fee of FB 11,743,000 should be paid by any club that sought to sign Bosman. As a result, Bosman found it impossible to find employment as a football player and therefore challenged the practice of the application of transfer fees in the Court of Justice.

Brandt, Willy (1913–92)

A German Social Democrat who was Chancellor of the Federal Republic of Germany from 1969 to 1974 (resigning in April 1974 after the discovery that a close aid, Gunther Guillaume, had acted as an East German spy). Previously mayor of West Berlin from 1957 to 1966 (developing an international profile during the 1961 **Berlin Wall** crisis) and foreign minister from 1966 to 1969. He was leader of the Social Democratic Party (SDP) from 1964 to1987, and was awarded the Nobel Peace Prize in 1971. During his time as Chancellor his greatest interest was foreign policy, which led to greater openness towards central and eastern Europe. This policy of **Ostpolitik** included an agreement with the German Democratic Republic that permitted East German products to enter the **European Community** (EC) through the Federal Republic of Germany. This policy therefore emphasized a shift away from the 'policy of strength' of **Konrad Adenauer**, although that did not mean that the Federal Republic under Brandt was less committed to organizations such as the EC and the **North Atlantic Treaty Organisation** (NATO). In this context, Brandt favoured a less insular approach to the Community and along with the French president, **Georges Pompidou**, advocated **enlargement**, which eventually resulted in the accession of Denmark, Ireland and the UK in 1973. In 1971 Brandt was awarded the Nobel Peace Prize for his Ostpolitik efforts.

Bretton Woods

A conference at which an agreement was signed in July 1944 by 44 countries in support of an international monetary system of stable exchange rates. After the conference a number of key organizations were created, including the International Monetary Fund (IMF) and the International Bank for Reconstruction and Development (IBRD) (or World Bank).

Briand, Aristide (1862–1932)

As French foreign minister, Aristide Briand proposed to the **League of Nations** on 5 September 1929 a scheme to create a federal union between European states. Briand was one of the first individuals to advocate such a system and some months later in May 1930 he outlined his ideas in the **Briand Memorandum**. It argued that 'the peoples of Europe, if they are to enjoy security and prosperity, must establish a permanent regime of joint responsibility for the rational organization of Europe'. The proposals were of considerable importance, but other European nations were unwilling to offer the support that Briand had hoped for. A lack of interest from the likes of Britain, Germany and Italy, combined with Briand's death in March 1932, brought to an end Briand's proposals.

British budget problem

When Britain eventually joined the EEC on 1 January 1973 (after two failed applications in 1961 and 1967), the issue of membership was supposed to have been resolved. The opposite was the reality. In February 1974 the Labour Party led by **Harold Wilson** won the general election partly on the back of a campaign that sought to renegotiate the terms of entry that **Edward Heath** had obtained. This included a readjustment of Britain's budgetary contributions. This **renegotiation** was influenced by a 1970 EC **budget** agreement to provide the Community with its **own resources** which included (among other aspects) a combination of agricultural levies charged on the importation of agricultural products from **third countries** and customs duties levied on industrial products imported into the Community. The 1970 agreement meant that Britain faced a requirement on its **accession** to the Community of having to pay significant sums into the Community budget, while at the same time it received little back in the way of funding from the **Common Agricultural Policy** (CAP) because it had a large industrial base and a smallest agricultural sector. All in all, this meant that Britain would become a **net contributor** to the Community and this disparity between Britain's low rate of economic growth and high budgetary contributions laid the basis for the subsequent budgetary disagreements that lasted from 1974 to 1984.

Britain's initial effort to solve this budgetary problem in the 1974 renegotiation of its membership terms resulted in a 'corrective mechanism' whereby a rebate would be given to any net contributor state that met a rather complex **European Commission** formula. For this to happen a member state would have to meet certain criteria that related to its balance of payments, growth rate and share of GNP. The exact nature of the rebate would be two-thirds of the difference between its share of GNP and its budget contributions, although not more than its total VAT contributions. In the end, however, the 1975 rebate mechanism failed to overturn Britain's status as a significant net contributor to the Community budget (the other being Germany), and when combined with the escalating costs of the CAP it ensured that the question of Britain's budget contributions remained a key issue.

When **Margaret Thatcher** was elected prime minister in 1979 one of the first issues that she focused on was the question of Britain's budgetary contributions. But, whereas she considered the existing funding arrangement of the Community budget to be 'demonstrably unjust', other member states were somewhat lukewarm to her demands. As such, the discussion over Britain's budgetary contributions became a key political battle in the early 1980s, whereby it dominated the work of the Community and the inability to achieve a satisfactory outcome was one of the factors which limited the opportunity for the Community to progress out of the **eurosclerosis** that had dominated the 1970s. In the end, a solution was finally achieved at the June 1984 Fontainebleau **European Council**. The **Fontainebleau agreement**, which is technically known as the abatement, provided Britain with an immediate lump-sum payment of 1000 million European Currency Units (**ECU**) for 1984, while in subsequent years Britain would obtain a rebate that amounted to two-thirds of the difference between what it contributed in VAT and what it received from the Community budget. The settlement also led to Britain agreeing to a general increase in EC revenue from 1 to 1.4 per cent of national VAT receipts so as to remedy a general deficit in budgetary resources. While Thatcher considered the outcome to be a just one, it came at the price of reducing Britain's status within the Community as other member states considered it to be an awkward partner.

In the period since the Fontainebleau meeting, successive British governments have defended the relevance of the budget rebate, with the Berlin European Council of March 1999 producing agreement that the rebate would continue until 2006. The 2004 **enlargement** of the EU brought to the fore discussions about the fairness of the rebate. But, while the UK in 2005 was a more prosperous country than it was in 1984, the British government has nonetheless stressed that its justness lies in the fact that the UK receives a low per capita share of EU receipts and does not, for instance, benefit in a significant way from the support of the CAP. To this end, if the rebate did not exist it would have paid 15 times more than France and 12 times more than Italy into the EU (and even with the rebate it has paid 2.5 times as much as France and Italy). Such points were the basis of the UK's arguments during the discussion of the budget with regard to the future financing of the EU for the period 2007–13 (**financial perspectives**) that dominated the UK's Presidency of the EU between July and December 2005. The **Council Presidency** eventually produced agreement at the 15–16 December 2005 Brussels European Council on a budget deal which resulted in a commitment by the UK to forgo €10,500m from its rebate over the 2007–13 period (amounting to £1,000m a year for seven years). But, while this will mean that there will be a 63 per cent net increase in the UK's contributions to the budget, the agreement also resulted in the contributions of countries with similar wealth to the UK also increasing. This particularly applied to France, whose input to EU funds has traditionally been lower. Indeed, over the 2007–13 period French contributions will increase by 116 per cent. In return for the UK's commitment to reduce its budget rebate, it got a commitment that the CAP would be reviewed in 2008–9.

Brittan, Leon (b. 1939)

Appointed by Prime Minister **Margaret Thatcher** as the UK's senior European Commissioner in 1989, the now Baron Brittan remained a member of the **European Commission** until 1999. During that time he was an extremely influential member of the Commission, being given the responsibility of **competition policy** within **Jaques Delors'** Commission from 1989 to 1992. He played an important role in eradicating uncompetitive business practices within the Community. From 1989 to 1993 Brittan also held the post of Commission Vice-President, and from 1993 to 1994 he was responsible for external economic affairs and trade policy. Although Brittan sought to succeed Jacques Delors as President of the Commission, there was an appreciation among the member states that it was not Britain's turn to provide the President. Instead, **Jacques Santer** from Luxembourg succeeded Delors and, while Brittan retained the post of Vice-President of the Commission with responsibility for commercial policy and external relations from 1995 to 1999, his influence was not as significant as it had been under the Delors Commission. Prior to his European Commission appointment, Brittan was UK Home Secretary (1983–85) and Secretary of State for Trade and Industry (1985–86) in the Conservative government led by Margaret Thatcher.

Bruges speech

In a speech delivered at the College of Europe in Bruges (Belgium) on 20 September 1988, the then UK prime minister, **Margaret Thatcher**, outlined her vision of the future of European integration. Although the speech was regarded as an attack on the federal visions of **Jacques**

Delors (the then President of the **European Commission**), Thatcher also advocated the need to enlarge the European Community to the countries of central and eastern Europe. Thatcher stressed that Britain should be a full member of the Community: 'And let me be quite clear. Britain does not dream of some cosy, isolated existence on the fringes of the European Community. Our destiny is in Europe, as part of the Community.' Yet, at the same time, she emphasized that the importance of the nation state should not be lessened in the face of the growing strength of the Community institutions in Brussels: 'To try to suppress nationhood and concentrate power at the centre of a European conglomerate would be highly damaging and would jeopardize the objectives we seek to achieve. Europe will be stronger precisely because it has France as France, Spain as Spain, Britain as Britain, each with its own customs, traditions and identity. It would be folly to try to fit them into some sort of identikit European personality. . . . working more closely together does *not* require power to be centralized in Brussels or decisions to be taken by an appointed bureaucracy. . . . We have not successfully rolled back the frontiers of the state in Britain only to see them re-imposed at a European level, with a European super-state exercising a new dominance from Brussels.'

Brussels

Capital of Belgium and regarded as the 'capital of Europe' because it is the location of many EU institutions, as well as being the base of the **North Atlantic Treaty Organisation** (NATO). Brussels is often used to indicate the EU and its decision-makers, in the sense that 'Brussels' has decided.

Brussels Treaty see *Treaty of Brussels*

Budget

Includes revenue obtained from **own resources**, money spent upon common policies and the costs of running the EU institutions. The largest element of the budget has traditionally been the price support system of the **Common Agricultural Policy** (CAP).

Budgetary deficit

Happens when governmental expenditure exceeds revenue.

Budgetary discipline

This basically refers to the constraints that are imposed on the EU **budget** to ensure that there is a balance between revenue and expenditure.

Bulgaria

Population: 7.5m (2005)
Capital: Sofia
Having been dominated by the Soviet-led Eastern bloc since the end of the Second World War, Bulgaria held its first free elections for over 40 years in June 1990. Along with a process of democratization, Bulgaria began to move towards a market economy with its attentions focused on western Europe. In 1993 it signed a **Europe Agreement** with the EU that came into effect on 1 February 1995. In December 1995 Bulgaria applied for EU membership. Yet, in contrast to other **central and eastern European states** that also sought EU membership, Bulgaria was one of the poorest countries and had not made the same degree of progress in establishing stable democratic institutions. With this in mind, the **European Commission** noted in its **Opinion** of July 1997 that Bulgaria had not met the requirements of the **Copenhagen criteria** for EU **accession**. Thus, Bulgaria was not one of the 10 countries that joined the EU on 1 May 2004. It did, however, join the **North Atlantic Treaty Organisation** (NATO) in 2004. While there is an expectation that Bulgaria (and **Romania**) will join the EU in 2007 (an objective endorsed by the EU at the Thessaloniki **European Council** of 2003), there continues to be a need for improvements in its economic performance. In 2003 its GDP per capita was only 29 per cent of the EU-25 average, which was a mere 3 per cent increase since 1997. There has also been a need for Bulgaria to develop the capacity of its administrative offices and judiciary to ensure that it is able to implement the *acquis communitaire*.

Bundesbank

Established in 1957, the Bundesbank is the central bank of Germany and has enjoyed considerable autonomy from the national government in the conduct of monetary policy. The renewed strength of the German economy from the 1960s onwards was viewed as being heavily influenced by the policies pursued by the Bundesbank. Its strength, and the strength of the German mark, resulted in the Bundesbank having a considerable influence on the western European economic system. To this end, the Bundesbank played a leading role in the **European Monetary System** (EMS) and its relative influence was one of the factors that motivated the desire of the French government to advocate the creation of a single currency that would be managed by a **European Central Bank** (ECB) as a means of ensuring that other **central banks** would have an input to key economic decisions (because the influence of the Bundesbank would decline). The Bundesbank was, however, cautious about the prospect of a **single currency** because it was concerned that any new currency would be less stable than the Deutschmark. But, while the German government was conscious of the need to ensure that a future single currency would be stable, by insisting on **convergence criteria**, the pursuit of the single currency for the German government was primarily a politically motivated project.

Butter mountain

Just like the **wine lake**, this popular phrase described one effect of the **Common Agricultural Policy** (CAP). The price guarantee and intervention system in the area of dairy farming resulted in the overproduction of butter which was then accumulated in storage facilities. This problem was tackled by limits being placed on dairy farming through the introduction of milk quotas, thereby reducing the demands made on the CAP. Butter in storage was then sold at a discounted price.

C

Cabinet

Each member of the **European Commission** has a private office (*cabinet*) that comprises a small group of officials whose role is to provide policy advice. Because of their close working relationship with the **European Commissioner**, members of the *cabinet* play a significant role that extends beyond the particular responsibilities that they have been allocated. A notable example of this was Pascal Lamy, who was in charge of **Jacques Delors'** *cabinet* and who himself became a European Commissioner.

Candidate country

This applies to those countries whose application to join the EU has been officially recognized. There are four candidate countries: Croatia, Hungary, Romania and Turkey.

CAP Reform

Since the **Common Agricultural Policy** (CAP) was introduced in 1960, it has led to the production of surpluses of a number of products, in particular barley, beef, milk and wine. A combination of these surpluses and the payment of subsidies to European farmers were influential in the desire of some member states and the **European Commission** to advocate the reform of the CAP. This willingness to reform was also shaped by a desire to reduce the CAP's share of the total EU **budget** (see **Butter mountain** and **Wine lake**).

Cartel

A cartel occurs when several businesses unite together with a view to controlling a market by establishing a monopoly. One of the aims of European integration has been to create open competition and to rule against the existence of cartels.

Cassis de Dijon

This is the judgment of the **European Court of Justice** in the 1979 case of *Rewe-Zentrale AG* v. *Bundesmonopolverwaltung für Branntwein* (case 120/78), known as 'Cassis de Dijon'. It established that it was not possible for restrictions to be imposed on a product lawfully manufactured and on sale in one member state when it was imported into another member state, being based on the principle of **mutual recognition**, and was therefore important in the creation of the **single market**. The judgment specifically noted that 'It is clear from the foregoing that the requirements relating to the minimum alcohol content of alcoholic beverages do not serve a purpose which is the general interest and such as to take precedence over the requirements of the free movement of goods, which constitutes one of the fundamental rules of the Community. . . . There is therefore no valid reason why, provided that they have been lawfully produced and marketed in one of the member states, alcoholic beverages should not be introduced into any other member state; the sale of such products may not be subject to a legal prohibition on the marketing of beverages with an alcohol content lower than the limit set by the national rules.'

Cecchini Report

Throughout 1986 and 1987 the Italian economist, Paolo Cecchini, led a group of researchers who considered the 'costs of non-Europe'. Published in 1988 at the request of the **European Commission**, the report examined the economic consequences of the plan to establish the **single market** by 1992. It suggested that the removal of frontier barriers, including those of a technical nature and frontier controls, would be likely to produce savings of some 200 thousand million **ECU**. This would in turn result in greater economic growth and increased employment. The summary of this report was also published by Cecchini in 1988 as a book entitled *The European Challenge: 1992*.

CE mark

Products that are manufactured in the EU are given the CE mark to highlight that they conform with the necessary standards **directives**. As such, the introduction of the CE mark in the late 1980s was primarily aimed for the benefit of customs and regulatory authorities and served as a means of helping to promote the **single market** programme by eliminating technical **barriers to trade**.

CELEX

A constantly updated multilingual EU database containing official legislation and other documentation, including proposals from the **European Commission** and ruling of the **Court of Justice.**

CEN/Cenelec

Acronyms for European Committee for Standardization (CEN) and European Committee for Electrotechnical Standardization (Cenelec). Both organizations are based in Brussels and aim to establish joint European standardization, embracing the EU, **European Free Trade Association** (EFTA) and national standards.

Censure motion

The **European Parliament** has the ability to sack the **European Commission** only if a motion of censure is passed by two-thirds of the votes cast which represent an absolute majority of **Members of Parliament** (MEPs).

Central and eastern European states (CEES)

The relationship between central and eastern European states and the EC was of a limited nature throughout the **Cold War** due to the bipolar division of Europe. Central and eastern Europe was dominated by the **Warsaw Pact** and the **Council for Mutual Economic Assistance** (CMEA), while western Europe was dominated by the EC and the **North Atlantic Treaty Organisation** (NATO). Where cooperation did exist, it was of a limited nature, such as West Germany's policy of **Ostpolitik**. In the latter years of the 1980s there began a process of closer relations between the EC and the CEES, evidenced by the conclusion of a joint declaration that established diplomatic relations in June 1988. This was followed by trade and cooperation agreements between the EC and individual states, such as Poland (1989), Bulgaria and Czechoslovakia (1990) and Romania (1991).

The end of the Cold War, signified by the November 1990 **Charter of Paris**, brought with it greater Community involvement in central and eastern Europe. In 1989 the **Council of Ministers** established the **PHARE** programme of aid to Poland and Hungary, which was subsequently extended to include a broader group of CEES. Alongside PHARE, the EU has helped to finance technical assistance projects through the **TACIS** programme, while finance for infrastructure and industrial projects has been provided by the **European Bank for Reconstruction and Development** (EBRD). Later in December 1991 the EC embarked on the first **Europe Agreements** with Czechoslovakia, Hungary and Poland which subsequently embraced many other countries with a view to promoting trade liberalization.

Many of the CEES wished to join the Community and in June 1993 the Copenhagen **European Council** established a series of criteria for the accession of countries from central and eastern Europe to the EU (**Copenhagen criteria**). Of the 10 countries of central and eastern Europe that have applied for membership of the EU in the 1990s (Bulgaria, Czech Republic, Estonia, Hungary, Latvia, Lithuania, Poland, Romania, Slovakia and Slovenia), with the exception of Bulgaria and Romania, all of the countries became EU members in 2004.

Central bank governors

The governors of the central banks of EU member states have played an important role in European financial affairs through the **European Monetary System** (EMS) and were crucial to the shaping of the **Treaty on European Union** provisions on **Economic and Monetary Union** (EMU), where the committee of central bank governors was one of the main negotiating bodies alongside the monetary committee and finance ministers. Under the provisions of the Treaty, in January 1994 the Committee of Central Bank Governors merged with the **European Monetary Cooperation Fund** (EMCF) to form the **European Monetary Institute** (EMI). In June 1998 the EMI was transformed into the **European Central Bank** (ECB). The central bank governors that are members of the ECB play a key role in determining the monetary policy of the **single currency,** particularly with regard to the setting of **interest rates**.

Central banks

Refers to the central banks of EU member states that play an important role in the coordination of both national and European monetary policy. Central bank governors are especially crucial. National central banks continue to exist and play an important role under **Economic and Monetary Union** (EMU). Along with the **European Central Bank** (ECB), they form the **European System of Central Banks** (ESCB). National central banks retain operational responsibility for the policy that is determined by the governing council of the ECB. If it is required, national central banks will also intervene in foreign exchange markets.

Some central banks have been more independent than others, such as the **Bundesbank** in Germany, while the UK Bank of England has traditionally been perceived to suffer from political influence. The latter has changed as a result of the 1997 reforms by the Labour government that provided the Bank of England with more independence, notably regarding the setting of **interest rates**. For those member states that participate in the **single currency**, decisions on the taking of the setting of interest rates are made by the ECB rather than national central banks. For some member states, this transfer in **decision-making** away from the national level constitutes an unacceptable loss of **sovereignty** and creates a situation whereby the interest rate for the **eurozone** may not reflect the needs of a particular member state. While it is true that even within those member states who continue to be independent of the **eurozone** the national interest rate policy does not always reflect the needs of everyone within the country, this concern over who has responsibility for interest rate decisions has been an important argument used by some governments against joining the single currency.

CERN

The Geneva based European Organization for Nuclear Research which was established in 1954 with the aim of promoting cooperation between European nations in research on nuclear energy and related policies. The acronym comes from the previous French title of Conseil européen pour la recherche nucléaire.

Chamber

The division in which the **Court of Justice** sits when it is not sitting in plenary.

Chapter

This term is used to signify a subdivision of a **Title** in a EU Treaty, of which a Chapter can in turn be further divided into **Sections**.

Charter of Fundamental Rights

The June 1999 Cologne **European Council** took the decision to commence work on the drafting of a charter of fundamental rights. This was with a view to ensuring that the fundamental rights applicable at the EU level should be set within a single document. Such a decision took place in the wake of the fiftieth anniversary of the Universal Declaration of Human Rights in December 1988. At the Tampere European Council of October 1999 member states agreed to entrust the work on the drafting of the Charter of Fundamental Rights to a Convention that was chaired by the former president of Germany, Roman Herzog. The outcome of this Convention was presented at the Biarritz European Council of October 2000 and was adopted by member states at the Nice European Council of December 2000. The Charter, which is divided into 54 articles, sets out fundamental rights that relate to **citizenship**, dignity, equality, justice, liberty and solidarity. But, although the Charter had been adopted in December 2000, member states were unable to reach agreement on how to incorporate it into the existing treaties and thereby ensure that it would be legally binding. It was therefore agreed that the **intergovernmental conference** of 2003–4 would examine this issue and at the Brussels European Council of June 2004 member states were able to agree on the incorporation of the Charter within the context of the EU **Constitutional Treaty**.

Charter of Paris

The signature by members of the **Conference on Security and Cooperation in Europe** (CSCE) of the Charter of Paris for a New Europe on 21 November 1990 is generally considered to be the formal end of the **Cold War** as a result of the collapse of the Soviet satellite states in eastern Europe. The Charter emphasized the concepts that were established in the **Helsinki Final Act**, while it also demonstrated the transformation of the CSCE into a permanent organization which resulted in its name changing to the **Organization for Security and Cooperation in Europe** (OSCE).

Chef de Cabinet

The personal political adviser to a member of the **European Commission** who heads the *cabinet* of officials.

Chirac, Jacques (b. 1932)

Gaullist politician and president of France since 1995, having previously been prime minister from 1974 to 1976 and 1986 to 1988. Born in Paris, he was educated at the prestigious Ecole National d'Administration and after military service in Algeria served in numerous government departments, including the position of Secretary of State for Economy and Finance (1968–71). Between 1986 and 1988 he was a Conservative prime minister at a time of a Socialist president, which was referred to as a period of cohabitation. This period in office was marked by international differences, while President **François Mitterrand**, who retained control over foreign policy, constantly challenged him. Chirac stood as a candidate in the 1988 presidential elections and managed to see off the challenge of the centrist Raymond Barre in the first round, though being defeated in the second round by Mitterrand. By 1995 Chirac had established a firmer base of power than in 1986, which provided the platform for his election as president in 1995 and subsequent re-election in 2002. Chirac experienced cohabitation as president when the 1997 parliamentary elections failed to secure a Conservative majority, resulting in the appointment of Lionel Jospin as prime minister. The 2004 **enlargement** of the EU brought with it the potential for new alliances among the member states and raised the potential for a decline in the traditional Franco-German relationship to play a dominant role in shaping the path of European integration. Such a state of affairs therefore posed a challenge to Chirac's ability to dominate the EU, with his influence being weakened further by the no vote that was recorded in the French **referendum** on the **Constitutional Treaty** in May 2005.

Christian democracy

The largest grouping of centre and centre-right political parties in post-war Europe, of which the German Christian Democratic Union (CDU) has been the most influential. Christian democracy was particularly important to European integration, embracing figures such as **Konrad Adenauer, Alcide de Gasperi, Walter Hallstein** and **Helmut Kohl**. At a European level, Christian democratic political parties in the **European Parliament** form the Group of the European People's Party, and the leaders of Christian democrat political parties form an important caucus in the establishment of points of consensus.

Churchill, Sir Winston (1874–1965)

Churchill served as prime minister from 1940 to 1945 and 1951 to 1955. As prime minister he inspired the nation during the Second World War. During that period he also supported policies for the future development of the country, including the Beveridge Plan for social insurance (1942) and the Butler Education Act (1944). He made a significant development to European affairs in the post 1945 period, despite having lost the premiership in that year. At a speech in Fulton, Missouri, in March 1946 Churchill emphasized the beginning of the **Cold War** when he noted that 'From Stettin in the Baltic to Trieste in the Adriatic, an iron curtain has descended across the continent. Behind that line lie all the capitals of the ancient states of central and eastern Europe. Warsaw, Berlin, Prague, Vienna, Budapest, Belgrade, Bucharest and Sofia, all these famous cities and the populations around them lie in the Soviet sphere and all are subject in one form or another, not only to Soviet influence but to a very high and increasing measure of control from Moscow.' Some months later in September 1946, Churchill urged the construction of a **United States of Europe** in a speech in Zurich, while he also provided backing to the International Committee of the Movements for European Unity. Churchill would later act as President of the sessions of the 1948 Congress of Europe (**Hague Congress**), in the wake of which he became one of the patrons of the **European Movement**. However, he did not perceive the UK as being part of an integrated Europe, which he considered would rather be based upon the reconciliation of France and Germany. Therefore, when he returned to power as prime minister in 1951 he continued to advocate the policy of the previous Labour government that saw the UK as only being involved in intergovernmental cooperation. This led to the UK under his leadership not taking part in the developments, which were pursued by **the Six**.

Citizenship

Citizenship of the EU was introduced in the Maastricht **Treaty on European Union**, whereby 'every person holding the nationality of a member state shall be a citizen of the Union'. In the **Treaty of Amsterdam** it was further noted that 'Citizenship of the Union shall complement and not replace national citizenship'. It is relevant in the granting of four key rights to EU citizens: (1) the freedom to live anywhere in the EU; (2) the ability to vote and stand in local government and **European Parliament** elections in the country of residence; (3) the ability to receive diplomatic and consular protection from any EU member state if a situation were to arise where the member state of nationality were not represented in a non-EU country; and (4) the right to refer points of concern to the **Ombudsman**. These rights are also contained in the **Charter of Fundamental Rights**.

Civil society

This is a general term that is used to denote the associations and organizations which represent interests within society but which are not part of government. Among the various groups that constitute civil society, some of the most prominent are trade unions, environmental groups and employers' associations.

Closer cooperation

Refers to the introduction of specific methods that have permitted some member states to engage in closer cooperation and thus deeper integration in a limited number of policy areas. The concept of closer cooperation was stressed in the **Treaty of Amsterdam**, although the Treaty did note that a member state could refuse closer cooperation in a specific area because of national political significance. The **Treaty of Nice** made additional refinements to the use of closer cooperation: (1) the minimum number of member states required for closer cooperation was set at eight; (2) a member state could no longer prevent closer cooperation; (3) the **European Parliament**'s consent is necessary in policy areas that are subject to **co-decision**; (4) closer cooperation should not impact on the **internal market** or social and economic cohesion; (5) it could be possible for closer cooperation to extend to **common foreign and security policy** (CFSP), with the exception of issues that had a military or defence consideration.

Cockfield, Lord (Arthur) (b. 1916)

A British member and Vice-President of the **European Commission** from 1985 to 1989 who was key to the implementation of the **internal market** programme that fell within his policy portfolio. In June 1985 he produced a **White Paper** with a timetable for completing the **single market** in response to the request of the Brussels **European Council** in March 1985. This included some 300 measures relating to the removal of **barriers to trade** of a physical, technical and fiscal nature, of which the report recommended the removal of frontier barriers by 1992. His tenure as a **European Commissioner** was stopped by **Margaret Thatcher** who refused to reappoint him in 1988, partly because of his pro-integrationist position. He was succeeded as a UK Commissioner by Sir **Leon Brittan**.

Codetermination

As a legislative framework requirement in the operation of works councils in several member states, it stipulates the various areas where the agreement of employee representatives is essential before any action can be taken by management. This includes the monitoring of employee performance.

Co-decision procedure

The co-decision procedure was introduced in the Maastricht **Treaty on European Union** to provide the **European Parliament** with greater powers in the decision-making process, thereby going considerably beyond the **cooperation procedure** that was introduced in the **Single European Act** (SEA). The co-decision procedure essentially provides the European Parliament with the power to veto legislative measures in instances when an agreement could not be reached between it and the **Council of Ministers.** This procedure was based on an existing procedure for the **Budget**, whereby the European Parliament and the Council of Ministers sought to reach agreement in a **conciliation committee**, and when such a agreement could not be reached then the Parliament could reject the **budget** by an absolute majority vote of its members.

In practical terms, the co-decision procedure consists of three readings and ensures that the adoption of legislation involves both the Council of Ministers and the European Parliament (Fig. 4.1). Moreover, the presence of a conciliation committee and the need for the

European Commission issues a proposal
Normally this is done after consultation has taken place with interest groups and other relevant actors. The proposal is then forwarded to the

↓

European Parliament (and often the Committee of the Regions and the Economic and Social Committee)
It issues its opinion. The opinions are then forwarded to the

↓

European Commission
It takes a view on the opinion of the other institutions and forwards them to the

↓

Council of Ministers
It creates a Common Position that is then forwarded to the

↓

European Parliament
The European Parliament has the option to approve the proposal, which would then subsequently be approved by the Council of Ministers. Otherwise, the European Parliament proposes amendments that are then subject to opinions by the European Commission and are thereafter forwarded to the

↓

Council of Ministers
The Council of Ministers has the opportunity to accept the amendments (by QMV if the European Commission supports the amendments or by unanimity if the European Commission opposes the amendments). If the Council of Ministers fails to accept all the amendments proposed by the European Parliament, it then convenes a

↓

Conciliation Committee
The committee comprises 25 members from the Council, 25 members from the European Parliament and 1 member from the European Commission (with no right to vote).
If a joint text is agreed and approved within six weeks the legislation is adopted (QMV of Council members/simple majority of European Parliament members).
If there is a failure to agree or a lack of time to reach agreement then the legislation is not adopted.

Figure 4.1 Co-decision procedure.

Parliament and Council to work together has ensured that there has both been a strengthening in the number of contacts between these institutions and to some extent a weakening in the influence of the **European Commission**. The procedure initially embraced decisions on consumer protection, culture, education, free movement of workers, health, the right of establishment, freedom to provide services, the **single market** and the adoption of guidelines or programmes covering trans-European networks, research and the environment.

The **Treaty of Amsterdam** extended the procedure to include public health, the fight against fraud, social exclusion, general principles of transparency, incentive measures for employment, the majority of measures taken under **environment policy**, and discrimination on grounds of nationality. At the same time the Treaty also simplified the co-decision procedure. This included the provision that where the Council does not amend the Commission proposal, or where the Parliament's amendments are accepted by the Council, it is possible for the measure to be adopted without a second reading.

The co-decision procedure was further widened in the **Treaty of Nice** to include judicial cooperation on civil matters; **economic and social cohesion** actions; measures relating to visas, asylum and immigration; the statute for European political parties; incentives to combat discrimination; and a number of industrial support measures (Table 4.4). If the EU **Constitutional Treaty** is ratified, the co-decision procedure would be established as the normal legislative procedure which would in turn cover virtually every aspect of EU law.

Table 4.4 Policies subject to co-decision

Non-discrimination on the basis of nationality

Right to move and reside

Free movement of workers

Social security for migrant workers

Right of establishment

Transport

Internal market

Employment

Customs cooperation

Fight against social exclusion

Equal opportunities and equal treatment

Implementing decisions regarding the European Social Fund

Education

Vocational training

Culture

Health

Consumer protection

Table 4.4 Continued

Trans-European networks
Implementing decisions regarding the European Regional Development Fund
Research
Environment
Transparency
Preventing and combating fraud
Statistics
Setting up a data protection advisory body

Cohesion Fund

Established in 1993 as a result of the Maastricht **Treaty on European Union**, the Cohesion Fund was created to reduce the differences in living standards between EU member states (as well as regions) and thereby to assist in promoting economic and social progress within the EU. This Cohesion Fund was required because the Maastricht Treaty's commitment to **Economic and Monetary Union** (EMU) stressed that, for monetary union to be achieved, member states would have to reduce budget deficits and to limit public debt. This in effect limited the ability of the least prosperous member states to undertake investment (often through public debt) so as to catch up with the more developed EU countries. To remedy this situation, the Cohesion Fund provided specific financial assistance to assist with financing projects in the least prosperous member states, which in the 1990s were Greece, Ireland, Portugal and Spain. Major projects financed through the Cohesion Fund have included improvements to road networks, bridge building, airports and the supply of drinking water. As the Cohesion Fund is designed to assist the least prosperous EU member states, the 2004 **enlargement** of the EU has meant that there has been an increase in the number of states that receive aid from the fund: the 10 new member states as well as Greece, Portugal and Spain (Ireland received funding until the end of 2003). Of the financing provided by the Cohesion Fund, one-third of the available funding was reserved for the new member states between 2004 and 2006.

Cohesion policy

A lessening of the gap between richer and poorer regions is a key objective of the EU. It is an issue that the EU has faced for a considerable period of time and has been exacerbated by successive **enlargements**. It was first highlighted by the accession of Ireland on 1 January 1973. The subsequent expansion of the Community to include Greece (1981) and Portugal and Spain (1986) resulted in a more active attempt by the

European Commission to level the differences between the richer and poorer regions. The commitment in the **Single European Act** (SEA) to complete the **single market** was followed by a reform of the **structural funds** that was aimed at providing greater levels of assistance to poor regions within the Community, with these changes having been influenced by the 1987 **Padoa-Schioppa Report**. Just as the process of enlargement and the **single market** programme had influenced thinking on cohesion policy in the 1970s and 1980s, the key determining factor that influenced policy-makers in the early 1990s was movement towards **Economic and Monetary Union** (EMU) and the creation of a **single currency**. This would later be followed by the need to respond to the challenge of enlargement to include **central and eastern European States** (CEES).

Cold War

A phrase developed in the late 1940s to highlight the tension that developed in the wake of the Second World War between the USA and USSR, particularly in the European arena. The reality of Soviet dominance over eastern Europe by 1948 resulted in the freezing of relations between both nations, evidenced by the **Berlin blockade** of 1948–49 and the subsequent erection of the **Berlin Wall** in August 1961. The division between East and West was further highlighted by the construction of a system of Western collective defence through the signing of the 1949 Treaty of Washington which founded the **North Atlantic Treaty Organisation** (NATO). The 1990 **Charter of Paris** is generally considered to signify the formal end of the Cold War.

Collective defence

Both the **Treaty of Brussels** (Article V) and **Treaty of Washington** (Article 5) stress that signatory states are required to provide assistance in the event of aggression. In the period since 1949 the main guarantee of European security has been provided by the **North Atlantic Treaty Organisation** (NATO).

College of Europe

Established in 1949 in Bruges (Belgium), the College of Europe provides postgraduate courses in areas that are of relevance to European integration. An additional campus exists in Natolin (near Warsaw). The College became famous for the so-called **Bruges speech** given by **Margaret Thatcher** in September 1988 in which she was critical of the supranational influence of the EU institutions and at the same time stressed the importance of expanding the EU to include **central and eastern European states** (CEES).

Collegiality

This is the principle whereby the decisions taken by one become the collective responsibility of the group. It is generally used in reference to the workings of the **European Commission**, whereby Commissioners are supposed to be viewed as equal in terms of their status.

Colombo, Emilio (b. 1920)

An Italian politician who served in various posts within different governments, including Minister of Foreign Trade 1958–59, of Industry and Commerce 1959–60, Treasury 1963–70, and prime minister between 1970 and 1972. He was subsequently appointed Minister of Finance 1973–74, of the Treasury 1974–76, and of Foreign Affairs 1980–83 and 1992–93. During his period of office between 1980 and 1983, he lent his name and supported proposals for a draft European Act. This extended to supporting the draft declaration on economic integration advanced by the German foreign minister, **Hans-Dietrich Genscher**. This eventually resulted in the 1981 **Genscher–Colombo** Plan. Otherwise he was a member of the **European Parliament** between 1976 and 1980 and its President from 1977 to 1979.

COM Documents

A **European Commission** document generally used for publishing proposed legislation.

Comecon see *Council for Mutual Economic Assistance*

COMETT

Acronym for Community Action Programme in Education and Training for Technology. Having been established in 1987 to develop cooperation between universities and industry through exchanges and training partnerships, it was absorbed into the **Leonardo** programme in 1995.

Comitology

This refers to the various committee procedures that oversee the implementation of EU law. Although the **European Commission** is responsible for implementing legislation within the EU, the executive activities of the Commission are monitored by the **Council of Ministers** via advisory, management or regulatory committees, which are composed of national experts. The power of advisory committees is limited to making non-binding recommendations to the European Commission. By contrast, management committees have the ability to refer the implementing measures of the European Commission back to the **Council of Ministers** for a decision within a set period of time. Measures are suspended in the intervening period. If a decision is not reached by the Council in the set time, the European Commission is able to implement the measures. European Commission measures can also be suspended and referred back to the Council by regulatory committees. However, in those areas where the Council has not taken a decision within the time limit, the European Commission is only able to adopt the measures if the Council has not rejected them. It can do this by a simple majority. The Council has tended to prefer using the regulatory procedure which it is able to choose whenever it likes, much to the aggravation of the European Commission.

Committee for a People's Europe

The 1984 Fontainebleau **European Council** established a committee to 'suggest ways of strengthening the identity of the Community at the individual level and of improving the image of the Community among the national populations'. The committee, which was chaired by the Italian **Member of the European Parliament** (MEP), Pietro Adonnino, and comprised the personal representatives of member states, produced an initial report in March 1985 which was followed by a more detailed report in the Milan European Council of June 1985. A central part of the report related to citizens' rights, including the right to participate in direct elections to the **European Parliament** through a uniformal process and the right to live in another member state on the same conditions as those available to national citizens.

Committee of Central Bank Governors

This was established in 1964 to assist with the cooperation of EU **central banks**. The progress towards monetary union increased the work of the Committee, resulting in the formation of various sub-committees and working groups to tackle specific areas of policy, such as monetary policy and banking supervision. The Maastricht **Treaty on European Union** made provision for central bank governors to play a key role in **Economic and Monetary Union** (EMU) as it merged with the **European Monetary Cooperation Fund** (EMCF) in 1994 to form the **European Monetary Institute** (EMI). At the end of Stage 2 of EMU, the EMI became the **European Central Bank** (ECB).

Committee of inquiry

The Maastricht **Treaty on European Union** provided the **European Parliament** with the ability to establish temporary committees of inquiry 'to investigate, without prejudice to the powers conferred by this Treaty on other institutions or bodies, alleged contraventions or maladministration in the implementation of Community law'. Committees of inquiry can be established by a request of one-quarter of **Members of the European Parliament** (MEPs).

Committee of Permanent Representatives (Coreper)

This comprises senior officials from the member states who examine draft legislation before it is examined in the **Council of Ministers** (Table 4.5). A proposal that has been agreed by Coreper becomes item A on the Council's agenda and is adopted without debate, while issues that are not agreed become item B and are debated. Coreper I consists of Deputy Permanent Representatives, while Coreper II consists of Permanent Representatives who are the ambassadors of the member states. In this context, Coreper I tends to tackle technical issues to be deliberated in the Council, whereas Coreper II focuses on matters relating to foreign policy and economic affairs.

Table 4.5 Structure of Coreper

Coreper I	Deputy Permanent Representatives	Employment, Social Policy, Health and Consumer Affairs; Competitiveness (internal market, industry, research and tourism); Transport, Telecommunications and Energy; Agriculture and Fisheries; Environment; Education, Youth and Culture (including audiovisual)
Coreper II	Permanent Representatives	General Affairs and External Relations (including European security and defence policy and development cooperation); Economic and Financial Affairs (including the budget); Justice and Home Affairs (including civil protection).

Committee of the Regions (CoR)

The **Treaty on European Union** included a provision to establish an advisory committee to consist of 'representatives of regional and local bodies'. It comprises representatives of local and regional authorities (the same as the **Economic and Social Committee**) who are appointed by national governments and not directly by any regional authority. It membership is extremely diverse, with powerful regional leaders from Germany sitting beside less powerful representatives from the UK. It is consulted by the **European Commission** and the **Council of Ministers** in areas that affect local and regional interests, such as the environment, culture, **economic and social cohesion**, education, energy, public health, social policy, telecommunications and transport. The **Treaty of Nice** provided for its membership to increase from 222 to 344 so as to take into consideration an enlarged EU of some 27 states.

Committees

The institutions of the EU are assisted in their work by a plethora of committees which are involved in every stage of the legislative process. They vary in terms of remit and size. The work of the **Council of Ministers** is assisted by committees and working parties, while various permanent committees serve the interests of Members of the **European Parliament**. Otherwise, the **European Commission** regularly consults committees of experts with a view to obtaining specialized advice prior to the advancement of a new legislative proposal.

Common Agricultural Policy (CAP)

A price and structural support system for agricultural production within the EU that continues to account for a dominant share of the EU **budget**. The CAP was established in 1962 to improve agricultural production and guarantee food supply. This policy has, however, led to overproduction and to reduce farm spending a 1992 reform severed the link between production and farm income. This has helped to reduce the agriculture share of the EU budget from 60 per cent in the 1980s to 43 per cent in 2005.

Common Commercial Policy (CCP)

The Common Commercial Policy is a key aspect of the EU's activities, reflected in the fact that the EU is the world's largest trading bloc, accounting for some 20 per cent of all global imports and exports. The CCP is a policy where the **European Commission** negotiates on behalf of the member states. Traditionally the EU has been in favour of free trade and there has generally been considerable coherence between the member states on matters relating to **trade policy**.

Common currency area

A term that is often used to describe the operation of a **single currency**. There are various economic arguments to support a common currency area. In the first instance, **interest rates** can be equalized with the removal of the possibility of currency movements. Secondly, in a common currency area there is no likelihood of an individual country trying to solve problems by means of **inflation**. Finally, an absence of exchange rates means that business and trade can prosper because of the removal of transaction costs.

Common External Tariff (CET)

Goods that are imported into the EU are subject to a duty that takes the form of the Common External Tariff, which is managed by the **European Commission** within the remit of the **Common Commercial Policy**. Income that is obtained from these duties constitutes part of the EU's **own resources**.

Common Fisheries Policy

A central part of the EU, the Common Fisheries Policy was intended to promote the conservation of fish stocks, establish a similar system of price support systems to the **Common Agricultural Policy** (CAP) and modernize the industry. However, in pursuing these objectives it has attracted much criticism. Legislation on the conservation of fish stocks (total allowable catch) combined with the ability of fishing fleets to fish freely within EU has had a severe impact on many traditional fishing ports. This has been particularly evident within the UK and in recognition of these difficulties the reforms that were made to the **structural funds** as part of the **Agenda 2000** process specifically stressed that areas dependent on fishing were to be granted support (see **Factortame Judgment**).

Common Foreign and Security Policy (CFSP)

The **Treaty on European Union** included a provision in Title V to establish a CFSP which replaced the previous method of **European Political Cooperation**. Despite a great deal of optimism, the CFSP did not prove as effective at coordinating the policies of member states throughout the 1990s and there was a notable distinction between what was expected of the CFSP and the reality of what could be achieved (the 'capabilities–expectations gap'). A desire to increase the effectiveness of the CFSP prompted member states to agree in the 1999 **Treaty of Amsterdam** to establish a Policy Planning Unit and appoint a **High Representative for CFSP**. The December 1999 Helsinki **European Council** moved towards the establishment of a **European Security and Defence Policy** (ESDP) and set a target of establishing a multinational corps of 60,000 forces with the capability of mounting an autonomous European mission. Further changes were made in the 2001 **Treaty of Nice**, including the provision for closer cooperation on CFSP, while the **Constitutional Treaty** that member states agreed to in 2004 stressed – subject to ratification – that a new post of EU Minister for Foreign Affairs would be created which would combine the existing positions of the Council's High Representative for CFSP and the **European Commissioner** for external relations. Such a strategy was shaped by a desire to provide greater coherence to the CFSP.

Common market

A general term that refers to the **customs union** established by the **Treaties of Rome** which aimed to provide free movement of capital, goods, persons and services, in addition to the establishment of common policies. This necessitated, for instance, the removal of customs duties between the member states (completed on 1 July 1968) and led to the creation at the end of 1992 of a **single market**.

Common position

This refers to when the **Council of Ministers** reaches consensus in the **cooperation procedure** and **co-decision procedure**.

Common transport policy

A precondition for the freedom of movement within the **single market** is the efficient transportation of goods and persons. The EU's common transport policy includes road transport, railways, waterways, shipping and aviation. This establishes common rules that relate to the passing of international transport across one or more member states, as well as the setting of rules that relate to the operation of non-resident carriers within member states. Since the introduction of the **Treaty of Amsterdam**, decisions relating to the common transport policy are taken on the basis of the **co-decision procedure**.

Commonwealth

The Commonwealth is a voluntary association of 53 countries with a combined population of 1.8 thousand million people, which is just over a quarter of the total world population (Table 4.6). Members of the Commonwealth are former members of the British Empire (plus Mozambique) who seek to strengthen cooperation between each other. Although the process of Commonwealth membership began with the 1931 Statute of Westminster, the majority of members have joined in the post-1945 period, reflecting the decision of the British govern-

Table 4.6 Members of the Commonwealth

1931	Australia, UK, Canada, New Zealand
1947	India, Pakistan (left 1972, rejoined 1989)
1948	Sri Lanka
1957	Ghana, Malaysia
1960	Nigeria
1961	Cyprus, Sierra Leone
1962	Jamaica, Trinidad and Tobago, Uganda
1963	Kenya
1964	Malawi, Malta, Tanzania, Zambia
1965	The Gambia, Singapore
1966	Barbados, Botswana, Guyana, Lesotho
1968	Mauritius, Nauru, Swaziland
1970	Fiji (left 1987, rejoined 1997), Tonga, Western Samoa
1972	Bangladesh
1973	Bahamas
1974	Grenada
1975	Papua New Guinea
1976	Seychelles
1978	Dominica, Solomon Islands, Tuvalu
1979	Kiribati, St Lucia, St Vincent and the Grenadines
1980	Vanuatu, Zimbabwe (suspended 2002, left 2003)
1981	Antigua and Barbuda, Belize
1982	Maldives
1983	St Kitts and Nevis
1984	Brunei
1990	Namibia
1994	South Africa (left 1961, readmitted on 1 June)
1995	Cameroon
1995	Mozambique

ment to guide its dependent territories towards self-government and independence. The Commonwealth provides an opportunity for the heads of state and government of its members to meet on a regular basis (every two years) and has resulted in common views being formulated in communiqués and declarations (such as the 1989 declaration on South Africa). The interests of Commonwealth members was an important issue which dominated all three of Britain's applications to join the European Community, and proved influential behind the 1975 **Lomé Convention.**

Commonwealth of Independent States (CIS)

Established in December 1991, it is a broad association that comprises the majority of the former republics of the Soviet Union.

Communitization

This is a process that refers to the transfer of a policy area to within the institutional framework of the EU. This has particularly been applied to the '**pillars**' that were established by the **Treaty on European Union**, whereby within the context of the **third pillar** of **justice and home affairs** (JHA) aspects relating to freedom of movement across frontiers were transferred to the **first pillar** by virtue of the **Treaty of Amsterdam**. Thus, at the heart of communitization is an understanding that the transfer of the policy will result in increased involvement by the supranational institutions in **decision-making**.

Community initiatives

Aid or action programmes established to complement the operation of the **structural funds** in certain specific areas. While coordinated and implemented under national control, they are initially drawn up by the **European Commission**. Community initiatives embrace a number of policy areas, including cross-border cooperation, rural development, industrial change and encouraging small- and medium-sized firms.

Community law

This embraces three forms: (1) the Treaties and related instruments, including the **own resources** decision; (2) legislation that consists of **regulations**, **directives** and **decisions**; (3) case-law that is materialized in decisions of the **Court of Justice**.

Community method

This refers to the most common method of EU **decision-making**, by which the **European Commission** puts forward a proposal that is then examined by the **Council of Ministers** and the **European Parliament**, often resulting in amendments being made before it becomes law.

Community preference

A part of the **Common Agricultural Policy** (CAP) whereby member states are expected to give preference to agricultural products from within the EU over those from outside.

Community support framework (CSF)

Coordinates the regional activities of the EU. At times this involves the **structural funds** and the **European Investment Bank**.

Competence

This term is generally used in the context of determining the extent of the power and influence of European institutions vis-à-vis national authorities.

Competition policy

Free competition is one of the main principles of the EU's **single market** programme: the removal of **barriers to trade** and the need for new sets of regulations to be created to govern the single market. At the same time, the increased potential for pan-European mergers meant that there was a need for them to be regulated. In order to ensure that free competition is practised, the member states have a common competition policy that rests on a number of fundamental rules, for example:

- companies are prohibited from entering into agreements that obstruct, restrict or distort competition (for instance, price-fixing or market-sharing);
- companies are not allowed to abuse a dominant market position;
- merger controls are in operation. The **European Commission** has the authority to approve or reject intended corporate mergers.

It is the task of the Commission to ensure that these rules are observed in all member states. Exceptions to the rules can be made if sufficiently strong grounds can be cited. The Commission may impose fines on countries or companies failing to comply with the competition regulations.

Competitiveness

Refers to the ability of both member states to compete with each other and with outside states, while also highlighting the ability of the economic strength of the EU versus other trading nations and trading blocs. The **European Commission**'s 1994 **White Paper on growth, competitiveness and employment** contained guidelines for a policy of global competitiveness.

Compulsory expenditure

Budgetary expenditure over which the **Council of Ministers** has greater power than the **European Parliament**. It is primarily aimed at the **Common Agricultural Policy** (CAP).

Concentric circles

A concept of European integration which involves states being grouped depending on the levels of integration achieved. The circles could involve both broad topics embracing all member states, such as legal policies, while there might also be additional circles dealing with more specialized subjects, such as defence policy.

Conciliation committee

A conciliation committee can be established under the **co-decision procedure**. It consists of members of the **Council of Ministers** or their representatives and an equal number of representatives of the **European Parliament**. It is referred to in the event of disagreement between the two institutions on the outcome of a co-decision procedure. The rationale is to ensure that a text is agreed which is acceptable to both sides. The draft of such a text must then be ratified within six weeks by **qualified majority voting** (QMV) in the Council and by an absolute majority of the members of the European Parliament. But if one of the two institutions does not approve the proposal then it is not adopted.

Conference on Security and Cooperation in Europe (CSCE)

Established by the signing of the Helsinki Final Act on 1 August 1975, it represented an attempt to reconcile the differing interests of the **North Atlantic Treaty Organisation** (NATO) and the **Warsaw Pact**, with all European countries apart from Albania initially taking part in the negotiations, in addition to Canada and the USA. The initial membership comprised 35 nations, of which Western nations were primarily interested in promoting human rights in the East, while Eastern nations hoped to benefit from economic and technological cooperation with the West. Such aims were emphasized in the various 'baskets' that the Final Act was divided into. Basket 1 focused on security and disarmament. Basket 2 was concerned with economic, scientific and technological cooperation and environmental protection. Basket 3 dealt with humanitarian cooperation and basket 4 dealt with means by which the commitments entered into by the signatory states would be followed up. But, while there was a steady expansion in the membership of the CSCE, until 1990 it primarily operated as a series of meetings and conferences that extended the commitments of the participating member states.

The end of the **Cold War** provided the CSCE with a new lease of life and the **Charter of Paris** for a New Europe that was agreed at the Paris Summit of November 1990 stressed that the CSCE should play a key role in tackling the challenges of the post-Cold War period. As a result, the CSCE obtained permanent institutions and obtained operational capabilities. However, the very establishment of a Secretariat and supporting institutions as well as an increased regularity in the holding of meetings meant that the work of the CSCE became far more structured. This in turn meant that the CSCE was more than just a 'Conference' and consequently at a summit meeting in Budapest in 1994 agreement was reached on a name change to the **Organization for Security and Cooperation in Europe** (OSCE) to reflect a more proactive institution.

Congress of Europe see *Hague Congress*

Consensus

A number of EU decisions require a consensus (unanimity) of all parties.

Constitutional Treaty

At the Brussels **European Council** of June 2004 member states reached agreement on a Constitutional Treaty that had been subject to formal negotiation in an **intergovernmental conference** (IGC) since October 2003. The Treaty had been shaped by the draft Constitutional Treaty that had been presented to the Thessaloniki European Council of June 2003 as a result of the work conducted under the **Convention on the Future of Europe**. The new Constitutional Treaty was influenced by a desire to provide a clearer structure and focus to the EU through the consolidation of all the previous treaties into one single document so as to provide the EU with a simpler and more accessible set of rules. The Treaty is, however, more than just a mere 'tidying up' exercise, and made a number of important changes. These include:

- The creation of a new post of EU President, to be elected by heads of government for a term of two and half years. Such a change was prompted by concerns that the previous system of a six-monthly rotation of the Presidency among all member states hindered the continuity of EU policies and created confusion for non-member states.

- The creation of a new EU Minister for Foreign Affairs that would combine the existing positions of the Council's **High Representative for CFSP** and the **European Commissioner** for external relations. This resulted from concern over the EU's international identity.
- Providing more scope for defence cooperation among member states.
- Incorporating the EU **Charter of Fundamental Rights** (including the right to strike).
- Getting rid of the national **veto** in some areas, such as immigration and asylum policy (although the veto was maintained on matters relating to financing the EU **budget**, tax, and defence and foreign policy).
- A fairer distribution of votes among member states with regard to the provision for **qualified majority voting** (QMV) in the **Council of Ministers**, and a system of double majority voting whereby a 'yes' vote requires 15 member states that comprise a minimum of 65 per cent of the population.
- Providing national parliaments with the ability to ensure that EU law does not encroach on the rights of member states.

Yet, despite the member state governments agreeing to the Treaty, the implementation of the Treaty has been hampered by the Treaty having been rejected in **referendums** in France in May 2005 and the Netherlands in June 2005.

Constructive abstention

This procedure permits member states to abstain in the EU **Council of Ministers** on decisions relating to **Common Foreign and Security Policy** and thereby not block a unanimous agreement.

Consultation procedure

The consultation procedure stipulates that the **European Commission** needs to send its proposals to both the **Council of Ministers** and the **European Parliament**. For many years, the European Parliament's influence was limited to the consultation procedure whereby, although it had the right to make its views known, neither the European Commission nor the Council of Ministers was required to take into consideration these views. In practical terms, after a proposal has been made by the European Commission, the Council of Ministers has to consult the European Parliament and is unable to act before an opinion has been issued by the European Parliament. Overall, the Council of Ministers acts as the sole decision-maker on the proposal. In recent years the influence of the European Parliament has been strengthened further, first through the **cooperation procedure** and thereafter through the **co-decision procedure**.

Consumer policy

While the **Treaties of Rome** did not mention consumer policy, both the **European Parliament** and numerous **interest groups** have campaigned for such a policy. This resulted in the **Council of Ministers** launching a consumer information and protections programme in April 1975 which embraced economic justice, health and safety issues, consultation, remedy for damages, and education and information.

However, it was not until the introduction of the Maastricht **Treaty on European Union** that consumer policy was given a legal base for 'specific action which supports and supplements the policy pursued by the member states to protect the health, safety and economic interests of consumers and to provide adequate information to consumers'. This has included, for instance, a 1998 law that banned tobacco advertising.

Contact group

Refers to the meetings of representatives of France, Germany, Russia, the UK and the US concerning the former Yugoslavia, the purpose of which was to act as a vehicle to present a united front to the warring parties. The first such meeting took place in London on 26 April 1994, with the contact group being key to the brokering of a ceasefire in Bosnia in 1995 and in the negotiation of the Dayton Peace Accords.

Contributions and receipts

Refers to the difference between the contributions of a member state to the EU **budget** and the benefits (receipts) that it obtains from the budget.

Convention on the Future of Europe

A declaration on the future of the European Union was adopted by member states at the Nice **European Council** of December 2000, with a view to progressing with institutional reform beyond the **intergovernmental conference** (IGC) negotiations that had concluded with the **Treaty of Nice**. This was to be achieved by a three-stage process:

*   the start of a debate on the future of the EU;
*   the establishment of a Convention on institutional reform;
*   the convening of an IGC to discuss these matters.

At the Laeken European Council of 15 December 2001, member states adopted a Declaration on the Future of the European Union. Commonly known as the Laeken Declaration, it called for the EU to be more democratic, effective and transparent. With this in mind, a Convention was convened under the chairmanship of former French president **Valéry Giscard d'Estaing** to examine key questions about the future of the EU. The Convention met between March 2002 and June 2003 and set out its recommendations in the form of a draft **Constitutional Treaty** that was presented to the Thessaloniki European Council of June 2003. The proposals that were set out in the draft both replaced and made changes to the existing Treaties. The proposals in turn formed the basis for the 2003–4 IGC negotiations on the EU **Constitutional Treaty**.

Convergence criteria

The Maastricht **Treaty on European Union** established a number of convergence criteria that each member state must make before they can take part in stage 3 of **Economic and Monetary Union** (EMU):

1 The ratio of government deficit to GDP must not exceed 3 per cent.
2 The ratio of government debt to GDP must not exceed 60 per cent.
3 A sustainable degree of price stability and an average inflation rate has to be observed over a period of one year prior to examination. It should not exceed by more than 1.5 percentage points that of the three best performing member states in terms of price stability.
4 Long-term nominal interest rates should not exceed by more than 2 percentage points that of the three best performing member states in terms of price stability.
5 Member states should have respected the normal fluctuation margins provided for by the **Exchange Rate Mechanism** (ERM) for at least the last two years before examination.

On 2 May 1998 the **Council of Ministers** concluded that 11 member states had met the criteria to participate in the **single currency** (Austria, Belgium, Finland, France, Germany, Italy, Ireland, Luxembourg, the Netherlands, Portugal and Spain). Of the remaining member states, Denmark, Sweden and the United Kingdom were unwilling to participate in the single currency and the economic conditions in Greece were such that its economy had not sufficiently converged. Greece was, however, subsequently able to meet the convergence criteria and on 1 January 2002 it adopted the **euro**.

Convertibility

The degree to which one currency can be exchanged for another.

Cooperation procedure

Introduced in the **Single European Act** (SEA), it provided the **European Parliament** with a greater say in the legislative process and therefore helped to reduce the **democratic deficit**. The cooperation procedure stipulates that the European Parliament needs to be consulted twice before a legislative proposal from the **European Commission** takes effect. In specific terms, if the **Council of Ministers** does not take into account the initial European Parliament opinion in its common position, then the European Parliament is able to reject it at the second reading. Thereafter, it is only possible for the Council to overturn the position of the European Parliament by means of a unanimous decision. But, as it is not always possible to obtain unanimity, the Council can seek conciliation with the European Parliament to ensure proposals are not rejected. In recent years the cooperation procedure has largely been superseded by the **co-decision procedure** that was introduced in the **Maastricht Treaty** and which was extended to cover more policies in the **Treaty of Amsterdam**. To this end, the cooperation procedure is now limited to the area of **Economic and Monetary Union** (EMU). Such limited use of the procedure resulted in the **Constitutional Treaty** which member states agreed to in 2004 (subject to a process of ratification) proposing the abolition of the procedure, with it to be replaced by the co-decision procedure or by non-legislative acts of the Council.

Copenhagen criteria

The June 1993 Copenhagen **European Council** established criteria that would have to be fulfilled for the countries of **central and eastern European states** to be able to join the EU:

- stable institutions that guarantee democracy, the rule of law, human rights and respect for and protection of minorities (political criterion);
- a functioning market economy and the capacity to cope with competitive pressure and market forces within the EU (economic criterion);
- the ability to take on the obligations of membership, including adherence to the aims of political, **Economic and Monetary Union** (EMU) (criterion concerning the adoption of the *acquis communitaire*).

Cordis

This acronym for the Community Research and Development Information Service is a database which provides information on all of the research projects that are currently being undertaken within the EU.

Core Europe

Refers to a small group of countries that are willing to enter into **closer cooperation** with each other. The term is often used in reference to the core countries of France, Germany, Belgium, Luxembourg and the Netherlands.

Coreper see *Committee of Permanent Representatives*

COREU

The system which allows the Foreign Offices of EU member states to exchange information in the form of faxes, telex messages and telegrams. This process is supervised by political directors and their assistants, known as European correspondents, and was initially introduced as a component of **European Political Cooperation** (EPC).

COSAC

Acronym for Conference of European Community Affairs Committees, which consists of members of the relevant national parliaments committees and of members of the **European Parliament**. The six-monthly meetings (since 1988) are important in providing a framework where views can be exchanged between national parliaments and the **European Parliament**, the pertinence of which has increased with the transfer to the EU of some policies which were purely a national preserve.

COST

Acronym for the Committee on European Cooperation in the Field of Scientific and Technical Research. It is a funding framework for the implementation and promotion of collaborative scientific research in the fields of agriculture, environmental protection, oceanography, telecommunications and transport that was set up in 1971.

Costa v. ENEL

In 1964 the **Court of Justice**'s ruling in the case of *Costa* v. *ENEL* established the primacy of Community law over national law by stressing that 'the law stemming from the Treaty . . . (cannot) be overridden by domestic legal provisions'.

Cotonou Agreement

The Cotonou Agreement, which was signed in Cotonou (Benin) on 20 June 2000 by representatives of the 15 EU member states and the 78 **African, Caribbean and Pacific** (ACP) states, replaced the **Lomé Convention** (which had operated since 1975) as the mean vehicle for the EU's **development policy**. The Cotonou Agreement mirrors the Lomé Convention in terms of institutional structure, with there being an ACP–EU Council of Ministers; a Committee of Ambassadors in Brussels; and an ACP–EU Joint Parliamentary Assembly to meet twice a year. The Cotonou Agreement establishes the general framework for ACP–EU development cooperation relations for the next 20 years, with mid-term reviews taking place every five years. Although the Agreement builds on the work of the Lomé Convention by providing economic assistance and trading opportunities for the ACP countries, it also makes a number of notable improvements. This particularly applies to attaching importance to political dialogue, whereby emphasis has been given to eradicating poverty, promoting non–governmental organizations and the role of civil society within the context of good governance. At the same time, the Cotonou Agreement provides for tighter financial controls and greater transparency with regard to the disbursement of development aid.

Coudenhove-Kalergi, Count Richard (1894–1972)

Throughout the 1920s and 1930s Coudenhove-Kalergi was one of the most prominent advocates of a united Europe. The son of an Austro-Hungarian diplomat, he founded the Pan-European Union in 1922 as a vehicle to advance his view that peace could only be guaranteed by the creation of a political union. Such views were outlined in his 1923 book *Paneuropa*, in which he argued for the creation of a European federation. In the aftermath of the devastating impact of the First World War, the Pan-European Union acquired a loyal following that included individuals who shaped European integration in the post-1945 era, such as **Konrad Adenauer, Georges Pompidou, Aristide Briand** and **Winston Churchill.**

Council for Mutual Economic Assistance (CMEA)

Commonly referred to as Comecon, it was established in 1949 as a means of promoting economic cooperation among the communist states of central and eastern Europe. The collapse of communism and the end of the **Cold War** eroded the need for Comecon, which formally ceased to exist in September 1991. In the period since then most of the members of Comecon have applied for EU membership and many became EU members at the time of the 2004 **enlargement**.

Council of Europe

The establishment of the Council of Europe, based in Strasbourg, in May 1949 had been greatly influenced by the **Hague Congress** of May 1948. But, while the federalists who had been influential behind the Hague Congress had sought to promote stronger cooperation among European nations, the Council of Europe was based on intergovernmental structures that did not involve the transfer of power and influence away from nation states. In this context, its aims were rather vague and wide-ranging, with Article 1(a) noting that 'the aim of the Council of Europe is to achieve a greater unity between its Members for the purpose of safeguarding and realising the ideals and principles which are their common heritage and facilitating their economic and social progress'. The end product is that while the Council of Europe (which is not part of the EU) has contributed to fostering European integration its members have not been faced with having to take decisions that impinge on national sovereignty. The Treaty does, for instance, stress that 'Matters relating to national defence do not fall within the scope of the Council of Europe'. The main institutions of the Council of Europe are:

• Secretariat;
• Committee of Foreign Ministers;
• Parliamentary Assembly;
• Congress of Local and Regional Authorities of Europe;
• European Commission of Human Rights;
• European Court of Human Rights.

The membership of the Council of Europe initially comprised 10 countries: Belgium, Denmark, France, Ireland, Italy, Luxembourg, the Netherlands, Norway, Sweden and the UK. Over time this membership would expand, to 15 nations by 1956 and to 21 nations by 1983. With the end of the **Cold War** and the removal of the division between eastern and western Europe, its membership had increased to 37 nations by 1995 and by 2005 to 46 nations (Table 4.7).

Table 4.7 Members of the Council of Europe

Albania	Germany	Norway
Andorra	Greece	Poland
Armenia	Hungary	Portugal
Austria	Iceland	Romania
Azerbaijan	Ireland	Russian Federation
Belgium	Italy	San Marino
Bosnia and Herzegovina	Latvia	Serbia and Montenegro
Bulgaria	Liechtenstein	Slovakia
Croatia	Lithuania	Slovenia
Cyprus	Luxembourg	Spain
Czech Republic	former Yugoslav Republic	Sweden
Denmark	of Macedonia	Switzerland
Estonia	Malta	Turkey
Finland	Moldova	Ukraine
France	Monaco	United Kingdom
Georgia	Netherlands	

Council of Ministers

The EU's main **decision-making** institution consisting of national ministers. Legislating and decision-making are the most important powers of the Council of Ministers, providing member states with ultimate control over the destiny of the EU. The majority of decisions are taken by **qualified majority voting** (QMV). The business of the Council is organized by the member state which holds the **Council Presidency** (which rotates twice a year: January to June; July to December). The task of managing the Presidency includes the setting of agendas and drafting texts during **intergovernmental conference** (IGC) negotiations. In exercising these duties, the Presidency is assisted by the **Council Secretariat**, whose staff assist with the resolution of compromises. This includes the writing of Council minutes and offering impartial legal advice. Such assistance is of greater importance to smaller member states who do not always have the necessary resources in their Brussels **Permanent Representations** to fully exercise the duties of the Presidency. The business of the Council of Ministers is divided into Council meetings that are organized on sectoral lines, including agriculture, finance, the internal market and transport. The General Affairs Council, which consists of foreign ministers, is the most important Council. The number of Councils has grown over the years to keep pace with the expansion of the activities of the EU.

Council Presidency

The **Council of Ministers** and the **European Council** have traditionally had a rotating Presidency, whereby each member state was in the chair for a period of six months (January until June, July until December). The Presidency's role is particularly important as it is responsible for arranging and presiding over all meetings at which it must find acceptable compromises and solutions to problems. In this connection it is important to ensure that continuity and consistency are maintained in the decision-taking process. The Presidency is assisted in its work by the **Friends of the Presidency** group, which comprises a representative from every **permanent representation** and is chaired by the official whose nation holds the Presidency. They assist policy development by providing a clearing ground for topics, thereby ensuring that more senior staff, such as the permanent representative or government ministers, are not burdened with unnecessary work. In this context, their work is similar to the **Antici group** which assists permanent representative meetings throughout the year by providing a clearing ground for policies.

Deputy and Permanent Representatives have to chair meetings of their fellow negotiators in the **Committee of Permanent Representatives**, as do ministers of state and those officials that staff the various EU Committees and Working Groups (except those chaired by the **European Commission**). A significant addition to these tasks has been the increased number of meetings between the Presidency and the **European Parliament**, whereby the latter is kept fully informed of developments. There has been a marked increase in the number of visits by the Presidency to the European Parliament, with the former no longer just presenting a 'report' at the start of its term of office, but rather being subjected to a more rigorous questioning and examination by the Parliament throughout the Presidency. In practical terms, this has been reflected, particularly since the 1997 **Treaty of Amsterdam**, in each Presidency spending more time with the Parliament than the previous Presidency did.

The increased amount of work which the assumption of the Presidency brings to a member state, and the Permanent Representation in particular, ensures that a great deal of effort is attached to its planning. It is therefore not surprising that a 'Presidency unit' tends to be established within a Permanent Representation at least a year before it assumes the Presidency, while there is a further tendency for staffing levels to increase. The extra burden means that in most cases additional ministers and officials have to be brought in to the Permanent Representation as national spokesmen so that the normal representative can move into the chair. For those that occupy the chair, they have the important task of creating compromises and brokering packages among member states, with their role also being crucial to the smooth running of the Presidency.

Although these range of duties attaches prominence to the member state (and leader) holding the Presidency and gives prestige to small member states, the rotating basis of the position has nonetheless been subject to criticism. The workload of the Presidency is a considerable strain on the resources of most national governments, with this being true for small member states. Moreover, the six-monthly change has not always helped to promote continuity of EU policies, especially those with an international dimension. In response, the EU **Constitutional Treaty** has proposed three new developments. First, the abolishment of the rotating basis of the Presidency, and to instead for the European Council to elect an individual for a term of two and a half years whose job will be to run the activities of the Council. It is an argument that was supported by many of the large member states, including France, Germany and the UK, who all stressed the benefits of having one individual that can offer stability and be able to represent the interests of the member states on an international basis. Second, the Constitutional Treaty provided for a 'Team Presidency' of three member states of 18 months to replace the existing six-monthly rotating Presidency. The practical reality of such a proposal is that one member state would preside over all the Council meetings for six months, with support provided by the other member states in the Team. Third, the Constitutional Treaty established a new post of EU Minister for Foreign Affairs, with there being a merger of the existing roles of the **European Commissioner** for External Relations and the **High Representative for CFSP**. The intention of such a merger is that the Foreign Minister would be able to ensure that there was greater consistency to the foreign policy of the EU.

Council secretariat

This is the professional civil service whose primary task is to act as a support service to the member state that chairs the **Council Presidency**. The Council secretariat, which comprises approximately 2,500 staff (and which is considerably smaller than the staff of the **European Commission**) provides briefings to government ministers and officials, gives legal advice and helps to prepare the agenda and organize Council meetings as well as to draft Council minutes. Small member states are often more reliant on the support functions of the Council secretariat. In the **Treaty of Amsterdam** provision was made for the secretary-general of the Council to become the **High Representative for CFSP**, which in turn signified that the secretary-general would play a greater role in political matters.

Council Working Groups

The majority of negotiations on EU legislation take place in working groups that comprise officials from national capitals and/or permanent representations.

Court of Auditors

Established in 1975 by the **Treaty of Brussels**, its main role is to audit the accounts of the institutions of the EU and other Union bodies. Comprising 25 members, it examines whether revenue and expenditure have been properly handled and checks if sound financial management has taken place.

Court of First Instance

A division of the **Court of Justice** which was created under the terms of the **Single European Act** (SEA). It entered operation in 1989 as a means of reducing the burden of work on the **Court of Justice**.

Court of Justice

Based in Luxembourg, it is the supreme court of the EU comprising 25 judges and eight Advocates General. It is only concerned with EC law and thereby ensures that the Treaties are applied and respected.

Crocodile group

Established in 1980, the crocodile group was created by **Altiero Spinelli** and other Members of the **European Parliament** who believed that there should be an acceleration in the process of European integration. The Crocodile initiative eventually resulted in the 1984 Draft Treaty on European Union being adopted by the European Parliament which assisted the momentum towards the **Single European Act** (SEA). The Crocodile initiative is also known as the Spinelli initiative, while the group's name comes from the Strasbourg restaurant where the first meeting took place.

Cross-border transactions

This refers not just to the exchange of currencies, but also a shift from one payment system to another. Prior to the introduction of the **euro**, the domestic payments system in each member state did not inter-operate between member states; as a result the costs associated with transactions increased. The introduction of the euro as a **single currency** will therefore result in a reduction in costs. This is because the euro will no longer involve foreign exchange transactions, and thus many of the associated costs, such as commission charges on exchanging currency, will no longer exist. In a similar sense, card transactions will also benefit because a fixed conversion rate will apply. A second benefit will be an acceleration in the processing of payments because there will be a reduction in payment delays with an absence of currency exchange transactions.

Cultural policy

The Maastricht **Treaty on European Union** formally recognized culture in the context of European integration. It noted that 'The Community shall contribute to the flowering of the cultures of the member states, while respecting their national heritage and regional diversity and at the same time bringing the common cultural heritage to the fore.'

Customs union

Refers to the merger of several customs areas into a single whole, resulting in the lifting of duties between participating countries. In this situation, members are not allowed to levy their own duties on imports from countries outside the Union, which contrasts with a **Free Trade Area** (in a customs union a **common external tariff** is set). Within the context of the EU, the creation of a customs union was a principal objective of the **Treaties of Rome**, with a full customs union being realized in 1968. Key aspects in the promotion of a customs union included the elimination of all customs duties among member states; the introduction of a common external tariff that would be applicable to all goods imported from **third countries**; and the creation of a **common commercial policy** as a vehicle for ensuring that the EU spoke as a whole in external affairs.

Cyprus

Population: 0.76m (2005)
Capital: Nicosia
Cyprus is a former British colony which received independence in 1960. It has a history of tensions between the majority Greek Cypriot community and the Turkish minority community. This tension was evident throughout the 1960s and early 1970s. In 1974 Turkey invaded Cyprus in the wake of a Greek-sponsored attempt to take control of the government, which resulted in Cyprus being divided into two, with a Turkish Republic of Northern Cyprus essentially controlling a third of the island. The dividing line between Turkish and Greek Cypriot communities has been patrolled by the United Nations (UN) and over a number of years the UN has attempted to broker talks between both communities. Despite these tensions, Cyprus signed an Association Agreement with the Community in 1973 and a formal application for membership was submitted on 4 July 1990. The initial **European Com-**

mission opinion of July 1993 was in favour of Cyprus joining the EU and at the June 1994 Corfu **European Council** it was stressed that 'the next phase of **enlargement** would involve Cyprus'. **Accession** negotiations commenced on 31 March 1998 with Cyprus joining the EU on 1 May 2004. Despite the fact that it is only the Greek Cypriot-controlled Republic of Cyprus which is a member of the EU, every Cypriot in possession of a Cyprus passport nonetheless benefits from the status of a EU citizen. Turkish Cypriots have benefited from this provision, but EU rules will not be applicable in the Turkish Republic of Northern Cyprus.

Czech Republic

Population: 10.27m (2005)
Capital: Prague
In the aftermath of the Second World War Czechoslovakia fell within the Soviet sphere of influence. Attempts by Czech leaders to offer 'socialism with a human face' were met with harsh repression when Warsaw Pact troops invaded Czechoslovakia in 1968, thereby ending what has become known as the 'Prague spring'. The collapse of Soviet authority in 1989 provided Czechoslovakia with a further opportunity of freedom during a period that was known as the 'Velvet Revolution'. On 1 January 1993, Czechoslovakia split into its two national components of the Czech Republic and Slovakia, and in the same year the Czech Republic signed a **Europe Agreement** with the EC that set out the possibility of membership and superseded the previous Europe Agreement that had been signed in 1991 with Czechoslovakia. In 1996 the Czech Republic made a formal application for EU membership which the EU favourably considered in 1997 with accession negotiations commencing in 1998. In 1999 the Czech Republic joined the **North Atlantic Treaty Organisation** (NATO), and along with Slovakia it joined the EU on 1 May 2004.

D

Davignon, Viscount Etienne (b. 1932)

As political director of the Belgian Foreign Ministry in the early 1970s, he played a major role in the development of **European Political Cooperation** (EPC) by chairing the committee of permanent representatives which devised the plan. He was later appointed a member of the **European Commission** from 1977 until 1985, under the leadership of **Roy Jenkins** and **Gaston Thorn**. During that time he was responsible for industry policy and was an active participant in encouraging greater competitiveness within member states.

Davignon Report

This is the name that is given to the report that emanated from the decision taken at the December 1969 **Hague Summit** to establish a committee that would investigate the possibility of achieving closer political integration. The initiative for the summit came from the French president, **Georges Pompidou**, who hoped to achieve a relaunch of the process of European integration. The committee established at the Hague to investigate political integration was chaired by the senior Belgian Foreign Ministry official, **Etienne Davignon**. Having been instructed by the Hague summit 'to study the best way of achieving progress in the matter of political unification, within the context of **enlargement**' of the EC, the November 1970 Davignon Report recommended that foreign policy coordination 'should be the object of the first practical endeavours to demonstrate to all that Europe has a political vocation'. In focusing on foreign policy, the Davignon Report stressed that the Community needed to have a stronger presence in international affairs that was to be achieved through the creation of an intergovernmental system of **European Political Cooperation** (EPC) to facilitate foreign policy harmonization and coordination among member states.

de Gasperi, Alcide (1881–1954)

A founding father of Europe, he was prime minister of Italy from 1945 to 1954, the first and longest-serving prime minister of the post-war period, during which time he pursued the modernization of the Italian economy. He was a member of the dominant Christian Democratic Party (Democrazia Cristani) and steered a pro-Western foreign policy, being a committed supporter of greater European integration. He advocated the economic development of Italy but also suppressed extreme political challenges, particularly from the Italian Communist Party (Partito Communista Italiano).

de Gaulle, Charles (1890–1970)

As the London-based leader of the Free French during the Second World War, he proved to be a key figure in French politics in the post-war period, being the first leader of the liberated nation. His retirement from office in 1946 through discontent over the Fourth Republic's constitution reduced his influence upon French politics. This marginalization continued until he became the first leader of the Fifth Republic in 1958, serving as president until 1969. During this time he placed great emphasis on restoring France's position in international affairs. This included a move away from any reliance on the USA and the assertion of a policy which maintained national **sovereignty** as well as French leadership of the EC. Within the Community his aims were reflected in the 1963 **Treaty of Friendship** between France and Germany, whereas his emphasis on national **sovereignty** resulted in the **empty chair crisis** in the second half of 1965 when he withdrew French participation in the Council of Ministers. This difficulty was eventually resolved by the 1966 **Luxembourg compromise** which reasserted the importance of member states and their ability to use the **veto**. On a wider level he personally vetoed the UK's application to the Community in 1963 and 1967, partly because he considered it would result in a large degree of US influence. He withdrew French forces from the integrated military structure of the **North Atlantic Treaty Organisation** (NATO) in 1966, resulting in the removal of NATO's political and military headquarters from France to Belgium.

Decision-making

Within the EU there are a number of decision-making procedures. Legislative decisions involve the **European Commission, European Parliament** and **Council of Ministers**. Although the majority of all legislation is now subject to the **co-decision procedure**, decisions can also be taken using the **assent, consultation** and **cooperation** procedures. Other types of decisions, such as those on **Common Foreign and Security Policy** (CFSP) and **justice and home affairs** (JHA) have traditionally been based on intergovernmental methods. In areas of trade policy the European Commission has **decision-making** responsibility.

Decision

This is one of the acts adopted by the **Council of Ministers** and the **European Commission**. Decisions have **direct effect** in law, referring to specific individual cases and may be addressed to firms, individuals or a particular member state.

Declaration

A statement by the EU that tends to be of limited judicial importance. Declarations can also be attached to a Final Act, or be a minor part of a Treaty, whereby its signatories express certain intentions. In this context it is not as significant as a protocol.

Decolonization

Refers to the process whereby European states retreated from their colonies throughout the twentieth century. Many of the former colonies are members of the **African, Pacific and Caribbean** (ACP) states and benefit from the **Cotonou Agreement**, and prior to that the **Lomé Convention**.

Debate on the future of the European Union

The 2000 **intergovernmental conference** (IGC) negotiation that resulted in the **Treaty of Nice** called for a more detailed discussion on the future of the EU. The Nice Declaration that was annexed to the Treaty of Nice noted the need for a broad debate that would incorporate a wide body of interested parties, including representatives of **national parliaments** and representatives of **civil society**, universities and political and commercial organizations. At the Laeken **European Council** of December 2001 member states agreed to the **Laeken Declaration** on the Future of the European Union that established a Convention that would be chaired by the former French president, **Valéry Giscard d'Estaing**. The Convention met between March 2002 and June 2003 and set out its recommendations in the form of a draft **Constitutional Treaty** which in turn formed the basis for the 2003–4 IGC negotiations that resulted in agreement on a Constitutional Treaty at the June 2004 European Council.

Deepening

A process of strengthening particular policies that may also produce certain institutional reforms that further European integration. While this process is considered by some member states to be necessary prior to **enlargement**, other member states have traditionally perceived the enlargement of the Community as not necessitating deepening, and therefore developing a debate between **widening** versus deepening.

Definitive Conversion Rate

When a member state joins the **single currency** the value of its national currency is set against the **euro** at a fixed rate.

Delors, Jacques (b. 1925)

As President of the **European Commission** between 1985 and 1995 he played a major role in the development of the Community. During his period of office the Community expanded from 10 to 15 members, while he oversaw reform through the **Single European Act** (SEA) and Maastricht **Treaty on European Union**. His efforts to foster closer political integration ensured that he was the most active President since

Walter Hallstein. His influence included being a prominent figure in drafting the 1989 **Charter of Fundamental Rights** and being the chair of the committee which examined the prospect of **Economic and Monetary Union** (EMU), producing the **Delors Report** in April 1989. During his period of office he fostered a workmanlike attitude within the Commission, where he was renowned for having a clear perception of where the Community should go. That often meant he worked closely with immediate colleagues, including members of his own *cabinet*, and prompted concern that more peripheral European Commissioners were not able to exercise the influence that their position merited. Among member states, he had frequent clashes with **Margaret Thatcher**, despite the fact that she approved his appointment as President of the European Commission and as chair of the committee which examined the prospect of monetary union. Thatcher was especially vociferous in attacking the introduction of a social dimension to the Community. However, the relationship between Delors and other leaders was by no means easy; in particular, contacts with **François Mitterrand** were often tense. This partly stemmed from Delors' own experience of French politics; he had been finance minister between March 1983 and July 1984.

Delors I Budget Package

A 1987 **European Commission** proposal to reform Community financing, reduce agricultural spending, increase the **structural funds** and reconsider the **budget** management rules. It formed the basis for the agreement reached at the February 1988 Brussels **European Council**.

Delors II Budget Package

In the wake of the signature of the Maastricht **Treaty on European Union**, the **European Commission** presented a **budget** package in February 1992 with the aim of securing the financing of the EU in the medium term. To allow the implementation of the decisions taken at the Maastricht **European Council** meeting with regard to the Treaty on European Union, budget resources were increased, being particularly pertinent to ensuring cohesion between member states. The package was subsequently approved by the Edinburgh European Council in December 1992, and provided for an increase in the **own resources** of the Community to 1.27 per cent of GDP in 1999, while also establishing the **Cohesion Fund** and providing greater resources for the **structural funds**.

Delors Report (12 April 1989)

Published in April 1989, it proposed a three-stage transition to **Economic and Monetary Union**:

1 This involved completion of financial details of the **single market**, with for instance the establishment of free capital movements among member states. At the same time all member states would participate in the narrow band of the **Exchange Rate Mechanism (ERM)**, closer monetary and macroeconomic cooperation between member states and their **central banks**, whilst usage of the **ECU** would be further developed.
2 Of the three stages, the second was the most vague. It was essentially a transition stage when the new institutions that would be required for the third stage would be developed. It was envisaged that realignments of the ERM would be gradually reduced and in effect the system would become fixed, while in line with the goal of establishing a **European Central Bank** in the third stage the national central banks would become operationally independent.
3 The third stage of the Delors Report advocated that exchange rates of member states would be irrevocably fixed and that a European Central Bank would have full authority for establishing economic and monetary policy which would result in the creation of a **single currency**. At the same time, so as to ensure convergence of national economies, rules would be established governing budget deficits, whilst poorer regions would be given subsidies.

The Delors Report presented EMU as being necessary to achieve effective economic integration through further developing the **single market**. In focusing on the importance of the argument that the single market was a significant factor in advancing the cause of EMU, such an approach could in the first instance be viewed as being reflective of the **neofunctionalist** idea of **spillover**. Such an approach emphasized the importance of sector-by-sector expansion of integration, being driven by **interest group** pressure.

Democratic deficit

Refers to the belief that the EU does not have sufficient democratic and parliamentary supervision, with its complex method of **decision-making** resulting in it appearing to be inaccessible to ordinary citizens. This is based on a view that the EU has been dominated by a **European Commission** that lacks democratic legitimacy and a **Council of Ministers** which combines both legislative and government powers. At the same time, the **European Parliament** (which has since 1979 directly represented the interests of European citizens) has been excluded from the decision-making process. Various attempts have been made to improve the democratic legitimacy of the EU, for the most part concentrating on strengthening the influence of the European Parliament. This included granting the European Parliament the power of **co-decision** in the **Treaty on European Union**, which ensured that the Parliament would be able to veto those legislative proposals that were governed by this procedure if its interests were not taken into consideration. The subsequent **Treaty of Amsterdam** and **Treaty of Nice** extended the remit of the co-decision procedure, while the **Constitutional Treaty** notes that the procedure should (with a number of small exceptions) be the norm for taking decisions in the EU.

Denmark

Population: 5.37m (2005)
Capital: Copenhagen
Denmark joined the Community in 1973 along with Ireland and the UK, with support for membership having been confirmed in an October 1972 **referendum** wherein 63.3 per cent of votes cast were in favour of joining the Community. As with the UK, membership was motivated primarily by economic rather than political factors, not least because the fact that a significant proportion of Denmark's trade was with the UK so it was imperative that it followed Britain's application for Community membership. But, while Denmark has been a committed member state, taking care to implement the required legislation, it has nevertheless been sceptical of the transfer of too much power away from Denmark to the European institutions. This position has been reflected among the electorate and was highlighted in the result of the June 1992 referendum on the Maastricht **Treaty on European Union**, when the Danish people voted against the Treaty (by a majority of less than 2 per cent). After a number of changes were made to the Treaty to reflect Danish concerns (including **subsidiarity**, non-participation in the **single currency**, and refusal to participate in decisions with a defence dimension), this 'no' vote was overturned in a second referendum on 18 May 1993, with 56.8 per cent of the vote in favour of the Treaty. Although a 1998 referendum on the **Treaty of Amsterdam** produced a narrow vote in favour of the Treaty, Denmark nevertheless decided not to participate in the single currency. Despite the presence of an undercurrent **Euroscepticism**, Denmark has nevertheless benefited from EU membership, not least through the **Common Agricultural Policy** (CAP) and **single market**.

Depression

An economic downturn that is of greater significance than a recession.

Deregulation

Refers to the removal of qualitative and quantitative restrictions to trade that impeded the implementation of the **single market** by creating barriers.

Derogation

A temporary waiver from a **regulation** or a **directive**, which is generally only granted by a unanimous agreement of the **Council of Ministers**. It has generally been the case that derogations have been granted to new member states for a period of five or ten years under the terms that have been set out in the treaty of **accession**.

Détente

Describes the relaxation of the tension between the Soviet Union and the United States as a result of foreign and defence policy decisions. It is most commonly associated with the 1970s as a result of the deliberate efforts by west European governments and the USA to improve relations with China and the USSR. Relevant initiatives included the visit by US President Nixon to China as well as the emergence of formal diplomatic relations between the USA and China during President Carter's period in office. Among west European governments, the West German policy of **Ostpolitik** that was advanced by Chancellor **Willy Brandt** was of particular importance, as too was the 1975 **Helsinki Final Act**. By the end of the 1970s the policy of intervention by the USSR (for example in Angola and Afghanistan) and the refusal of the USSR and Eastern bloc states to observe human rights provisions led to a deterioration in relations with the West, and when US president Ronald Reagan took office in 1981 the period of détente essentially came to an end. This was, however, relatively short-lived as a period of détente once again emerged when **Mikhail Gorbachev** acceded to power in the USSR a few years later. This final period lasted until the end of the **Cold War** in 1990.

Development policy

The EU plays an important international role as the largest donor of humanitarian aid in the world, and has cooperative agreements with many developing countries. In the early years after the signature of the

Treaties of Rome, the EC's development policy was primarily focused on the member states' overseas territories and beneficiaries through the **Lomé Convention**. The **enlargement** of the Community has, however, widened the scope of cooperation to include other countries, including those belonging to the **African, Caribbean and Pacific** (ACP) grouping. The June 2000 **Cotonou Agreement** has further strengthened the EU's relationship with developing countries. The EU also plays an important role through the work of the **European Community Humanitarian Office** (ECHO) that was established in 1992.

The EU and its member states therefore play an important role in providing aid and development to the 'South' or 'Third World'. The two forms of EU aid and development are, first, regional agreements and, second, action throughout the world, including financial and technical aid, trade agreements with Asian and Latin American countries and the system of generalized tariff preferences. The EU's role also extends to providing a market for the exports of developing countries, among which the ACP countries obtain preferential terms of access, while also attempting to ensure the provision of democratic government and erosion of poverty in the countries it has a relationship with.

In terms of institutional dynamics, international aid and development agreements are adopted by the **Council of Ministers** (in some cases by qualified majority) and generally require the assent of the **European Parliament**. The **European Commission** proposes legislation and policy initiatives, negotiates international agreements, manages policies and programmes and participation in the decision-making of the ACP–EU Council of Ministers and the Committee of Ambassadors.

Differentiated integration

A process of integration in which member states choose to progress at different speeds, possibly towards common objectives. This therefore contrasts with the perception of all states moving towards the same objectives at a similar speed.

Diplomacy

The means by which conflict is reduced or cooperation promoted by the use of dialogue of compromise and persuasion between interested parties.

Direct action

Legal proceedings of a contentious nature that commence and terminate in the **Court of Justice**.

Direct effect

This refers to an EU provision that becomes law in a member state without needing additional national enactment.

Direct elections see *European elections*

Direct implementation

The putting into effect of European legislation other than by national governments.

Directive

A legal instrument by which the **Council of Ministers** or **European Commission** can require member states to amend or adopt national legislation by a specific deadline so as to achieve the aims established in the directive.

Directorates general (DGs)

They are the principal bureaucratic ministries of the **European Commission**, carrying out EU policy and administering allocations from the **budget** to different policy areas and the **structural funds**.

Dooge Committee

An ad hoc committee on institutional affairs was established by member states at the June 1984 Fontainebleau **European Council** to examine amendments to the **Treaty of Rome**, under the chairmanship of the former Irish foreign minister, Jim Dooge. The committee made use of the 1981 Genscher–Colombo plan and the **Draft Treaty on European Union** proposed by the **European Parliament**, with the report providing the basis for the decision by member states at the June 1985 Milan European Council to establish an **intergovernmental conference** (IGC). That decision eventually produced the **Single European Act** (SEA).

Draft Treaty on European Union

The name of a document which came from **Altiero Spinelli** and other **Members of the European Parliament** (MEPs) in the wake of the first direct elections to the **European Parliament**. They formed an action group (the Crocodile group) which aimed to reform the institutional dynamics of the Community. The European Parliament appointed an institutional committee in 1981 to construct a draft Treaty on political union under the chairmanship of Spinelli. Its contents were approved by a majority of MEPs in February 1984. It advocated enlarged powers for the **European Commission,** including the preparation and implementation of the **budget,** and making it the sole executive which would be accountable to both the European Parliament and the **Council of Ministers.** It additionally suggested that the use of **qualified majority voting** (QMV) would be extended in the Council.

Dual circulation of currencies

This refers to the situation that took place for a short period immediately after the introduction of **euro** notes and coins on 1 January 2002. At this point both euros and national currency notes and coins were in circulation within each member state in the **eurozone.** By 30 June 2002, old national bank notes and coins were withdrawn from circulation.

Dual mandate

This refers to those politicians who are members of both the **European Parliament** and a national parliament. Prior to the introduction of **direct elections** in 1979, the dual mandate was the normal method as **Members of the European Parliament** (MEPs) were selected from representatives of **national parliaments.**

Dublin Asylum Convention

In 1997 common formal arrangements relating to **asylum** within the EU entered into practice. The introduction of such arrangements reflected the concern of member states that the combination of the **single market** and the provisions of freedom of movement that it created would result in significant numbers of individuals seeking asylum in the EU.

Dumping

This term refers to the selling of products at below cost prices. Such practices are outlawed within the EU.

Dunkirk Treaty see *Treaty of Dunkirk*

E

Eastern bloc

A term from the **Cold War** that was used to refer to the Soviet Union and its allies and satellite states in central and eastern Europe.

Economic and Financial Committee

On 1 January 1999 the Economic and Financial Committee took over the functions of the **Monetary Committee**. To this end, the Economic and Financial Committee is responsible for preparing the meetings of EU finance ministers as well as those of the **Eurogroup**. It is composed of two representatives from each member state, two representatives from the **European Commission** and two from the **European Central Bank**.

Economic and Financial Council of Ministers (Ecofin)

This is the second most important part of the **Council of Ministers** after the Foreign Affairs Council. The meetings, which are composed of national finance ministers, take place every month. With the introduction of **Economic and Monetary Union** (EMU), it has been responsible for general economic guidelines. However, only those finance ministers who are part of the **eurozone** are able to vote on the external exchange rate policy of the **euro** and on the use of sanctions against those member states that are not meeting the necessary fiscal conditions necessary for EMU.

Economic and Monetary Union (EMU)

Although the objective of EMU was initially established in 1969 at a meeting of **the Six** and thereafter outlined in the 1970 **Werner Report**, it was not until the 1989 **Delors Report** that EMU became more of a reality. It led to the decision to convene an **intergovernmental conference** (IGC) on monetary union, the decisions of which formed a key part of the **Treaty on European Union**. The Delors Report detailed three stages for currency union: linking the currencies together through strengthening existing procedures; integration between states through a new Treaty; and finally the creation of a **European Central Bank** (ECB) resulting in the transfer of monetary policy from national authorities, and the irrevocable locking of currencies. Member states at the June 1989 Madrid **European Council** decided the Delors Report provided a basis for further work. In so deciding, the Council launched the process leading to EMU, with agreement that the first stage of the realization of EMU should begin on 1 July 1990. The second stage began on 1 January 1994, with a coordinating role being taken on by the newly established **European Monetary Institute** (EMI). The third stage commenced on 1 January 1999, with 11 member states having met the **convergence criteria** (Greece subsequently joined in 2001).

Economic and social cohesion

The objective of an economic and social cohesion policy can be traced back to the preamble of the 1957 **Treaties of Rome**, which referred to reducing regional disparities. Little significant progress took place until the **Single European Act** (SEA) established economic and social cohesion as an objective of the Community, with the subsequent Maastricht **Treaty on European Union** incorporating the policy in the EC Treaty. Economic and social cohesion policy is aimed at promoting balanced economic growth throughout the EU, whereby structural distinctions between regions are reduced and individuals are given equal opportunities. After the **Common Agricultural Policy** (CAP), economic and social cohesion is the next largest **budget** item for the EU. The 2004 **enlargement** of the EU has necessitated the focusing of economic and social cohesion objectives because a significant number (approximately 60 per cent) of the regions that have lower levels of economic growth are to be found in the new member states of central and eastern Europe.

Economic and Social Committee (ESC)

Established in 1957 by the **Treaties of Rome** with the aim of involving economic and social **interest groups** in the establishment of the **common market**. Based in Brussels, its primary purpose is to advise the **European Commission** and the **Council of Ministers** on social and economic matters. It comprises 317 members representing employers and employees as well as other groups such as consumers and farmers, who are appointed for a four-year term of office by the Council after having been nominated by national governments. The main task of members is to issue opinions on matters referred by the European Commission and the Council. In certain cases it is mandatory for the European Commission and the Council to consult the ESC, being optional in others, while it may also adopt opinions on its own initiative. These roles were reinforced by the **Single European Act** (SEA) and the **Treaty on European Union**, especially new policies such as **environment policy** and **regional policy**. This process was continued by the **Treaty of Amsterdam** providing for the ESC to be consulted by the **European Parliament**. The **Treaty of Nice** made a slight change to the description of ESC members, noting that the Committee should

comprise 'representatives of the various economic and social components of organized civil society'. The Treaty of Nice provided for its
membership to increase from 222 members to 344 members in an enlarged EU of 27 states.

Economic convergence

Member states who wish to participate in the **single currency** have
to ensure that their economies are broadly operating within the same
conditions, such as having low levels of debt. In this context the **Treaty
on European Union** specifically set **convergence criteria** that member
states have to meet for them to join the **eurozone**.

Economic union

This refers to an area where there are no **barriers to trade**, or for that
matter to the movement of capital and labour. Thus, the **single market**
programme made a significant contribution to the achievement of a
European economic union. It is possible for an economic union to exist
with (or without) a **monetary union**. The main benefit of an economic
union over a monetary union is for nations to be able to determine
economic policy. But, at the same time, the economic union does not
deliver the trade and investment benefits associated with a monetary
union, which are generally perceived to outweigh the loss of national
sovereignty with regard to the control of economic policy.

ECU

This acronym refers to the European Currency Unit. Prior to the introduction of the **euro**, the ECU acted as the accounting and currency
unit of the Community and as such it was used to calculate the accounts
of the Community (replacing the **European Unit of Account**). The
ECU became effective when the **European Monetary System** (EMS)
was established in 1979, and as a primary element of the EMS the ECU
was used for establishing the differences of fluctuation between Community currencies, while the member states that participated in the **Exchange Rate Mechanism** (ERM) of the EMS had a bilateral exchange
rate that was set against the ECU. Beyond this it was used as a unit
of account for settling trade balances between member states' **central
banks**. The overall EC **budget** was represented in ECUs, as too were
the grants distributed by the Community and the fines that were levied
by the **Court of Justice**. On 1 January 1999 it was replaced by the **euro**
at the rate of 1 ECU = 1 euro.

Education policy

Although the **Treaties of Rome** did not include much reference to education policy apart from an arrangement for member states to reciprocally recognize diplomas, professional qualifications and vocational training, there have recently been an increase in the number of programmes relevant to education. These have included **Erasmus, Socrates** and **Tempus**.

Effective date

This is the date given in an EU **directive** as the deadline for its incorporation into national legislation.

Employment policy

In the wake of the 1993 **White Paper on growth, competitiveness and employment**, the December 1994 Essen **European Council** outlined five key areas to promote employment within the EU:

1   a focus on vocational training;
2   the reduction of non-wage costs;
3   improving the effectiveness of labour market policies;
4   increasing growth rates;
5   focusing on sectors of the population that are badly affected by unemployment.

Thereafter, the **Treaty of Amsterdam** included a new chapter on employment that stipulated that job creation was a formal goal of the EU. Subsequent European Councils, such as at Lisbon in March 2000, have focused on ways of tackling this goal.

Empty chair crisis

In 1965, **Walter Hallstein**, the President of the **European Commission**, advanced a proposal that sought to provide a financial basis for the **Common Agricultural Policy** (CAP) with a requirement that budgetary expenditure should be subject to parliamentary approval. Hallstein believed this proposal to be necessary because the existing method of financing the relatively small Community **budget** out of national contributions was inadequate. However, the French president, **Charles de Gaulle**, disliked the proposal because it involved the transfer of more authority to the Commission away from the member states. De Gaulle's hostility to **supranationalism** was also emphasized in his concern over the **Treaty of Rome**'s provision to move from unanimity to **majority voting** in certain areas of the **Council of Ministers** work from 1966 onwards. This change in voting procedure represented a strengthening of the supranational design of the Community and would in turn result in a reduction of national control.

An inability to resolve differences of opinion over these issues led de Gaulle to prohibit his ministers from attending Council meetings from July to December 1965, a period commonly known as the 'empty chair crisis'. In the end, the crisis was finally resolved in January 1966, with the Hallstein Plan being abandoned in favour of the '**Luxembourg Compromise**': member states agreed to an interim financial regulation for the CAP, to limit the powers of the Commission and the **European Parliament**, and to introduce the procedure of majority voting with the provision that 'where very important interests are at stake the discussion must be continued until unanimous agreement is reached'. It would not be until 1970 that the Community budget would be financed via a system of **own resources**.

Energy policy

Despite the existence of **Euratom**, a coherent European energy policy (as first suggested in 1974) has proved problematic, partly because it is directly relevant to national interests. Nevertheless, targets were established in 1986 on levels of consumption, nuclear energy, oil imports and the development of alternative energy sources up until 1995, and a European energy charter was signed by member states in 1991. In March 2000 at the Lisbon **European Council** member states called for the creation of a genuine **single market** for energy. As a result, in March 2001 the **European Commission** set in place a number of measures that were aimed at opening up the electricity and gas markets by the end of 2005.

Enhanced cooperation

Used in the same breath as '**closer cooperation**', it refers to the decision of specific member states to work together on particular policies when other member states are unwilling or unable to participate in the policy. The **Treaty of Nice** that was agreed to by member states at the Nice **European Council** of December 2000 stressed that the minimum number of member states necessary to establish enhanced cooperation was eight (instead of a majority). The authorization for using enhanced cooperation rests with the **Council of Ministers**, with the decision being based on **qualified majority voting**, and where enhanced cooperation impacts on a policy area that makes use of the **co-decision procedure** then the **European Parliament**'s assent is necessary.

Enlargement

The concept and process of enlargement is not a new phenomenon with regards to the EU. The preamble of the **Treaties of Rome** contained reference to the determination 'to lay the foundations of an ever closer union among the peoples of Europe'. Over the years there have been several enlargements whereby the EU has expanded from **the Six** members that signed the 1957 Treaties of Rome to the 25 member states that concluded the 2004 **Constitutional Treaty** negotiations (Table 4.8). There have been five enlargements:

* 1973: Denmark, Ireland and the UK
* 1981: Greece
* 1986: Portugal and Spain
* 1995: Austria, Finland and Sweden
* 2004: Cyprus, the Czech Republic, Estonia, Hungary, Latvia, Lithuania, Malta, Poland, Slovakia and Slovenia

Prior to 1990, enlargement primarily focused on the applicant states from the southern periphery of the Community or northern **European Free Trade Association** (EFTA) countries. Recent enlargement of the EU is a response to the end of the **Cold War** as signalled by the dramatic events of 1989–91 that witnessed the collapse of the Soviet Union and brought an end to the bipolar division of Europe. The process of enlargement has increased the weight that the EU plays in the global economy to the extent that the EU is the largest **single market** in the world. Enlargement has also helped to ensure that more countries are

Table 4.8 History of EU enlargement

The Six	The Nine	The Ten	The Twelve	The Fifteen	The Twenty-Five	Applicant countries
1957	1973	1981	1986	1995	2004	
Belgium	UK	Greece	Portugal	Austria	Cyprus	Bulgaria
France	Denmark		Spain	Finland	Czech	Croatia
Germany	Ireland			Sweden	Republic	Romania
Italy					Estonia	Turkey
Luxembourg					Hungary	
Netherlands					Latvia	
					Lithuania	
					Malta	
					Poland	
					Slovakia	
					Slovenia	

bound into structures which promote peace, democracy, stability and prosperity. In addition, the enlargement of the EU has helped to improve environmental standards in a number of countries and as a result reduce trans-border crime. Today, there are only three significant states in western Europe that are not members of the EU: Norway (which rejected membership by **referendums** in 1972 and 1992), Switzerland and Iceland (which considered Community membership in 1972 but rejected the concept on the grounds of 'political' difficulties).

EU cooperation is based on treaties that stress that any European country may apply for membership. However, admission is also based on the fulfilment of certain criteria. During an EU summit in Copenhagen in 1993, the member states agreed on a set of requirements that should apply to all prospective EU states (the '**Copenhagen Criteria**'):

- They must have stable institutions that can guarantee democracy, the rule of law, human rights and protection of minorities (political criterion).
- They must be functioning market economies with the capacity to cope with competitive pressure and market forces within the EU (economic criterion).
- They must be equipped to take on the obligations of membership and to adhere to the aims of political union and **Economic and Monetary Union** (EMU) (criterion regarding the adopting of the EU *acquis communitaire*).

The third criterion means, in practice, that a **candidate country** must accept the EU's common regulatory framework, be able to incorporate it into national legislation and ensure that it is observed. In turn, this means that the country in question must have an efficient public administration and a well developed judicial system.

Considerable changes have had to be made by the candidate states before they meet the conditions for EU membership. During the past decade, the countries of central and eastern Europe have carried out comprehensive reforms to introduce democratic political systems and market economies. At the same time, the EU has also had to make changes so as to enable it to function efficiently. This has included the need to adjust the weighting of votes in the **Council of Ministers** for decisions taken by **qualified majority voting** (QMV). While the process of enlargement has enhanced the EU's influence on economic and political issues, it has also resulted in an EU that is more diverse and where the process of **decision-making** is often lengthier.

Environment policy

Since the EU's environmental policy was established in 1972 there has developed a substantial body of environmental law to protect against pollution (water, air, noise) as well as to impose controls on certain industries (chemical, biotechnology and nuclear). In 1993 a **European Environmental Agency** was set up. Today the EU plays an important role in matters relating to the environment throughout Europe and indeed the world by participating in global negotiations on the environment, including the **Kyoto Protocol** on Climate Change.

Equal opportunities

The principle is a fundamental part of the EU and refers to the provision of equal pay for men and women with the intention of being applicable to all areas, but especially the economic, cultural and social field. Since 1975 **directives** have been aimed at employment, career progression, training and working conditions so as to reduce discrimination between men and women in the workplace. The principle of equal treatment was subsequently extended to social security, statutory schemes and occupational schemes.

Erasmus (European Community action scheme for the mobility of university students)

Since its establishment in 1987 this scheme has supported student and teacher exchanges throughout the EU. In 1991 the scheme was widened to include **European Free Trade Association** (EFTA) countries. Students who participate in the scheme have the period that they study abroad recognized by the students' home university through a credit transfer scheme.

Esprit

Acronym for European Strategic Programme for Research and Development in Information Technology. It was created in 1984 as a means of promoting cooperation in information technology research and development.

Estonia

Population: 1.37m (2005)
Capital: Tallinn
After centuries of Danish, Swedish, German and Russian rule, Estonia attained independence in 1918. Forcibly incorporated into the USSR in

1940, it regained its freedom in August 1991, with the collapse of the Soviet Union. Since the last Russian troops left in 1994, Estonia has been free to promote economic and political ties with western Europe. It joined both the **North Atlantic Treaty Organisation** (NATO) and the EU in the spring of 2004.

Ethnic cleansing

Refers to a practice whereby the members of any ethnic group are forcibly removed from an area controlled by another group. This was a practice that took place during the war in Bosnia in the early 1990s when Croats and Muslims were removed (often killed) from their territories by Serbs who claimed the areas inhabited by Croats and Muslims to be part of 'greater Serbia'. Throughout this period the EU was ineffective in providing a cohesive and robust response to halt some of the worst atrocities that had taken place since the Second World War.

Euratom see *European Atomic Energy Community*

Eureka

Acronym for the European Research Coordination Agency which was established in 1985 in Brussels. It was created under the initiative of former French president **François Mitterrand** as a means of coordinating research and development in new technology.

Euro

The official name for the **single currency** that entered circulation on 1 January 2002, represented by the € symbol, and which replaced national currencies in the member states participating in the single currency on 28 February 2002. There are seven bank notes in denominations of 5, 10, 20, 50, 100, 200 and 500 euro and eight coins in denominations of 1, 2, 5, 10, 20 and 50 cents, 1 and 2 euro.

Euro-Mediterranean Partnership

Mediterranean countries are the EU's third-largest trading partner, after the **European Free Trade Association** (EFTA) and the United States. Their importance has been illustrated by the replacement of individual bilateral agreements with an overall 'new Mediterranean policy', which covers a region with over 200 million people from Algeria, Egypt, Israel, Jordan, Lebanon, Morocco, the Palestinian authority, Syria, Tunisia and Turkey (Libya has had observer status since 1999). A desire to export stability to Mediterranean countries – many of which had a history of ties with EU countries such as France, Spain, Italy and the UK – resulted in the Euro-Mediterranean Partnership which emerged out of the **Barcelona Declaration** of 12 November 1995. In seeking to guarantee security in the Mediterranean region, the Euro-Mediterranean Partnership had two key aims: first, to strengthen cohesion and develop economic ties between the EU and the Mediterranean countries; second, to promote cooperation between these countries and their regional integration. In addition, the **European Commission** proposed the creation of a Euro-Mediterranean free trade area by the year 2010, covering between 30 and 40 countries with a population of between 600 and 800 million, with the possible subsequent development of a Euro-Mediterranean Economic Area. The three primary elements of the EU's policy with these countries are:

1 the promotion of trade to ensure free access for manufactured goods from these countries to the European market and the liberalization of agricultural imports;
2 increased cooperation in such sectors as agriculture, industry, research, the environment, fisheries, energy, and support for democracy and human rights;
3 financial support in the form of grants from the **European Investment Bank** (EIB).

In assessing the significance of the Euro-Mediterranean Partnership, it is evident that it represented an attempt by the EU to promote stability in the region through trade and investment which would in turn assist with fostering economic growth, democracy, an improvement in human rights and at the same time a reduction in conflict and terrorism. The reality is, however, that not all of the objectives have been met and it is unlikely that the objective of a Euro-Mediterranean free trade area will be attained by the year 2010. Moreover, the changed geopolitical climate that has been evident since the terrorism attacks of September 2001 in the US has meant that the EU's attention has often been directed towards issues relating to political stability rather than human rights, with EU financial aid (20,000m in grants and loans by 2005) not always being conditional on reform.

Eurobarometer

This refers to the public opinion surveys conducted in EU member states twice a year on behalf of the **European Commission**.

Eurocorps

Established in May 1992 at the fifty-ninth Franco-German summit in La Rochelle, and originating from a joint Franco-German brigade that was created in 1991. The 60,000 strong corps was subsequently joined by Belgium and Spain in 1993 and Luxembourg in 1996. Based in Strasbourg, it has been operational since November 1995 and is relevant to the concept of a European security and defence identity. Its remit provides for it to operate within the limits of Article V of the **Western European Union** (WEU) and Article 5 of the **North Atlantic Treaty Organisation** (NATO). It is under the political control of the WEU, while it is also committed to NATO. The corps can be activated for missions involving humanitarian relief, the evacuation of member state nationals and peace-keeping and peace-making operations. The last two fall under the United Nations or the **Organization for Security and Cooperation in Europe** (OSCE). The first operation mission of the corps took place on 23 June 1998 when 150 troops flew to Sarajevo from their Strasbourg base. Since June 2001 the Eurocorps has become part of the **European Rapid Reaction Force**.

Eurocrat

A term denoting an official that works in one of the bodies or institutions of the EU.

Eurogroup

Refers to the informal meetings of the **euro** area ministers of finance which deal with issues relating to the **single currency**. The meetings, which are also open to attendance by representatives of the **European Commission** and the **European Central Bank**, tend to take place prior to meetings of the **Economic and Financial Council of Ministers** (Ecofin).

Eurofighter

A joint project conceived in the late 1970s by Germany, Italy, Spain and the UK to develop and construct a European fighter aircraft. The project encountered problems in the early 1990s when the German government announced its withdrawal from it in June 1992, citing cost and lesser security needs in the post-**Cold War** environment. However, an agreement in December 1992 by the defence ministers of Germany, Italy, Spain and the UK resulted in emphasis being placed on a less costly aircraft, with overall project costs being reduced by 30 per cent. Agreement on the production phase was reached in December 1992 when the defence ministers of the four countries signed a deal for the £42,000m project.

Europe à la carte see À la carte Europe

Europe agreements

This refers to the agreements between the EU and **central and eastern European states**, whereby the EU sought to provide specific economic and political assistance to prepare the countries for EU membership (Table 4.9).

Table 4.9 Europe agreements

Country	Europe agreement signed	Europe agreement came into force	Application for EU membership	Joined the EU
Czech Republic	October 1993	February 1995	January 1996	May 2004
Estonia	June 1995	February 1998	November 1995	May 2004
Hungary	December 1991	February 1994	March 1994	May 2004
Latvia	June 1995	February 1998	October 1995	May 2004
Lithuania	June 1995	February 1998	December 1995	May 2004
Poland	December 1991	February 1994	April 1994	May 2004
Slovakia	October 1993	February 1995	June 1995	May 2004
Slovenia	June 1996	February 1999	June 1996	May 2004

Europe Day

On 9 May 1950 **Robert Schuman** proposed **Jean Monnet**'s idea for the creation of the organization that became the **European Coal and Steel Community** (ECSC). This has been symbolized as the birth of what has become the European Union. As a result, 9 May is recognized as Europe Day.

Europe of the Regions

This phrase came to prominence in the 1980s and referred to the involvement of local and regional authorities in matters relating to European integration. The Maastricht **Treaty on European Union** specifically recognized these bodies through the creation of a **Committee of the Regions.**

European Agency for the Evaluation of Medicinal Products (EMEA)

Established in 1995 and based in London, the Agency has three main aims: first, to harmonize the work of national drug regulatory bodies: second, to reduce the costs incurred by drug companies having to obtain individual approvals from each member state: third, to eliminate the protectionist tendencies of member states that are unwilling to provide approval to new drugs that could possibly challenge those already being produced by domestic drug companies.

European Agricultural Guidance and Guarantee Fund (EAGGF)

Established in 1962, the EAGGF has been the largest single item in the Community **budget**. Its resources are jointly provided by member states. It comprises two parts, of which the Guarantee Section finances Community expenditure under the policy on prices and markets, including the **Common Agricultural Policy** (CAP), compensatory payments and the accompanying measures. By far the greater part of EAGGF expenditure goes on the Guarantee Section, of which half is spent on direct payments to farmers. By contrast, the far smaller Guidance Section contains the Community resources allocated to the structural funds, including aids for the modernization of holdings, the installation of young farmers, aids for processing and marketing and diversification. This component also finances rural development actions along with the **European Regional Development Fund** and **European Social Fund**. Such measures are planned and executed in a decentralized manner in cooperation with individual member states or regions, while the principle of co-financing is applicable. In addition to national financial contributions to the Community budget and revenues from customs duties, the CAP plays a major role in the provisions of revenues through duties on farm trade and sugar levies. The total expenditure on agriculture is decided by the **Council of Ministers** and the **European Parliament** under the general budgetary procedure. The overall proportion of the EU budget devoted to agriculture has been on a downward trend with it representing less than 50 per cent of total spending.

European anthem

The EU adopted from the **Council of Europe** the anthem 'Ode to Joy' from Beethoven's Ninth Symphony, thereby constituting one of the **European symbols**.

European arrest warrant

This is based on a June 2002 Council decision that has been aimed at bolstering cooperation between the judicial authorities of EU member states. This is with a view to doing away with the need to use extradition procedures among member states because of an acceptance of mutual recognition of decisions on criminal matters.

European Atomic Energy Community (Euratom)

Established as a result of a treaty signed in Rome on 25 March 1957 by **the Six**, Euratom commenced operating on 1 January 1958 with the aim of conducting research and developing nuclear energy, creating a **common market** for nuclear fuels and supervising the nuclear industry. The creation of Euratom had been influenced by an appreciation of the significance of atomic energy as the basis of conflict (in a similar manner to coal and steel) and also as a potential method of energy supply. A common community for atomic energy would therefore limit the potential for it to be the root of war (France was anxious about the possibility of Germany possessing nuclear weapons) and also act as a means of reducing the dependence of western Europe's energy requirements on the Middle East. As a result, it was agreed at the 1955 Messina conference to examine the possibility of creating a **customs union** and an atomic energy community. These proposals were investigated by the Spaak Committee and resulted in the **Treaties of Rome**.

Euratom was based on the same institutional structure as the **European Coal and Steel Community** (ECSC), with there being a Commission, a Council of Ministers, a Court of Justice and an Assembly. On 1 July 1967 the institutions of Euratom, ECSC and the EEC were merged. During its time of existence the Euratom Commission had three Presidents: Louis Armand (1958–59), Etienne Hirsch (1959–62) and Pierre Chatenet (1962–67) (Table 4.10). The Euratom Commission consisted of five representatives, with one each from Belgium, France, Germany, Italy and the Netherlands. Because Luxembourg did not have a nuclear power programme it did not have a member of the Commission.

Table 4.10 Presidents of the Commission of the European Atomic Energy Community (Euratom)

Period in office	President	Nationality
1958–59	Louis Armand	France
1959–62	Etienne Hirsch	France
1962–67	Pierre Chatenet	France

European Bank for Reconstruction and Development (EBRD)

Established in April 1991 (at the initiative of the former French president, **François Mitterrand**), the London based EBRD was created in response to the collapse of communism in central and eastern Europe. As a result, the EBRD grants loans for private and commercial risks and infrastructure projects that aid the transition to a free market economy in **central and eastern European states**. The EBRD was troubled by controversy in 1993 when it materialized that it had spent more on furnishing its headquarters in London and on expense accounts than it had provided in loans.

European Capital of Culture

From 1985 until 1999 this programme was known as the European City of Culture. It is one of the best-known examples of the EU **cultural policy**. Traditionally there has been a strong contest among cities for the award of this title, which was based on the decisions of member states and for which the chosen cities receive a subsidy from the **European Commission**. In recent years the capitals of culture have included: Weimar (1999); Avignon, Bergen, Bologna, Brussels, Krakow, Helsinki, Prague, Reykjavík, and Santiago de Compostela (2000); Porto and Rotterdam (2001); Bruges and Salamanque (2002); Graz (2003); Genoa and Lille (2004). So as to allow a more equal distribution of capitals of culture among member states, in 1999 a decision was taken to introduce a rotation system to ensure that each member state would host the event, with member states being invited to submit their application for one (or more) cities at least four years in advance. The scheduled rotation is Ireland (2005), Greece (2006), Luxembourg (2007), the United Kingdom (2008), Austria and Lithuania (2009), Germany and Hungary (2010), Finland and Estonia (2011), Portugal and Slovenia (2012), France and Slovakia (2013), Sweden and Latvia (2014), Belgium and the Czech Republic (2015), Spain and Poland (2016), Denmark and Cyprus (2017), the Netherlands and Malta (2018), Italy (2019).

European Central Bank (ECB)

Based in Frankfurt, the ECB took over the responsibility for carrying out the monetary policy of the Community on 1 January 1999, with instructions coming from the decision-making bodies of the Executive Board and Governing Council and the Executive Board. It supervises the **European System of Central Banks** (ESCB), which conducts foreign exchange operations, administers money in circulation, ensures the smooth operation of the payment systems and manages the official reserves of member states. The precursor to the ECB was the **European Monetary Institute**, founded in 1994.

European Coal and Steel Community (ECSC)

The creation of the ECSC in 1952 had been influenced by the efforts of **Jean Monnet** and **Robert Schuman**. On 9 May 1950 the **Schuman Plan** had argued the need for Franco-German coal and steel production to be placed under one common authority. This **functionalist** approach to European integration was based on the gradual transfer of **sovereignty** from nation states. Apart from France and Germany, there was support for the Schuman Plan in Belgium, Italy, Luxembourg and the Netherlands. By contrast, Britain did not wish to participate in a process that involved decisions being imposed on the participating member states. This fear of the erosion of sovereignty proved to be a recurring theme in UK policy towards European integration. As a result, the UK did not participate in the negotiations which commenced in June 1950 to discuss the implications of the Schuman Plan and which resulted in the founding treaty of the ECSC being signed in Paris on 18 April 1951. The **Treaty of Paris** was signed by Belgium, France, Germany, Italy, Luxembourg and the Netherlands, who in turn would become referred to as '**the Six**'.

The Treaty sought to promote 'economic expansion, growth of employment and a rising standard of living' within the member states through the creation of a **common market** for coal and steel. The **supranational** design of the ECSC meant that it was distinct from previous initiatives to foster European integration such as the **Council of Europe**. The four institutions that governed the ECSC were a High Authority (subsequently the **European Commission**), Council of Ministers, Court of Justice and Common Assembly. The ECSC was significant because it was the first attempt to integrate European states

Table 4.11 Presidents of the High Authority of the European Coal and Steel Community

Period in office	President	Country of origin
1952–55	Jean Monnet	France
1955–58	René Mayer	France
1958–59	Paul Finet	France
1959–63	Piero Malvestiti	Italy Resigned May 1963
1963	Albert Coppe	Belgium
1963–67	Rinaldo Del Bo	Italy Resigned March 1967
1967	Albert Coppe	Belgium

into a structure that was distinct from intergovernmental cooperation. In 1967 the institutions of the ECSC, the **European Economic Community** (EEC) and **European Atomic Energy Community** (Euratom) were amalgamated into a single institutional structure.

European Commission

While the **Council of Ministers** is the EC's **decision-making** centre, the European Commission plays an important role as the dynamic engine of the Community's legislation and action. The Council is sometimes portrayed as the blocking institution which represents national governments, while others consider that the European Commission has attempted to both centralize and take power away from the member states. The European Commission has responsibility for initiating legislation and oversees the implementation of common policies, decision being taken by a simple majority. The European Commission is also the guardian of the Treaties and the *acquis communitaire*. It provides a mediation role between member states in order to reach a compromise and acts as the diplomatic representative of the Community in third countries and in many international organizations. Each Commissioner is assisted by a **directorate general** (DG). The **European Parliament** must give its approval to the appointment of the European Commission.

European Commission of Human Rights

Established in 1953, this body operates under the authority of the **Council of Europe** which is based in Strasbourg. Despite the fact that the European Commission of Human Rights has no formal connection with the EU, the EU nevertheless recognizes the role that the former plays in the area of human rights.

European Commissioner

An individual responsible for one or more policy areas within the **European Commission**.

European Communities (EC)

Collective term for the **European Coal and Steel Community** (ECSC), **European Economic Community** (EEC) and **European Atomic Energy Community** (Euratom)

European Community Humanitarian Office (ECHO)

The European Community Humanitarian Office was established in 1992 to provide emergency humanitarian aid such as food and medicine to victims of disasters or wars. It supplies free assistance to all countries outside the EU suffering from conflicts or disasters, with aid being directly targeted at people in distress. In this context over 80 per cent of the humanitarian projects are carried out in partnership with specialized organizations like the United Nations, thereby assisting such countries as Afghanistan, Angola, Armenia, Azerbaijan, Burundi, Cuba, Haiti, Rwanda, Sudan, Tajikistan and the former Yugoslavia.

European Community Investment Partners (ECIP)

A programme which supports European investment and exports to Asia, Latin America and the Mediterranean, of which 300 million **ECU** was devoted to this task from 1992–97. Aid is granted to four complementary areas: the identification of projects and partners, operations prior to the formation of a joint venture, the financing of capital needs and the provision of management training or assistance for joint ventures.

European Convention see *Convention on the Future of Europe*

European Convention on Human Rights

Signed on 4 November 1950 by members of the **Council of Europe**, it established a **European Commission of Human Rights** and a **European Court of Human Rights** in Strasbourg to ensure the observation of human rights. The rights which they undertook to protect included life, liberty and security of the person, the right to respect for private and family life, the right to a fair trial, the right to freedom of accession and assembly, the right to freedom of thought, conscience and religion, and the banning of torture, slavery and forced labour.

European Correspondent

The junior Foreign Office official appointed by each member state who supervises and directs the communication of faxes and telegrams associated with **European Political Cooperation** (EPC) and is the main assistant to the Political Director.

European Council

Composed of Heads of State or Government of the member states and the President of the **European Commission**. Meets two or three time a year. Such meetings have taken place since 1974, although the European Council's existence was only legally noted in the **Single European Act** (SEA). By this time, it had established itself as an important negotiating body by providing political direction to the EU.

European Court of Human Rights

Not to be confused with the **Court of Justice**, it is a body based in Strasbourg within the **Council of Europe** and hears cases relating to states that have ratified the **European Convention on Human Rights**.

European Currency Unit see *ECU*

European Defence Community (EDC)

In October 1950 the premier of France, René Pléven, put forward a plan (which had been devised by Jean Monnet) that suggested that France, Germany and any other countries should establish a supranational European Army of 100,000 soldiers. Thus, just as the **Schuman Plan** sought to control German industry via the **European Coal and Steel Community** (ECSC), the **Pléven Plan** attempted to tackle the question of German rearmament via the EDC. The Pléven Plan, which built on the 1947 **Dunkirk Treaty** and 1948 **Brussels Treaty**, centred on the belief that Germany's capacity for independent action would be limited because of the constraints of a European defence system. Belgium, France, Germany, Italy, Luxembourg and the Netherlands signed the EDC Treaty on 27 May 1952. The Treaty advocated the creation of a European army that would consist of 14 French divisions, 12 German divisions, 11 Italian divisions and three divisions from the Benelux states. The Treaty also proposed an institutional structure that was similar to the design of the European Coal and Steel Community (ECSC):

- a Commission;
- an Assembly;
- a Council to represent the interests of the member states where the voting power of each state would be in accordance with the level of its contribution to the European army.

As with the ECSC negotiations, the UK government chose not to participate because of the supranational design of the Treaty. Article 1 stressed that 'The High Contracting Parties, by the Present Treaty, set up among themselves a European Defence Community, supranational in character, comprising common institutions, common Armed Forces, and a common budget'. Article 3 emphasized the common defence element of the Treaty: 'Any armed attack against any of the member states in Europe or against the European Defence Forces shall be considered an armed attack on all member states'.

A concern over supranationalism proved to be an influential factor in the 1951 French elections which subsequently resulted in France adopting a more nationalist foreign policy that called for a diluting of the supranational element of the EDC. The leaders of the other member states were, however, unwilling to accept these demands and thus on 30 August 1954 the French National Assembly refused to ratify the EDC Treaty. This signalled the end of the attempt to create a defence community. As a result of the failure of the EDC, plans for the creation of a European Political Union also came to an end, which in turn appeared to signify the end of the process of European integration. In an effort to move beyond the EDC and create a body capable of coordinating European defence policy, the British foreign secretary, **Anthony Eden**, suggested that the 1948 Brussels Treaty should be expanded to include Germany and Italy to create a new defence organization that would be known as the **Western European Union** (WEU). A key advantage of this proposal for Britain was that the WEU was based on **intergovernmental** methods of cooperation and therefore did not include the supranational aspects of the EDC.

European Development Fund

Established in 1957, it promotes economic and social development in the **African, Caribbean and Pacific** (ACP) states and funds schemes to promote export marketing and sales, technical cooperation projects and in special cases emergency aid.

European Documentation Centres

This refers to information centres containing EU documents which are normally based in university libraries.

European Economic Area (EEA)

Comprises the territory of **European Free Trade Association** (EFTA) and the EU after an agreement signed in 1992 and provides for free movement of capital, goods, services and workers. To ensure compliance of rules and regulations, EFTA countries agreed to accept over 80 per cent of the Community's rules pertaining to the **single market**. Nevertheless, the agreement does not include Switzerland, a decision caused by a no vote in a referendum. This delayed the ratification process and therefore meant that the EEA Treaty did not come into being until 1 January 1994. But its significance was soon diminished by the entry into the EU of three EFTA countries on 1 January 1995 (Austria, Finland and Sweden).

European Economic Community (EEC)

One of the founding treaties of the European Community. Established by the 1957 **Treaties of Rome**, providing common trade, agriculture, transport and competition policies, in addition to cooperation in economic and monetary affairs and closer political union. The Maastricht **Treaty on European Union** stressed that the EEC would in future be known as the European Community.

European elections

Refers to the direct elections to the **European Parliament** as provided for in the **Treaties of Rome**, and agreed to by Heads of State and Government at the Paris **European Council** meeting of 9–10 December 1974. Taking place every five years, the first elections were held in June 1979. Prior to the first direct elections that took place in 1979, the European Parliament comprised **Members of the European Parliament** (MEPs) appointed by **national parliaments**. Despite a desire to have a uniform day upon which the **European elections** take place, it has proved impossible to reach agreement among the member states and so the elections take place over several days and votes do not start to be counted until the polls have closed in all the member states. There is in addition a lack of uniformity with regard to the method of electoral system used, with each member state using for the most part the same system as used in national elections. Within the UK a method of proportional representation was introduced in the June 1999 elections that differed from the first-past-the-post system that continues to be used in national elections within the UK.

   The number of MEPs within each member state broadly reflects the differing population levels within the EU. Germany has the largest number of MEPs (99) and this is in accordance with it having the greatest population. By contrast, Malta, with a population of fewer than half a million, has the smallest number of MEPs (5), although in real terms it has more MEPs per head of population than Germany. Once elected, MEPs join alliances with other MEPs who share similar political views. In the case of the UK, MEPs who are elected under the banner of the Labour Party form part of the Party of European Socialists within the European Parliament. This is significant because it highlights the transnational nature of the political groupings within the European Parliament, whereby MEPs are supposed to reflect political and not national priorities.

   It is evident from Table 4.12 that there exists a wide divergence of voting patterns within EU member states. The UK has traditionally had

Table 4.12 Voter turnout in European Parliament elections, 1979–2004

State	1979	1981	1984	1987	1989	1994	1995	1996	1999	2004
Belgium	91.4		92.2		90.7	90.7			91	90.81
France	60.7		56.7		48.7	52.7			46.8	42.76
Germany	65.7		56.8		62.3	60.0			45.2	43
Italy	84.9		83.4		81.5	74.8			70.8	73.1
Luxembourg	88.9		88.8		87.4	88.5			87.3	89
Netherlands	57.8		50.6		47.2	35.6			30	39.3
Denmark	47.8		52.4		46.2	52.9			50.5	47.9
Ireland	63.6		47.6		68.3	44.0			50.2	58.8
UK	32.2		32.6		36.2	36.4			24.0	38.83
Greece		78.6	77.2		79.9	71.2			75.3	63.22
Portugal				72.4	51.2	35.5			40	38.6
Spain				68.9	54.6	59.1			63	45.1
Austria								67.7	49.9	42.43
Finland								60.3	31.4	39.4
Sweden							41.6		38.8	37.8
Cyprus										71.19
Czech Republic										28.32
Estonia										26.38
Hungary										38.5
Latvia										41.34
Lithuania										48.38
Malta										82.37
Poland										20.87
Slovakia										16.96
Slovenia										28.3
EU	63		61		58.5	56.8			49.8	45.7

Extracted from website: http://www.elections2004.eu.int

the lowest turnout. By contrast, other member states have experienced a higher voter turnout, particularly Belgium, Italy and Luxembourg. There are some clear reasons for these differences. Nations such as Belgium and Luxembourg generally have a high degree of support for the EU. This is not surprising as both countries receive large financial injections from having EU institutions based there and accordingly public apathy and discontent are less relevant. By contrast, the high turnout in Italian elections can be explained from a public desire to support a democratic European Parliament in the face of domestic corruption. However, it is very important to note that voting is compulsory in Belgium, Greece and Luxembourg and, while not so in Italy, it is still regarded to be a public duty. Where turnout is declining, it is worth considering that voting apathy is influenced by the perceived need to participate in other, domestic, elections, such as local and regional, which are often held at the same time as European elections. But, irrespective of the turnout within each member state, European elections face the additional problem of being used as a sounding board for national policies, especially when the European election falls within a government's term of office.

European Energy Charter

This document, which was signed at The Hague in 1991, provides a set of principles and objectives for the achievement of pan-European cooperation in the field of energy with a view to achieving greater security in European energy supplies by creating a grid of supply lines that would link the resources available in eastern Europe to western Europe. Eastern European countries would in return receive investment from western Europe.

European Environmental Agency

Its establishment in 1993 mirrored the increasing importance attached to the protection of the environment within the EU. Based in Copenhagen, its primary task is the composition of environmental data that is central to the creation of a EU **environmental policy**. The agency currently comprises 31 member countries and was the first EU body to welcome the applicant nations from central and eastern Europe. The 31 countries of the agency are:

- the 25 member states of the EU;
- the three EU candidate countries of Bulgaria, Romania and Turkey;
- Iceland, Liechtenstein and Norway (all members of the **European Economic Area**).

European flag

In 1986 the EC adopted the design of 12 five-pointed stars set against an azure background as the European flag. The same flag has been used by the **Council of Europe** since 1955.

European Free Trade Association (EFTA)

An organization that was established in 1960 as a means of offering an alternative to the **European Economic Community** (EEC) for Austria, Denmark, Norway, Portugal, Sweden, Switzerland and the UK. All seven countries signed the Treaty of Stockholm in 1960, and Finland and Iceland joined at a later date. The primary aim of EFTA was to promote free trade among its members without the loss of sovereignty that the EEC involved or the erection of a **common external tariff** (which had implications for countries such as the UK who had extensive trading links outside western Europe). EFTA was, however, unable to offer a rival to the more integrated economies of the EEC, who throughout the 1960s experienced faster rates of economic growth. This was influential behind the decision of the British government of **Harold Macmillan** to seek entry to the EEC, which in turn influenced Denmark's decision also to join. As Britain and Denmark were among the most important EFTA countries, their joining of the EEC in 1973 severely weakened EFTA. Although a policy of closer cooperation between EFTA and the Community has been of importance, with the creation of a **European Economic Area** (EEA), the EU has nevertheless proved to be a significant draw for EFTA members: Portugal joined in 1986, and Austria, Finland and Sweden joined in 1995. As a result, the membership of EFTA has been reduced to Iceland, Liechtenstein, Norway and Switzerland.

European Fund

The **European Monetary Agreement** (EMA) provided for a European Fund to help finance temporary deficits in the balance of payments of a country emanating from a decision to make their currencies convertible into dollars.

European Health Insurance Card (EHIC)

From 1 January 2006 the EHIC has entitled European citizens to free medical treatment (or at a reduced cost) when travelling within the **European Economic Area** and **Switzerland**. The EHIC replaced the E111 form which ceased to be valid on 31 December 2005.

European Investment Bank (EIB)

Established by the **Treaties of Rome** as a non-profit development bank with the primary aim of promoting long-term loans and guarantees for investment in industry and infrastructure projects in priority areas. These include less developed regions, industrial modernization and joint industrial projects. The activities of the EIB have expanded beyond the EU and now embrace **African, Caribbean and Pacific** (ACP) nations and other countries which have association agreements with the EU. The Bank's operations are financed by borrowing on both the international and EU capital markets.

European Investment Fund

Established in June 1994 by the **European Investment Bank** (EIB), the EU and a group of 76 banks and financial institutions from EU member states as a means of tackling economic problems, including unemployment. It helps finance trans-European infrastructure projects and supports small and medium-sized businesses by guaranteeing loans.

European Monetary Agreement

Approved by the Council of the **Organisation for European Economic Co-operation** (OEEC) in August 1955, the agreement demonstrated a willingness of European nations to gradually make their currencies convertible into dollars. This replaced the **European Payments Union** when the agreement was implemented in December 1958. The **Bank for International Settlements** became the agent for financing operations.

European Monetary Cooperation Fund (EMCF)

Although the EMCF was established in 1973 as part of the Community's early drive towards **monetary union**, the lack of progress in this area meant that the EMCF suffered from a lack of use until its 1979 revival when the **ECU** became part of the **European Monetary System** (EMS). To this end, member states who participated in the EMS reached agreement that they would deposit 20 per cent of their gold and dollar reserves with the EMCF, which in exchange issued ECUs. The EMCF also regulated central bank interventions on the exchange markets of the **Exchange Rate Mechanism** (ERM), while the EMCF could additionally provide short-term financial credits to assist with member states' balance of payments difficulties. With the firm commitment to monetary union that was established by the Maastricht **Treaty on European Union**, the EMCF's operations finished on 1 January 1994 when its tasks were taken over by the **European Monetary In-**

stitute (EMI) as part of the second stage of **Economic and**
Union (EMU).

European Monetary Institute (EMI)

Based in Frankfurt, it was established under the terms of the **Trea**
on European Union to coordinate the monetary policy of the **centra**
banks of member states within the **European System of Central Banks**
(ESCB). It assisted the preparation of the third stage of **Economic**
and Monetary Union (EMU), with a European **single currency** introduced in 1999, at which point the EMI was renamed the **European**
Central Bank (ECB).

European Monetary System (EMS)

Established in 1979 as a 'zone of monetary stability', whereby exchange
rates would be for all intents and purposes stable with a small degree
for adjustment. Participants in the system would coordinate exchange
rates through the **Exchange Rate Mechanism** (ERM). The technicalities of the system were that currency rates were established in relation
to the **European Currency Unit** (ECU) at meetings of finance ministers, and in the intervening period member states support the agreed
value of the currencies within the system by drawing on the resources
of the **European Monetary Cooperation Fund** (EMCF). The EMS
had three key elements:

1   Exchange Rate Mechanism (ERM). This was a parity grid whereby
    currencies were given central value in relation to the ECU. Prior
    to 1993 states were not allowed to let their currencies diverge from
    the central valuation by more than 2.25 per cent (Italy, Spain and
    the UK had 6 per cent bands). Member states had to intervene
    by means of interest rates and intervention on foreign exchange
    markets if their currency reached a level of three-quarters of the
    fluctuation margin.
2   European Currency Unit (ECU). A basket currency of weighted
    amounts of each member currency that acted as the denominator
    of the ERM.
3   European Monetary Co-operation Fund (EMCF). A pool of 20
    per cent of each members' gold and dollar reserves that acted as a
    credit facility.

European Movement

A pro-European integration political lobby that was formed in October 1948, having received impetus from the May 1948 meeting of the

...gress of Europe (**Hague Congress**). The Movement drew up the ...rst draft of what became the **Council of Europe**.

European Ombudsman

Investigates complaints about maladministration by institutions and bodies of the EU and is not able to deal with complaints regarding national, regional or local administrations of the member states.

European Parliament

There are 732 **Members of the European Parliament** (MEPs) who are directly elected for a five-year term of office from each member state, with the number of national MEPs being in proportion to population. The most important area of the European Parliament's influence is its power to amend and adopt legislation through the **co-decision procedure** which ensures that it is a co-legislator with the **Council of Ministers** on the vast majority of European legislation. The European Parliament also plays a significant role in the monitoring and setting of EU spending. The importance of the European Parliament is also influenced by the fact that its approval is necessary for appointments to the **European Commission**.

European passport

Member states (Denmark, Ireland and Luxembourg) started to introduce European passports on 1 January 1985 after agreement had been reached in 1981 on the size and shape of a burgundy coloured passport which would have 'European Community' on the cover. In the course of 1985 most of the rest of the then 10-member Community introduced this style of passport, although both Germany and the UK did not do so until 1987.

European Payments Union

Established in 1950 by the **Organisation for European Economic Co-operation** (OEEC), it replaced the intra-European payments agreements of 1948 and 1949. The EPU allowed the multilateral settlement of deficits or surpluses between European states and facilitated policies of trade liberalization by offering automatic credit facilities to participants which encountered deficits in their balance of payments.

European Police Office (Europol)

Based in The Hague, the European Police Office is a liaison organization whose task is to assist the police forces of member states in the exchange and analysis of information. In this way, Europol serves as a tool for member states to enable them to prevent and combat cross-border crime more effectively. The convention establishing Europol was eventually signed in July 1995 and became fully operational on 1 July 1999. Europol took over the work of the European Drugs Unit that had been created in January 1994 as a means of providing a practical angle to police cooperation. Although the Unit initially focused upon drug trafficking and money laundering, its remit was widened to embrace immigration networks, money laundering and trafficking in radioactive and nuclear substances; trade in human beings was added at a later date. The **Treaty of Amsterdam** gave additional tasks to Europol, including the ability to coordinate and implement investigations conducted by the authorities of member states. Europol's remit was further widened in December 2001 to embrace all types of international crime as set out in the annex to the Europol Convention.

European Political Community

This refers to the provision in the **European Defence Community** (EDC) Treaty for the **European Coal and Steel Community** (ECSC) Parliamentary Assembly to prepare plans for the development of a common external policy for the then six participating member states. The ECSC set up an ad hoc assembly in September 1952 with the task of drawing up a draft Treaty establishing a European Political Community. The Treaty, which was adopted by the ECSC Assembly on 10 March 1953, provided for the establishment of a federal community that would control the proposed European army. This would include the creation of a European Executive Council, a two-chamber Parliament and a Council of Ministers that would assist with the coordination of the financial, foreign and monetary policies of the member states. However, the failure of the French National Assembly to ratify the EDC in August 1954 meant that the proposals for the European Political Community also collapsed.

European Political Cooperation (EPC)

Refers to cooperation by EC foreign ministers whose origins lay in 1970 **Davignon Report** which recommended that an intergovernmental system of EPC be established to facilitate foreign policy harmonization and coordination among member states. EPC aimed to promote greater understanding of international issues among the member states through the exchange of information and the holding of regular meetings. It was hoped that this process would result in the coordination of foreign policy objectives and in certain instances lead to the establishment of a common EC position. In May 1971 the first joint ministerial statement was issued, which in that instance applied to the Middle East.

Although the EPC played an important role in promoting cooperation among the member states, it was nevertheless not based on the founding treaties and as such it developed outside the EC institutional framework. As such, EPC developed on an intergovernmental basis and was therefore devoid of any supranational input (the **Davignon Report** deliberately avoided the establishment of a Secretariat that would manage foreign policy coordination). Coordination was principally through six-monthly meetings of foreign ministers (to be chaired by the **Council Presidency**), the establishment of a Political Committee (comprising the political directors of the national foreign ministries), and the linking of foreign ministries through a direct telex network. The **Single European Act** (SEA) recognized the position of EPC, provided it with a small secretariat in Brussels and committed the member states to 'endeavour jointly to formulate and implement a European foreign policy'. The Maastricht **Treaty on European Union** changed the position of EPC, replacing it with the **common foreign and security policy** (CFSP).

European Regional Development Fund (ERDF)

The largest of the EU's **structural funds**, it was established in 1975 to provide financial assistance to development projects in poor regions so as to reduce imbalances between regions of the Community. The majority of ERDF expenditure is attached to infrastructure development projects that are advanced by the member states. Although bids for ERDF support can only be made by member state governments, it often the case that the genesis of these requests lies in regional and local initiatives or other public and private bodies. Funding that is provided by the ERDF operates on the basis of **additionality**, which means that the maximum that can be provided by the ERDF is 50 per cent of the project costs and therefore the member states need to finance the outstanding amount.

European security and defence identity (ESDI)

Refers to the concept of a European defence identity in relation to the challenges which the EU has faced and faces from neighbouring conflicts such as Bosnia–Herzegovina and Chechnya at a time when there has been a decline in the number of United States troops based in Europe. This has prompted suggestions by states such as Belgium and France that the EU should fill this gap. The January 1994 Brussels **North Atlantic Treaty Organisation** (NATO) Council stressed the need to define a ESDI. The consequence of this was the establishment of a Combined Joint Task Force (CJTF) at the June 1996 Berlin NATO Council. In the wake of the **Treaty of Amsterdam**, the EU has established military and political structures to assist with the management of crises. Thereafter, in December 2002 the EU and NATO signed a crisis management strategic partnership agreement whereby the EU had access to the logistical and planning resources of NATO to assist the creation by 2003 of a 60,000 strong EU rapid reaction force as set out in the December 1999 Helsinki **European Council**.

European Security and Defence Policy (ESDP)

Since the late 1990s the EU has sought to play a greater role in defence and military matters, having been influenced by the failure of the EU to take a significant part in the Kosovo conflict (in that campaign, a third of all aircraft sorties and 20 per cent of all strike sorties were flown by European nations). The concept of an ESDP was discussed at the first meeting of EU defence ministers which took place in Vienna on 4 November 1998. In December 1998 the UK and France reached agreement on the need for this policy at a meeting in St Malo. Thereafter, at the Cologne **European Council** of 3–4 June 1999, EU member states agreed to provide the EU with a defence capacity by means of transferring the majority of the **Western European Union**'s (WEU) functions to it. The Cologne meeting committed member states to a common policy on security and defence to provide the EU with 'the capacity for autonomous action backed up by credible military forces, the means to decide to use them, and a readiness to do so, in order to respond to international crises without prejudice to NATO'. At the same time, member states also agreed to appoint **Javier Solana**, the former NATO Secretary General, as the first EU **High Representative for CFSP** for a term of five years from 18 October 1999.

The need to establish the military assets that an EU defence force would require was discussed at the Helsinki European Council of 10–11 December 1999, which reached agreement that the EU should establish a multinational corps of 50,000 to 60,000 forces by 2003 with the capability of mounting an autonomous European mission if NATO declined to get involved in a crisis situation. In terms of institutional dynamics, agreement was also reached at Helsinki on the establishment of three military and political bodies that would be responsible to the **Council of Ministers**:

- A standing Political and Security Committee (PSC), meeting once a week, consisting of senior national officials having responsibility for all areas of the CFSP, including ESDP. The PSC will essentially have political control of military operations in a crisis situation.
- A European Military Committee (EMC) comprising national Chiefs

of Defence to be represented by appointed military delegates, with Chiefs of Defence meetings taking place as and when required. The EMC offers military advice to the PSC, whilst also giving directions to the European Military Staff.

- A European Military Staff as part of the structures of the Council to give military support to the ESDP. The Staff has responsibility for providing situation assessments, early warning and strategic planning for the Petersberg tasks.

The Treaty of Nice, which entered into force in 2001, stressed that, while the Council would have responsibility for crisis management operations, the PSC would nonetheless take charge of these operations. In light of the fact that not all member states have the similar military capabilities (or share the same desire to develop an ESDP), the **Constitutional Treaty** stressed that military tasks could be assigned to a group of member states or that a 'permanent structured cooperation' could be established which would allow a number of member states to progress at a quicker pace to the objective of a common European defence. At the same time, in response to the changed security environment of the twenty-first century, the defence element of the ESDP was strengthened in the Constitutional Treaty through the provision for a mutual defence clause and a solidarity clause that would apply in the event of terrorist attacks or in response to disasters (whether natural or man-made).

European Social Fund (ESF)

Established in 1960, it is the main mechanism of Community **social policy** providing financial assistance for retraining, job-creation schemes and vocational training. The **Delors II budget package** significantly increased the resources available to the ESF, while the focus was directed towards the reintegration of unemployed people into working life and the improvement of the functions of the labour market. Finance provided by the ESF operates on the principle of **additionality**, whereby the ESF generally only provides 50 per cent of the expected costs of the proposed scheme, with the remainder having to be met by the member state government.

European Space Agency (ESA)

Established in 1975 as a means of coordinating the efforts of European governments in the field of space exploration and technology and the development of cooperation with NASA (USA space agency). The 14 members of the ESA are Austria, Belgium, Denmark, Finland, France, Germany, Ireland, Italy, the Netherlands, Norway, Spain, Sweden, Switzerland and the UK.

European symbols

Refers to the public identity of the Union, which since 1986 has been represented by the **European flag** of 12 gold stars on a blue background and the **European anthem** of 'Ode to Joy' from Beethoven's Ninth Symphony.

European System of Central Banks (ESCB)

It is responsible for managing **Economic and Monetary Union** (EMU). Its primary objective is maintaining price stability, while it shares the right to propose new policies with the **European Commission**. Independent of national governments and EC institutions, it consists of the **European Central Bank** (ECB) and national banks. The governing council of the ECB is composed of members of the executive board and **central bank governors** of the member states, with the executive board consisting of four members plus a president and vice-president, all of which are appointed for eight years by the **European Council**. By contrast, national central bank governors have to be appointed for a minimum of five years, with the ability to appeal to the **Court of Justice** in the event of dismissal.

European Trades Union Confederation (ETUC)

Established in 1973 and based in Brussels, it is an umbrella organization for the national trades unions of the member states. The ETUC is represented on a number of EU committees and has played an important role in promoting and defending the rights of workers, such as with regard to the **Social Charter**. The ETUC plays an important role as one of the three **social partners**, alongside the **Union of Industrial and Employers' Confederations of Europe** (UNICE) and the **European Commission**.

European Union (EU)

While the preamble of the **Treaties of Rome** called for 'an ever closer union' among the peoples of Europe, with the **Single European Act** (SEA) thereafter naming European Union as the ultimate goal of European integration, it was the **Treaty on European Union** (TEU) which established the concept. It stated that it was founded upon the European Communities and supported by **justice and home affairs** (JHA) and **common foreign and security policy** (CFSP). The objectives of the Union included strengthening the identity of **citizenship** and promoting economic and social progress.

European Unit of Account (EUA)

This was used within the Community as a book-keeping mechanism to determine the relative value of payments into and out of the accounts of the Community. It was replaced in 1981 by the **ECU**, which was in turn replaced by the **euro** in 1999.

European University Institute (EUI)

Based in Florence and established in 1975. It is a postgraduate teaching and research institute dealing with European integration and focuses upon economics, history and civilization, law and political and social sciences.

Europeanization

This is a term that is used to highlight the impact of the EU on member states as well as non-member states. This has particularly been with regard to the impact on domestic legislation, administrative structures and policy priorities.

Eurosceptic

Individuals who are opposed to European integration, often favouring economic independence rather than European integration and being against the loss of national legislative **sovereignty**. While there are many sceptical organizations in every member state, it is the UK which has often been perceived to harbour the greatest number of sceptics. This has been influenced by the attitudes of successive governments towards Europe and in recent years has been hardened by the negotiating position of **Margaret Thatcher**. Of UK Eurosceptic groups, the Conservative Party has given birth to some of the most famous, including the Bruges Group. Other organizations have included the UK Independence Party.

Eurosclerosis

This term is generally used in reference to the 1970s when there was little growth in the pace of European integration. The December 1969 Hague Summit had attempted to inject new dynamism into the Community after the **Luxembourg compromise** by resolving the question of **enlargement** and providing impetus on political and economic integration. This led to the publication of the **Davignon Report** and **Werner Report**, which respectively focused on the development of foreign policy cooperation (**European Political Cooperation**) and monetary union. However, these objectives were hampered by the unwillingness of member states to support new initiatives at a time of international economic instability caused by **oil crises**. At the same time, the supranational institutions of the Community, particularly the **European Commission**, appeared to be unable to deal with the challenges that the Community faced. Although the appointment of **Roy Jenkins** as President of the European Commission in 1977 – after **François Ortoli**'s lacklustre presidency – appeared to signal a renewed sense of purpose and dynamism in the Community's activities, for all intents and purposes the Community's fortunes had not been substantially revived by the early 1980s. Yet, despite the general malaise that dominated the decade, there were some notable developments. These included the decision of the Paris summit of 1974 to establish the **European Council** and confirm the principle of direct elections to the **European Parliament**.

Overall, the combined difficulties that the EC encountered during the 1970s have led to the decade being categorized as a 'dark age' of European integration. Just as internal factors – such as the leadership qualities of the European Commission – and external developments – such as oil crises – lay at the root of the difficulties of the 1970s, the ability of the Community to progress beyond this stagnation in European integration would be determined by internal and external circumstances. Yet, for all intents and purposes, the initial years of the 1980s did not signal a dramatic change in the Community's fortunes, thereby leading some commentators to conclude that the limit of European integration had been reached.

Eurostat

The Statistical Office of the EU based in Luxembourg, which publishes statistical analysis to assist the taking of decisions by institutions of the EU, while also providing information upon which the wider public can be informed about EU issues.

Eurozone

Member states participating in the third stage of **Economic and Monetary Union** (EMU) form a zone where the **euro** has been adopted as the **single currency**.

Excessive deficit procedure

Introduced in the **Treaty on European Union** as one of the **convergence criteria** under the provisions of **Economic and Monetary Union** (EMU). The Treaty provided for member states not to have excessive government deficits, with Article 104c and the protocol on the excessive deficit procedure stating that member states should have a budget deficit not exceeding 3 per cent of GDP and a public debt not exceeding 60 per cent of GDP. An important inclusion within the procedure was the reference to 'gross errors' in Article 104c(2), which ensured that the excessive deficit procedure should only occasionally come into being by taking account of cyclical developments. Emphasis on flexibility was further signified by Article 104c noting that allowance could be made if a country's deficit had 'declined substantially and continuously' or 'is only exceptional and temporary'. Hence, the **convergence criteria** were both tough and flexible.

Exchange Rate Mechanism (ERM)

In conjunction with the **ECU**, the ERM was a central component of the **European Monetary System** (EMS) that had been established in 1979 to provide a zone of monetary stability. Within the EMS, the ERM acted as the specific mechanism for reducing currency fluctuations among the participating member states. Each currency that participated in the ERM was given an exchange rate that was set in relation to the **ECU**. As a result it was possible to create a system of bilateral central rates that covered all of the participating currencies. This in turn provided the framework whereby the participating currencies were allowed to fluctuate around the central rates with there also being a divergence indicator inserted at the top and bottom of the margins of fluctuation so as to highlight if the permissible bands of fluctuation were likely to be breached. When these divergence indicators were triggered, intervention was required by the central banks on the exchange markets to bring the currency back within the margins of fluctuation. In most cases, the permitted range of fluctuation was set at ±2.25 per cent, although a broader band of ±6 per cent was allowable for some countries. In addition to this strategy of intervention, the value of currencies could also be realigned through a devaluation or revaluation.

When the ERM started operation in 1979 eight member states took part in the system: Belgium, Denmark, France, Germany, Ireland, Italy, Luxembourg and the Netherlands. For much of the 1980s the ERM was successful in reducing the fluctuations in the level of exchange rates and in inducing the reduction and convergence of member states' inflation rates. It therefore provided a framework within which member countries were able to pursue counter-inflationary policies at a lesser cost in terms of unemployment and lost output than would have been possible otherwise. Whereas most governments decided to participate in the ERM, successive British governments declined as they did not want to be committed to maintain the value of sterling within a fixed system. However, towards the end of the 1980s the case for British independence from the ERM became harder to defend. But, when Britain eventually joined the ERM in October 1990, it did so at a time when the pressure of movement towards **Economic and Monetary Union** (EMU) meant that the system became more rigid.

Events thereafter conspired against the success of the ERM. First, because of the costs of reunification the German government increased interest rates to control inflation. This had a knock-on effect of making it less likely for other European economies (who were not necessarily suffering from inflation) to emerge from recession, as their interest rates tended to follow Germany's, which meant that their currencies were artificially high and consequently exposed to speculators. Second, the Danish no vote in its **referendum** on the **Treaty on European Union** in the summer of 1992 was a catalyst for a period of uncertainty in exchange markets. This in turn sparked considerable speculation against ERM currencies which, despite considerable intervention by central banks, resulted in Italy and Britain withdrawing from the ERM in September 1992. In Britain the withdrawal is known as **Black Wednesday**. Subsequently, pressure on the French franc led to a decision in August 1993 to widen ERM fluctuation bands to 15 per cent for all but the Deutschmark and Dutch guilder severely damaged the credibility of the ERM. Although a number of countries subsequently joined the ERM (Austria in 1995) and others were readmitted (Italy in 1996), for those countries that had chosen to progress towards EMU, the very need for the ERM came to an end when the final stage of EMU commenced on 1 January 1999. But for those countries outside EMU the ERM continued as **Exchange Rate Mechanism II** from 1 January 1999 to provide a vehicle for coordinating the relationship between the **euro** and those countries that had chosen not to participate in the euro.

Exchange Rate Mechanism (ERM) II

On 1 January 1999 the ERM II was established to provide a method of coordinating the exchange rates between the **euro** system and those EU member states that were not members of the euro. Membership of the ERM II is voluntary. As with its predecessor, the **Exchange Rate Mechanism**, the ERM II involves setting a central rate for a particular country's exchange rate against the euro and then establishing a band of fluctuation around the central rate. Although the general fluctuation band is ±15 per cent, it is possible for a narrower fluctuation band to be agreed. Countries participating in the ERM II can receive support from foreign exchange intervention and financing at the margins as a means of helping to maintain the currency's participation within the fluctuation bands.

Exemption

This is the field of application where a treaty, **regulation** or **directive** is not applicable.

Exclusive agreements

The **European Commission** banned this style of relationship between companies because it contravened the EU's competition policy.

Exclusive competence

This refers to the Community's ability to act, as in the field of the **Common Agricultural Policy** (CAP), while mixed competence refers to the mix between the Community and member states. The Community has explicit responsibility in the arena of the **common commercial policy**.

External relations

A general term used to describe the trading relationships that the Community has with third countries, such as **association agreements** and cooperation agreements. In addition, external relations is also used to describe the security and defence aspects of the Community.

External tariff

The gradual establishment of a **customs union** within the EEC resulted in the abolition of separate national customs tariffs by 1968, being replaced by a **common external tariff**. All revenue from the common external tariff has gone to the EU **budget** since 1975.

External trade

Trade between a **third country** and the EU.

F

Factortame judgment

This 1990 judgment by the **Court of Justice** in a Spanish fishing case involved the UK government. The case centred on the fact that Spanish fishermen had purchased British fishing vessels and with them the quotas that were attributable to Britain and as such the Spanish fishermen were using British quotas under the **Common Fisheries Policy** to land fish that they had caught in Spain. The UK government challenged this situation by passing the 1988 Merchant Shipping Act, which required 75 per cent of the shareholders and directors of a company to be British for the company to be able to register itself as British. The implication of this was that the Spanish fisherman could no longer operate on the basis of using the British quotas. However, the Spanish fishermen responded by claiming that this action was a breach of their rights to be given equal status as EC citizens. It was a view that the Court of Justice sympathized with when it ruled that the 1988 Merchant Shipping Act was a breach of EC law on the ground of equal treatment of citizens and the ruling consequently overturned the Merchant Shipping Act. In this context, the Court's decision confirmed that national legislation needs to be suspended when it is in conflict with EU law.

Federalism

A political system where there is a constitutional division of power between different levels of government, such as Canada, Germany, Switzerland and the United States. It is has often been used within the context of European integration by **Eurosceptics** as a means of criticizing the concentration of supranational power in the EU institutions and diluting the role of member states.

Financial perspectives

These are the multi-annual **budget** programmes of the EU. The first covered the period 1989–92 and is generally referred to as the **Delors I Budget Package.** The second financial perspective covered the years 1993–99 and is generally referred to as the **Delors II Budget Package**. At the March 1999 Berlin **European Council** a third financial perspective was agreed with regard to financing the **enlargement** of the EU during the period 1999–2006. The December 2005 Brussels European Council reached agreement on the budget programme for the period 2007–13, which included a commitment by the UK to forgo €10,500m of the rebate that it has received from the EU (£1000m a year for seven years). The UK had originally obtained the rebate in 1984 as a response to the **British budget problem**, whereby its contributions to the EU were far in excess of the benefits that it received from the **Common Agricultural Policy** (CAP) that dominated the EU budget. The agreement reached at the December 2005 Brussels European Council also increased the amount of contributions paid to the EU from other member states, in particular France.

Finland

Population: 5.2m (2005)
Capital: Helsinki

In the post-1945 era Finland played a rather minimal role in initiatives towards European integration. This was a product of the 1948 Finno-Soviet Pact of Friendship, Cooperation and Mutual Assistance, which essentially meant that Finland pursued a policy of neutrality so as not to engage in any activities that might be construed to violate the terms of its treaty with the Soviet Union. As a result, Finland had little interest in participating in the initiatives that led to the **Treaties of Rome**. But, while many other Nordic countries were also unwilling to get involved in the creation of the European Communities, Denmark, Norway and Sweden nevertheless did participate from the outset in the **European Free Trade Association** (EFTA). Indeed, it was only in 1986 that Finland became a member of EFTA. Thereafter, developments moved swiftly, with Finland being a full participant in the negotiations over the **European Economic Area** and in 1992 it formally submitted an application to join the Community. Finland subsequently joined what by then had become the European Union on 1 January 1995 along with Austria and Sweden. It subsequently joined the **European Monetary System** (EMS) on 14 October 1996 and was considered by the **European Commission** in March 1998 to have met the **convergence criteria** of the **single currency** to enable it to participate in **Economic and Monetary Union** (EMU) from 1 January 1999. This belated recognition of the importance of European integration has been heavily influenced by the need for Finland to benefit from access to the **single market**.

First pillar

This is the European Community pillar of the EU, with the majority of all policies falling within it. The 2004 **Constitutional Treaty** (subject to ratification) stressed that the pillar system would be altered and the three **pillars** would be merged together. A reservation was, however, provided so as to protect particular procedures relating to the **common foreign and security policy** (CFSP) (including defence policy).

Flexibility

This term is generally used within the context of highlighting different approaches to European integration, such as **à la carte Europe**, **two-speed Europe** and **multi-speed Europe**. The mechanisms for **enhanced cooperation** that were introduced in the **Treaty of Amsterdam** also come under the general heading of flexibility.

Fontainebleau agreement

A compact reached at the Fontainebleau **European Council** of June 1984 that resolved the dispute over the UK's contribution to the Community's **budget**, this being an issue that had particularly dominated **Margaret Thatcher**'s period as prime minister. She considered that Britain was contributing too much to the Community in relation to its overall wealth. **The British budget problem** was solved by an agreement that gave the government an **abatement** on the portion of its annual contribution based on **value added tax**.

Food safety

As the EU is the world's biggest food importer and the second largest exporter, food safety is an important consideration. Traditionally, the focus attached to food safety was in relation to the **Common Agricultural Policy** (CAP) and the need to protect the interests of consumers (**consumer policy**). Whereas the initial emphasis of the CAP was on the mass production of food to ensure an adequate supply within the Community, this in time gave way to concerns about the quality of mass produced food with the use of fertilizers and in some instances the genetic modification of crops (thereby prompting changes to the CAP). In recent years there has been a growing concern about food safety, not least because of outbreaks of such diseases as BSE and foot-and-mouth (**beef crisis**). There has at the same time been greater emphasis attached to the labelling of products and the promotion of organically produced food. Concern over food safety resulted in the publication of a **White Paper** on food safety in January 2000 which included the development of a legal framework that covered 'from the farm to the fork'. The White Paper was adopted in February 2002 and also founded the European Food Safety Authority (EFSA), which is tasked with providing independent advice on food safety issues.

Fouchet plan

A draft Treaty for political union published on 2 November 1961 by a committee chaired by Christopher Fouchet of France. The initiative emanated from the French president, **Charles de Gaulle**, who considered that **the Six** should explore ways of achieving political union. In this context, it proposed the creation of a council of Heads of Government or foreign ministers where decisions would only be taken by unanimity; the establishment of an international secretariat composed of officials taken from national foreign ministries; the creation of four permanent intergovernmental committees to deal with foreign affairs, commerce, defence and cultural matters; and the development of an appointive European assembly. However, such a scheme was opposed by all member states apart from France, which meant that the plan was essentially abandoned by 1962.

Fortress Europe

This phrase is often used in the context of defending the EU from outside influences, such as **asylum** seekers, and in the context of EU rules on trade protection that favour member states over non-EU states.

Founding fathers

This expression highlights the influence that individuals such as **Jean Monnet** and **Robert Schuman** had in the integration of Europe after the Second World War.

Four freedoms

Refers to the **free movement of capital, free movement of people, free movement of goods** and **free movement of services** (see **single market**).

France

Population: 59.34m (2005)
Capital: Paris
France played a significant role in the shaping of European politics in the postwar period, **Robert Schuman** being the instigator of the Community while **Jean Monnet** helped shape its development. During the early years of the Community France essentially regulated the pace of integration, being insistent on the inclusion of the **Common Agricultural Policy** (CAP). This emphasized the French perception of integration as an economic goal, which was further demonstrated by the 1965 **empty chair crisis** when President **Charles de Gaulle** refused to accept the introduction of **qualified majority voting** (QMV) as a method of **decision-making** in the **Council of Ministers**. That episode further illustrated the ability of de Gaulle to influence events, as when he was instrumental in refusing to allow the UK to become a member. His replacement by **Georges Pompidou** in 1969 marked a transition in this policy, with the **enlargement** of the Community to include Denmark, Ireland and the UK in 1973. In later years, during the 1980s, France under the leadership of **François Mitterrand** was especially influential within the Community when it supported greater European integration. He was important to the **single market** programme and **Single European Act** (SEA) and was the principal motivator behind

the 1990–91 **intergovernmental conference** (IGC) on **Economic and Monetary Union** (EMU). The setting of a timetable of 1999 for the introduction of a **single currency** was his principal objective at the December 1991 Maastricht **European Council** which produced agreement on a **Treaty on European Union**. A particular feature of this period was the strong alliance he developed with the German chancellor, **Helmut Kohl**. This alliance with Kohl was continued when Mitterrand's successor, **Jacques Chirac**, was elected president in 1995 and it was further maintained between Chirac and **Gerhard Schröder**, who succeeded Kohl as chancellor in 1998. The closeness in this relationship was most evident in recent years when both countries opposed the US led **Iraq war** in 2003, but the special Franco-German axis looks likely to weaken with **Angela Merkel** succeeding Schröder as German Chancellor in 2005.

In 1998 France was deemed to have met the **convergence criteria** for participation in the single currency and therefore became a founder member of it on 1 January 1999. Yet in the years that have followed the French economy has suffered from a lack of dynamism. Critics have often highlighted French labour laws as being a contributory factor. Not surprisingly the possibility of economic reform through a change to 'Anglo-Saxon' working practices – which would result in longer working hours and less job security – has concerned the French electorate. This state of affairs, combined with its traditional opposition to Turkey's **accession** to the EU, proved to be influential factors behind the no vote that was recorded in the French **referendum** on the **Constitutional Treaty** in May 2005.

Francovich Judgment

In the 1990 case of *Francovich et al.* v. *Italy* the **Court of Justice** ruled against the Italian government which had been accused of not implementing the rules of the EC. The significance of the ruling was that the Court of Justice established the principle that individuals could challenge a member state for the non-implementation of EC law on the basis of the infringement of their individual rights. Moreover, the judgment also stressed that fines could be levied on member states that were found to be guilty.

Fraud

In the 1990s the concept of fraud became an important issue within the EU, particularly with regard to the **budget** where there was concern that significant sums of money were being lost through fraud. Such concerns were highlighted in the reports of the **Court of Auditors**. In 1999 allegations of corruption forced the downfall of the **European**

Commission that was led by President **Jacques Santer**. As a direct result of these concerns an **Anti-Fraud Office** (OLAF) was established within the European Commission in 1999.

Free movement of capital

The principle of free movement of capital is directly linked to the right to provide services in another member state. It means that EU citizens and companies with operations in the EU may open bank accounts anywhere in the EU and transfer unlimited sums of money from one EU country to another. Capital movements were fully liberalized within the EU on 1 July 1990 (see **four freedoms**).

Free movement of goods

An essential component for the functioning of the **single market**, requiring harmonized customs duties and taxes, uniform rules on the protection of health, consumers and the environment and the removal of all other **barriers to trade**. This principle ensures that a product manufactured and marketed lawfully in one member state shall be approved for sale in the other member states. At the same time, countries are not allowed to impose quantitative restrictions that place limits on the volume of particular goods that can be imported (see **four freedoms**).

Free movement of people

This provides the right for EU citizens to move and reside freely within the EU. In other words, EU citizens should receive the same treatment in all member states. This applies, for example, to employment, pay and working conditions and social and fiscal benefits, and it is not permissible to discriminate against EU citizens on account of their nationality. At the same time, free movement of persons has also been reflected in the partial removal of checks on persons at border crossings between EU member states. Although progress in this area can be traced back to 1985, when a number of member states agreed to gradually phase out controls of persons at internal borders and to develop police and judicial cooperation in the form of the **Schengen agreement**, not all member states have accepted the wisdom or the need to remove all border checks (see **four freedoms**).

Free movement of services

The free movement of services is aimed at ensuring that EU citizens and businesses may provide services in other member states. The free movement of services is closely connected with the freedom of establishment. This type of freedom entitles EU citizens to start and run a company in another EU country on the same conditions as citizens of that country. Free movement of services is a broader concept encompassing activities in which a company in one member state provides services in another. It is often companies providing financial services that enjoy this 'freedom', for example, banks and insurance companies. Companies in the energy and telecommunications sectors are also included in this group (see **four freedoms**).

Free trade agreement

A contract to eliminate all customs duties and prevent trade restrictions between signatory nations, as established between the EC and the **European Free Trade Association** (EFTA) in 1972–73.

Free trade area

Denotes a situation where customs duties and other restrictive trading measures have been removed between two or more customs territories. National customs duties are retained for trade with third countries and this therefore differs from a **customs union** which has a common external customs tariff. Examples of a free trade area include the **European Free Trade Association** (EFTA) and the North American Free Trade Area (NAFTA). The problem with free trade areas is that the presence of distinct national external tariffs on goods that are imported from countries that are outside the FTA ensures that goods are often imported in to the FTA via the country with the lowest external tariff. Thus, in an FTA between Britain and Ireland, if Ireland has a lower tariff than Britain on oranges, companies in Britain will import oranges via Ireland so as to pay the lower tariffs. The benefit of a customs union is that there exists a **common external tariff**.

Freedom of establishment

Refers to the right of EU citizens to establish themselves in other member states to run a business, farm or work in a self-employed capacity.

Friends of the Presidency

A group of officials comprising a representative from the permanent representation of each member state to the EU, being chaired by the official from the country which has the Presidency of the **Council of Ministers**. The group's primary task is to act as a clearing ground for issues before they reach permanent representative or ministerial level. It is particularly effective at coordinating policy during **intergovern-**

mental conference (IGC) negotiations and is similar to the **Antici group** (see **Council Presidency**).

Functionalism

The founding father of the functional approach was the Romanian born scholar, David Mitrany. He regarded nationalism as a major threat to world and European peace and believed that states should restructure their working relationships in order to reduce regional and thereby global tensions that could lead to war. Mitrany's thoughts were influenced by two historical events: the First World War of 1914–18 and the apparent success of the Danubian Commission, which was a multi-state body that managed to control traffic on the Danube river despite the strong national interests of the bordering states. As a result, Mitrany argued that states should cooperate in such policy sectors as agriculture, science and transport. Supranational high authorities would then be established where technocrats would make decisions.

The functional approach to integration is based on a strategy that encourages integration through technical cooperation in specific policy areas, such as agriculture or coal, with these sectors governed by supranational institutions. Functionalists considered that governments would be prepared to surrender **sovereignty** in these technical areas because they did not threaten the nation state. Governments would also appreciate the benefits of cooperating on these matters at a regional or world level. Moreover, the success of cooperation in one sector would create pressures that would result in a demand for more integration in other areas. The end result would be that such cooperation would ensure that the capacity for governments to undertake independent action would lessen. For Mitrany, functional cooperation would therefore provide a means of bringing different nations together and the experience of cooperation would ensure that the potential for nationalist tendencies would reduce.

In this approach, Mitrany argued that it would be possible to separate functional cooperation from politics. Yet the reality has been the reverse, as political disputes have affected many technical bodies. As a consequence, a significant weakness of this approach was the lack of appreciation that the technical bodies would inevitably be political entities and that they would therefore be faced with making political decisions. Consequently the functional approach was subsequently overtaken by the more realistic **neofunctional** approach.

Future financing

An argument over the financing of the Community took place between 1986 and 1992, revolving around the **Delors I Budget Package** and

Delors II Budget Package. The UK especially advocated that there should be tighter controls on the expenditure of the **Common Agricultural Policy** (CAP) while there should be greater budget discipline. A final solution emerged at the Edinburgh **European Council** of December 1992 which included a modest increase in the **budget**.

G

General Affairs Council

This body, which comprises the regular meetings of national foreign ministers, is regarded as the senior meeting within the **Council of the European Union**.

General Agreement on Tariff and Trade (GATT)

Signed in 1947 by 23 countries, GATT has aimed to promote trading relationships among the signatory states. To achieve these ends GATT introduced a number of key principles, including non-discrimination, a ban on quantitative restrictions, a ban on dumping and export subsidies, and the objective of a general and progressive reduction in customs duties. As the **Treaties of Rome** stressed that the member states should be represented by the EC in matters relating to external trade, it has therefore been the **European Commission** which has represented the member states in GATT negotiations. To achieve the aim of dismantling national **trade barriers** there have been a number of rounds of GATT negotiations:

*   the Dillon Round (1961–62);
*   the Kennedy Round (1964–67);
*   the Tokyo Round (1973–79);
*   the Uruguay Round (1986–93);
*   the Doha Round (2001–6).

In 1995 GATT was replaced by the **World Trade Organization** (WTO).

Genscher, Hans-Dietrich (b. 1927)

As foreign minister of the Federal Republic of Germany from 1974 until 1992 he proved to be a major force within his own nation where he was chairman of the influential Free Democratic Party. His decision to switch the coalition partnership from the Social Democrats to Christian Democrats in 1982 resulted in **Helmut Schmidt** being removed as Chancellor and **Helmut Kohl** taking his place. Genscher's later resignation as foreign minister in 1992 consequently weakened the political position of Kohl. As foreign minister he attempted to maintain the policy of developing links with eastern Europe that had been initiated by **Willy Brandt**, while being committed to the Community and the **North Atlantic Treaty Organisation** (NATO). But during the **Cold War** atmosphere of the early 1980s this policy drew some criticism from the USA and the UK. Within the Community he was the main architect of the 1981 **Genscher–Colombo Plan**.

Genscher–Colombo Plan

This refers to a 1981 political union initiative advanced by the German and Italian foreign ministers, **Hans-Dietrich Genscher** and **Emilio Colombo**. They suggested that there should be more common policies, particularly in the field of foreign affairs; that the **European Council** should report annually to the **European Parliament**; that **qualified majority voting** (QMV) should be increased in the **Council of Ministers**; and that there should be more cultural and legal cooperation. A primary aim was to make the institutions more explicit, especially the European Council which had developed outside the **Treaties of Rome**. However, the proposals were objected to by some member states because they envisaged an extension of QMV and an expanded **budget**.

German reunification

The collapse of the former Soviet Union and its satellite states in eastern Europe throughout 1989 and 1990 provided the opportunity for the former General Democratic Republic to be incorporated into West Germany, as provided for in Article 23 of the latter's constitution. This was accepted at the Dublin **European Council** meeting of April 1990, with reunification being achieved on 3 October 1990 after the establishment of a State Treaty on 1 July 1990.

Germany

Population: 82.43m (2005)
Capital: Berlin
Just as France was instrumental to the establishment of the **European Community**, Germany has been its most important member since 1957. It has consistently been a strong supporter of European integration, not least because such a process was perceived as a means of tying the nation into the Community. This was a view adopted by the first postwar chancellor of Germany, **Konrad Adenauer**, and was emphasized by **Helmut Kohl** upon reunification in 1990. During that period Germany established a close relationship with France, illustrated by the

1963 **Treaty of Friendship** signed by Adenauer and **Charles de Gaulle**. Thereafter, **Helmut Schmidt** and **Valéry Giscard d'Estaing** cemented the Franco-German axis, which was further strengthened by Helmut Kohl and **François Mitterrand**. By contrast, Willy Brandt's tenure between 1969 and 1974 witnessed a significant change of policy with the pursuit of **Ostpolitik**. This referred to a series of agreements negotiated between Germany and the states of eastern Europe, of which the most significant was with the German Democratic Republic.

Giscard d'Estaing, Valéry (b. 1926)

As president of France between 1974 and 1981 he played an important role within the European Community and developed a strong relationship with the German chancellor, **Helmut Schmidt**, who entered office at roughly the same time. That Franco-German alliance further developed the relationship which had been grounded in the 1963 **Treaty of Friendship**, with both leaders meeting regularly. He played a key role in the institutionalization of summit meetings of Heads of State and Government, arguing in 1974 for their development into the **European Council**. He was also a strong supporter of the **European Monetary System**. He did not want to accelerate Spain's accession to the Community. After the 1981 election of **François Mitterrand** as president, Giscard d'Estaing continued to be a member of the French parliament until 1989 when he entered the **European Parliament** and subsequently led the Liberal group. Within the European Parliament he proved to be a regular campaigner for granting it increased powers, which he incidentally opposed when president of France. He played an important role in recent reforms to the EU, having chaired the discussions on the **Convention on the Future of Europe** that took place between March 2002 and June 2003, and which provided the basis for the **Constitutional Treaty** that member states agreed to at the June 2004 European Council.

Glasnost

Refers to a process of 'openness' that was one of the key principles adopted by **Mikhail Gorbachev** when he was appointed General Secretary of the Communist Party of the Soviet Union in 1985. For Gorbachev, glasnost was a means of debating formerly closed issues in Soviet society, such as the role of women, as well as issues relating to the environment (a point that was particularly relevant after the Chernobyl nuclear disaster of 1986). Glasnost spread to encompass other issues, including freedom of speech and publication and led to the toleration of criticism of Soviet history and the role of its leaders, including Lenin and Stalin. In conjunction with perestroika, glasnost was significant in promoting reform throughout central and eastern Europe, which in the end brought about the downfall of the Soviet Union.

Globalization

The challenge of responding to globalization is one of the most important issues that the European Union faces and has played a major part of EU discussions on **competition policy, environment policy** and **trade policy**. At the same time, the EU and its member states have been drawn into global developments that require a foreign policy response and which have therefore been the focus of the **common foreign and security policy** (CFSP). The process of globalization is signified by a combination of factors that include rapid technological developments and the liberalization of world trade that has been initiated by the **World Trade Organization** (WTO). As a result, there has been a gradual removal of **trade barriers** between the countries and regions of the world, with the producers of many goods relocating to countries where there are lower labour costs. Yet, although many developing countries, such as China and India, have had phenomenal rates of growth in recent years, the process of globalization has not been without its critics and as a result there has emerged a significant 'anti-globalization movement'.

Gorbachev, Mikhail (b. 1931)

General Secretary of the Soviet Union from 1985 until his resignation in 1991. A reforming leader of the Soviet Union, Gorbachev sought to change the planned economy and the role of the Communist Party. This led to changes that established the principles of a free market economy and parliamentary elections which even resulted in the Communist Party losing its monopoly on political power. But, while Gorbachev deemed political openness (**glasnost**) and economic reform (perestroika) to be central to the future of the Soviet Union, the changes also gave rise to nationalism which culminated in a campaign for independence in many of the Soviet Republics, especially the Baltic Republics. Gorbachev's attempts to reform at a measured pace brought criticisms from individuals such as Boris Yeltsin who advocated a more rapid transition to a market economy, and from hard-liners who opposed the reform process. Such was the hard-liners' concern that they launched a coup in August 1991, during which time Gorbachev spent three days under house arrest. Gorbachev returned to power, but it was the defiance of Boris Yeltsin that had brought about the coup's collapse, and Yeltsin was increasingly in control of power structures within the Soviet Union. As a consequence, Gorbachev found himself ever more powerless, a situation which led to his resignation. Thus, in the end, although Gorbachev's reforms brought him prominence among the international community, they did not assist his popularity at home. It was a state of affairs that was marked by Gorbachev only receiving 0.5 per cent of the votes in the June 1996 Russian presidential elections.

Greece

Population: 10.6m (2005)
Capital: Athens
Having applied for membership of the Community in the mid-1970s after the collapse of the military regime, it did not obtain accession until 1981. That time lapse was caused by the **European Commission**'s perception that the Greek economy was initially not strong enough to join, a problem that continued into the 1980s. Throughout that decade the Greek Socialist government of Andreas Papandreou proved to be a constant disruptive voice to the future development of the Community, particularly in the field of **European Political Cooperation**. Indeed, the UK's acceptance of an extension of **qualified majority voting** (QMV) in the **Single European Act** (SEA) was motivated by a concern that Greece would be able to veto the development of the single market if unanimity voting procedures were maintained. However, the return to power of a Conservative government in late 1980s brought with it an attempt to construct a more positive relationship with the Community, although Greece continued to prevent the Community developing better relations with Turkey. Such a stance was motivated by a dispute over Cyprus, where a Turkish-backed government controlled the northern section of the island. A primary feature of Greece's membership of the Community has been its weak economy, highlighted when the European Commission did not include it in March 1998 as one of the 11 member states which met the **convergence criteria** of **Economic and Monetary Union** (EMU). Greece's determination to participate in EMU resulted in it subsequently meeting the criteria for joining and it acceded to EMU in 2001.

Green Paper

A set of proposals advanced by the **European Commission** with the aim of fostering discussion by establishing a range of possible ideas, such as **social policy**, the **single currency** and telecommunications. This contrasts with a **White Paper**, which is an official set of proposals in a given policy area.

Group of Eight (G-8)

Refers to the meetings of finance ministers, heads of **central banks** and heads of government of the most advanced industrial economies. The meetings are a means to discuss issues relating to the state of the global economy, with particular reference to exchange rates and issues that relate to the countries concerned. Other issues that have been discussed included the cancellation of debt relief to Third World countries. The G-8 comprises Canada, France, Germany, Italy, Japan, UK, USA and since 1991 Russia. The EU is also represented at G-8 meetings, in the form of the President of the **European Commission** and the Presidency of the **European Council**.

Guidelines

These are acts of law, whereby the **European Commission** or the **European Council** binds member states to implement the objectives that are set out in the guidelines and to ensure that their own national legislation is in turn altered within a specified time period.

Gulf War

Iraq's invasion of Kuwait on 2 August 1990 resulted in the massing of coalition forces from over 25 countries to liberate Kuwait. The USA and UK had particularly large contributions. The expiry on 16 January 1991 of the United Nation's deadline for Iraq's withdrawal from Kuwait resulted in the commencement of nearly six weeks of continuous air bombing under Operation Desert Storm. The land offensive started on 24 February 1991 and ended on 26 February, at which point Saddam Hussein accepted that Kuwait was not part of Iraq. The war was notable not just for its brevity, but for the reassertion of the dominant role of the USA in providing global security. It went some way to imparting a more realistic tone to the debate over the development of a **European security and defence identity** (ESDI), as particularly advocated by France during the 1991 **intergovernmental conference** (IGC) negotiations which resulted in the **Treaty on European Union** (TEU). In this connection, it was notable that Belgium refused to sell the UK ammunition during the conflict, a point which reinforced the latter's scepticism towards the development of an ESDI.

Gymnich meetings

EU ministers tend to have few informal meetings throughout a year when a limited number of officials and interpreters are present. The intention of such fireside discussions is to provide a relaxed atmosphere where compromises can be reached on outstanding issues. They bear the name of the first such meeting in April 1974 at Schloss Gymnich near Bonn (see **Council of Ministers**).

H

Hague Congress (May 1948)

The Congress was influenced by federalist approaches to European integration that had been reflected in the formation of the European Union of Federalists in December 1946. The federalist approach envisaged the creation of a federal constitution for Europe whereby a federal parliament, government and court would be entrusted with certain powers over such policy areas as security and trade, with the remaining policies to be dealt with by the different levels of government within the member states. This desire to establish an appropriate constitution therefore resulted in the decision to hold a conference which took place in The Hague in May 1948. Some 750 delegates attended the Congress, of which the Honorary President was **Winston Churchill** who had himself called for a '**United States of Europe**' in 1946. The final resolutions of the Congress included a call for a united and democratic Europe. This in turn provided some impetus to the establishment of the **Council of Europe** one year later.

Hague Summit (1969)

The French president **Georges Pompidou** called a special meeting of the leaders of the six member states to be held at The Hague in December 1969 in order to 'relaunch' the Community. The summit provided an important opportunity to resolve a number of issues, including the question of **enlargement** (paving the way for subsequent applications from Britain, Denmark, Ireland and Norway). The meeting also provided the momentum for member states to reach agreement in April 1970 to provide the Community with its own financial resources, which represented a move away from direct national contributions. These **own resources** extended beyond the remit of financing the **Common Agricultural Policy** (CAP) and were designed to ensure the Community had sufficient income to satisfy all the policies that the Commission administered. In addition to resolving the CAP funding, the meeting was significant for its agreement to deepen the Communities' activities with a view to extending cooperation within the economic and political fields. As a result, two committees were established to examine the case for deeper economic and political integration. The premier of Luxembourg, **Pierre Werner**, was given the responsibility of leading a committee to examine the case for monetary union (**Werner Report**), and the Belgian diplomat (and future **European Commissioner**), **Étienne Davignon**, led the committee which investigated the possibility of achieving closer political integration (**Davignon Report**).

Hallstein, Walter (1901–82)

He was the first President of the **European Commission** and is to date the second longest serving, having held office from 1958 until 1967. Before then he led the West German delegation to the 1950 conference that discussed the **Schuman Plan**, and participated in the 1955 **Messina conference** which produced agreement on the establishment of a common market. His view of the European Commission acting as the engine of European integration produced several clashes with the French president **Charles de Gaulle**, and provided a great deal of the motivation behind that government's action with respect to the **empty chair crisis**. A reason for this was because Hallstein proposed that the completion of the **Common Agricultural Policy**'s (CAP) financial settlement should be linked to the granting of increased budgetary power to the **European Parliament**, with the European Commission being given executive authority. Hallstein also played an important role in German politics and was the author of the **Hallstein Doctrine,** which stressed that Germany should not have diplomatic relations with the German Democratic Republic (GDR).

Hallstein Doctrine

This referred to the claim by the Federal Republic of Germany (FRG) that it was the sole representative of Germany because, in contrast to the government in the German Democratic Republic (GDR), the FRG's government had been democratically elected. Named after its author, **Walter Hallstein**, the Doctrine was set out in the 'Government Declaration' of **Konrad Adenauer** on 23 September 1955. But, while the Doctrine stressed that the FRG would not have diplomatic relations with the GDR, a question mark arose over its viability and it was succeeded by the policy of **Ostpolitik** (relations with the East) which came to prominence after the election of **Willy Brandt** as Chancellor in 1969.

Hard core

A concept of integration embracing a small group of countries that wish to have closer cooperation with each other. It relates to the context of **flexibility** of European integration.

Hard ECU

A currency proposal launched by the UK in January 1991 in an attempt to provide clarification on stage two of the **Delors Report**'s proposals for **Economic and Monetary Union** (EMU) as well as providing the UK with greater influence in the 1990–91 **intergovernmental conference** (IGC) negotiations. The plan envisaged the hard **ECU** being created and managed by a European Monetary Fund, while it would float alongside existing currencies in the **Exchange Rate Mechanism** (ERM) of the **European Monetary System** (EMS). However, it received little support from other member states, except temporary Spanish interest, and was effectively sunk by the summer of 1991. This was primarily because it did not envisage the creation of a **single currency**, as desired by a majority of member states, and it was additionally perceived to be a delaying tactic.

Harmonization

Coordination of member states' economic policies and legal and administrative rules so as to ensure that the rules set by the EU are applied in each member state.

Health and safety

The EU has for a long time been concerned with matters relating to health and safety, especially the provision of acceptable conditions in the workplace. Notable initiatives have included the **Social Chapter** and the **Working Time Directive**.

Heath, Edward (1916–2005)

A committed pro-European, Heath served as a British Conservative prime minister for less than four years (1970–74) and was a member of parliament for more than half a century (1950–2001). His support for European integration was based on a belief that there should not be a future conflict in which Europe tore itself apart. Heath was in charge of the negotiations for Britain's first application to the Community, which commenced in October 1961 and lasted for 15 months until they broke down. As prime minister one of his most significant achievements was securing Britain's entry into the **European Economic Community** (EEC) in 1973. During the negotiations for entry, Heath's major concern was for the Community to develop a strong regional policy. He perceived this to be a means of both benefiting the UK economy and at the same time helping to offset the costs of membership which would result from participation in the **Common Agricultural Policy** (CAP).

However, his premiership became hampered by industrial unrest which eventually resulted in electoral defeat and the coming to power of the Labour Party in March 1974. In the wake of election defeat he was challenged for the leadership of the Conservative Party by **Margaret Thatcher**, with her victory in the first ballot ensuring that Heath refused to stand in the second round. His relationship with Thatcher was from then on a difficult one, with Heath being opposed to her **Eurosceptic** outbursts in the 1980s. Upon Thatcher's election as prime minister in 1979 he refused her offer of the post of Britain's ambassador to the US, although this was not surprising as Heath had chosen as prime minister to place less reliance on the **special relationship** with the US.

Helsinki Final Act

Refers to the agreement that was drawn up by the 35 nations which took part in the 1975 Helsinki **Conference on Security and Cooperation in Europe** (CSCE). The agreement was signed by all European states (with the exception of Albania), Canada and the USA. The meeting established the CSCE, which provided a forum whereby the communist states of eastern Europe and the capitalist states of western Europe along with Canada and the USA could meet to discuss matters of common concern. As such, the forum was of considerable importance and was until 1990 the only means for such meetings to take place. With the collapse of communism in eastern Europe in 1989/1990, the significance and relevance of the CSCE came into question. This resulted in its remit and scope of membership being widened and it being renamed the **Organization for Security and Cooperation in Europe** (OSCE).

High Authority

Created by the Treaty of Paris on 18 April 1951, the High Authority was the executive body of the **European Coal and Steel Community** (ECSC) whose members were Belgium, France, Germany, Italy, Luxembourg and the Netherlands. Based in Luxembourg, it commenced operating on 10 August 1952. The High Authority was one of four institutions that governed the ECSC (the others were the **Council of Ministers**, **Court of Justice** and Common Assembly). Designed as a supranational body, the High Authority was independent of the member states. It was responsible for administering the common market for coal and steel in **the Six** member states. The nine members of the High Authority comprised two each from France and Germany, and one each from Belgium, Luxembourg, Italy and the Netherlands. The ninth member was co-opted by the other eight members. During its period of existence it had five Presidents: **Jean Monnet** (1952–55), René Meyer (1955–57), Paul Finet (1958–59), Piero Malvestiti (1959–63) and Rinaldo Del Bo (1963–67). Although its activities were at times limited by the influence of national governments, it was nevertheless of importance in promoting the importance of supranational institutions. It existed as an independent institution until the **merger treaty** joined it with the **European Atomic Energy Community** (Euratom) Commission and the **European Economic Community** (EEC) Commission on 1 July 1967.

High Representative for CFSP

The Treaty of Amsterdam included a provision to create a new position of High Representative for **Common Foreign and Security Policy** (CFSP) to be held by the Secretary General of the Council. By creating the post the intention was to provide greater cohesiveness to the EU's CFSP. The June 1999 Cologne **European Council** appointed **Javier Solana** as the first High Representative for the CFSP.

Historical institutionalism

This theory of integration attempts to account for evolution of a policy or an institution by the environment and circumstances in which they take place. Students of historical institutionalism therefore stress that institutional settings have a significant impact on policy decisions, whereby the environment acts as a constraint. In other words, the initial structure of a policy has a determining impact on its further development and so a kind of 'path dependency' influences the evolution of the policy. A notable example of this is the **Common Agricultural Policy** (CAP), which was initially designed to ensure adequate food production and to guarantee farm income. A linkage between farm income and food production resulted in the supply of food (**butter mountains** and **wine lakes**) over and above what was required. But, because of the vested interests of the farming community, the CAP has proved an extremely difficult policy to reform.

Human rights

The establishment of the **Council of Europe** in 1949 had as one of its basic objectives the maintenance and development of human rights. This provided a great deal of motivation behind the signing of the European Convention on Human Rights in 1950. However, the **Treaties of Rome** made little reference to human rights although subsequent reforms such as the **Single European Act** (SEA) included reference to human rights in the preamble and therefore it became part of the *acquis communitaire*.

Humanitarian aid

The combination of the activities of the **European Commission** and the member states has ensured that the EU is one of the most important donors of humanitarian aid in the world. In recent years the EU's provision of humanitarian aid has become more important because of the increased number of world crises. As a response to this situation the **European Community Humanitarian Office** (ECHO) was established in 1992 with the purpose of providing emergency relief, such as goods and services, to disaster areas and conflicts outside of the EU. Partners of ECHO, such as non-governmental organizations and the United Nations humanitarian agencies, play the leading role in distributing the aid.

Hungary

Population: 10.01m (2005)
Capital: Budapest
After the end of the Second World War Hungary fell under communist rule. A 1956 uprising against communist authority (in which it was announced that Hungary would withdraw from the **Warsaw Pact**) was greeted with massive military intervention from Moscow. As a result, Hungary continued to be dominated by communist rule for the next three decades, although under the leadership of János Kadar in 1968 Hungary started a process of a partial liberalization of its economy, resulting in what would be referred to as 'goulash communism'. With the fall of the communist regime in 1989 and the end of the **Cold War,** Hungary quickly announced its intention of forging a closer relationship with the European Community with a view towards eventual membership. As a result, Hungary signed a **Europe Agreement** in 1991, while the Community accepted the principle that Hungary could become an EC member state so long as its economy underwent a process of reform and it was able to meet the *acquis communitaire*. In March 1994 Hungary submitted a formal application, with accession negotiations commencing in 1998. The following year Hungary joined the **North Atlantic Treaty Organisation** (NATO) and it became a member of the EU in 2004 at the time of the historic **enlargement** to include the 10 countries of central and eastern Europe.

I

Immigration policy

For a long time immigration policy was of little concern to the European Communities, with member states being able to pursue their own policies. It was not until the mid-1980s that progress towards the coordination of immigration policy took place. This included the creation of the **Trevi Group** in 1986 to promote greater cooperation among member states with regard to the granting of visas and as a means of improving controls at the EC's external borders. Although the changes that swept through central and eastern Europe in 1989–90 were influential in promoting greater awareness of the need to tackle matters relating to immigration, the subsequent Maastricht **Treaty on European Union** (TEU) established only visas as an EU competence. By contrast, other matters relating to immigration were part of the intergovernmental pillar of the **justice and home affairs** (JHA) provisions. This state of affairs was partly tackled in the **Treaty of Amsterdam** which raised matters relating to **asylum** and **immigration policy** to the **supranational** level. This included an agreement to establish an **area of freedom, security and justice**, with the **third pillar** being renamed **police and judicial cooperation in criminal matters**.

Implementation

This is a particular important aspect of the process of European integration as it refers to the carrying out and putting into effect of EU policies. Laws that are agreed to at the EU level have to be implemented at the national level, and there has been a dramatic increase in the number of such laws since the 1980s. Member states did, for instance, have to implement a significant amount of legislation to achieve the goal of creating a **single market**. The issue of implementation is, however, often a contentious one as some member states who do not agree with a specific piece of legislation may attempt to resist or delay implementation. It is the responsibility of the **European Commission** to ensure that implementation takes place.

Independent European Programme Group (IEPG)

Established in 1976 to provide European members of the **North Atlantic Treaty Organisation** (NATO) with a forum where they could formulate policies that would assist cooperation in the procurement of armaments. Its functions were dissolved in December 1992 when European Defence Ministers decided to incorporate its activities into the **Western European Union** (WEU).

Indirect implementation

This is when the putting into effect of European legislation is dependent on the actions of national governments.

Inflation

This term refers to an increase in the amount of money that is in circulation and is demonstrated by an increase in prices and depreciation in value.

Inner core

This term is often used when referring to a group of member states that wish to pursue deeper European integration at a speed that is quicker than all member states would agree to.

Institution

A part of the Community or Union with significant status, such as the **European Commission**.

Institutional balance

Refers to the relationship between the **European Commission, Council of Ministers** and **European Parliament** and the extent to which there is a balance of powers between them. A particular focus of concern has been the influence of the European Parliament, whose influence has been strengthened in recent years via the **co-decision procedure** as set out in the **Treaty on European Union, Treaty of Amsterdam**, and **Treaty of Nice**. The **Constitutional Treaty** of 2004 notes that the co-decision procedure will be the primary means of **decision-making** within the EU.

Institutional reform

The reform of the EU's institutions has been one of the most important issues that the EU has faced in recent years. From the signing of the **Treaties of Rome** in 1957 until the mid-1980s there were relatively few institutional reforms, with one of the main early reforms having been the establishment of a single institutional structure in July 1967. In the 1970s the role of the **European Parliament** was altered through the introduction of direct elections in 1979. The introduction of the **Single European Act** (SEA) in 1987 further enhanced the powers of the European Parliament with the introduction of the cooperation procedure and was part of an attempt to remedy the so-called **democratic deficit** in the EU **decision-making** procedures. The SEA also increased the use of **qualified majority voting** (QMV) in the **Council of Ministers**. The **Treaty on European Union** (TEU) made further changes to the role of the European Parliament through the introduction of the co-decision procedure and there was an increase in the number of policies that fell under this procedure in the **Treaty of Amsterdam**. The use of QMV was also increased in both of these Treaties. The prospect of **enlargement** to the countries of central and eastern Europe was a key factor behind the **Treaty of Nice** as it sought to ensure that the EU institutions took into consideration the implications of enlargement. This not only applied to the distribution of European Parliament seats in an enlarged EU, but also included the size and composition of the **European Commission** as well as the use of QMV in the Council of Ministers. The Treaty of Nice did, however, fail to fully address all of the questions relating to institutional reform. This directly resulted in the holding of a **Convention on the Future of Europe** that led to member states agreeing on a **Constitutional Treaty** which sought, among other factors, to provide the EU with a clearer institutional structure.

Integrated Mediterranean Programme

Created in 1985 as a response to the **accession** of Greece who felt that its particular needs were not reflected in its terms of membership. This was addressed in the decision by the **European Council** in March 1984 to establish a programme for the duration of seven years from 1986 to 1992 that would tackle the problems of the southern parts of the Community, especially the whole of Greece, the south of France and the majority of southern Italy. Funding came from **structural funds**, a loan from the **European Investment Bank** and the **budget**. It has not been renewed, but the **Cohesion Fund** addresses the needs of Greece, Ireland, Portugal and Spain.

Integration theory

The process of European integration has been subject to considerable debate (primarily among political scientists) who have sought to attempt to explain the factors that have determined the manner in which the EU has evolved. While there has developed over a number of years a large number of explanations of European integration, there is, however, general agreement that there is no single theory that is capable of explaining the whole process. For the most part, the main divisions are between the two approaches of **intergovernmentalism** and **supranationalism**. The key difference between these approaches is that, whereas intergovernmentalism asserts that member states are the key actors which determine the nature of the evolution of European integration, supranationalism by contrast considers that it is the supranational institutions that have played the main role in shaping integration.

Interdependence

Refers to the situation whereby the actions of one state impact on others.

Interest groups

They attempt to exercise influence on policy-making and **decision-making** within the EU. The expansion in the number of policies that are dealt with by the EU has resulted in a significant increase in the number of interest groups that have focused their **lobbying** effort at the EU level and have in themselves become important actors in the EU integration process. Interest groups essentially have a twofold role: first, to provide information to the EU institutions and other member states that reflect the objectives of the interest group (proactive role); second, to gather information about **European Commission** initiatives or EU directives for the benefit of the interest group (reactive role). Some interest groups purely reflect a national position, such as the British Confederation of British Industry (CBI) while others are organized on a Europe-wide basis, such as the **European Trades Union Confederation** (ETUC).

The main type of interest groups within the EU are business, public and regional. Business interest groups represent the interests of firms that have responded to the increased importance that has been attached to the centralized nature of EU decision-making since the **single market** programme. Regional interest groups represent the views of regions that are increasingly drawn into national and European level decision-making. Devolution within the UK has, for instance, ensured that the Scottish Executive exercises control over a range of specific policies, while at the same time EU funding has been targeted at particular regions through the **structural funds**. The significance of regions to the EU has also been emphasized by the creation of the **Committee of the Regions**. Finally, the emergence of public interest groups is reflective of the growing involvement of the EU in matters relating to the environment and social affairs as well as impacting on the interests of the consumer. Public interest groups such as Friends of the Earth also play an important role in counterbalancing the views of business interest groups.

Some interest groups are inevitably more influential than others and business interest groups have typically had more influence than public and regional interest groups. This has been not least because business interest groups have tended to benefit from better organization and resources, but it is also because they often have a stronger and more concentrated constituency base. By contrast, public interest groups often have more a more diffuse constituency base. For instance, while the general public might all agree on the need for less pollution, it is often easier for the polluters to present a collective position because their vested interests are often greater because of the direct costs involved. Nevertheless, there are some areas where the general public have been able to exercise considerable influence, including the concern expressed against genetically modified organisms.

Interest rate

This applies to the rates applicable to savings and borrowings. Interest rates are increased so as to dampen down **inflation** by means of decreasing demand in an economy as the cost of borrowing increasing. By contrast, interest rates are reduced so as to increase demand in an economy. A common interest rate exists for all members of the **single currency**.

Intergovernmental bargaining

Refers to bargaining that takes place between governments, normally within the EU **Council of Ministers** and at **European Council** summits. **Intergovernmental conference** (IGC) negotiations are another example. The supranational actors, such as the **European Commission** and the **European Parliament** play no substantive part in such negotiations.

Intergovernmental conference (IGC)

The practice of holding an IGC to examine the working practices of the EU and make changes to the Treaties is not a new development. IGC negotiations involve representatives of member states and take place outside of the formal framework of the EU institutions. They have been a regular feature of European integration throughout the last 20 years and have emphasized the extent to which the EU **decision-making** process has reflected intergovernmental rather than supranational design. Because all member states have to be in agreement with the final Treaty for it to become a reality, individual leaders inevitably have to compromise on many of their initial negotiating positions. This process of negotiation has a tendency to produce Treaties that broadly serve the interests of all participants and which crucially permit national leaders to 'sell' the outcome to their electorates. The important point here is that EU leaders are able to stress that the agreement defends the national interest and that 'victory' has therefore been achieved.

Overall, there have been seven IGC negotiations:

- The first IGC negotiation commenced in May 1950 and resulted in the establishment of the **European Coal and Steel Community** (ECSC).

- The second IGC negotiation opened in April 1955 in Messina and led to the setting up of the **European Economic Community** (EEC) and the **European Atomic Energy Community** (Euratom).
- The third IGC negotiation took place in 1955 and led to the **Single European Act** (SEA), setting out a timetable for the completion of the **single market**.
- The fourth and fifth IGCs took place in 1990–91: the parallel negotiations on monetary and political union that culminated in the Maastricht **Treaty on European Union** (TEU).
- The sixth IGC was launched in 1996 and concluded in June 1997 with agreement on a **Treaty of Amsterdam** that sought to reform the institutional design of the EU with a view to future **enlargement**.
- The seventh IGC took place in 2000 and resulted in the **Treaty of Nice** which, like the **Treaty of Amsterdam**, also focused on institutional reform.
- The eighth IGC in 2003–4 produced the **Constitutional Treaty** which consolidated all the previous treaties into one single document to provide the EU with a simpler and more accessible set of rules.

The various IGC negotiations have therefore made a number of significant changes to the EU, including altering the decision-making structure and extending its remit into new policy areas. Such changes have been prompted by a number of factors, including the desire to make the EU more competitive vis-à-vis such countries as the United States and Japan. But at the same time, the expansion of EU membership from six to 25 member states has been a further factor important factor influencing change.

Intergovernmental cooperation

This is cooperation that involves nation states and does not involve supranational actors.

Intergovernmental organizations

These are international institutions that comprise groups of member states.

Intergovernmentalism

This theory of European integration highlights the role played by national governments (member states) in the process of European integration. This approach was influenced by the work of Stanley Hoffman, who gained inspiration from realist approaches to international relations. In essence, this approach stressed three points. First, that integration only takes place as a result of the decisions taken by national governments that are primarily concerned with protecting the 'national interest'. Second, that, while integration might take place in technical policy areas, the process of integration would not extend to areas of high politics such as national defence policy. Third, that integration would not follow the path of spillover as proposed by **neofunctional** accounts. As such, the emphasis attached to the importance of the role played by national governments differed from the neofunctional approach to European integration.

Internal market

The difference between the economic activity within EU member states and external trade, which has particular relevance to allowing the free movement of capital, goods and persons. See **single market**.

Internal security

The **Treaty on European Union** included a provision for **justice and home affairs** (JHA) that was strengthened in the **Treaty of Amsterdam** (which also incorporated the **Schengen agreement** into the EU framework).

Inter-institutional agreements

Agreements made between two or more institutions of the Community.

Inter-institutional conference

A formal conference between the **European Parliament, European Commission** and **Council of Ministers**. The Council tends to be represented by the **Council Presidency**. The conference is a means of allowing the European Parliament's voice to influence **intergovernmental conference** (IGC) negotiations, from which it is excluded.

International organizations

A general view of an international organization is a body that aims to coordinate the interests of its members who participate on a voluntary basis. Such cooperation does, however, tend not to extend to making the international organization autonomous of the members; nor is it the case that international organizations are able to impose decisions on their members. In this sense, the EU is quite distinct from an international organization because it has the ability through its institutions to take decisions that are binding on the member states, while EU law (by virtue of the decisions of the **Court of Justice**) has primacy over national law.

Interpol

An organization which gathers and exchanges information among police forces, also acting as a forum for discussing issues of common interest, such as terrorism and police training. Its foundations rest in the International Criminal Police Commission which was established in Vienna in 1923, but has been known as Interpol since 1956.

Intervention

Represents a part of the **Common Agricultural Policy** (CAP) price support system whereby a product will be purchased and stored for the future if it cannot be sold at an agreed price during the year in question, as demonstrated by the **butter mountain** and **wine lake**. The cost of this process is borne by the **budget**.

Intra-community trade

Trade between EU member states.

Investiture

The action whereby the **European Commission** is provided with the authority to act on behalf of the Community.

Inward investment

The creation of jobs through outside investment in one member state. Funds can come either from a source within another EU member state or from outside.

Ioannina compromise

Refers to the decision taken on **qualified majority voting** (QMV) at an informal foreign ministers meeting in the Greek city of Ioannina on 27 March 1994. The aim of the meeting was to reach an agreement on the level of votes required to pass (or to block) legislation in an enlarged EU of 16 member states because Austria, Finland, Norway and Sweden had applied for membership. However, Norway's decision not to join the EU meant that the compromise that was reached at Ioannina had to be adjusted to reflect an EU of 15 member states. The outcome was a compromise which stipulated that where a vote in the **Council of Ministers** fell between 23 votes (the old blocking minority threshold) and 26 votes (the new threshold) and therefore signified opposition by certain states to a Council decision, then the Council would do everything in its power to reach a satisfactory solution that could be adopted by at least 65 votes out of a total number of 87 votes.

Iraq conflict

On 20 March 2003 a US-led coalition officially commenced military operations to remove the Iraqi regime of Saddam Hussein on the basis of a view that Iraq possessed weapons of mass destruction (WMD). The history behind the conflict can be traced back to the 1990 **Gulf War**, when an international coalition under US leadership (although crucially with United Nations backing), was galvanized by the need for Iraq to withdraw from Kuwait. But, while the conflict had removed Iraqi forces from Kuwait, it had not removed Saddam Hussein from power. Although Iraq agreed to peace terms imposed by the coalition, including a commitment not to develop or possess WMD, in subsequent years Saddam Hussein's regime made every effort not to conform with the peace terms and did not fully cooperate with UN weapons inspectors.

For much of the 1990s Iraq's attempts to work against the terms of the 1991 peace agreement resulted in little decisive action by the international community. This state of affairs dramatically changed after the 11 September 2001 terrorist attacks on the US. Such attacks produced a change in US foreign policy, whereby threats to national security would be eliminated by a policy (or doctrine) of pre-emptive conflict as part of the administration's 'war on terrorism'. This was most notably demonstrated by the removal of the Taliban regime in Afghanistan on the basis that it had provided a safe haven for terrorist groups. US attention thereafter shifted to Iraq, which President George Bush accused in January 2002 of forming an 'axis of evil' along with Iran and North Korea.

By stressing that Iraq had failed to fully comply with the terms of the 1991 ceasefire, the US attempted to widen the war on terrorism to include Iraq. The US specifically accused Iraq of developing and possessing WMD of a biological and chemical nature and not complying with UN weapons inspectors, who had been forced to leave Iraq in 1998 (although weapons inspectors were operating in Iraq again until the eve of the invasion). The key argument behind the use of force (and the removal of Saddam Hussein) was therefore that Iraq had concealed WMD from the weapons inspectors and by doing so had deliberately sought to deceive the international community. In advancing this case, both Britain and the US stressed that the taking of action was justified because of the threat level posed by Iraq.

This Anglo-American position differed from the viewpoint held by many other states in the international community. The latter were of the opinion that the proper course of action was for the weapons inspectors to continue with their work and that if further time was granted then the concerns over Iraq's WMD could be resolved in a peaceful manner. France, Germany and Russia were among the most vociferous advocates that matters should be resolved in a peaceful way. It was therefore notable that there existed significant divisions among European nations and between Europe and the United States over how best to resolve the Iraqi situation.

Having won the war, the key question that has faced coalition forces in post-conflict Iraq is the extent to which they are able to secure the peace. Since the conflict ended, the Iraq that was ruled by the iron fist of Saddam Hussein has witnessed an upsurge in lawlessness as the coalition forces have struggled to maintain peace and stability in the country and rebuild essential services, such as power stations, that were destroyed during the conflict.

Ireland

Population: 3.88m (2005)
Capital: Dublin

In the post-1945 period Ireland was reluctant to get involved in developments relating to European integration, a decision that reflected its neutral status. Moreover, the close linkage between the Irish and British economies meant that Irish foreign policy priorities were greatly shaped by its relationship with the UK. Thus, as Ireland's economy was intrinsically linked to Britain's, it had little choice but to follow Britain's application for membership of the Community. Policy-makers in Dublin were, nevertheless, hopeful that Community membership would in the longer term help Ireland to become less dependent on Britain by developing economic and political links with a wider group of countries. Both countries joined along with Denmark in 1973, after which the Irish economy underwent a period of remarkable growth, especially in the 1980s and 1990s.

Membership immediately proved beneficial to the Irish agricultural community via the **Common Agricultural Policy** (CAP), while it has also benefited from financial support via the **structural funds**. The advent of the **single market** brought with it fresh opportunity for a highly educated English speaking nation which proved attractive to inward investment. In broader terms, Community membership also allowed Ireland to pursue a more independent foreign policy that was not dominated by the UK, while ensuring that Anglo-Irish relations, especially regarding the dispute over Northern Ireland, could be set in a multilateral context. Ireland's economic success meant that it was named in March 1998 by the **European Commission** as one of the 11 member states that met the **convergence criteria** to enable it to join **Economic and Monetary Union** (EMU) from 1 January 1999. Ireland has, as a result, undergone a significant transformation through EU membership and it has also been the case that Ireland has for the most part supported deeper economic and political integration. Moreover, the Irish electorate has been one of the most supportive of European integration among member states, even despite the initial no vote against the **Treaty of Nice** in a June 2001 **referendum** (overturned by a subsequent yes vote).

Italy

Population: 58.02m (2005)
Capital: Rome

Italy's position as a founder member of the Community had an immediate impact on the economic and political aspects of the nation. Access to wider Community markets resulted in a greater focus on competitiveness, from which the northern industrial sector benefited while the more rural southern sector continued to have economic difficulties. Nevertheless, membership proved to be a valuable means of providing Italian politicians and civil servants with contact to member states suffering from less corruption. This helped to create a less corrupt government bureaucracy. In broader terms, Italy has consistently advocated for a stronger **European Commission** and **European Parliament**, although the latter has been motivated by domestic political weakness. Italian membership of the **Exchange Rate Mechanism (ERM)** helped to stabilize the lira throughout the 1980s, although the nation suffered during the 1992–93 European currency crisis. In a similar manner, the drive towards **Economic and Monetary Union** (EMU) provided a further means of injecting some stability into the Italian economy and as a result Italy was one of 11 member states that took part in EMU from 1 January 1999.

J

Jenkins, Roy (1920–2003)

A former UK Labour Party Home Secretary and Chancellor of the Exchequer, he was appointed President of the **European Commission** from 1977 to 1981. A committed European, he previously led a minority section of the Labour Party in supporting UK membership of the

Community in 1971 during a vote within the House of Commons. His time as President of the European Commission was dominated by complaints from the UK about its **budget** contribution, although he was a prime motivator behind greater European integration where he helped to develop the **European Monetary System** (EMS), while he also obtained the right for the Commission President to represent the Community at one of the sessions of the annual Western economic summits – although this was done very much despite the reluctance of France. After his period as President he proved to be a key figure in UK politics, winning the Hillhead by-election and breaking away from the Labour Party to be a founder member of the Social Democratic Party.

Joint actions

The procedure established in the **Treaty on European Union** (TEU) for member states to take action in the area of **common foreign and security policy** (CFSP) and **police and judicial cooperation in criminal matters**. Where a joint action is agreed member states are bound to uphold the agreed position in the actions they take and views they express. While it is the case that joint actions, which commit the member states, are normally adopted by **unanimity**, within the remit of the CFSP it is possible in certain circumstances to adopt joint actions by **qualified majority voting** (QMV). In respect to police and judicial cooperation in criminal matters the **Treaty of Nice** replaced joint actions with framework decisions and ordinary decisions.

Joint Interpreting and Conference Service

A department of the **European Commission** that deals with the translation of written and spoken texts and the organization of conferences.

Joint Parliamentary Committee

Committees established with the parliaments of states that have association agreements with the EU or those states where negotiations for accession have commenced.

Justice and home affairs (JHA)

The Maastricht **Treaty on European Union** (TEU) included provision for cooperation in this new area of policy so as to increase cooperation among member states on matters of **asylum** policy, the crossing of the external borders of member states, **immigration policy**, combating drugs, combating international fraud, judicial cooperation in civil and criminal matters, customs cooperation and police cooperation. Reform took place in the **Treaty of Amsterdam** through the establishment of an **area of freedom, security and justice**, and resulted in a number of aspects of the JHA provisions of the **third pillar** being incorporated in the regular **first pillar** provisions of the EU. This specifically applied to those matters that related to the free movement of people, including matters relating to asylum, immigration and visas. The **Schengen agreement** on the free movement of persons between member states was also incorporated into the first pillar provision of the EU. The effect of these changes was that the third pillar was renamed **police and judicial cooperation in criminal matters**.

Justiciable

It is possible for disputed issues to be submitted for decision to the **Court of Justice** and **Court of First Instance**.

K

Kangaroo group

A group of **Members of the European Parliament** (MEPs) that have traditionally advocated a frontier-free Europe.

Kennedy Round

A series of negotiations on tariff reductions held by the **General Agreement on Tariffs and Trade** (GATT). They commenced in May 1964 and finished on 15 May 1967. Named after President John F. Kennedy of the USA, it was the first time that the **European Commission** had been the sole Community spokesman, producing agreement on reducing the **common external tariff** by an average of 35 per cent.

Kirchberg Declaration

The **Western European Union** (WEU) Council of Ministers declaration of May 1994 gave nine central and eastern European countries the status of 'associate partners', which was distinct from the associate membership of Iceland, Norway and Turkey. The meeting produced a system of variable geometry with there being three different levels of membership, as well as observer status. Members are all WEU members that are also members of both the EU and the **North Atlantic Treaty Organisation** (NATO). Secondly, WEU associate members are members of NATO but not the EU. Thirdly, WEU associate partners are members of neither the EU nor NATO. Finally, WEU observers can be members of NATO and/or the EU. The product of this reform was that the forum of consultation with central and eastern European nations established in 1992 by the **Petersberg Declaration** was abolished.

Kohl, Helmut (b. 1930)

Chancellor of the Federal Republic of Germany from 1982 until October 1998. A graduate of the Universities of Frankfurt and Heidelberg (where he got his DPhil in 1958), he became a member of the Rhineland Palatinate Parliament in 1959. He continued in that position until 1976, during which time he was leader of the Christian Democrat Union Party (CDU) of the Rhineland Palatinate Parliament from 1963 to 1979 and Chairman from 1966 to 1974. Between 1969 and 1976 he was Minister-President of the Rhineland Palatinate Parliament and from 1976 to 1982 he was leader of the opposition in the Bundestag. He was leader of the national CDU Party from 1973 to 1998, and his strength within the Party was demonstrated in the 1988 election campaign when the CDU campaigned solely on Kohl's personality. His election as Chancellor of the reunified Germany in 1990 proved to be one of the most significant aspects of his period of office. **German reunification** was also of significance in terms of the attitudes of other member states; the UK under **Margaret Thatcher** appeared to resist, while France under **François Mitterrand** was unequivocal in support, and the prime minister of the Netherlands, Ruud Lubbers, provided a lukewarm response. The attitude of Lubbers could be said to have influenced Kohl's decision to **veto** his nomination to succeed **Jacques Delors** as President of the **European Commission**. However, with reunification established, Kohl sought further European political integration, partly as a means of tying Germany into the EC, while at the same time France sought monetary integration as a means of countering the strength of the Deutschmark. A bargain was therefore struck between the two leaders over these issues which essentially formed the agenda for the 1990–91 **intergovernmental conference** (IGC) negotiations that eventually produced the **Treaty on European Union** (TEU). In the wake of the implementation of the Treaty, Kohl played an important role in pressing the EU towards **Economic and Monetary Union** (EMU) and the **enlargement** of the EU. In the 1998 German elections **Gerhard Schröder** defeated him, and thereafter the potential for him to play the role of an elder statesman in German politics was hampered by a political scandal relating to financial irregularities during his period as leader of the Christian Democrat party which therefore tarnished his reputation.

Kyoto Protocol

This Protocol to the United Nations Framework Convention on Climate Change was adopted by the EU in December 1997 and subsequently ratified by the EU on 31 May 2002. The Protocol calls for industrialized countries to reduce greenhouse gas emissions over the period 2008–12 by 5 per cent in comparison with 1990 levels. The six greenhouse gases are carbon dioxide, methane, nitrous oxide, hydrofluorocarbons, perfluorocarbons and sulphur dioxide. By 2000 emission rates for these gases was 3.5 per cent lower than 1990 levels.

L

Laeken Declaration

At the Laeken **European Council** of 15 December 2001, member states adopted a Declaration on the Future of the European Union. Commonly known as the Laeken Declaration, it called for the EU to be more democratic, effective and transparent. With this in mind, a **Convention on the Future of Europe** was convened under the chairmanship of former French president **Valéry Giscard d'Estaing** to examine key questions about the future of the EU. The Convention met between March 2002 and June 2003 and set out its recommendations in the form of a draft **Constitutional Treaty** that was presented to the Thessaloniki European Council of June 2003. The proposals that were set out in the draft both replaced and made changes to the existing Treaties. The proposals in turn formed the basis for the 2003–4 **intergovernmental conference** (IGC) negotiations on the EU Constitutional Treaty.

Latvia

Population: 2.37m (2005)
Capital: Riga
After a brief period of independence between the two World Wars, Latvia was annexed by the USSR in 1940. It re-established its independence from the Soviet Union in August 1991 following the breakup of the Soviet Union. Although the last Russian troops left in 1994, the status of the Russian minority (some 30 per cent of the population) has been a concern of Moscow. In 1994 Latvia concluded a **free trade agreement** with the EU and in 1995 signed a **Europe Agreement** which led to the formal submission of an application for EU membership on 27 October 1995. Although the EU offered a supportive opinion (**avis**) on Latvia's application in 1997, it nevertheless did not recommend the start of **accession** negotiations because it considered that not enough progress had been made in reforming the Latvian economy. In the end,

the December 1999 Helsinki **European Council** recommended that Latvia be invited to negotiate terms for EU membership. It joined the EU in May 2004.

League of Nations

Created in 1920 by the Treaty of Versailles, the League of Nations was an international organization that aimed to promote peace and security throughout the world. A central tenet of the League was that the members should preserve the territorial integrity and political independence of each state against armed aggression. Although the League of Nations comprised 45 members in 1920, the failure of the United States to ratify the Treaty of Versailles meant that it stood detached. Its membership subsequently expanded to include additional countries such as Germany and the Soviet Union. Nevertheless, the League of Nations proved unable to adequately tackle the aggressive behaviour that was evidenced on the part of such states as Japan, Germany and Italy in the period after the First World War. It was moreover incapable of preventing the Second World War. In the end, the League of Nations was disbanded in 1946 to be replaced by the United Nations.

Legal personality

The situation that allows a body to take actions in international law on an autonomous basis instead of having to allow governments to act on its behalf. In this context, the legal status of the EU is pertinent because it does not have the international legal right to conclude agreements with third countries, otherwise referred to as Treaty-making powers.

Legal service

A department of the **European Commission** providing advice on legal matters, assisting the drafting legislative proposals and initiating legal proceedings in the **Court of Justice**. In addition, it checks whether affairs and actions of the EU countries are in accordance with, authorized, or required by the law or EU Treaties.

Legislation

The EU has a rather complex process for enacting legislation. The **Council of Ministers** and the **European Parliament** or the **European Commission** are able to issue three different types of legislation: **decisions**, **directives** and **regulations**. A fourth source of legislation is the rulings that are made by the **Court of Justice**.

Legitimacy

In recent years the legitimacy of the EU has been challenged by a number of developments which have centred on a criticism of the direction of European integration. This was evidenced by the difficulties that surrounded the ratification of the **Treaty on European Union** (TEU), **Treaty of Nice** and most recently the **Constitutional Treaty**. One of the most commonplace concerns has been that the domestic electorate in member states feel increasingly isolated from the decisions that are taken about the nature of European integration and there has therefore been a lack of identification with the EU. A second area of concern has been the intrusion of the EU's competence into areas of policy that have traditionally rested with the member states' governments.

Leonardo

The Community programme for vocational training which replaced various programmes, including COMETT (cooperation on training and further training between universities and industry) and PETRA (initial vocational training).

Liberal intergovernmentalism

This theoretical account places emphasis on the manner in which the EU has been transformed by a series of intergovernmental bargains. Based on the work of Andrew Moravcsik, this theory offered a more developed approach to European integration than **intergovernmentalism**. In this sense, liberal intergovernmentalism stressed three points. First, that the key developments in European integration reflected the choices of national governments and not the views of supranational institutions. Second, that the choices favoured by national governments emphasized economic interests rather than the security concerns of a nation or the preferences of individual politicians. Third, that the final outcome of the negotiations highlighted the bargaining strength of individual nation states to achieve a satisfactory agreement. But, while Moravcsik has applied these conclusions to a study of key episodes in the history of European integration (particularly **intergovernmental conference** (IGC) negotiations), liberal intergovernmentalism has been criticized for focusing too much attention on 'history-making' decisions and neglecting the importance of day-to-day decisions in the process of European integration.

Liberalization

The process of removing restrictions placed by member states on the free movement across frontiers of goods, capital, payments and services. Apart from the EU, other organizations which are dedicated to this process include the **General Agreement on Tariffs and Trade** (GATT) and the **Organisation for Economic Co-operation and Development** (OECD).

Liberalization of financial services

This is a key aspect of **monetary policy** which had previously been hampered by exchange controls regulating capital imports and exports, while the existence of different regulatory frameworks within member states proved to be a barrier to the provision of services such as banking and insurance across national borders. This was an issue which particularly concerned the UK and proved to be a significant motivation behind it supporting the **single market**, the consequence of which has been three broad strategies pursued by the EU in liberalizing financial services:

1 removing exchange controls;
2 harmonization of essential regulations and the acceptance of mutual recognition of other national regulations. Banks are therefore able to operate across national borders, while scrutiny of their activities rests with authorities in the home country;
3 harmonization of tax rates.

However, while there has been a deregulation of financial services and the removal of exchange controls, little progress has been achieved in the field of harmonizing tax rates. One reason why the **European Commission**'s efforts have been diminished in this area is because tax rates are central to the national interest.

Lingua

Established in 1990 as a means of improving and promoting the teaching of foreign languages within the EU. It was merged in 1995 into the **Socrates** and **Leonardo** programmes.

Linkage

The process where agreement on one particular issue is dependent on obtaining a satisfactory outcome on another. There is greater room for negotiation of this sort when decisions are taken purely by **unanimity** and states are therefore provided with a **veto**.

Lisbon strategy

In March 2000, EU member states committed themselves at a meeting in Lisbon to become 'the most competitive and dynamic knowledge-based economy in the world, capable of sustainable growth with more and better jobs and greater social cohesion'. To achieve this goal, member states agreed on a 'Lisbon strategy' that includes the reform of national social protection systems with a view to making them sustainable for the future.

Lithuania

Population: 3.69m (2005)
Capital: Vilnius
Lithuania was annexed by the Soviet Union in 1940 and remained under Soviet control for the next 50 years. After the end of the **Cold War** and the collapse of the Soviet system of satellite states, Lithuania formally became independent in 1991. This was followed by the signature of a free trade agreement with the EU in 1994 and a **Europe Agreement** in 1995. But, although a formal application for EU membership was submitted in December 1995, the **European Commission**'s opinion (**avis**) on its application expressed concern about Lithuania's economic readiness to become an EU member state. As a result, it was not included in the first wave of countries from central and eastern Europe that were invited to open accession negotiations in 1998. Nevertheless, one year later at the December 1999 Helsinki **European Council** Lithuania was formally invited to commence negotiations for EU membership which resulted in it joining the EU in May 2004 at the time of the historic **enlargement** which increased the EU member states from 15 to 25.

Lobbying

There has been a vast expansion in the lobbying of both the institutions of the Community and national-based permanent representations. This can be by private enterprises, trade unions and regional bodies such as the German Länder.

Lomé Convention

The Preamble to the **Treaties of Rome** contained an obligation for **European Economic Community** (EEC) member states to create links with their former colonies. As a result the EEC concluded the **Yaoundé Convention** in 1963 with 18 former colonies, thereby granting them privileged rights to export products to the EEC. With the expansion of the Community in 1973 to include the UK there was a need to ensure that a new arrangement covered former British colonies. This in turn resulted in the first Lomé Convention of 1975 (Lomé I), which provided for free trade between 44 former colonies and the EEC. Over a period of years the Convention has been renewed with Lomé II in 1980, Lomé III in 1985 and Lomé IV in 1990. In 2000 a further agreement was signed and resulted in Lomé V which is otherwise known as the **Cotonou Agreement**. Today there are over 70 countries covered by these agreements that embrace the **African, Caribbean and Pacific** (ACP) states, covering multilateral trade and development agreements between them and the EU. The nations are provided with associate status to the EU, including financial assistance and trading advantages, while Lomé IV also embraced agreements for the protection of human rights and democratic development and Lomé V has the aim of creating a **free trade area** by 2020.

Louvre Accord

An agreement on 22 February 1987 among the Group of Seven countries to stabilize the US dollar.

Luxembourg

Population: 0.45m (2005)
Capital: Luxembourg
A founder member and the smallest nation in the Community, Luxembourg has advocated greater European integration. Its own international profile has been increased through membership, while the location of numerous Community institutions within Luxembourg has resulted in nearly one-quarter of its working population being employed in Community work. But, while it has campaigned for the extension of **qualified majority voting** (QMV) in the **Council of Ministers** and a stronger **European Parliament**, it has been a pragmatic member state when it has occupied the position of **Council Presidency**. It successfully chaired the 1985 **intergovernmental conference** (IGC) which produced the **Single European Act** (SEA) and imparted a realistic negotiating position during its chairing of the first six months of the 1991 IGC which resulted in the **Treaty on European Union** (TEU). A pragmatic position during the latter contrasted with the position of the Netherlands, who advocated a maximalist position. Luxembourg was one of the 11 member states considered by the **European Commission** in March 1998 to have met the **convergence criteria** requirements for the adoption of the **single currency** and therefore participated in **Economic and Monetary Union** (EMU) from 1 January 1999. But, while its status as a pro-EU nation was further reflected in Luxembourg's electorate supporting the EU constitution in a July 2005 **referendum** by 56.5 per cent to 43.5 per cent, the fact that there was a significant

'no' vote was partly influenced by a concern that the EU constitution would not be good for smaller countries as they would lose some voting privileges.

Luxembourg compromise

An informal agreement established by **the Six** at an extraordinary session of the Council in Luxembourg on 28–29 January 1966. The agreement stressed that, where 'very important interests of one or more partners' were at stake, the member states would try to reach unanimous solutions. The compromise resolved the stalemate of the **empty chair crisis** that had engulfed the Community from July to December 1965 as a result of the decision of French president **Charles de Gaulle** to prohibit his government ministers from attending meetings of the **Council of Ministers**. Although the Luxembourg compromise served the interests of member states, it is nevertheless widely accepted that it limited the opportunity for further European integration over the next two decades. In this sense, as a result of the crisis, the Community's future development assumed the structure that it would maintain for the next 20 years. Indeed, it would not be until the 1987 **Single European Act** (SEA) that the Community would engage in a process of reform that significantly went beyond the Luxembourg compromise.

M

Maastricht Treaty

Term that is generally used to describe the **Treaty on European Union** (TEU) because the Treaty was concluded in the Dutch town of Maastricht in December 1991.

MacDougal Report

The 1972 decision to establish **Economic and Monetary Union** (EMU) by 1980 led to the publication of a report authored by Sir Donald MacDougal which examined the role of public finance if EMU was to be created. Published in 1977, it suggested that it would be necessary for public expenditure at the Community level to play a significant role in the redistribution of wealth if EMU was to have any chance of succeeding. However, because aspirations for EMU did not materialize in the 1970s, the report was not adopted.

Macmillan, Harold (1894–1986)

UK Conservative prime minister from 1957 to 1963, having succeeded **Anthony Eden** after the **Suez crisis**. In July 1961 he stressed that the

UK would seek membership of the **European Economic Community** (EEC). Although unsuccessful, the UK's position had altered primarily because of the change in its own economic circumstances, with the **European Free Trade Association** (EFTA) not proving to be a vigorous market. Yet membership was also perceived by Macmillan as a means of maintaining and strengthening the nation's influence in world affairs and negotiations were therefore conducted for practical reasons. That was not lost on the French president, **Charles de Gaulle**, who took the UK's obtaining the Polaris nuclear missile from the USA in December 1962 as a demonstration that London would only be acting as a Trojan horse for Washington. In that context, as well as from a desire to maintain French dominance within the Community, de Gaulle chose to **veto** the UK's application in January 1963.

Macsharry, Ray (b. 1938)

As Irish member of the **European Commission** with responsibility for Agriculture and Rural Development from 1989 to 1992, Ray Macsharry oversaw a significant reform of the **Common Agricultural Policy** (CAP), which had become a huge drain on the **budget** of the Community. The need to reform was influenced both by a desire to reduce the CAP's share of the EC budget and by external pressures in the form of the pressure from the **General Agreement on Tariffs and Trade** (GATT) to reduce the protection provided to the EC agricultural sector as part of a process of liberalizing world trade.

Major, John (b. 1943)

Having beaten Douglas Hurd and Michael Heseltine in the November 1990 UK Conservative Party leadership election, he succeeded **Margaret Thatcher** as prime minister on 28 November. On appointment, he was the youngest prime minister in the twentieth century and the first Conservative to become prime minister by winning a leadership election. He was previously Secretary of State for Foreign and Commonwealth Affairs (July–October 1989) and Chancellor of the Exchequer (October 1989–November 1990). Few expected that he would become prime minister, as which he continued to serve until the Conservative Party was defeated in the general election of May 1997. He was succeeded as prime minister by **Tony Blair**. Although as prime minister he initially attempted to chart a more constructive position within the EC, and managed to secure a satisfactory agreement in the **Treaty on European Union** (TEU), his position was weakened by a **Eurosceptic** Conservative Party. This was particularly evident after the 1992 general election, which the Conservatives won with a reduced majority. From 1992 to 1997 the UK's standing within the EU worsened, culminating in the debate over the reweighting of **qualified majority voting**

(QMV) in 1994, the 1995 **beef crisis** and the subsequent policy of non-cooperation. By the end of his tenure, his government was officially a minority one, isolated within the EU and pandering to Eurosceptic interests at home.

Majority voting

While some decisions of the **Council of Ministers** are taken by **unanimity**, others are taken by either simple or **qualified majority voting** (QMV). Majority voting was extended by the **Single European Act** (SEA) to cover **single market** procedures, with a further widening of policy competences taking place under the **Treaty on European Union** (TEU).

Malfatti, Franco (b. 1927)

A former Italian politician and government minister, he replaced Jean Rey as President of the **European Commission** in July 1970. His period in office was undistinguished, primarily because the Commission remained weakened in the aftermath of the empty chair crisis of 1965–66. His own tenure as President was relatively short, as he resigned two years early in March 1972 to enable him to pursue a career in Italian politics.

Malta

Population: 0.39m (2005)
Capital: Valletta
A member of the Commonwealth, Malta obtained its independence from the UK in 1964. It thereafter proceeded to join the **Council of Europe** in 1965 and on 5 December 1970 concluded an **Association Agreement** with the Community. But little emerged out of this relationship with the Community (primarily as a result of domestic politics in Malta) and as a result Malta submitted its application for Community membership only on 16 July 1990. Although this was met by a favourable opinion (**avis**) from the **European Commission** in June 1993, Malta froze its application in 1996 after the Maltese Labour Party won the election. Indeed, it was not until the re-election of the Nationalist Party in September 1998 that Malta's application was reactivated and in February 1999 the European Commission produced a further opinion that was broadly in favour of Malta joining the EU. As a result Malta became a formal EU member state in May 2004 when it was part of the historic **enlargement** that increased the EU's membership from 15 to 25 member states.

Mansholt, Sicco (1908–95)

During his lengthy tenure as a member of the **European Commission** from January 1958 until January 1973, Mansholt played a part in a number of key developments, from the creation of the Community to the establishment of a **customs union** in 1968. During that time, the Community also enlarged to nine member states and overcame the difficulty of the 1965–66 **empty chair crisis**. Towards the end of his period in office, Mansholt occupied the post of President from March 1972 until January 1973 as a result of the resignation of Franco Malfatti. Mansholt made a significant contribution to European integration through implementing the **Common Agricultural Policy** (CAP) and proposing the **Mansholt Plan**.

Mansholt Plan

Sicco Mansholt, a member of the **European Commission** with responsibility for agriculture, proposed on 18 December 1968 to significantly reform the **Common Agricultural Policy** (CAP). Central to the plan was an attempt to reduce agricultural surpluses and create a new policy on production structures that would replace the system of price supports. The overall intention was to increase the economic viability of the European agricultural sector. In order to do this Mansholt argued in favour of:

- encouraging small farmers to leave the land;
- the creation of large units of agricultural production;
- cutting price levels to force inefficient farmers off the land;
- the setting aside of land so as to avoid overproduction;
- culling cows over eight years of age to avoid milk surpluses;
- providing financial incentives that would include grants, pensions to farmers over 55 and the provision of assistance to help young farmers find new jobs.

Regardless of the need to make some changes to the agricultural sector, the plan received a hostile reception among the farming community, particularly in France and Germany. Mansholt submitted a revised version of his plan in 1969 which was then subjected to further amendments. In the end, the **Council of Ministers** agreed to a small number of modernization measures, including the provision of training to farmers and the closure of the smallest farms. While Mansholt considered that this agreement at least signified the beginning of a process of modernization, the failure to obtain support for his initial proposals was a significant setback for him. Moreover, the anticipated programme of reform that Mansholt had expected to emerge out of his proposals never materialized, not least because of the economic difficulties of the

1970s which meant that member state governments did not want to increase unemployment rates by forcing people off the land.

Marjolin, Robert (1911–86)

A senior member and Vice-President of the **European Commission** led by **Walter Hallstein**, Marjolin was a pragmatic individual committed to the process of European integration. A French national, he worked closely with **Jean Monnet** on the French Nationalization Plan in the post-war period and was subsequently appointed Secretary-General of the **Organisation for European Economic Co-operation** (OEEC) until 1955. During his period as a European Commissioner he advocated a more restrained approach to integration and suggested that the Commission should not attempt to press for extra powers, advice which was not accepted and ultimately provoked the 1965 **empty chair crisis**. Later in life, at the suggestion of the French president **Valéry Giscard d'Estaing**, Marjolin proved to be an influential figure by assisting in the preparation of a report on Community reform as one of the **'Three Wise Men'**. The report, which was published in 1980, put forward a number of suggestions to improve decision-making within the Community, but crucially failed to make the argument for the stronger **European Council** that Giscard had wanted.

Marshall Plan

In June 1947 the US Secretary of State George Marshall proposed a plan that would aid the rebuilding of European economies in the wake of the Second World War. Known as the European Recovery Programme, the plan offered financial aid as well as other forms of assistance to the war-ravaged countries of western Europe. Between 1948 and 1951 the plan distributed just over $12,500m in aid. The plan stressed that 'Europe's requirements for the next three or four years of foreign food and other essential products – principally from America – are so much greater than her present ability to pay that she must have substantial additional help or face economic, social, and political deterioration of a very grave character'. In proposing the plan, the US was concerned that the difficult economic conditions in western Europe could lead to support for communist parties and stall attempts to recover world trade, which would in turn impact on the US economy. Although the plan was open to the Soviet Union, it was nevertheless rejected by them. As a result the plan further signified the division between east and west Europe when the 16 countries of western Europe began to benefit from it. To administer the plan, the **Organisation for European Economic Co-operation** (OEEC) was created, which in due course was transformed into the **Organisation for Economic Co-operation and Development** (OECD). The Marshall Plan played an important role in helping to foster the economic and political recovery of Europe, and was of considerable importance in promoting the concept of European integration as well as liberalizing intra-European trade.

MED-Campus

This programme aims to further develop the human resources of Mediterranean countries by encouraging cooperation between universities in the EU and these countries through teacher training, continuing education, training courses and temporary secondment, applied research and the purchase of small items of equipment for training projects.

MED-Invest

A EU decentralized cooperation project aimed at providing joint funding for Mediterranean countries through financing business contacts and implementing pilot projects to support small businesses.

MED-URBS

Aimed at the developing cooperation between EU local authorities and Mediterranean countries so as to encourage the transfer of skills and knowledge through the establishment or consolidation of trans-Mediterranean cooperation networks and the fostering of lasting cooperation ties between network partners. Projects have to involve at least two local authorities from different member states and at least two local authorities from a Mediterranean country.

Member of the European Parliament (MEP)

An MEP is directly elected form member states, with the total number from each nation related to the size of population. The first democratic election took place in 1979, with **European elections** held every five years. They do not sit in national delegations within the **European Parliament**, but rather take part in transnational political groupings.

Member state

A term used to denote the countries that are members of the EU. Since 1 May 2004 there have been 25 EU member states: Austria, Belgium, the Czech Republic, Cyprus, Denmark, Estonia, Finland, France, Germany, Greece, Hungary, Ireland, Italy, Latvia, Lithuania, Luxembourg, Malta, the Netherlands, Poland, Portugal, Slovakia, Slovenia, Spain, Sweden and the United Kingdom.

Table 4.13 Member states and the EU

Member state	Accession to ECSC/EC/EU	Population (million)	Votes in Council	Number of MEPs
Austria	1995	8.14	10	18
Belgium	1952	10.31	12	24
Cyprus	2004	0.27	4	6
Czech Republic	2004	10.27	12	24
Denmark	1973	5.37	7	14
Estonia	2004	1.37	4	6
Finland	1995	5.20	7	14
France	1952	59.34	29	78
Germany	1952	82.43	29	99
Greece	1981	10.6	12	24
Hungary	2004	10.01	12	24
Ireland	1973	3.88	7	13
Italy	1952	58.02	29	78
Latvia	2004	2.37	4	9
Lithuania	2004	3.69	7	13
Luxembourg	1952	0.45	4	6
Malta	2004	0.39	3	5
Netherlands	1952	16.10	13	27
Poland	2004	38.64	27	54
Portugal	1986	10.34	12	24
Slovakia	2004	5.40	7	14
Slovenia	2004	1.99	4	7
Spain	1986	40.41	27	54
Sweden	1995	8.91	10	19
United Kingdom	1973	60.11	29	78

Merger Treaty

Signed in Brussels on 8 April 1965, the Merger Treaty established a single institutional structure for the three Communities: the **European Atomic Energy Community** (Euratom), the **European Coal and Steel Community** (ECSC) and the **European Economic Community** (EEC). The Treaty came into force on 1 July 1967 and established a common **Council of Ministers** and a Commission that served all three Communities.

Merkel, Angela (b. 1954)

On 22 November 2005 Angela Merkel became the first female Chancellor of Germany. As leader of the Christian Democratic Union (CDU), Merkel had been unable to obtain an outright victory in the September 2005 election and the intervening period was dominated by negotiations with the Social Democratic Party (SDP) who ruled before under the leadership of **Gerhard Schröder**. The outcome of these discussions was for Merkel to lead a CDU/SPD coalition. Merkel, who has been chairwoman of the CDU since 2000, is not only the first female Chancellor of Germany, but also the first former citizen of the German Democratic Republic (East Germany) to lead the reunified Germany. A physicist by training, Merkel was a leading figure in the CDU when it was in opposition after the 1998 general election and became the leader of the opposition in 2000. Her election as Chancellor was on the back of a reform agenda with regard to the German economic and social system, with her having a more free-market position. It is a position that was influenced by Germany having experienced feeble economic growth during the late 1990s and the early years of the twenty-first century, with it having an unemployment rate of 11 per cent in 2005. Outwith the domestic reform agenda, Merkel has advocated a stronger partnership with the United States, having offered support for the US-led **Iraq conflict** on the basis of it being unavoidable, and as such offers a contrasting viewpoint to that of her predecessor, Gerhard Schröder, who opposed the Iraq war.

Messina conference

At a conference attended by the foreign ministers of the six nations of the **European Coal and Steel Community** (ECSC) in Messina on 1–2 June 1955 the participating parties agreed to a declaration which set out to further advance the cause of European integration. The declaration specifically noted that 'the Governments of the Federal Republic of Germany, Belgium, France, Italy, Luxembourg and the Netherlands believe the time has come to make a fresh advance towards the building of Europe. They are of the opinion that this must be achieved, first of all, in the economic field. They consider that it is necessary to work for the establishment of a united Europe by the development of common institutions, the progressive fusion of national economies, the creation of a common market and the progressive harmonization of their social policies.' To take these matters forward the foreign ministers also agreed at Messina to establish an intergovernmental committee under the chairmanship of the Belgian foreign minister, **Paul-Henri Spaak**. The ensuing **Spaak Report** provided the basis for the two Treaties establishing the **European Economic Community** (EEC) and the **European Atomic Energy Community** (Euratom).

Mitterrand, François (1916–96)

As president of France between 1981 and 1995 (succeeded by **Jacques Chirac**), he was an active campaigner for closer European integration, while continuing to maintain France's national interest. He played a key role in the resolution of the **British budget problem** at the June 1984 Fontainebleau **European Council**, and he would later be a prime instigator behind moves to develop a European **single currency**. In that context, he provided much of the motivation behind the convening of an **intergovernmental conference** (IGC) on **Economic and Monetary Union** (EMU) which took place in 1991, while a joint letter from him and Chancellor **Helmut Kohl** in April 1990 provided the impetus behind the convening of a second IGC on political union. During these negotiations, he obtained the crucial French objective that EMU would commence by 1999. However, the ratification of the **Treaty on European Union** (TEU)proved more problematic for him, when he decided to hold a **referendum** on its acceptance in September 1992 as a means of demonstrating support for the treaty in the wake of the Danish no vote in May 1992. But that gesture nearly proved fatal, with the referendum only being approved by 50.4 per cent to 49.6 per cent. Domestically, his period as president was marked by the initial failure of his experiment with socialism from 1981 to 1983, with the government thereafter adopting a capitalist economic strategy. Mitterrand was faced with right-wing prime ministers in 1986–88 (Jacques Chirac) and 1993–95 (Edouard Balladur) because of their victory in elections to the National Assembly. This accordingly reduced his influence over the wider scope of government affairs, although he continued to maintain control of foreign and defence policy.

Monetary Committee

The **Treaty of Rome** established a Monetary Committee with the purpose of providing advice on matters of economic and financial affairs to the **Council of Ministers.** However, at the start of the third stage of **Economic and Monetary Union** (EMU) in January 1999 the Monetary Committee was replaced by a new **Economic and Financial Committee.** In the intervening period, the Monetary Committee (which had been composed of two high-level officials from each national finance ministry and central bank, and two officials from the **European Commission**) had been consulted on all major financial issues by the Council of Ministers. The Committee also played an important role in the operation of the **Exchange Rate Mechanism** (ERM), helping to determine exchange rate parities after currency realignments, including agreeing to the temporary suspension of the Italian lira from the ERM in September 1992. The work of the Monetary Committee also included monitoring the progress that each member state made towards the **convergence criteria** required for stage 2 of EMU. Moreover, the committee was heavily involved in the EMU negotiations during the 1990–91 **intergovernmental conference** (IGC) which resulted in the **Treaty on European Union** (TEU). Indeed, during that negotiation it was evident that a sub-group of alternates of the monetary committee (comprising more junior officials) was heavily involved in technical aspects, notably what became the monetary and economic chapters of the Treaty, especially the **convergence criteria** and **excessive deficit procedure**, with the full Monetary Committee generally endorsing its work.

Monetary Compensatory Amounts (MCAs)

Introduced into the **Common Agricultural Policy** (CAP) as a means of temporarily easing the difficulties encountered by the decision to retain common agricultural prices at their original level of exchange.

Monetary policy

This is concerned with the supply, value and cost of money in the economy. Within the **eurozone** monetary policy is conducted by the **European System of Central Banks** (comprising the **European Central Bank** and national central banks). The main means by which monetary policy can be used to achieve an objective of price stability (low **inflation**) is through changes to short-term **interest rates**.

Monetary union

In contrast to an **economic union**, a monetary union is a situation where there is either a **single currency** or locked exchange rates, though a single currency is the preferable option to achieve the credibility of the monetary union. It is also important that the monetary union is centrally managed so as to achieve common macroeconomic objectives. For a monetary union to be completely effective it is necessary for financial markets to be integrated, for capital transactions to be liberalized and for there to be flexible labour markets. A monetary union has certain benefits over an economic union. These include the elimination of exchange rate fluctuations between the countries participating in the system, thereby reducing the risks for trade within the European Union. In a similar vein, the existence of a single currency creates benefits by means of reducing transaction costs that would otherwise be incurred through changing one currency for another. Both of these cases are advantageous to investment and trade. A monetary union does, however, involve certain costs, of which a loss of national **sovereignty** over an area of economic policy is often cited as one of the most important. Because each member of a monetary union is subjected to the same monetary policy, it is possible that some policies will not suit each member of the monetary union. Nevertheless, it is also true that the national economic policies of those countries that are not part of a monetary union often result in policy decisions that are more detrimental to some areas of the economy.

Monnet, Jean (1888–1979)

Commonly regarded as a **founding father** of Europe, Monnet was a key figure in the European integration process after 1945, being appointed head of the French Planning Commission that was responsible for the Modernization Plan. His analysis suggested that it was impossible for any European nation to independently plan for economic growth and prosperity and he considered that the loose intergovernmental structure of the **Organisation for European Economic Co-operation** (OEEC) lacked the necessary supranational structures to bring long-term changes to the economic and political situation in western Europe. It was a view shared by **Robert Schuman** (French foreign minister from 1948 to 1953). Monnet argued that integration in one sector could **spill over** into another. He was instrumental behind the **Schuman Plan** of 9 May 1950 which advocated the creation of an organization which would take responsibility for Franco-German coal and steel production (and which would be open for other countries to join). This resulted in the establishment of the **European Coal and Steel Community** (ECSC).

Monnet was appointed the first President of the **High Authority** of the ECSC when it began operating on 10 August 1952. He additionally provided impetus behind the **Pléven Plan** that led to the **European Defence Community** (EDC), although the latter's collapse raised concerns about the future of European integration and proved to be influential in his decision to resign from the High Authority on 10

June 1955. By then Monnet had already proposed in April 1955 with **Paul-Henri Spaak** that a new Community for civilian nuclear power should be established. This belief, in conjunction with a proposal by the Dutch foreign minister, Johan Willem Beyen, for a common market (**Beyen Plan**), accordingly formed the basis of the **Treaties of Rome** which established the **European Economic Community** (EEC) and the **European Atomic Energy Community** (Euratom). After his departure from the High Authority, Monnet decided to establish the **Action Committee for a United States of Europe** (ACUSE) in October 1955 as a means of bringing together the leaders of political parties and labour unions to campaign, until it was dissolved in 1975, for closer European integration.

Multilevel governance

This is a theory that has been developed to analyse the nature of European integration. The theory of multilevel governance emerged as a result of research on EU structural policy and it sought to categorize the different levels of governance within the EU – supranational, national, regional and local. In many senses the theory harked bark to **neofunctionalist** approaches to European integration, as it stressed that the process of European integration was not in the control of individual governments. As such, the theory also offered a critique of **realism** (which stressed the centrality of government action). Scholars of multilevel governance have pointed to the constraints that are imposed on individual governments as a result of collective **decision-making** within the EU (such as the nature of **qualified majority voting** (QMV) which ensures that any government can be outvoted). As the theory attaches emphasis to the role of subnational and supranational governments in EU decision-making, it consequently points to declining role for national governments. In this sense, it is argued that policies, such as **regional policy**, are the product of bargaining between actors at all levels.

Multi-speed Europe

Recent changes to the European Union include an expansion in membership and a deepening of the policy areas covered by the EU. Such changes have resulted in some member states advocating a faster pace of reform. However, other countries have traditionally been reluctant to support such rapid changes, and instead they have tended to want to reduce the pace of integration. As a response to these tensions, the idea of a multi-speed Europe has been suggested, with this being a method of **differentiated integration** where common objectives are pursued by a group of states, with the intention that the other states will achieve the same goal at a later date.

Mutual recognition

The process whereby member states are obliged to recognize each other's rules of qualifications as the same if they fulfil a similar purpose. This was the principle used by the **Court of Justice** in the 1979 **Cassis de Dijon** case. As the volume of Community legislation has grown, increasing importance has been attached to the principle of mutual recognition.

N

National parliaments

They play an important role in the process of European integration by, among other factors, passing legislation so as to implement **directives**, and members of the **European Parliament** were selected from national parliamentarians before the introduction of direct elections in 1979. National parliaments are additionally involved in the **ratification** of treaties, such as the **Treaty of Nice**. An involvement in these and other aspects of European integration means that national parliaments play an important role in helping to scrutinize the EU and it is with this in mind that specialized committees have been created in national parliaments to specifically examine EU issues. There has, nevertheless, been some concern that many EU policies are decided by governments with little involvement from national parliaments, this being one aspect of the **democratic deficit**. Moreover, as more and more policies are dealt with at a EU level, there has been growing concern about the extent to which the influence of national parliaments has declined.

Negative integration

This is method of European integration that involves the removal of obstacles between member states for the free movement of goods. Examples include the removal of tariff barriers, such as **quotas**, and non-tariff barriers, such as distinct technical standards.

Neofunctionalism

This theory of European integration moved forward the **functionalism** approach that had derived from the work of David Mitrany. A considerable amount of the research on neofunctionalism took place during the emerging stages of European integration in the 1950s and 1960s, of which the leading exponents of the theory were the American academics Ernst Haas, Leon Lindberg and Philippe Schmitter. Neofunctionalists stressed that the integration process involved bargaining and compromise and argued that cooperation in the less contentious areas of low politics could lead to cooperation in the more politically sensitive areas of high politics. In this sense, neofunctionalists advanced the concept of **spillover** of integration from one sector to another. In other words, economic or functional spillover takes place when there emerges a pressure for integration in those areas where the absence of integration undermines the effectiveness of the policy.

Apart from the fact that the neofunctional approach was a more detailed method of integration than the functional approach, and that it was specifically designed for the experiences of the European Community rather than being a grand theory, the main distinction between neofunctionalism and functionalism were that in the neofunctional approach the role of politics and governments were accounted for. The decline in the pace of European integration in the mid-1960s somewhat undermined the neofunctional approach as it could not explain the 1966 **Luxembourg compromise** which provided member states with the ability to veto initiatives that impinged on their national interest. Nevertheless, the approach once again found favour in the 1980s at a time of the relaunch of European integration. In this sense, it is possible to argue that the desire to create **Economic and Monetary Union** (EMU) was directly the result of the spillover pressure from the **single market** programme. Thus, it could be argued that the single market was hampered by the presence of competing national currencies and currency conversion costs and therefore the single market would only be complete when the EU had a **single currency**.

Neorealism

This is a further development of the realist account of international relations (**realism**). Both realists and neorealists conceptualize the state as a cohesive actor pursuing a set of policies that reflect the national interest. Whereas the realist account emphasizes the dominance of the state system because of the anarchic nature of international relations, the neorealist account stresses that the state system is maintained because of structural factors rather than the specific character of states.

Net contributor

Refers to the differences between what a country pays into the **budget** of the EU and what it gets back. Countries which tend to benefit the most are those that are major farm producers as the **Common Agricultural Policy** (CAP) dominates a large proportion of EU finances. The largest net contributor is Germany.

Netherlands

Population: 16.10m
Capital: Amsterdam (The Hague is the seat of government)
The Netherlands was a founder member state of the Community and has proved to be a strong supporter of European integration, a position equally reflected by its **Benelux** partners. The Netherlands contributes most per head to EU funds. Within the Community it has been a consistent supporter of greater powers for the **European Parliament** and an extension of **qualified majority voting** (QMV) within the **Council of Ministers**. In that context, its desire not to have intergovernmental cooperation meant that upon taking over the **Council Presidency** during the 1991 **intergovernmental conference** (IGC) it rejected the Luxembourg proposal for a pillar structure. That had envisaged **justice and home affairs** (JHA) and **common foreign and security policy** (CFSP) operating as intergovernmental policies. Therefore the Netherlands attempted to incorporate them into a single pillar whereby they would be subjected to influence from all the institutions of the Community. However, that strategy failed which meant that the Dutch government had to adopt a pillar structure as represented in the **Treaty on European Union** (TEU). Despite having an integrationist position on institutional policies, the Dutch government has been a strong supporter of the **North Atlantic Treaty Organisation** (NATO) and therefore has tended to adopt a similar position to the UK on foreign and defence policy. Although it met the **convergence criteria** requirements of **Economic and Monetary Union** (EMU) in March 1998 and has been a participant in EMU since 1 January 1999, the electorate nonetheless rejected the **Constitutional Treaty** in a **referendum** vote on 1 June 2005.

Nine see *The Nine*

Noël, Emile (1922–96)

Appointed Executive Secretary of the Commission of the **European Economic Community** in 1958 and served as the first Secretary General of the **European Commission** from 1968 until 1987. A committed European, he had previously been secretary of the General Affairs Committee of the Consultative Assembly of the **Council of Europe** between 1949 and 1952 and prior to his appointment in 1958 was the chief personal assistant to Guy Mollet when he was president of the Consultative Assembly of the Council of Europe and president of France. During his time as Secretary General of the European Commission he served under Presidents **Walter Hallstein, Jean Rey, Franco Malfatti, Sicco Mansholt, Francois-Xavier Ortoli, Roy Jenkins,**

Gaston Thorn and **Jacques Delors**. His position as the most senior administrator in the European Commission, combined with his length of tenure, meant that he helped to shape and consolidate the administrative machinery of the European Communities and overcome difficulties such as the 1965 **empty chair crisis**. After leaving the European Commission, where David Williamson replaced him, he was appointed president of the **European University Institute**.

Non-compulsory expenditure

The section of the EU **budget** which refers to policies that are not directly provided for by the **Treaties of Rome**.

Non-discrimination principle

Within the EU discrimination is not permitted on the basis of nationality in areas covered by EU legislation.

Non-governmental organization (NGO)

Refers to **interest groups**, companies, consumer groups and trade unions that attempt to influence policy.

Non-paper

A draft negotiating text that may establish a compromise. It especially denotes those texts in the **Council of Ministers** which emanate from either the **Council Presidency** or secretariat general and are particularly apparent during **intergovernmental conference** (IGC) negotiations.

Non-state actors

Generally applies to actors other than governments.

North Atlantic Assembly

An inter-parliamentary forum of the Alliance members that is independent of the **North Atlantic Treaty Organisation** (NATO). The Assembly, which meets twice a year in plenary session, provides a link between **national parliaments** and the **Atlantic Alliance** by providing a forum where both European and North American legislators are able to discuss common concerns. Meetings take place in national capitals through a strict rotation system, while the Assembly's work is principally directed through five committees: civilian affairs, defence and security, economic, political, and scientific and technical.

North Atlantic Cooperation Council (NACC)

The November 1991 Rome meeting of the **North Atlantic Treaty Organisation** (NATO) resulted in agreement on the establishment of the NACC as a means of providing a forum where NATO members could discuss security issues with **central and eastern European states** as well as those of the Baltic. The first meeting of the NACC took place in Brussels in December 1991.

North Atlantic Treaty Organisation (NATO)

A desire to establish a common defence system had been set out in the 1948 **Brussels Treaty**. The **Berlin blockade** in the summer of 1948 accelerated the momentum towards widening the security and defence relations of the **Treaty of Brussels**, and so the North Atlantic Treaty (**Treaty of Washington**) was signed on 4 April 1949 by Belgium, Canada, Denmark, France, Iceland, Luxembourg, the Netherlands, Norway, Portugal, the UK and the USA and entered force in August of that year. Subsequent members included Greece and Turkey (1952), the Federal Republic of Germany (1955), Spain (1982), and the Czech Republic, Hungary and Poland (1999). Today, there are 19 members. A key aspect of the Treaty is the commitment to collective defence that is embodied in Article 5: 'The Parties agree that an armed attack against one or more of them in Europe or North America shall be considered an attack against them all and consequently they agree that, if such an attack occurs, each of them, in exercise of the right of individual or collective self-defence recognized by Article 51 of the Charter of the United Nations, will assist the Party or Parties so attacked by taking forthwith, individually and in concert with the other Parties, such action as it deems necessary, including the use of armed force, to restore and maintain the security of the North Atlantic area.'

Norway

Population: 4.52m (2005)
Capital: Oslo
For the most part Norway has been rather wary towards European integration, favouring **intergovernmental cooperation** rather than supranational integration. To this end, it was, along with other Nordic countries, not involved in the negotiations that led to the **Treaties of Rome** and instead favoured membership of the **European Free Trade Association** (EFTA) when the latter was established in 1960. Nevertheless, the attraction of Community membership of other members of EFTA, such as the UK, meant that Norway made an application for membership in 1962. France's rejection of the UK's application in 1963 and 1967 meant that no progress was made on Norway's application throughout the 1960s. Although negotiations resumed in 1970 (along

with the UK, Denmark and Ireland), a **referendum** in September 1972 produced a no vote (53 per cent) against Community membership. Thereafter, Norway expressed little interest in joining the Community and it was not until the end of the 1980s that Norway began to reconsider joining, primarily as a result of the perceived economic benefits of the **single market**. This was initially reflected in the advocation of participation in the **European Economic Area** (EEA). The decisions of Finland and Sweden to seek Community membership meant that Norway applied to become a member in 1992. The **accession negotiations** were concluded in 1994 but a subsequent referendum rejected the concept of membership. In the period since then, Norway's relationship with the EU has been based on its involvement in the EEA and **Schengen agreement**.

Nyborg Agreements

The decisions taken in Nyborg (Denmark) by EU finance ministers in November 1987, whereby they relaxed the practice of intra-marginal interventions inside the **Exchange Rate Mechanism** (ERM). Previous adjustments had to be made with the consent of the central bank of the affected country, with repayment made in the currency of the creditor. However, the agreement ensured that repayments could be made in **ECU**s.

O

Official Journal

Decisions adopted by the institutions are published daily in the Official Journal.

Official languages of the EU

Since 1 May 2004 there have been 20 official EU languages: Czech, Danish, Dutch, English, Estonian, Finnish, French, German, Greek, Hungarian, Italian, Latvian, Lithuanian, Maltese, Polish, Portuguese, Slovakian, Slovenian, Spanish and Swedish.

Oil crises

The first significant oil crisis took place in 1973–74 when Arab oil-producing states exercised their influence over world oil production by cutting off supplies of oil to states that had offered strong support to Israel in the Arab–Israeli war that had started in October 1973. This reduction in the output of oil had a dramatic impact on the world price of oil, which quadrupled, and consequently had a knock-on effect on the economies of many developed states in the 'West' (as well as those in the communist bloc) whose economic growth was heavily dependent on access to oil. As a result, many countries experienced a period of negative economic growth and an increase in unemployment rates. Some countries, such as the UK and USA, also experienced an increase in inflation rates. Within the European context, the oil crisis decreased the appetite for further European integration among member state governments whose main priority was to tackle domestic economic problems. Arab states were also influential in creating a second oil crisis in 1979 after the overthrow of the Shah of Iran, when oil prices doubled. These oil crises, and subsequent disturbances in oil production, such as during the **Gulf War** of 1990–91 and in 2000 (when oil producers limited production to counter a decline in oil prices) have demonstrated the extent to which world economic growth is dependent on oil, particularly from Arab states. Many governments have therefore sought to develop alternative sources of production, including the massive oil resources in Russia and former Soviet states such as Azerbaijan.

Ombudsman

The **European Parliament** appoints an Ombudsman for the lifetime of the Parliament. The Ombudsman serves as the primary point of contact for all complaints that relate to instances of maladministration in the activities of the EU institutions or bodies. The only exceptions to this rule are the **Court of Justice** and **Court of First Instance**.

Opt-out

This refers to the decision to grant a member state the ability to not take part in a specific EU policy area. The benefit of granting an opt-out is that it allows the EU to make progress where there would otherwise be a stalemate because of the reluctance of a member state(s) to accept a particular policy. Examples of opt-outs include the decision to allow the UK not to participate in the third stage of **Economic and Monetary Union** (EMU) and agreements with Denmark on EMU, defence policy and European **citizenship**.

Organisation for Economic Co-operation and Development (OECD)

The Convention on the Organisation for Economic Co-operation and Development (OECD) was signed in Paris on 14 December 1960. It included Canada and the United States and replaced the **Organisation for European Economic Co-operation** (OEEC) that had been created in 1948 as a result of the **Marshall Plan**. Based in Paris, the OECD commenced operation on 30 September 1961 with the aim of promoting international co-operation between industrialized countries with free-market economies. The primary aim is to coordinate economic, trade and development policy. The organisation has 30 members: Australia, Austria, Belgium, Canada, the Czech Republic, Denmark, Finland, France, Germany, Greece, Hungary, Iceland, Ireland, Italy, Japan, Korea, Luxembourg, Mexico, the Netherlands, New Zealand, Norway, Poland, Portugal, Slovakia, Spain, Sweden, Switzerland, Turkey, the United Kingdom and the United States.

Organisation for European Economic Co-operation (OEEC)

Developed from the 1947 European Economic Recovery programme initiated by the **Marshall Plan**, when the 16 nations who had established the Committee of European Economic Cooperation to administer the European Economic Recovery Programme realized that there was a need for a permanent coordinating agency. The OEEC was created by virtue of the signing of the Convention on European Economic Cooperation in Paris on 16 April 1948. Although the initial task of the OEEC was to administer the distribution of American aid provided by the Marshall Plan, it helped to reduce trade restrictions between the member states and also provided a clearing bank that would process payments between the participating nations. Based on an intergovernmental method of cooperation, the OEEC managed to lower trade barriers among European nations and provided the first small step towards European economic cooperation. In 1961 the OEEC was replaced by the **Organisation for Economic Co-operation and Development** (OECD) with the accession of Canada and the USA.

Organization for Security Cooperation in Europe (OSCE)

The OSCE is a pan-European security body whose origins lie in the **Conference on Security and Cooperation on Europe** (CSCE) that was created in 1975 during the era of détente. Whereas the CSCE had operated primarily as a series of meetings up until 1990, the ending of the **Cold War** resulted in the CSCE being charged with taking a greater role in managing the post-Cold War period. This resulted in the CSCE acquiring permanent institutions and specific operational capabilities. Yet this very institutional support, combined with an increased regularity of meetings, meant that the CSCE had become more than just a 'Conference' and as a result a decision was taken at the 1994 Budapest Summit to change its name to the Organization for Security and Co-operation in Europe (OSCE).

With some 55 participating countries (Table 4.14), the OSCE tackles a wide range of security concerns that include arms control, human rights, confidence and security building measures, democratization, counter-terrorism, confidence and security-building measures, as well as economic and environmental matters. In many ways the OSCE is unique when compared with other organizations, such as the **North Atlantic Treaty Organisation** (NATO), as the OSCE comprises a broad membership from the Atlantic to Eurasia.

Table 4.14 OSCE states

Albania	Italy	Switzerland
Andorra	Kazakhstan	Tajikistan
Armenia	Kyrgyzstan	Turkey
Austria	Latvia	Turkmenistan
Azerbaijan	Liechtenstein	Ukraine
Belarus	Lithuania	United Kingdom
Belgium	Luxembourg	United States of America
Bosnia and Herzegovina	former Yugoslav Republic	Uzbekistan
Bulgaria	of Macedonia	*Partners for cooperation*
Canada	Malta	Afghanistan
Croatia	Moldova	Japan
Cyprus	Monaco	Republic of Korea
Czech Republic	Netherlands	Thailand
Denmark	Norway	Mongolia
Estonia	Poland	*Mediterranean partners for*
Finland	Portugal	*cooperation*
France	Romania	Algeria
Georgia	Russian Federation	Egypt
Germany	San Marino	Israel
Greece	Serbia and Montenegro	Jordan
Holy See	Slovakia	Morocco
Hungary	Slovenia	Tunisia
Iceland	Spain	
Ireland	Sweden	

Organization of Petroleum Exporting Countries (OPEC)

Established in 1960 at a Baghdad conference of petroleum exporting states, OPEC has aimed to coordinate petroleum prices among the participating countries. The original members of OPEC were Iran, Iraq, Kuwait, Saudi Arabia and Venezuela. Subsequent members have included Qatar (1961), Indonesia and Libya (1962), the United Arab Emirates (1967), Algeria (1969), Nigeria (1971), Ecuador (1973–92), and Gabon (1975–94). OPEC has managed to control petroleum prices by increasing and decreasing supply. On occasion, OPEC has clashed with western industrialized nations whose economies are heavily dependent on oil, as evidenced by the **oil crises** of the 1970s.

Origin

Used in the description of imported goods. A good is considered to have originated in another country if it was produced there. By contrast, goods which have been produced in more than one country are regarded as having originated in the country where they were last manufactured.

Ortoli, François Zavier (b. 1925)

As President of the **European Commission** between 1973 and 1977 he helped to direct the Community's progress during a period of **enlargement** and economic difficulties which were principally caused by the 1973–74 **oil crisis**. He was, however, a largely ineffective President, despite having had considerable experience as the French finance minister between 1968 and 1969. The economic difficulties which helped to stifle the Community's growth were not assisted by his cautious nature, with one of his most important initiatives as President being the introduction of the New Community Instrument. Despite being regarded as a poor Commission President, Ortoli continued to work in the Commission, occupying the post of Vice-President under **Roy Jenkins** and then **Gaston Thorn** until he finally left the Commission in 1984

Ostpolitik

Refers to the policy towards eastern Europe adopted by the coalition government of Social Democrats and Liberal Free Democrats that came to power in the Federal Republic of Germany (FRG) in 1969. The policy, under the leadership of Chancellor **Willy Brandt**, was described as 'change through rapprochement'. It set out to replace confrontation with the **eastern bloc** that had been a central feature of the **Hallstein Doctrine**, which had advocated the non-recognition of any western state which diplomatically recognized the German Democratic Republic (GDR). In 1971 Brandt was awarded the Nobel Peace Prize for his efforts. Ostpolitik was important to the development of **European Political Cooperation** (EPC), while the French president, **Georges Pompidou**, highlighted it as a reason for the **enlargement** of the Community.

Own resources

Whereas the EU **budget** was initially dependent on the financial contributions provided by member states, a decision was taken on 21 April 1970 to ensure that its finances would be based on its own resources. The significance of this initiative was that it provided the Community with financial autonomy and since 1 January 1978 the budget has been exclusively financed by its own resources. The own resources have four elements: (1) customs duties based on the imports from non-EU member states; (2) agricultural duties and the sugar and isoglucose levies; (3) the VAT resource based on a portion of the revenue of each member state's VAT; (4) and a percentage of the GNP of a member state (Table 4.15).

Table 4.15 The EU's own resources

	Budget 2005		Budget 2004	
Type of revenue	million euro	%	million euro	%
Agriculture duties and sugar levies	1613.03	1.5	1742.48	1.7
Customs duties	10,749.90	10.1	10,664.40	10.5
VAT based resource	15,313.49	14.4	13,579.91	13.3
GNP based resource	77,583.05	73.0	69,010.24	67.8
Miscellaneous plus surplus from previous year	1040.53	1.0	6809.58	6.7
Total	106,300.00	100	101,806.61	100

Source: European Commission, *General Budget of the European Union for the financial year 2005*, p. 24. http://europa.eu.int/comm/budget/pdf/budget/syntchif2005/en.pdf

P

Package deal

An overall proposal incorporating various measures that has been drawn up for universal adoption. The package is often drawn up by a Community institution as a means of breaking an impasse which has developed out of a difference of opinions between negotiators.

Padoa-Schioppa Report

The deputy director-general of the Bank of Italy, Tommaso Padoa-Schi-oppa, submitted a report to the **European Commission** in April 1987 entitled 'Efficiency, Stability and Equity: A Strategy for the Evolution of the Economic System of the European Community'. This was done at the request of **Jacques Delors**, the President of the European Commission, who wanted Padoa-Schioppa to examine the implications of the accession of Portugal and Spain, and the single market, on the economic system of the Community. In this context, the report stressed four priorities, the first of which was the need to complete the **single market**. The second included the development of a single monetary policy. The third was the need to promote cohesion, while the last was the necessity to establish a macroeconomic strategy. The significance of the report was emphasized by the decision taken at the February 1988 Brussels **European Council** to increase the size of the **structural funds** targeted at the poorer regions of the Community.

Paragraph

Subdivision of a Treaty Article, which tends to be numbered.

Parliamentary committees

Study groups within the **European Parliament** which examine policy proposals, including a committee of inquiry.

Partnership agreement

They were created to satisfy the demand of the former nations of the Soviet Union so as to provide political contacts at both ministerial and parliamentary level.

Partnership for Peace

An initiative of the **North Atlantic Treaty Organisation** (NATO) that was endorsed by the North Atlantic Council at Brussels in January 1994 when leaders announced that 'We have decided to launch an immediate and practical programme that will transform the relationship between NATO and participating states. This new programme goes beyond dialogue and cooperation to forge a real partnership – a Partnership for Peace.' Aimed at the countries of central and eastern Europe and the Baltic states, it is a military complement to the **North Atlantic Cooperation Council** (NACC). The agreement permits partner states to establish liaison offices with NATO headquarters as well as with the 'Partnership Coordination Cell' at the Supreme Headquarters Allied Powers Europe (SHAPE). Cooperation with the partner states takes place in military exercises, peacekeeping exercises, joint planning, search and rescue and humanitarian operations, and in promoting democratic control of defence ministries.

Path dependence

This view considers that decisions taken in the past influence (and limit) decisions taken in the present.

Permanent representation

Every member state has a permanent representation to the EU which acts as the Brussels arm of national governments, thereby advocating national policy and informing officials and ministers at home of policy developments (see **Committee of Permanent Representatives**).

Petersberg Declaration

This was issued in June 1992 at a meeting of **Western European Union** (WEU) foreign and defence ministers that was held at the Petersberg Hotel (near Bonn). The Declaration established the guidelines for the WEU's future development, as had been set out in the **Treaty on European Union** (TEU). Members gave their support to conflict prevention and peacekeeping efforts, while a WEU planning cell was established. A forum of consultation was also established with the foreign and defence ministers of eight **central and eastern European states**, namely Bulgaria, Czechoslovakia, Estonia, Hungary, Lithuania, Latvia, Poland and Romania. This was later abolished by the **Kirchberg Declaration**.

Petersberg tasks

This refers to the tasks that were established in the **Petersberg Declaration** of June 1992 which related to the future development of the **Western European Union** (WEU). The member states of the WEU noted their willingness to utilize military units from the whole range of their conventional armed forces for military tasks that would be conducted under the authority of the WEU. Apart from the task of contributing to the **North Atlantic Treaty Organisation**'s (NATO) principle of collective defence, WEU member states agreed to specifically engage in three key areas: (1) humanitarian and rescue tasks; (2) peacekeeping tasks; (3) tasks to combat forces in crisis management, including peacekeeping (*sic*).

Petitions

Every EU citizen enjoys the right to address a petition to the **European Parliament** on any subject that falls within the activities of the EU. The European Parliament's Committee on Petitions determines whether such requests are admissible, and may put a question to the **Ombudsman** where it sees correct.

PETRA

Established in 1989, it is an action programme of the Community for the vocational training of young people with the purpose of improving the quality of training in tandem with the needs of the **single market**. It was replaced by the **Leonardo** programme.

PHARE

A programme of aid that was set up in 1989 to provide aid to Poland and Hungary so as to improve the process of democratic and political reform. The acronym literally means lighthouse. The programme was subsequently extended to include Bulgaria, the former East Germany, the former Czechoslovakia, Albania, Romania, Slovenia and the Baltic states of Latvia, Lithuania and Estonia. The programme has provided upwards of 25 per cent aid of the total cost for direct investment in infrastructure and public sector undertakings, while assistance has also been given to restructure agriculture and banking and insurance industries. The **European Investment Bank** provides finance to any country covered by the PHARE programme, with funds having been mainly aimed towards the rehabilitation of major communications infrastructure systems or the restructuring of undertakings. See **TACIS**.

Pillars

This is a term that has been used to describe the structure of the EU. The first pillar includes **European Communities**, where the **European Commission**, **European Parliament**, and **Court of Justice** are able to exercise their full powers. The second and third pillars are essentially based on intergovernmental cooperation. Pillar 2 includes the **common foreign and security policy** (CFSP) and pillar 3 **justice and home affairs** (JHA). The latter was amended in the **Treaty of Amsterdam**, whereby it is now concerned with **police and judicial cooperation on criminal matters**, while the Treaty also transferred matters relating to the free movement of persons from the **third pillar** to the **first pillar**. The 2004 agreement by member state governments on a **Constitutional Treaty** (subject to ratification) stressed that the pillar system would be altered, whereby the three pillars would be merged together. A reservation was, however, provided so as to protect particular procedures relating to the CFSP (including defence policy).

Plenary

Describes the entire **European Parliament** or one of its part-sessions, occasionally referred to as plenary sessions.

Pléven Plan

The French prime minister, René Pléven, put forward a proposal for the creation of a **European Defence Community** (EDC) on 24 October 1950 as a means of tackling the issue of German rearmament. The EDC proposal subsequently failed in 1954 because of the unwillingness of the French National Assembly to ratify as a result of concerns over its supranational design. In this context, the Plan stressed that 'The creation of a European Army cannot result from a simple joining up of national military units. This would in reality only conceal a coalition of the old type. For tasks which are inevitably common ones, only common institutions will do. The army of a united Europe, composed of men coming from different European countries, must bring about, as near as possible, a complete fusion of its human and material components under a single political and military authority.' Moreover, the Plan stressed that the ensuing European army would be financed from a common budget and that a 'European minister of defence would be responsible for the implementation of existing international obligations and for the negotiation and implementation of new international engagements on the basis of directives received from the council of ministers'.

Pluralism

This principle acknowledges that there are a diversity of interests within society and that the process of government should therefore reflect the bargaining between the groups that reflect these interests, such as employers and trade unions.

Poland

Population: 38.64m (2005)
Capital: Warsaw
At the end of the Second World War Poland became a satellite state of the Soviet Union. Labour unrest in 1980 led to the creation of Solidarity, an independent trade union that became an important political force throughout the 1980s. With the end of the **Cold War** and the breakup of the Soviet Union, a new democratic government led by Solidarity took office after 1989. This in turn led to the opening of negotiations with the Community which resulted in the signing of a **Europe Agreement** in December 1991. At the same time the Polish economy commenced a period of significant structural reform and in 1994 Poland submitted a formal application to join the EU. In 1997 the **European Commission** gave its formal approval to the application, albeit at the same time noting that further administrative changes would need to be made for Poland to accept the *acquis communitaire*. Thereafter accession negotiations commenced in 1998, with Poland formally becoming a EU member state on 1 May 2004. (Poland had already joined the **North Atlantic Treaty Organisation** (NATO) in March 1999.) But, although Poland was eager to join the EU, the initial period of membership has resulted in increasingly disquiet among an electorate that are unhappy about the modest benefits of EU membership. This state of affairs was reflected in a paltry turnout of 20.87 per cent in the 2004 Polish elections to the **European Parliament**.

Police and judicial cooperation in criminal matters

The **Treaty of Amsterdam** transferred a number of policy areas to the **first pillar** which were previously set within the **justice and home affairs** (JHA) provisions of the **third pillar**. The intention of this was to ensure that the EU had a greater capability to respond to issues relating to terrorism, drug trafficking, arms trafficking, corruption and fraud, trafficking in human beings, and crimes against children. Such aims are achieved in three main ways. First, by ensuring that there is **closer cooperation** between national customs authorities and police forces through the **European Police Office** (Europol). Second, through closer cooperation between national judicial authorities through the European Judicial Cooperation Unit (Eurojust) that was established by the **Treaty of Nice**. Finally, the approximation (where applicable) within member states of rules on criminal matters.

Policy

A series of legislative decrees with the intention of fulfilling specific objectives such as in relation to the **Common Agricultural Policy** (CAP).

Political groups

Members of the **European Parliament** sit in political groups dependent on their political allegiance, such as the Party of the European Socialists which includes the UK Labour Party.

Political directors

Senior foreign ministry officials who were provided with the responsibility of coordinating the **European Political Cooperation** (EPC) process in 1970.

Pompidou, Georges (1911–74)

As president of France from 1969 until his death in April 1974, Georges Pompidou did not find the task of succeeding **Charles de Gaulle** to be particularly easy. Pompidou had previously served as prime minister of France from 1962 until 1968, at which point de Gaulle dismissed him at a time of student unrest. Despite Pompidou's close association with de Gaulle, there were clear distinctions between the two leaders. This particularly applied to Pompidou's acknowledgement of the need to accept the **enlargement** of the Community and in so doing overturn the Gaullist **veto**. It was, however, a position that was shaped by necessity, with France being pressurized into accepting British membership by the other five member states. Moreover, by the end of the 1960s French leadership of the Community was threatened by a resurgent Germany. A combination of these and other issues influenced Pompidou's belief for the need for a French initiative in the Community which duly resulted in the meeting of heads of state and government that took place in The Hague in December 1969. The **Hague summit** – as it came to be known – provided the Community with a fresh sense of direction and purpose and established the basis for enlargement from **the Six** to **the Nine** member states in 1973. Although the summit also demonstrated that Pompidou was not as rigid in his views as de Gaulle had been, there were nonetheless strong similarities between the two leaders. For instance, Pompidou shared de Gaulle's hostility towards **supranationalism** (and thereby further empowering the **European Commission** with greater authority) and at the same time supported the traditional French argument that member states should retain the ability to shape future developments. He considered **summit** meetings were a particularly valuable vehicle to achieve this objective.

Portugal

Population: 10.34m (2005)
Capital: Lisbon
Portugal entered the Community in 1986 along with Spain. It had previously been isolated from the mainstream of postwar European politics through an undemocratic government. However, the removal of the right-wing authoritarian government in the mid-1970s paved the way for Community membership, which was also perceived to be a means of bolstering the democratic basis of government. Upon accession to the Community Portugal has tended to side with the UK on a great majority of topics, including the **European Parliament** and foreign and defence policy. Despite this position, it is in favour of the **single currency** and was named in March 1998 by the **European Commission** as having met the convergence criteria which enabled it to participate in **Economic and Monetary Union** (EMU) from 1 January 1999. As a relatively poor EU member state, Portugal has received substantial financial support from the **structural funds** and the **Cohesion Fund**.

Positive integration

In contrast to **negative integration**, positive integration refers to a form of integration that involves the replacement of distinct national rules with a set of new EU rules and policies.

Potsdam conference

Immediately after the end of the Second World War, a conference was held in July 1945 in Potsdam (near Berlin) that involved the heads of government of the USSR, USA and UK with the purpose of deciding the principles upon which Germany should be governed by the occupying powers.

Pre-accession aid

Refers to the financial assistance that has been provided by the EU to an **applicant country**.

Preamble

The sentences at the start of a Treaty that establish the primary aims of the signatories. It is possible for the **Court of Justice** to draw on these when defining Community law.

Preliminary ruling

A **Court of Justice** decision on a point of Community law referred to it by a tribunal or national Court.

Preferential agreement

Any agreement in which preferential treatment in trade is granted by each country to the other.

Presidency see Council Presidency

Price convergence

It was anticipated that the introduction of the **euro** would result in the narrowing of price differentials between member states for the same product. This was because it would be simpler for comparisons to be made between member states.

Price support mechanism

This is the system of agricultural support for farmers that results in higher food prices.

Primacy

The primacy of Community law over national law as established in the **Court of Justice** ruling in the case of *Costa* v. *ENEL*, when the Court ruled that 'the law stemming from the Treaty . . . (cannot) be overridden by domestic legal provisions'.

Prodi, Romano (b. 1939)

Succeeded **Jacques Santer** as President of the **European Commission** from 2000 to 2004, during which time his energies were largely focused on reforming the EU policy-making process to take account of **enlargement**. In 2006 he was elected prime minister of Italy, having already held that position between 1995 and 1998. A graduate of the Catholic University of Milan, he is a trained economist and has served as Professor of Economics and Industrial policy at the University of Bologna. From 1978 to 1979 he was Minister of Industry. Between 1982 and 1989 he was chairman of IRI (Istituto per la Ricostruzione Industriale) in Rome, which was the largest Italian and European industrial and financial holding. From 1990 to 1993 he taught Industrial Organization and Industrial Policy at the University of Bologna. He was reappointed as chairman of IRI in 1993, a position he held until July 1994.

Proportional representation

In general terms this refers to the design of an electoral system which ensures that the proportion of votes cast for a political party are reflected in the proportion of seats obtained by the political party. It contrasts with traditional first-past-the-post electoral systems, whereby elections are determined on the basis of candidates who have the most votes in their electoral constituency, which does not necessarily mean that they have an overall majority of votes. As such, proportional representation is a means to ensure that the allocation of seats for a political party is representative of the votes that have been cast. There are a number of different methods of proportional representation.

Proportionality

The methods used to ensure that a given end should not exceed what is appropriate to achieve that end.

Protocol

A section of a Treaty which is attached to it but enjoys the same status. The reason for its attachment is because it often contains large amounts of material, such as the protocol on the **excessive deficit procedure** that was attached to the **Treaty on European Union** (TEU).

Provisions

The aims and contents of a Treaty.

Q

Quaestor

Officers who are responsible for administrative and financial matters that relate to **Members of the European Parliament** (MEPs). They work in accordance with guidelines provided by the bureau of the **European Parliament**.

Qualified majority voting (QMV)

This is one of the methods by which the **Council of Ministers** comes to a decision. Votes are divided among member states in proportion to the relative size of their population. Over a period of time there has been a gradual expansion in the number of policy areas that are covered by QMV. The taking of decisions by QMV has been an important means of speeding up a **decision-making** process which would otherwise have ground to a halt through a lack of agreement. The **Single European Act** (SEA) brought with it a major shift towards the use of QMV as a result of the need to complete the **single market**. Just as QMV ensures that it is possible to achieve a decision on the basis of a majority vote, it is also the case that a group of states can unite together to oppose a piece of legislation by acting as a 'blocking minority.' In the 25-member EU, there are a total of 321 votes. For a proposal to succeed under QMV it must achieve a minimum of 232 out of the 321 votes (72.3 per cent of votes). At the same time, a majority of states must also support the proposal and the overall votes supporting the proposal have to reflect at least 62 per cent of the total EU population. Just as a proposal needs to pass these hurdles, it can also be stopped by a blocking minority comprising at least four member states that represent a minimum of 35 per cent of the population. The **Constitutional Treaty** that was negotiated in 2004 (subject to ratification in the member states before it enters into force) slightly alters the method of QMV, whereby a proposal can succeed if it obtains 232 votes with support from 55 per cent of the member states and 65 per cent of the population. In the period since the **Treaties of Rome** were signed in 1957, the arrangements for the weighting of votes in the Council of Ministers have been adjusted on a pro rata basis on the occasion of **enlargements** (Table 4.16).

Quantitative restrictions

Measures that impose partial or total restraints on imports.

Quotas

A restriction on the volume of trade in a particular area.

R

RACE

Acronym for research and development in advanced communications technologies for Europe. It is a comprehensive telecommunications programme with the aim of fostering broadband communication technologies to ensure the concurrent broadcast of data, images and sound.

Rapporteur

The **European Parliament** Committee spokesman that drafts reports on proposed legislation to be adopted by the Parliament.

Ratification

This refers to the process regarding the approval of a treaty. All of the member states have to ratify treaties for it to come into force. In recent years there have been a number of ratification crises. This included the Danish 'no' vote to the **Treaty on European Union** (TEU) in June 1992 (subsequently overturned in May 1993), the Irish 'no' vote to the **Treaty of Nice** in June 2001 (subsequently overturned in the autumn of 2002), and the French 'no' vote to the **Constitutional Treaty** on 29 May 2005. This was followed by a **referendum** in the Netherlands rejecting the Constitutional Treaty on 1 June 2005. The combination of these results threw the ratification of the Constitutional Treaty into turmoil.

Table 4.16 Weighting of votes in the Council of Ministers

Country	Votes after the 2004 enlargement	Votes after the 1995 enlargement	Votes after the 1986 enlargement	Votes after the 1981 enlargement	Votes after the 1973 enlargement	Votes as set out in the Treaties of Rome
Germany	29	10	10	10	10	4
France	29	10	10	10	10	4
UK	29	10	10	10	10	
Italy	29	10	10	10	10	4
Spain	27	8	8			
Poland	27					
Netherlands	13	5	5	5	5	2
Greece	12	5	5	5		
Czech Republic	12					
Belgium	12	5	5	5	5	2
Hungary	12					
Portugal	12	5	5			
Sweden	10	4				
Austria	10	4				
Slovakia	7					
Denmark	7	3	3	3	3	
Finland	7	3				

	321 (25 countries)	87 (15 countries)	76 (12 countries)	63 (10 countries)	58 (9 countries)	17 (6 countries)
Ireland	7		3	3	3	
Lithuania	7					
Latvia	4					
Slovenia	4					
Estonia	4					
Cyprus	4					
Luxembourg	4	2	2	2	2	1
Malta	3					
Total votes	321 (25 countries)	87 (15 countries)	76 (12 countries)	63 (10 countries)	58 (9 countries)	17 (6 countries)
Majority	232 votes	62 votes	54 votes	45 votes	41 votes	12 votes
Blocking minority	4 member states that represent a minimum of 35 % of the population	26 votes	23 votes	19 votes	18 votes	6 votes

Realism

A theory of international politics that has played an important role in influencing academic debate since it was first advanced in the 1930s and 1940s. Realists consider power to be the key factor that shapes human action and that states are the primary actors in international relations. For realists, state action in international politics is influenced by a desire to defend their own interests, while international organizations do not have the ability to restrain state action. The end result is that, because states take action on the basis of serving their own self-interests, there is little chance of states cooperating with each other or acting in a manner that is influenced by moral concerns. Inevitably this view of international politics was not without its critics. In the 1970s realism was adapted into **neorealism**, according to which state action took place within an identifiable international system that inevitably placed certain constraints on state action.

Recommendation

A measure adopted by the **Council of Ministers** or **European Commission** that is not binding.

Referendum

In the context of the EU, referendums have been held by prospective member states on whether they should join the EU, and by existing member states on specific policy proposals (Table 4.17).

Reflection group

Such a group was established in June 1995 in accordance with the decision of the Corfu **European Council** in June 1994. The group's task was to prepare for the 1996–97 **intergovernmental conference** (IGC), and it consisted of a representative from each member state and the **European Commission** and **European Parliament**. The 18 members of the group were: Austria – Manfred Scheich (Permanent Representative to the EC); Belgium – Franklin Dehousse (professor of European law); Denmark – Niels Ersbøll (former Council Secretary General); Finland – Ingvar Melin (former defence minister); France – Michel Barnier (minister for European Affairs); Germany – Werner Hoyer (foreign affairs minister); Greece – Stefanos Stathatos (ex-diplomat); Ireland – Gay Mitchell (minister for Europe); Italy – Silvio Fagiolo (diplomat); Luxembourg – Joseph Weyland (ambassador to the UK); Netherlands – Michiel Patijn (minister for Europe); Portugal – Andre Goncalves (former foreign minister); Spain – Carlos Westendorp (minister for Europe); Sweden – Gunnar Lund (Secretary of State for

Table 4.17 Examples of referendums relating to European integration

Country	Date	Example	Result
Norway	25 September 1972	Referendum on joining the EU	Against joining
Denmark	2 October 1972	Referendum on joining the EU	In favour of joining
UK	5 June 1975	Referendum on staying a member of the EU	In favour of continuing membership
Finland	16 October 1994	Referendum on joining the EU	In favour of joining
Sweden	13 November 1994	Referendum on joining the EU	In favour of joining
Norway	28 November 1994	Referendum on joining the EU	Against joining
Denmark	2 June 1992	Referendum on Maastricht Treaty on European Union	Rejected the Treaty
Denmark	18 May 1993	Second referendum on Maastricht Treaty on European Union	Accepted the Treaty
Ireland	7 June 2001	Referendum on Treaty of Nice	Rejected the Treaty
Ireland	19 October 2002	Second referendum on Treaty of Nice	Accepted the Treaty
Malta	8 March 2003	Referendum on joining the EU	In favour of joining
Slovenia	23 March 2003	Referendum on joining the EU	In favour of joining
Hungary	12 April 2003	Referendum on joining the EU	In favour of joining
Lithuania	10–11 May 2003	Referendum on joining the EU	In favour of joining
Slovakia	16–17 May 2003	Referendum on joining the EU	In favour of joining
Poland	7–8 June 2003	Referendum on joining the EU	In favour of joining
Czech Republic	13–14 June 2003	Referendum on joining the EU	In favour of joining
Estonia	14 September 2003	Referendum on joining the EU	In favour of joining
Sweden	14 September 2003	Referendum on joining the single currency	Rejected
Latvia	20 September 2003	Referendum on joining the EU	In favour of joining
Spain	20 February 2005	Referendum on Constitutional Treaty	Accepted the Treaty
France	29 May 2005	Referendum on Constitutional Treaty	Rejected the Treaty
Netherlands	1 June 2005	Referendum on Constitutional Treaty	Rejected the Treaty
Luxembourg	10 July 2005	Referendum on Constitutional Treaty	Accepted the Treaty

Foreign Affairs); UK – David Davis (Minister of State for European Affairs); European Commission – Marcelino Oreja (Commissioner); European Parliament – Elisabeth Guigou (French Socialist MEP) and Elmar Brok (German Christian Democrat MEP).

Regional policy

The EU attempts to reduce social and economic disparities by channelling funds to poorer regions primarily through the use of the **European Regional Development Fund** (ERDF). The **Treaty on European Union** (TEU) included a **Cohesion Fund** to reduce economic disparities for Greece, Ireland, Portugal and Spain.

Regulation

One of three binding forms of EU legislation (others are **decisions** and **directives**). Regulations, which can by adopted by the **Council of Ministers** on its own, by the **European Commission** (in certain circumstances), and the Council and the **European Parliament** (**co-decision procedure**), are directly applicable and fully binding on those that the regulation is applicable to. This includes the administrations of member states.

Renegotiation

The process of challenging the sets of conditions of membership of an organization, such as the UK's 1974 renegotiation of membership.

Representative Office

The **European Commission** local office in individual states throughout the world.

Resolution

A form of Community legislation which is not binding (**acts of the Community institutions**).

Rey, Jean (1902–83)

His tenure as President of the **European Commission** between 1967 and 1970 was hampered by difficulties caused by the 1965 **empty chair crisis**, the problems of merging the three executives of the European Communities in 1967 and **Charles de Gaulle**'s resignation as president of France in 1969. His Presidency was notably cautious, as he attempted to ensure that a balance was maintained between the positions of different member states.

Right of initiative

The **European Commission** has the responsibility for drafting legislative proposals, although it may have been influenced by comments from the **Council of Ministers, European Council** and **European Parliament.**

Romania

Population: 22.3m (2005)
Capital: Bucharest
After the end of the Second World War Romania fell under the influence of the Soviet Union, resulting in the formation of a Communist 'people's republic' in 1947. From 1965 until the collapse of the Soviet system of satellite states in 1989 Romania was ruled by the dictator Nicolae Ceausescu. In 1989 Ceausescu was overthrown and executed. But, although Romania signed a trade and economic cooperation agreement with the European Community in 1990 and a **Europe Agreement** in 1993, former communists nevertheless continued to dominate the government until 1996. In 1997 Romania applied for EU membership, with the **European Commission** in its opinion later that year recommending the delay of **accession negotiations**. This was because the Commission considered that a significant number of changes were needed to be made to the economy, society, rule of law and administrative structures to enable Romania to implement the *acquis communitaire*. In 1999 Romania was eventually invited to commence accession negotiations, but the slow progress of these meant that it was not included in the 2004 EU **enlargement**. The net effect of this is that Romania (along with Bulgaria) is expected to become an EU member state in 2007.

Rural development

This policy is related to the **Common Agricultural Policy** (CAP) as well as measures designed to support employment. A key element of **Agenda 2000** was the reform of the CAP with a view to moving away from providing financial support on the basis of productivity to focusing on the quality and safety of farming products as well as the broader issue of rural development policy. A key aim has been to provide greater coherence at the local level in the framing of a relevant development strategy.

S

Santer, Jacques (b. 1937)

President of the **European Commission** from 1995 to 2000, having been prime minister of Luxembourg from 1984 to 1995, and Member of the **European Parliament** 1975–79 (Vice-President 1975–77). Santer's election to the Presidency of the European Commission was because of the failure of member states to agree on the Belgian prime minister, Jean-Luc Dehaene, at the Corfu **European Council** of June 1994. A further European Council was scheduled for July 1994 at which Santer was elected as a compromise candidate. As Commission President he proved to be less interventionist than his predecessor, **Jacques Delors**, while his style of leadership was less confrontational. Although agreement was reached at the June 1997 Amsterdam European Council on a **Treaty of Amsterdam**, it failed to tackle key subjects such as institutional reform. Much of the effort of the Santer Presidency was directed towards the achievement of **Economic and Monetary Union** (EMU) and developing links with applicant members from central and eastern Europe. His period in office was greatly affected by the March 1999 fraud report by a Committee of Independent Experts which criticized the operation of the Commission. In response to the report the Santer Commission decided to resign en bloc, but they were subsequently able to continue in their role until a new Commission could be appointed in 2000.

Schengen Agreement

Established in the Luxembourg town of Schengen on 14 June 1985, the agreement (which was initially formed outside the legal framework of the EU) aimed to remove border controls between EU member states. The full removal of borders was agreed to in March 1995 in the wake of the establishment of the Schengen Information System (SIS). This represented a significant delay on the initial goal of opening up borders by 1990. The **Treaty of Amsterdam** provided for the incorporation of the Schengen agreement within the EU's single institutional framework. Apart from the removal of internal borders, the Schengen Agreement includes common rules on asylum, joint initiatives on combating drug-related crime, the right of police to follow suspected criminals across borders in hot pursuit, the establishment of a common list of countries whose nationals require visas, the separation in airports of passengers who are travelling within the Schengen area from other passengers, and the establishment of the SIS, which permits access for police forces and consulates to a shared database of wanted people and stolen items.

Altogether 15 countries have agreed to the removal of internal borders by implementing the Schengen Agreement: Belgium, France, Germany, Luxembourg, the Netherlands, Portugal and Spain implemented the agreement in 1995, Austria and Italy in 1997, Greece in 2000, and Denmark, Finland, Sweden, Iceland and Norway in 2001 (of which the last two are non-EU member states). The 10 member states which joined the EU in 2004 (Cyprus, the Czech Republic, Estonia, Hungary, Latvia, Lithuania, Malta, Poland, Slovakia, Slovenia) have agreed to implement the Schengen Agreement by 2007. Notably, while Ireland and the UK are not part of the Schengen Agreement, they are as a result of the Treaty of Amsterdam able to participate in some areas of activity. As a result, in March 1999 the UK requested to take part in Schengen-based cooperation on matters relating to police and judicial cooperation on criminal matters, the campaign against drugs and the SIS. In a similar vein, in June 2000 and November 2001 Ireland also requested to take part in certain aspects of Schengen cooperation, including the SIS.

Schmidt, Helmut (b. 1918)

A socialist politician, he was Chancellor of the Federal Republic of Germany from 1974 until 1982 when **Helmut Kohl** succeeded him after Schmidt had received a constructive vote of no confidence. Schmidt was particularly influential in shaping the development of the **European Community**, notably with regard to being the main advocate of the **European Monetary System** (EMS) that was proposed by the President of the **European Commission, Roy Jenkins**. This eventually resulted in the **European Council** endorsing the proposal in 1978. Although a pragmatic individual who was often sceptical about the wider development of the Community, he established a fruitful alliance with the French president, **Valéry Giscard d'Estaing**.

Schröder, Gerhard (b. 1944)

Social Democratic Party (SDP) Chancellor of the Federal Republic of Germany from 1998 until 2005 (re-elected 2002). Having been unable to obtain outright victory in the September 2005 election, he announced after three weeks of negotiation that he would stand down as Chancellor in favour of **Angela Merkel** of the rival Christian Democratic Union. Schröder was the seventh Chancellor in post-war Germany and the first leader not to have personal experience of war. During his period as Chancellor, Schröder took the decision to deploy German troops to Kosovo and to Afghanistan. This was a significant decision because prior to his Chancellorship no German troops had been deployed outside the territory of the **North Atlantic Treaty Organisation** (NATO) since the end of the Second World War. But, whereas the early years of his Chancellorship were noted for a strong support for the USA (noting his support for the USA in the aftermath of the September 2001 terrorist attacks), Schröder nonetheless spoke out strongly in 2003 against the war in Iraq. His criticism of US (and UK) policy towards Iraq was shared by French president **Jacques Chirac** and reaffirmed the strength of the Franco-German alliance. Other significant foreign policies have included the cultivation of close ties with Russia, a policy that has in part been influenced by a German desire to secure Russian energy supplies.

Schuman, Robert (1886–1963)

Although born in Luxembourg, he was an important European statesman in the interwar period when he served as foreign minister of France. In the revolving governments of post-war France, Schuman served as finance minister in 1946 and 1947, prime minister from 1947 until June 1948, and foreign minister from July 1948 until December 1952. As foreign minister Schuman not only added stability to French politics, but also was particularly influential behind European integration and Franco-German reconciliation. This was emphasized on 9 May 1950 when he proposed that France and Germany should place their coal and steel industries under a common authority. The **Schuman Plan** therefore provided the basis for the establishment of the **European Coal and Steel Community** (ECSC), which in turn helped provided the momentum for the establishment of the **European Economic Community** (EEC). The first meeting of the Parliamentary Assembly elected him as President. His role in the advancement of European integration was emphasized in 1986 when the European Communities stated that 9 May (the day when he advocated the ECSC) would be referred to as **Europe Day**.

Schuman Plan

Published on 9 May 1950 by the French foreign minister, **Robert Schuman**, with the aim of fostering European integration, the Schuman Plan proposed to place Franco-German coal and steel production under a common supranational **High Authority**.

The Plan specifically noted that 'The French Government proposes that Franco-German production of coal and steel be placed under a common "high authority", within an organization open to the participation of the other European nations. The pooling of coal and steel production will immediately ensure the establishment of common bases for economic development as a first step in the federation of Europe, and will change the destinies of those regions which have long been devoted to the manufacture of arms, to which they themselves were the constant victims.' A central aspect of the Plan was the desire to ensure peaceful cooperation within Europe. Thus, the Plan stressed that 'The common production thus established will make it plain that any war between France and Germany becomes not only unthinkable, but materially impossible' and 'By pooling basic production and by creating a new high authority whose decisions will be binding on France, Germany and the other countries that may subsequently join, these proposals will lay the first concrete foundation for a European Federation which is so indispensable to the preservation of peace.'

The plan for coordinating coal and steel production was accepted by Belgium, France, Germany, Italy, Luxembourg, and the Netherlands (**the Six**), who signed the Treaty establishing the **European Coal and Steel Community** (ECSC) in Paris on 18 April 1951 (the **Treaty of Paris**). The ECSC Treaty came into force on 25 July 1952 for a period of 50 years. The four institutions that governed the ECSC were a **High Authority**, **Council of Ministers**, **Court of Justice** and Common Assembly. The success of the Schuman Plan and its seminal role in the process of European integration have resulted in 9 May being designated **Europe Day**.

Second pillar

Encompasses the **Common Foreign and Security Policy** (CFSP). The 2004 agreement by member state governments on a **Constitutional Treaty** (subject to ratification) stressed that the pillar system would be altered, whereby the three pillars would be merged together. A reservation was, however, provided so as to protect particular procedures relating to the CFSP (including defence policy) (see **Pillars**).

Secretariat General

The central bureaucratic department of the **European Commission**, headed by the Secretary General of the European Commission, which acts as the primary administrative link between the President and the overall work of the **Directorates General** and other agencies.

Section

In terms of the Treaty, this refers to the subdivision of a chapter.

Sectoral integration

A view of integration that takes an incremental approach sector-by-sector.

Semi-detachment

Principally refers to the UK's traditional hostility to closer integration, with successive governments placing emphasis on the defence of national sovereignty. Also relates to the slow adaptation of the UK to bargaining and negotiating procedures, while both the public and the political parties have not always shown a genuine preference for EU membership.

Set-aside

Introduced in 1988 so as to limit agricultural production under the **Common Agricultural Policy** (CAP) whereby farmers would be paid compensation if they took at least one fifth of their land out of production over a minimum of a five-year period.

Single currency

The single currency of the member states is the **euro**. There are a number of benefits to a single currency. In the first instance there will be an elimination of transaction costs caused by the conversion of one currency into another. There will also be transparency in prices because goods and services will be priced in the same currency. A single currency is further likely to provide a clear identity to the EU, with the currency competing against the US dollar and Japanese yen.

Single European Act (SEA)

The SEA emanated from an **intergovernmental conference** (IGC) negotiation in the second half of 1985 that sought to provide the first major review of European integration since the original **Treaties of Rome** were signed in March 1957. The cornerstone of the SEA was its provision for the creation of a **single market** by 31 December 1992. This programme would permit the free movement of goods, persons, capital and services throughout the member states. To achieve these aims, the SEA introduced a number of new measures, including **qualified majority voting** (QMV) for **decision-making** within the **Council of Ministers** on matters relating to the single market. Elsewhere, the powers of the **European Parliament** were strengthened by means of the introduction of the **cooperation procedure**. The SEA, which came into force on 1 July 1987, had the following key provisions:

- It established the objective of creating a single market by 31 December 1992 that would be the biggest market in the world. To achieve this aim, provision was made for individuals to live and work freely throughout the Community and for businesses to operate throughout the Community. At the same time, the position of monopolies was challenged and protectionism was banned.

- It introduced qualified majority voting (QMV) in the **Council of Ministers** for matters relating to the single market.
- It provided the institutions of the Community with influence over many policy areas, such as the environment, **regional policy**, and research and development.
- It augmented the legislative powers of the European Parliament via the cooperation procedure.
- It gave legal status to **European Council** meetings of Heads of State and Government.
- It created a **Court of First Instance**.
- It incorporated **European Political Cooperation** (EPC) into the treaty and therefore enabled member states to progress towards a stronger foreign policy.
- It stressed the objective of **Economic and Monetary Union** (EMU) in a **Preamble** to the treaty.

Single market

Refers to 'an area without frontiers in which the free movement of goods, persons, services and capital is ensured'. It represents the total amount of economic activity within member states, especially in relation to trade across frontiers. The **Cassis de Dijon** case had an important impact in the creation of the single market, as too did the report of the **Kangaroo Group** and the **White Paper on completing the internal market**. The single market had a notable impact in propelling European integration forward, has provided an enhanced regulatory role at the EU level and has brought about notable changes to the governance of the EU (see **four freedoms** and **single European Act**).

Slovakia

Population: 5.4m (2005)
Capital: Bratislava
Following the end of the Second World War Czechoslovakia became a communist nation within the Soviet system of satellite states. Soviet influence over Czechoslovakia continued until 1989, when the collapse of the Soviet Union brought with it independence. As a result, Czechoslovakia began to forge a policy of cooperation with the states of western Europe and in 1991 signed a **Europe Agreement**. On 1 January 1993 Czechoslovakia divided into Slovakia and the Czech Republic (in 1918 the Czechs and Slovaks had joined together to form Czechoslovakia) and as a result the 1991 Europe Agreement became obsolete. A consequence of this was that Slovakia applied for EC membership in 1993 and a further Europe Agreement was concluded with

Slovakia in October 1993. Slovakia's progress towards EU member-ship was, however, rather unstable for much of the 1990s, primarily a result of the authoritarian government of Vladimír Mečiar which was in power from 1993 to 1998. To this end, in 1997 the **European Com-mission** issued a critical report on Slovakia's membership application. However, the election of a new government in October 1998 brought with it improved relations with the EU and significant progress in its route to EU membership, which it finally obtained on 1 May 2004.

Slovenia

Population: 1.99m (2005)
Capital: Ljubljana
In the aftermath of the breakup of the former Yugoslavia, in 1991 Slov-enia was the first republic to declare its independence and in 1992 the EC officially recognized Slovenia. In 1995 Slovenia signed a **Europe Agreement** and in June 1996 it made a formal application for EU membership. Slovenia, which has strong ties to western Europe, made significant progress with reforms to its economy throughout the late 1990s and as a result was able to meet the criteria to enable it to join the EU on 1 May 2004.

Snake in the tunnel

The common name for a March 1972 agreement that limited the fluc-tuation of European currencies. This was a mechanism to permit a managed floating of currencies (the snake) within a slim band of fluc-tuation against the US dollar at a rate of 1.25 per cent on either side (the tunnel). The subsequent **oil crises** of the 1970s reduced the mo-mentum behind this project, with the majority of the snake's members leaving within two years. By 1976 the snake was reduced to a 'mark' area that consisted of Germany and the **Benelux** countries. Currency coordination shortly re-emerged in the form of the **Exchange Rate Mechanism** (ERM).

Social Chapter

Initially intended to form part of the **Treaty on European Union** (TEU), but the then UK prime minister, **John Major**, refused to accept its inclusion despite being offered a watered-down version. One reason for this was a role being given to the **social partners** in the formation of policy. The result was that the contents of the Social Chapter were taken out of the draft Treaty and included as a separate **Social Policy Agreement** that was signed by the other 11 member states, it itself be-ing annexed to the **Social Policy Protocol**. This was referred to as a UK

opt-out. The UK's exclusion from this area of policy resulted in the other member states and the **European Commission** attempting to include **social policy** issues under Articles 118A of the **Single European Act** (SEA) which provided for **qualified majority voting** (QMV), notably a **working time directive** which the **Court of Justice** determined was applicable to the UK in 1995. The arrival of the Labour government in May 1997 resulted in the UK accepting the Social Chapter in the **Treaty of Amsterdam**, thereby ending its exclusion.

Social Charter

Adopted by the **European Council** at Strasbourg on 9 December 1989 with the purpose of emphasizing the social dimension of the **single market**. Although the agreement was not legally binding, the UK voted against. The fundamental 12 rights of the Social Charter were: freedom of movement; employment and remuneration; social protection; improvement of living and working conditions; freedom of association and collective bargaining; worker information, consultation and participation; vocational training; equal treatment for men and women; health and safety protection at the workplace; elderly people – upon retirement everyone is entitled to a pension that will provide a decent standard of living; disabled people – so as to improve social integration people with disabilities are to be helped, especially with regard to housing, mobility and employment; protection of children and adolescents.

Social dialogue

A term used to describe European level meetings between labour and management representatives, otherwise known as the **social partners**. This involves discussion, joint action and on occasion negotiations between the European social partners, as well as discussions between the social partners and the institutions of the EU. This process started with meetings under the chairmanship of the **European Commission** in the mid-1980s between the **European Trade Union Confederation** (ETUC), **Union of Industrial and Employers' Confederations of Europe** (UNICE) and European Centre for Public Enterprises (ECPE).

Social dumping

This happens when a member state attracts or retains job creation programmes through lower labour costs or less restrictive labour practices. **Inward investment** was one of the reasons why the UK refused to accept the **Social Chapter** in the **Treaty on European Union** (TEU).

Social partners

Reflecting a corporatist strategy evident in many continental European countries, especially Germany, this refers to meetings of the two sides of industry, namely employers and employees. The UK partly refused to accept the **Social Chapter** set out in the **Treaty on European Union** (TEU) because it included a role for the social partners in the formation of **employment policy** (the Labour government subsequently accepted the Social Chapter in the **Treaty of Amsterdam**). The presence of the **Economic and Social Committee** does, however, provide a framework in which the social partners can debate issues.

Social policy

A term which represents employment policy, including labour law, working conditions and parts of vocational training.

Social Policy Agreement

The Social Policy Agreement was the product of the Maastricht **Treaty on European Union** (TEU). It represented the desire of all member states apart from the UK to make further advances in the field of **social policy** that had initially been set out in the 1989 **Social Charter**. The Social Policy Agreement was annexed to the **Social Policy Protocol**, which was in turn annexed to the EU Treaty. The **Treaty of Amsterdam** incorporated the Social Policy Agreement into the **Social Chapter**, with also a strengthening of provisions.

Social Policy Protocol

Adopted at the December 1991 Maastricht **European Council**, and annexed to the **Treaty on European Union** (TEU), the Protocol was devised so as to ensure that the 11 member states (excluding the UK) could make further advances in the field of **social policy** that were outlined in the **Social Policy Agreement** that was annexed to the Protocol. When Austria, Finland and Sweden joined the EU in 1995 they too became signatories of the Protocol. The UK Labour government, which was elected to office in May 1997, accepted the terms of the **Social Policy Agreement** and therefore there was no longer any need for the Social Policy Protocol.

Socrates

The Socrates programme of 1995–99 replaced the earlier **Erasmus** and **Lingua** schemes as the mechanism for administering student and teacher exchanges and language training that formed part of a broader **education** policy. From 2000 to 2006 the Socrates II programme has embraced all of the countries in the **European Economic Area** (EEA), although the Erasmus scheme has continued to operate as a particular aspect of the Socrates programme.

Soft law

Some non-legally binding documents can have a political impact. This situation is described as the result of soft law.

Solana, Javier (b. 1942)

A physicist by training, Solana served for 13 years as a minister in the Spanish government, including three years as Minister for Foreign Affairs (1992–95). In December 1995 Solana became Secretary General of the **North Atlantic Treaty Organisation** (NATO), replacing the Belgian politician Willy Claes who had been forced to resign because of a corruption scandal. Solana served as NATO Secretary General until 1999, during which time he took control of NATO's mission in the Balkans and played a crucial role in restructuring NATO's military and political structure to take account of the challenges of the post-**Cold War** era. In June 1999 the Cologne **European Council** appointed Solana to the newly created position of the EU's **High Representative for the CFSP** (Common Foreign and Security Policy), with him at the same time holding the position of Secretary General of the Council of the European Union. In June 2004 Solana was designated the EU's first Minister for Foreign Affairs, this being a post that would combine his position as head of the CFSP with that of the **European Commissioner** for Foreign Relations.

Solemn Declaration on European Union

Member states adopted a 'Solemn Declaration' at the June 1983 Stuttgart **European Council**. It stressed the international identity of the Community and a desire to more closely coordinate **European Political Cooperation** (EPC) matters, and had clearly been motivated by the 1981 **Genscher–Colombo** plan.

Sovereignty

Hardly a day passes without some discussion regarding sovereignty within the context of European integration, and particularly with regard to whether there has occurred a transfer of powers away from the member states to the EU institutions and therefore a concurrent reduction in the sovereignty of the member states. To this end, it is clear that because the EU institutions have the ability to take decisions that are binding on member states then there has occurred a transfer of sovereignty in those areas where the EU has responsibility. This is because, in the context of a state, sovereignty refers to the ability of the institutions of the state to take decisions and implement laws. Within the context of European integration, the most common argument made by a **Eurosceptic** is that there has been a loss of national sovereignty. But while at first glance this may appear to be true, it is nevertheless the case that the member states have joined the EU by voluntary means and have moreover played a leading role in shaping the powers of the EU institutions and determining the policies that are to be dealt with at the EU level. To this end, it is more correct to say that there has really just taken place a redistribution of sovereignty (in some policy areas) to the EU level. It is also important to note that there continue to be many areas of national policy where the EU has little or no involvement.

Spaak, Paul-Henri (1889–1972)

He held the offices of prime minister and foreign minister of Belgium on various occasions after 1945, during which time he acted as a driving force behind European integration. In this context, his initiatives included helping to establish the Belgian, Luxembourg and Netherlands economic union (**Benelux**) and the 1948 **Hague Congress**. Spaak was also a guiding light behind the **European Movement**. The latter provided the direction which established the **Council of Europe**, of which Spaak was elected the Assembly's first President. However, he resigned from that post in 1951, partly because of its lack of progress. Thereafter, he was a key figure at the 1955 **Messina conference**, which he attended as the Belgian foreign minister, and was empowered with the authority to chair a committee which would examine proposals for a European Community. The subsequent **Spaak Report** was accepted by **the Six** which resulted in the committee which he chaired being further entrusted with the task of drafting the **European Economic Community** (EEC) and **European Atomic Energy** (Euratom) treaties.

Spaak Report

Presented to the **European Coal and Steel Community** (ECSC) foreign ministers in April 1956 with the recommendation of establishing a **European Economic Community** (EEC) and a **European Atomic Energy Community**. The report had its origins in the 1955 **Messina conference**, which had asked the Belgian foreign minister, Paul-Henri Spaak, to chair a committee of experts to examine methods of advancing further European integration.

Spain

Population: 40.41m (2005)
Capital: Madrid

Spain's accession to the Community in 1986 along with Portugal marked the end of numerous failed attempts. Just like Portugal, who also joined in that year, Spain had suffered from an undemocratic and authoritarian government led by Francisco Franco between 1939 and 1975. Upon accession Spain has proved to be a strong supporter for greater European integration, contrasting with the more pragmatic attitude adopted by Portugal. In this context, Spain supported a greater foreign and defence policy and campaigned for the introduction of **citizenship** during the 1991 **intergovernmental conference** (IGC). It has benefited from the introduction of the **Cohesion Fund**. In March 1998 the **European Commission** named it as having met the **convergence criteria** requirements to enable it to participate in **Economic and Monetary Union** (EMU) from 1 January 1999. Spanish support for the EU has been influenced by an electorate which has for the most part directly linked their economic prosperity and democracy with EU membership. It is a situation that was reflected in the electorate overwhelmingly accepting the **Constitutional Treaty** in a **referendum** on 20 February 2005.

Special Committee on Agriculture (SCA)

A committee of member state representatives responsible for preparing the work of agriculture ministers that meet within the **Council of Ministers** and for fulfilling the tasks which the Council gives it.

Special Drawing Rights (SDR)

A country which is a member of the IMF has the ability to purchase an amount of currency that has been given to another member of the IMF under the SDR system and does not have any obligation to sell them back within a fixed time period.

Special relationship

The UK is considered to have a special relationship with the United States of America, particularly with regard to matters relating to defence and intelligence. For President **de Gaulle** of France, the closeness of this relationship was the basis for his 1963 **veto** of the UK's application for Community membership. The special relationship is, however, not just about defence issues, with the economic relationship being in many ways just as important. The UK is, for instance, the largest foreign investor in the US, while the US is the largest single investor in the UK. At the same time, the UK has received in excess of 40 per cent of all US investment into the EU. London and New York are also two of the world's leading financial centres. While such statistics may result in some commentators suggesting that the UK does not need to be a member of the EU, it is important to point out that since it joined in 1973 UK trade with other EU countries has grown at a faster rate than trade with countries outside the EU. Today, the EU accounts for in excess of 50 per cent of all UK trade in goods and services. The end product of this state of affairs has resulted in the UK government attempting to act as some form of bridge between the US and Europe.

Spillover

Neofunctionalism stressed that sectoral integration on one area would have an impact on other areas. This 'spillover' would therefore have a powerful force on European integration.

Spinelli, Altiero (1907–86)

A member of the **European Commission** from 1970 until 1976 who advocated a federal **United States of Europe**. He was later elected a Member of the **European Parliament** where between 1979 and 1986 he served as an independent on the Italian Communist list. In 1980 he established the **Crocodile group** that provided the motivation behind the **Draft Treaty on European Union**, of which he was the principal architect. He had previously been active in federalist organizations in the 1940s and 1950s, establishing the European Federalist Movement in Milan in 1943 and the European Union of Federalists (EUF) in 1946. Later he was the founder and director of the Institute for International Affairs in Rome during the mid-1960s.

Spokesman's Service

A department of the **European Commission** that supplies the press and other media with news of the Union and European Commission developments.

Stability and Growth Pact

Although the **Treaty on European Union** (TEU) included a provision that **Economic and Monetary Union** (EMU) could commence in 1997 if a majority of member states had met the **convergence criteria**, this objective proved too difficult to meet. In response to this situation and a concern about the economic costs of committing to the **single**

currency, the less developed member states of Greece, Ireland, Portugal and Spain obtained extra financial support via the **Cohesion Fund** to ensure that they could meet the requirements of the convergence criteria. At the same time, to ensure that member states participating in the single currency would maintain a stable level of economic progress (and therefore not jeopardize the single currency), the December 1996 Dublin **European Council** set out the conditions of a Stability and Growth Pact that required member states to adhere to detailed fiscal and budgetary measures so as to avoid excessive deficits. The pact, which was adopted in 1997, stressed that member states should respect two key annual criteria:

- an annual budgetary deficits to be below 3 per cent of GDP;
- an annual public debt lower than 60 per cent of GDP.

While the pact stressed that if a member state were to breach these limits then sanctions could be imposed, it was nonetheless subject to criticism because it was viewed as being too inflexible and the criteria needed to be applied over the economic cycle rather than just one year. Moreover, the imposition of sanctions on member states has proved to be impossible. For instance, France and Germany (both of which championed the creation of the stability pact) have in recent years run excessive deficits for which sanctions have not been applied against them. The combination of these factors led member states to reach an agreement at the EU summit of 22–23 March 2005 to relax the rules of the pact.

Stage 1 of Economic and Monetary Union (EMU)

Refers to the period from 1 July 1990 to 31 December 1993.

Stage 2 of Economic and Monetary Union (EMU)

Refers to the period from 1 January 1994 to 31 December 1998.

Stage 3 of Economic and Monetary Union (EMU)

Commenced on 1 January 1999. This was when the conversion rates of the then 11 participating currencies were irrevocably fixed and the **euro** became the **single currency**.

Stagiaire

An individual who is appointed on a short-term basis to the offices of the **European Commission**.

Standardization

National standards within member states have been replaced by European standards in line with the requirements of the **single market**. The creation of common standards is a means of reducing **barriers to trade**, the work of which is organized by the EU standards organizations **CEN** and **Cenelec**.

State aids

Finance provided from public funds to commercial enterprises that bend the principles of competition within the EU must be subjected to examination by the **European Commission**, which has the power to block them, or determine that repayment is necessary. The final arbiter of state aids is the **Court of Justice**.

Stockholm Convention

A document signed on 4 January 1960 by Austria, Denmark, Norway, Portugal, Sweden, Switzerland and the UK which established the **European Free Trade Association** (EFTA). While Finland participated in the discussions, it did not sign the Convention.

Strasbourg

The plenary sessions of the **European Parliament** are held in Strasbourg for one week each month (most business is conducted in Brussels). Strasbourg is also home to the **Council of Europe** and the **European Court of Human Rights** (both of which are not EU institutions).

Stresa Conference

A conference convened in 1958 by **Sicco Mansholt**, who was Vice-President of the **European Commission** and responsible for the **Common Agricultural Policy** (CAP). The aim of the gathering of European Commission officials, national experts and farmers' representatives was to examine means of implementing the goals of the CAP, an important conclusion of which was the decision to support agriculture through a system of guaranteed prices (see **Mansholt Plan**).

Structural funds

Administered by the **European Commission** with the purpose of aiding **economic and social cohesion**, there are four structural funds: (1) the **European Regional Development Fund** (ERDF) that was established in 1975 with the aim of providing infrastructure support for businesses and local development projects; (2) the **European Social Fund** (ESF) that was set up in 1958 to assist unemployed and disadvantaged sections of society through the provision of specific training policies; (3) the **European Agricultural Guidance and Guarantee Fund** (EAGGF) that was set up in 1958 to finance the Common Agricultural Policy; (4) the Financial Instrument for Fisheries Guidance (FIFG) that was established in 1993 to modernize fishing resources and at the same time provide opportunities to diversify the employment base of those areas of the economy that are traditionally dependent on fishing. As part of the **Agenda 2000** process (being adopted by the March 1999 Berlin **European Council**) reforms were made to the structural funds to reduce the number of priority areas from six to three:

1 providing assistance to underdeveloped regions of the EU that have a per capita income of less than 75 per cent of the EU average;
2 assisting areas with structural difficulties, including economic change; these include areas dependent on fishing, declining rural areas, difficult urban areas and areas with significant demographic or natural problems;
3 providing opportunities relating to education, training and employment for those regions that are not covered by Objective 1.

Subcontracting

Refers to the process whereby temporary labour is secured to complete projects on terms and conditions that are possibly inferior to those enjoyed by permanent employees. This practice is tackled by the 'Posting of Workers' directive, effective from 24 September 1999.

Subsidiarity

A concept that is of relevance to the European Union because of the multi-level nature of its operation, as well as being of note to traditional federal political systems. Subsidiarity is a principle which stresses that decisions should be taken by the lowest level of government and as such if it is not possible to take decisions at the lowest level then the decision should be passed up to the next, or most appropriate, level of government. The basic principles that underpin subsidiarity were initially defined by the Edinburgh **European Council** of December 1992. The concept of subsidiarity has been of particular importance in EU debates where there has been criticism over the centralization of **decision-making** within EU institutions. In her famous **Bruges speech** of 1988, UK prime minister **Margaret Thatcher** argued that EU decision-making should be concentrated at the level of member states rather than by the EU's supranational institutions. The actual principle of subsidiarity was set out in the Maastricht **Treaty on European Union** (TEU), with subsequent changes being made in the **Treaty of Amsterdam**.

Subsidy

Economic aids granted to businesses such as tax concessions and financial support, which clearly can upset **European competition**. For this reason subsidies which distort the market are forbidden by the EU.

Suez crisis

In July 1956 President Nasser of Egypt threatened to nationalize the Suez canal in response to the withdrawal of UK and US development funding for Egypt's Aswan Dam project. The canal was jointly owned by French and UK shareholders and until June 1956 British troops had been stationed in the canal zone. Nasser's proposed nationalization of the canal would have an impact on its economic and military importance to Western nations. In response, France and the UK conspired with Israel to create a legitimate reason to invade the canal zone, and Israel, which had been affected by an Egyptian naval blockade, invaded Egypt towards the end of October 1956. As a result, France and the UK invaded the canal zone a few days later under the pretence of protecting the viability of the canal. However, French and UK forces were quickly forced to withdraw because of economic and military pressure from the US (who had not been consulted on the Franco-British plan). The crisis had a significant impact on both France and Britain: some 18 months later the Fourth Republic collapsed in France and the British prime minister, Anthony Eden, was forced to resign. The upshot of the crisis was that it signified Britain's relatively weak international status.

Summit

Meetings of Heads of State and Government institutionalized in the **European Council**.

Supranationalism

In general terms this refers to a method of **decision-making** in international organizations whereby representatives of member states and independent officials exercise power in addition to the role that member state governments play. The institutions of the EU have autonomy from national governments, EU law has primacy over national law, while decisions can be taken by a majority vote. To this end, supranationalism has an impact on national sovereignty because it imposes certain limitations on member states. Supranationalism can be contrasted with **intergovernmentalism**, which is an approach that attaches greater emphasis to the role of member states in the decision-making process.

Surplus

A situation where an excess has been produced, notably within the agricultural sector. It is possible for the Community to restrict the production guarantee given to farmers.

Sweden

Population: 8.91m (2005)
Capital: Stockholm
In the post-1945 period Sweden adopted a policy of neutrality, only wishing to participate in **intergovernmental cooperation**. As such, in 1960 it was a founder member of the **European Free Trade Association** (EFTA). A preference for cooperation based on economic requirements led Sweden to sign a free trade agreement with the Community in 1972. For the next three decades this was the primary linkage between Sweden and the Community. The creation of the **single market** resulted in Sweden reassessing the nature of its relationship with the EC, with this being initially achieved through the **European Economic Area** (EEA). However, before negotiations on the EEA were formally completed, Sweden considered that the economic benefits of the internal market necessitated that it become a full EU **member state** and so it submitted a formal application to join the EU in 1991. Sweden's status as an advanced industrialized economy meant that the negotiations were swiftly concluded by 1994 and it joined the EU on 1 January 1995 (along with Austria and Finland). However, in contrast to Austria and Finland, Sweden has adopted a more sceptical position, with it deciding (like Denmark and the UK) not to participate in **Economic and Monetary Union** (EMU).

T

TACIS (Technical assistance to the Commonwealth of Independent States and Georgia)

Established in 1990 to provide technical assistance for economic reforms in the countries of the former Soviet Union (Armenia, Azerbaijan, Belarus, Georgia, Kazakhstan, Kyrgyzstan, Moldova, Uzbekistan, Russia, Tajikistan, Turkmenistan and Ukraine) and Mongolia. It is primarily concerned with providing foundations for the transition to democracy and a market economy.

Target price

The price which producers anticipate their products will obtain.

Tariff quotas

A means of allowing limited amounts of particular goods to be imported at either reduced or duty-free rates, thereby allowing member states to obtain particular essential goods without endangering the overall customs protection.

Tax harmonization

The question over the harmonization of tax across all EU members states is one of the most sensitive subjects that the governments of EU member states face. The issue of tax harmonization particularly applies to corporate tax, with the varying tax rates among EU member states being a factor that influences decisions relating to foreign direct investment. It is a situation that has been accentuated by the **accession** of 10 new countries to the EU in 2004, the majority of which have low rates of corporate tax. A direct impact of this is that many of the older member states face competitive pressures for inward investment. But, while member states with a low rate of tax have argued that it is appropriate for governments to compete for foreign investment, foreign investment is nevertheless dependent on other (often more important) factors such as infrastructure, and the skill, cost and availability of workers.

Technical barriers to trade

Obstacles to trade that emanate from national consumer safety and environmental standards that goods have to meet.

TEMPUS

Trans-European mobility scheme for University students of central and eastern Europe, providing financial assistance for joint projects established by organizations from EU member states with partners from central and eastern European countries. The programme initially embraced Bulgaria, Czechoslovakia and its successor states, Hungary, Poland and the former Yugoslavia; the second stage of the programme

(1994–98) included the nations of the former Soviet Union. It has paid particular attention to those studying applied economics; agriculture and agricultural economics; applied science, technology and engineering; business management; environmental protection; and modern European languages. The Tempus programme also provides grants for staff members from central and eastern Europe going to an EU country (and vice versa) for the purpose of attending practical courses and carrying out teaching or training duties.

Terms of entry

The conditions which applicant members achieve when they obtain membership of the EU.

Thatcher, Margaret (b. 1925)

UK Conservative prime minister between 4 May 1979 and 28 November 1990. Thatcher was a particularly dominant personality in the Community during her time in office, of which the early period was shaped by the dispute over the UK's contribution to the **budget**. The disagreement centred on the UK being the second largest **net contributor** to the budget although one of the poorer member states in terms of GDP per head, and was also related to Thatcher's perception that the **Common Agricultural Policy** (CAP) was wasteful. Agreement on a rebate was eventually reached at the June 1984 Fontainebleau **European Council** meeting. Although sceptical of the need to deepen European integration at the expense of national influence, Thatcher was a vigorous supporter of the **single market** programme which reflected her own liberal economic thinking. Her own opposition to the strengthening of the supranational powers of the **European Commission** came to a head in her 1988 **Bruges speech** when she criticized it for attempting to create an 'identikit' European personality. While this was emphasized by her opposition to social and monetary integration, members of her own government were concerned that such a position isolated Britain within the Community. A weakening in Thatcher's ability to dominate government was reflected in her accepting the need for Britain to join the **Exchange Rate Mechanism** (ERM) in October 1990, while the Conservatives' fear of losing the general election resulted in her losing a leadership contest the following month. Out of office, she proved to be a thorn in the side of the Conservative government led by **John Major,** especially after the negotiation of the **Treaty on European Union** (TEU) and her own elevation to the House of Lords in 1992.

The Fifteen

The **accession** of Austria, Finland and Sweden as members of the EU in 1995 meant that **the Twelve** became the Fifteen.

The Nine

The **enlargement** of the Community in 1973 to include Denmark, Ireland and the UK meant that **the Six** became the Nine.

The Six

Refers to the initial six countries which formed the **European Coal and Steel Community** (ECSC) in 1951 and thereafter established the EEC and Euratom under the 1957 **Treaties of Rome**, namely Belgium, France, Italy, Luxembourg, the Netherlands and Germany.

The Ten

The **accession** of Greece to the Community in 1981 meant that **the Nine** became the Ten.

The Twelve

The **enlargement** of the Community in 1986 to include Portugal and Spain meant that **the Ten** became the Twelve.

The Twenty-Five

The **enlargement** of the EU in 2004 brought in 10 additional member states: Cyprus, the Czech Republic, Estonia, Hungary, Latvia, Lithuania, Malta, Poland, Slovakia and Slovenia.

Third country

A state that is not a member of the EU.

Third pillar

Encompasses **police and judicial cooperation on criminal matters**.

Thorn, Gaston (b. 1928)

His Presidency of the **European Commission** between 1981 and 1985 proved not to be as dynamic as his predecessor, **Roy Jenkins**, or his successor, **Jacques Delors**. Prior to his appointment he had served as a Luxembourg government minister since 1969, during which time he was prime minister between 1974 and 1979. Thorn was therefore fully aware of the mechanics of negotiating within Brussels, but this experience proved to be of little assistance during a Presidency that was perceived to be a disappointment. But his task had not been an easy one, with the UK **budget** dispute dominating the agenda. It proved to be a difficult problem for the European Commission to manage, as did lengthy negotiations over the entry of Portugal and Spain, the question of institutional reform and the technological advancements made in Japan and the USA.

Three Wise Men

A report commissioned by the Brussels **European Council** of December 1978 to examine means of making the institutions of the Community more effective, particularly with the likelihood of future enlargement. The 'Three Wise Men' who conducted the report were Darend Biesheivel (a former prime minister of the Netherlands), Edmund Dell (a former UK Secretary of State for Trade in the Labour government) and **Robert Marjolin** (a former Vice-President of the European Commission). The 'Report on European Institutions' was published in October 1979 and formed the basis of some discussions by Foreign Ministers, though its actual recommendations were hardly adopted.

Threshold price

The minimum prices for the importation of farm products into the EU. Cheaper imports are increased to the threshold price by means of levies and customs duties, thereby protecting the European farming industry from cheaper competitors.

Tindemans, Leo (b. 1922)

As prime minister of Belgium from 1974 until 1978 he was an active proponent of greater European integration, as demonstrated in the 1975 **Tindemans Report**. It highlighted a desire to propel the Community out of a period of slow growth, but found little support from other member states. However, as foreign minister of Belgium from 1981 until 1989 he took part in the economic revival of the Community, using the Belgian Presidencies as a means of promoting the single market and advancing the **Single European Act** (SEA). After leaving the office of foreign minister in 1989 he became a Member of the **European Parliament**.

Tindemans Report

The December 1974 Paris Summit the member states requested the then prime minister of Belgium, Leo Tindemans, to undertake a study to analyse the ways in which a more integrated Europe could be achieved that was also closer to the citizen. The Report was published on 29 December 1975 and called for a consolidation of existing institutions and the development of common policies. This included proposals to reduce the number of members of the **European Commission**, a move away from **unanimity** to **qualified majority voting**, and the holding of direct elections to the **European Parliament**. In terms of specific policies, the Report advocated the development of a common foreign policy, the strengthening of social, regional and sectoral economic policies, as well as a stronger management of the currency **snake**. But despite these suggestions, the Report failed to produce any notable developments in the process of European integration.

Title

The subdivision of a Treaty below a part.

Trade barriers

While the desire to create the **single market** brought with it the removal of customs duties and quantitative restrictions in trade between member states, free trade was hampered by other non-tariff barriers including those of a technical nature due to differing laws between member states. This was particularly evident in the arena of foodstuffs, although the process of **harmonization** essentially removed all remaining **barriers to trade** by the commencement of the single market in 1992 (see **technical barriers to trade**).

Trade policy

Although the 25 member states of the EU represent 7 per cent of the world's population, they nevertheless account for in excess of 20 per cent of all global imports and exports and the EU is the largest trading bloc in the world. The combined economic strength of the member states means that the EU is able to play an important role in on matters relating to trade. Indeed, to ensure that the influence of the 25 member states is maximized, EU negotiations on trade policy are conducted by the **European Commissioner** responsible for trade rather than by individual member states (see **Common Commercial Policy**).

Trans European Networks (TENs)

They serve the purpose developing the full potential of the single market by assisting cross-frontier infrastructures in the areas of energy, environment, transport and telecommunications.

Transitional period

A period of time that new member states are given to allow them to progressively introduce and apply the rules of the EU, as determined by the process of **accession**.

Transnational

A term that is used to describe cooperation between businesses and organizations that are based in more than one country.

Transparency

This is a term that refers to a process of greater openness in the workings of the EU institutions. This involves greater access to information and documents concerning the EU, such as ensuring that EU documents are easy to read. This includes simplification of the Treaties and ensuring that EU legislation is drafted in a clear manner. In general terms, questions about transparency reflect a view that the decision-making mechanisms of the EU are inaccessible and remote. With this in mind, the **Treaty of Amsterdam** made specific reference to transparency to ensure that all EU citizens have the right to access **European Commission**, **European Parliament** and Council documents.

Transposition

The process whereby Community law is written into national legislation, being required for **Directives**.

Treaty base

Highlights the specific provision of the Treaty that determines a piece of legislation.

Treaty of Amsterdam

The June 1997 Treaty (entered into force in 1999) made policies on employment, consumer protection, human health protection and sustainable development formal EU objectives. Second, the Treaty reduced the role of the **cooperation procedure** and extended the use of the **co-decision procedure** and increased the number of policy areas that would be subject to **qualified majority voting** (QMV). Third, the Treaty ensured that policies dealing with asylum, immigration and visas would be subject to EU rules and procedures (Denmark, Ireland and the UK were granted an **opt-out**), while the Treaty also incorporated the **Schengen Agreement** into the Community. Fourth, the Treaty incorporated the **social policy protocol** and established an employment chapter. Finally, the Treaty attempted to improve the effectiveness of foreign policy cooperation through the creation of a policy planning unit, improving cooperation with the **Western European Union** (WEU), and appointing one member of the **European Commission** to have responsibility for the **external relations** of the EU.

Treaty of Brussels

Signed on 17 March 1948, the Treaty demonstrated a willingness on the part of Belgium, France, Luxembourg, the Netherlands and the UK to establish a common defence system and to strengthen their relationship with each other so that they would be able to thwart ideological, military and political threats to their security. The emphasis on a common defence system was stressed in Article 4 of the Treaty: 'If any of the High Contracting Parties should be the object of an armed attack in Europe, the other High Contracting Parties will, in accordance with the provisions of Article 51 of the Charter of the United Nations, afford the Party so attacked all the military and other aid and assistance in their power.' The need for such a system was within the context of threats to the sovereignty to various countries at this time, notably Greece, Norway and Turkey, while the **Berlin blockade** and a coup in Czechoslovakia took place in 1948. Such a desire to protect their own borders through a pact of collective security ultimately resulted in the April 1949 **Treaty of Washington** which established the **North Atlantic Treaty Organisation** (NATO).

Treaty of Dunkirk

France and the UK signed a 50-year Treaty of Alliance and Mutual Assistance at Dunkirk on 4 March 1947. The main aim of this Treaty was to counter against the possibility of renewed German aggression. The Treaty was subsequently replaced by the **Treaty of Brussels**.

Treaty of Friendship

French president **Charles de Gaulle** and German Chancellor **Konrad Adenauer** signed the Franco-German Treaty of Friendship and Cooperation on 22 January 1963. This was all that was rescued from the failure of the **Fouchet Plan** that had aimed to create greater political integration. The Treaty noted that 'the two Governments shall consult each other, prior to any decision, on all important questions of foreign policy, and particularly on questions of mutual interest, with a view to achieving as far as possible an analogous position'. In the years since the entering into force of the Treaty, the Franco-German relationship has proved to be a crucial axis behind the furthering of European integration, such as the progress towards **Economic and Monetary Union** (EMU). Although the closeness of the relationship has varied depending on such factors as the issues being discussed and the personalities of government leaders, few other member states have been able to unite to provide the same degree of influence.

Treaty of Luxembourg

An agreement that was signed by **the Six** on 22 April 1970 and came into effect on 1 January 1971. It amended the **Treaties of Rome** by providing the Community with its own resources and increased the power of the **European Parliament** with regard to the **budget**.

Treaty of Nice

The December 2000 Treaty (signed on 26 February 2001 and entered into force on 1 February 2003) concluded the work of the **intergovernmental conference** negotiations that commenced in February 2000 and focused on ensuring that the EU institutions took into consideration the implication of **enlargement**. The main changes introduced by the Treaty of Nice involved a limitation on the size and composition of the **European Commission** and the weighting of votes in the Council of Ministers. There was also an extension of the use of **qualified majority voting** (QMV) so that it applied to a greater number of areas. A Declaration on the Future of the Union was annexed to the Treaty, paving the way for the **Convention on the Future of Europe** which in turn resulted in the agreement on a **Constitutional Treaty** at the Brussels **European Council** of June 2004.

Treaty of Paris

The Treaty of Paris, which was signed on 18 April 1951, established the **European Coal and Steel Community** (ECSC). The Treaty had been influenced by the proposals set out in the **Schuman Plan** of 9 May 1950 that had sought to unite Franco-German coal and steel production under a common 'high authority'. The Treaty was signed by Belgium, France, Germany, Italy, Luxembourg and the Netherlands, and provided the first crucial step on the path to European economic and political integration.

Treaty of Washington

The product of formal negotiations to establish a collective security alliance which took place in Washington between December 1948 and April 1949, with the Treaty being signed on 4 April. It thereby established a defence organization that was known as the **North Atlantic Treaty Organisation** (NATO), of which the cornerstone was the commitment to collective defence that was set out in Article 5: 'The Parties agree that an armed attack against one or more of them in Europe or North America shall be considered an attack against them all and consequently they agree that, if such an attack occurs, each of them, in exercise of the right of individual or collective self-defence recognized by Article 51 of the Charter of the United Nations, will assist the Party or Parties so attacked by taking forthwith, individually and in concert with the other Parties, such action as it deems necessary, including the use of armed force, to restore and maintain the security of the North Atlantic area.' The Treaty marked a process which had commenced with the March 1948 **Treaty of Brussels** when its five signatories (Belgium, France, Luxembourg, the Netherlands and the UK) demonstrated a desire to establish a common defence system. Momentum towards widening the security and defence relations of the **Treaty of Brussels** had been accelerated by the beginning of the **Berlin blockade** in the summer of 1948, which highlighted a deterioration in the relationship between the United States and Soviet Union. The Treaty entered into force in August 1949, with the commitment to collective defence being embodied in Article 5.

Treaty on European Union

Otherwise known as the **Maastricht Treaty** after the conclusion of the Treaty negotiation in the Dutch town of Maastricht on 11 December 1991 (the Treaty was formally signed by the member states in Maastricht on 7 February 1992). The Treaty made a number of substantial changes to the EU institutions and increased the number of policies dealt with at the EU level. The Treaty, which came into force on 1 November 1993 (after **ratification** by the then 12 member states) was the product of two **intergovernmental conference** (IGC) negotiations that commenced in Rome in December 1990 and which concluded in Maastricht in December 1991. The main initiatives of the Treaty were:

* It transformed the Community into the European Union, with policies and responsibilities divided within a three-pillar structure that reflected the willingness (and unwillingness) of member states to tackle policies at a European rather than a national level. The **first pillar** comprised the three existing Communities (economic, atomic, and coal and steel) and provided for the full participation

of the EU institutions. The second and third pillars were designed on an intergovernmental basis, with cooperation to take place purely between the member states without **majority voting** or the involvement of EU institutions such as the **European Commission** and **Court of Justice**. Pillar 2 dealt with cooperation for the new area of **common foreign and security policy** (CFSP), while pillar 3 focused on cooperation for the new area of **justice and home affairs** (JHA).

- It established a timetable for establishing **Economic and Monetary Union** (EMU), and therefore a **single currency**, by 1999.
- It extended EU responsibility into a range of new policy areas, including education, transport, public health policy, consumer protection and social policy. The UK government was, however, excluded from social policy cooperation until the Labour government accepted this policy at the 1997 Amsterdam European Council.
- It provided EU citizens with new rights and created the provision of 'European citizenship'.
- It made a number of changes to the EU institutions. The **European Parliament**'s powers were considerably strengthened by means of a '**co-decision**' procedure. This ensured that the European Parliament's opinion had to be taken into consideration in a number of policy areas because if it was not then it could exercise a right of veto over the specific policy under consideration.

Treaties of Rome

Signed on 25 March 1957 (entered into force on 1 January 1958), they established the **European Economic Community** (EEC) and **European Atomic Energy Community** (Euratom), as well as the additional protocols.

Trevi Group

Established in 1975 with the purpose of creating informal cooperation among EU ministers to tackle drug trafficking and international terrorism. Meetings took place twice a year. It was replaced by meetings of the EU interior and justice ministers when the new group met for the first time on 29 November 1993.

Troika

The primary role of the troika is that of representing the EU in its external relations that constitutes the **common foreign and security policy** (CFSP). Traditionally the 'troika' has referred to the member state that currently holds the **Council Presidency**, the **member state** that immediately preceded it and the member state to succeed it, whilst also being assisted by the **European Commission**. This grouping was established so as to inject stability into the Community framework in light of the rotating nature of the Council Presidency.

Truman Doctrine

Refers to the commitment made by US president Truman in 1947 to maintain freedom throughout the world by limiting the spread of communism, and as such was an example of the policy of 'containment'. In subsequent years the Doctrine was used as the basis for US involvement in the Greek civil war, the establishment of the **North Atlantic Treaty Organisation** (NATO) and the longer-term global presence of the US.

Turkey

Population: 68m (2005)
Capital: Ankara
An **Association Agreement** was signed between the Community and Turkey in 1963 and Turkey submitted a formal application for membership in April 1987. However, in its opinion of December 1999 the **European Commission** noted that it was at that time against the immediate opening of negotiations. In the **Agenda 2000** document of 1997, the Commission stressed that, while the **customs union** with Turkey that came into force on 31 December 1995 was working well, there were nevertheless difficulties with regard to financial cooperation and political dialogue, while the Commission also proposed that European assistance be given to improve Turkey's **human rights** record. The December 1997 Luxembourg **European Council** noted that Turkey was eligible for EU membership and on 4 March 1998 the Commission presented a communication to prepare Turkey for **accession**. This included the development and extension of the customs union. The 1999 Helsinki European Council noted that Turkey was a full candidate for EU membership, although it stressed that Turkey would have to meet the **Copenhagen Criteria**. These developments eventually led to the commencement of negotiations for membership in October 2005.

One of the most pressing issues concerning Turkey's candidacy for EU membership is its human rights record, with the electorates of a number of member states being opposed to Turkey joining the EU. A further issue that has impacted on talks concerning Turkey's membership of the EU has been its relationship with Cyprus, with the European Commission having called for the normalization of bilateral relations with Cyprus in the short term. This is because Turkey does not at present recognize the government of Cyprus, while Cyprus also has the potential to block Turkey's membership negotiations.

Beyond the technicalities concerning Turkey's membership, it is evident that there are a number of key arguments to support its membership of the EU. First, a democratic Turkey that is a member of the EU could act as a bridge to the Middle East and a link to the Muslim world. Second, the majority of Turkey's trade is already with the EU and it has a fast-growing economy that is supported by a young workforce (which contrasts with the ageing workforce in many EU member states). Third, its large army would support the **European Security and Defence Policy**. Against these arguments, critics of Turkey's membership point to the fact that the accession of a Muslim nation of some 70 million people would fundamentally alter the nature of the EU, while Turkey is itself not fully complying with the requirements for EU membership (not least in its refusal to recognize the government of Cyprus).

Two-speed Europe

A term that is used to describe a situation whereby a core group of member states may choose to advance at a faster pace of European integration than other member states. Some member states already engage in closer working practices under the method of **enhanced cooperation**.

'Two plus Four' talks

To prepare for the **German reunification**, between February and September 1990 discussions took place between representatives of the two German states and the four former occupying powers of France, the UK, the USA and the USSR. These discussions were of relevance because, as a result of no formal peace treaty having been concluded after World War Two, the former occupying powers had retained responsibilities (albeit in a limited, though formal way). There was therefore a need to ensure to obtain the consent of the four powers before reunification could take place. As a result a Treaty was signed in Moscow in September 1990 between the two German states and the four powers which was in essence a formal post Second World War peace treaty.

U

Unanimity

This term refers to the requirement that all member states have to be in agreement before a decision can be taken in the **Council of Ministers**.

Decisions requiring the use of unanimity therefore provide member states with the right of **veto**, with this primarily being a means of ensuring that national governments are able to retain influence over the most sensitive policy areas. Since the introduction of the **Single European Act** (SEA), decisions requiring the use of unanimity have been steadily reduced with more and more decisions making use of the practice of **majority voting**. This change has been a product of necessity, with the growth in the number of policy areas being tackled at the EU level and the expansion in member states ensuring that if unanimity were maintained then there would be huge potential for disagreement and therefore deadlock in the **decision-making** process.

Union of Industries of the European Community (UNICE)

Founded in 1958, it represents the interests of member confederations from the EU and **European Free Trade Association** (EFTA) and co-ordinates their policies on European affairs when lobbying member states and European institutions, and therefore acts as a key forum for linking business interests with the EU institutions.

United Kingdom

Population: 60.11m (2005)
Capital: London
The UK's accession to the Community in 1973 (along with Denmark and Ireland) was the third attempt at membership. The UK had suffered from economic decline in the postwar period and this brought with it a reduction in its global influence. Membership of the Community was supposed to mark a commitment to Europe, but instead the UK has consistently been an awkward member. This was emphasized as early as 1974 when it sought a renegotiation of its terms of membership, continuing into the 1980s with the **British budget problem** that was finally resolved at the 1984 Fontainebleau **European Council**. The resolution of the budgetary dispute paved the way for the creation of the **single market**, which reflected UK preferences for free trade. The UK was, however, less keen on subsequent developments, including the objectives of creating a **single currency** and developing a European **social policy**. This was because UK governments have traditionally taken the view that these policies should be the preserve of national governments, with for instance labour market flexibility being an important factor in the success of the UK economy. At the heart of these issues is a broader debate between **widening** and **deepening**; the UK has generally been in favour of EU **enlargement**, but has at times been reluctant to accept the need for the deepening of the EU's **decision-making**. In recent years, and particularly since the election of the

Labour government in 1997, the UK has been more willing to accept the need for changes in decision-making through the increased use of **qualified majority voting** (QMV), not least because in an enlarged EU of 25 member states it is impossible to achieve **unanimity.**

United States of Europe

The speech by **Winston Churchill** at Zurich University on 19 September 1946 was notable for the promotion of the objective of a 'United States of Europe'. In the dark and bleak post-war years, Churchill believed that the interests of European states were best served by joining forces together: 'And what is the plight to which Europe has been reduced? Some of the smaller States have indeed made a good recovery, but over wide areas a vast quivering mass of tormented, hungry, careworn and bewildered human beings gape at the ruins of their cities and homes, and scan the dark horizons for the approach of some new peril, tyranny or terror. ... Yet all the while there is a remedy which, if it were generally and spontaneously adopted, would as if by miracle transform the whole scene, and would in a few years make all Europe, or the greater part of it, as free and as happy as Switzerland is today. What is this sovereign remedy? It is to re-create the European family, or as much of it as we can, and provide it with a structure under which it can dwell in peace, in safety and in freedom. We must build a kind of United States of Europe.'

Uri, Pierre (1911–92)

As financial and economic adviser to the French Planning Commission between 1947 and 1952, he played an important role in the advancement of a warmer policy by France towards Germany. Uri played an influential role in the drafting of the **Schuman Plan** and the **European Coal and Steel Community** (ECSC) Treaty. From 1952 to 1959 he was a senior official within the ECSC, and in the wake of the recommendations of the Spaak Committee he was involved in the drafting of the **European Economic Community** (EEC) and **European Atomic Energy Community** (Euratom).

V

Value-added tax

A system of value-added tax was adopted by **the Six** in 1967. It subsequently constituted an important part of the **own resources** of the Community, evolving from the application of a standard rate to the VAT base which is settled in a uniform style for all member states.

Variable geometry

A method of **differentiated integration** which accepts that member states have European integration objectives that are so different that it necessitates a permanent separation between different groups of member states, although some may choose to join policy areas at a later date. This is a similar assumption to a **multi-speed** Europe because the **hard core** is open to those states that are willing and, in time, able to join. However, the likelihood is that the hard core would establish objectives themselves, thereby shifting the goal posts for other member states.

Veto

Provides any member state with the ability to block a decision, such as in the Council of Ministers, when decisions are taken by **unanimity**. Since the introduction of the **Single European Act** (SEA), the use of unanimity as a voting procedure has been progressively reduced and so there has been less room for member states to exercise the right of veto. For some governments, the veto has been regarded as an important mechanism of preserving their national interest and by extension their **sovereignty** within the EU.

Visegrad states

This term comes from the February 1991 meeting that took place in Visegrad (Hungary) between the leaders of Czechoslovakia, Hungary and Poland, at which they highlighted their desire for 'total integration into the European political, economic, security and legislative order'. In 2004 the Czech Republic, Hungary, Poland and Slovakia became members of the EU.

W

Warsaw Pact

The Warsaw Pact was established on 14 May 1955 as result of bilateral military cooperation treaties being signed between the Soviet Union and seven countries of eastern Europe: Albania, Bulgaria, Czechoslovakia, the German Democratic Republic, Hungary, Poland and Romania. (In 1951 Albania withdrew from the Warsaw Pact.) The Warsaw Pact alliance was basically the Soviet Union's response to the **North Atlantic Treaty Organisation** (NATO). Following the collapse of communism in central and eastern Europe in 1989 and the ending of the **Cold War**, the Warsaw Pact was dissolved on 1 April 1991.

Weighting of votes in the Council see *Qualified Majority Voting*

Werner Report

At the **Hague Summit** of December 1969 Heads of State and Government set up a High Level Group under the Luxembourg prime minister, Pierre Werner, to report on how **Economic and Monetary Union** (EMU) could be achieved by 1980. The final report of the 'Werner group' was submitted in October 1970 and set a three-stage process for the achievement of a complete **monetary union** within a 10-year period. This included the objective of the irrevocable conversion of member states' currencies, free movement of capital, the permanent locking of exchange rates and the possibility of replacing member states currencies with a **single currency**. The specific recommendations of the report were:

- Economic policy coordination was to be strengthened in parallel with the narrowing of exchange-rate fluctuations.
- Decisions on interest rates, exchange rates and the management of reserves were to be taken at Community level.
- It would be necessary to have fiscal harmonization and for cooperation in structural and regional policies to take place.
- In terms of institutional building, the report vaguely called for the creation of 'the centre of decision for economic policy' and of 'the Community system for the central banks'.

However, despite the fact that EMU would be reached in stages, of which the **snake in the tunnel** would be the first stage, its very failure meant that the objectives of the Werner Report were forsaken.

Western European Union (WEU)

The origins of the WEU began with the March 1948 **Treaty of Brussels** that committed Belgium, France, Luxembourg, the Netherlands and the UK to a system of collective defence. While part of the original purpose of the Treaty of Brussels was to demonstrate a European desire to cooperate in defence policy, the creation in 1949 of the **North Atlantic Treaty Organisation** (NATO) essentially made the Brussels Treaty superfluous. Some countries, such as France, nevertheless desired a European defence capability and this took the form of the **European Defence Community** (EDC). After the collapse of the EDC in 1954 the British government advocated an alternative security structure. The British proposal, which was advanced by the Foreign Secretary Anthony Eden, proposed that Germany and Italy should become members of the Brussels Treaty and thereby extend the system of collective defence. As a result, the WEU commenced operation on 6 May 1955 (based in London), with its institutions consisting of:

- a Secretariat;
- a Council of foreign and defence ministers;
- an Assembly comprising the member states' representatives to the Council of Europe Parliamentary Assembly.

Although the WEU was of importance in helping to tackle the question of Germany's security, the organization was nevertheless quickly overshadowed by NATO and it proved to be a rather lifeless institution. This however changed in the 1980s when a series of decisions were taken to 'reactivate' the WEU and resulted in it becoming an important link between the EC and NATO. The changed European security environment brought about by the end of the **Cold War** resulted in a strong debate among European countries during the Maastricht **Treaty on European Union** (TEU) negotiations about whether the WEU should replace NATO as the main means of providing Europe's defence. In the end, although the TEU stressed that NATO would remain the main means for Europe's defence, the Treaty also contained a declaration which stressed that the 'WEU will be developed as the defence component of the European Union and as the means to strengthen the European pillar of the Atlantic Alliance'. In the wake of the June 1999 Cologne European Council and the December 1999 Helsinki **European Council**, the WEU relinquished its military headquarters and its responsibility for crisis management after the EU member states announced their desire to establish a **European Security and Defence Identity** (ESDI) that would subsume the WEU.

White Paper

An official set of European proposals advanced by the **European Commission** in a specific policy. In some instances they follow a Green Paper as a means of launching a discussion process at the EU level. Examples include the **White Paper on completing the internal market,** the White Paper on approximation of the laws of the associated states of central and eastern Europe in matters that are of relevance to the internal market, and the **White Paper on growth, competitiveness and employment.**

White Paper on completing the internal market

While the initial aim was that a **common market** was to have been realized by the end of 1969, in reality this goal was only partially achieved and it was not until the mid-1980s that work to achieve a common market began in earnest. In 1985, the **European Commission** under the authorship of the UK European Commissioner **Lord Cockfield** drew up a **White Paper** outlining concrete action for the completion of the internal market. The White Paper contained a detailed programme of some 282 legislative proposals aimed at removing all border barriers between the member states. According to the White Paper, the elements that needed to be deregulated to enable the single market to function were of three types: physical, technical and fiscal (taxes).

- Physical barriers at the borders between member states consist mainly of customs and police controls.
- Technical barriers largely refer to various national rules for products and standards on goods.
- Fiscal barriers between member states relate to taxation in the form of excise duties and value-added tax on goods and services.

It was decided that all legislative proposals of the White Paper should be implemented by the end of 1992 so that the internal market could be completed by 1 January 1993 (see **single market**).

White Paper on growth, competitiveness and employment

This paper was published by the **European Commission** in 1994 and established a set of policy goals with the overall aim of reducing EU unemployment, including a call for market-orientated economic strategies. It acknowledged that high rates of unemployment on the continent were partly due to labour market rigidities which were not present in nations such as Japan and the United States. It proposed a 'social pact' in which productivity gains produced by limited deregulation of labour market are used to fund job creation and training. Emphasis was placed on job creation, flexibility, reduced non-wage labour costs, structural reforms of social security and taxation systems. It generally signalled a decline in Community activism, with attention directed towards consolidation rather than new initiatives and in sum marked a gradual move away from traditional social welfarism to the dual goal of protection and **flexibility**.

Widening

The enlargement of the EU is often used in the same breadth as **deepening**. Those who favour widening consider it imperative that the policies of the Union be strengthened, particularly the institutional design. By contrast, some states have traditionally advocated that widening does not necessitate deepening because such a process would make the process of enlargement more difficult, as all new member states would not just have to accept existing competences but also those envisaged in any deepening, given the requirement for all new entrants to accept the *acquis communitaire*. The UK, especially under the leadership of **Margaret Thatcher**, insisted that widening did not necessitate deepening.

Wilson, Harold (1916–95)

A UK Labour prime minister from October 1964 to June 1970 and March 1974 to April 1976, he previously held various government posts including Parliamentary Secretary in the Ministry of Works (1945–47), Secretary for Overseas Trade, (March–October 1947) and President of the Board of Trade (1947–51). During his first tenure as prime minister he oversaw the UK's second application for UK membership of the Community, although its failure owed much to the problems associated with the first application. Upon his return to office in 1974, he applied for a **renegotiation** of the terms of entry which **Edward Heath** had obtained, accepting the new terms in January 1975. That was later followed by a **referendum** on Community membership in 1975, during which Wilson allowed his own Cabinet a free vote. This resulted in seven of the 23 Cabinet Ministers voting against the terms of entry, including the future Labour Party leader, Michael Foot.

Wine lake

A phrase analogous to the **butter mountain**, which was equally effected by the price guarantee and intervention system of the **Common Agricultural Policy** (CAP). In this context, large amounts of wine were accumulated through overproduction. Agreement on reducing wine production was reached at the December 1984 Dublin **European Council**.

Withdrawal of national notes and coins

Those countries participating in the **eurozone** have to replace their national currency with the **euro**.

Working document

Generally a first stage in the drafting of reports in the **European Parliament**. In this context a **rapporteur** may submit an outline of their intended report or of the policy proposals that it is concerned with.

Working group

This is a body of officials which meets to settle details surrounding particular EU policies.

Working Time Directive

Refers to the basic hours, shift and overtime hours, rest periods and holiday entitlements applicable to employees in member states that are covered by a EU directive. It provides a minimum rest period of 11 consecutive hours a day, a rest break when the working day is longer than six hours, a minimum rest period of one day a week, a maximum working week of 48 hours on average including overtime, four weeks annual holiday and not more than eight hours a night on average engaged in night work. The directive does not cover workers in the transport sector – air, rail, sea, roads – or doctors in training. Other jobs, such as senior managers, family workers and jobs in hospitals and airports, docks and prisons, the emergency services, agriculture, electricity, gas and water are covered by special arrangements.

World Trade Organization (WTO)

Established in 1995 in the wake of the conclusion of the **General Agreement on Tariffs and Trade** (GATT) Uruguay Round, the WTO has 147 members. All GATT members now belong to the WTO, which furthers trade relations among its members and forms a basis for further multilateral trade discussions. The latest round of negotiations is the Doha Round, which commenced in 2001.

Wörner, Manfred (1934–94)

A former minister of defence of the Federal Republic of Germany from 1982 until 1988 who had been elected to the German Bundestag in 1965. He had special interests in security policy, having completed a doctorate in international law at the University of Munich in 1958 which dealt with the defence relations of allied countries. He chaired the Working Group on Defence of the Christian Democratic Union/ Christian Social Union (CDU/CSU) parliamentary party until 1976, was Chairman of the Defence Committee of the German Bundestag until 1980 and was Deputy Chairman of the CDU/CSU parliamentary party until 1982. After his tenure as minister of defence he succeeded Lord Carrington in 1988 as Secretary General of the **North Atlantic Treaty Organisation** (NATO). This proved to be an extremely turbulent period for the Alliance, caused by the collapse of the Soviet-dominated eastern Europe, the drive towards a separate European defence identity and the challenge of the 1991 **Gulf War**. During this period Wörner managed to ensure that NATO remained the primary European defence identity, with it proving crucial to the resolution of the conflict in the former Yugoslavia.

Y

Yalta conference

In February 1945 a conference was held in Yalta (in the Crimea) that involved the leaders of the Second World War allies before the war had formally ended. By that stage it was apparent that Germany would be defeated and so the key question was how a postwar Germany should be treated. The meeting decided that Germany should be divided into three zones of occupation (it was subsequently decided that France should have a zone of occupation taken from territory previously allocated to the UK and the USA). Agreement was also reached on the need for Germany to surrender unconditionally, for its total disarmament and that it should accept the establishment of the United Nations.

Yaoundé Convention

A trade agreement between **the Six** and the 18 nations of the Associated African States and Madagascar which was signed in 1963 in Yaoundé, Cameroon. Entering into force in 1964, the Convention was renegotiated in 1969 and thereafter was superseded by the **Lomé Convention**.

5   Chronology

1945

4–11 February	Yalta Conference.
8 May	End of Second World War in Europe.
26 June	Signing of the United Nations Charter in San Francisco.

1946

16 March	Winston Churchill's 'Iron Curtain' speech at Fulton, Missouri.
19 September	Winston Churchill urged Franco-German reconciliation within a United States of Europe in a speech at Zurich.

1947

4 March	Treaty of Dunkirk. France and the UK signed a 50-year Treaty of Alliance and Mutual Assistance.
12 March	Truman Doctrine. US President Truman said that 'it must be the policy of the United States to support free peoples who are resisting attempted subjugation by armed minorities or by outside pressure', and requested financial aid to Greece and Turkey.
5 June	US Marshall Plan for the economic rehabilitation of Europe that motivated the European Recovery Programme and helped form the Organisation for European Economic Co-operation (OEEC).
23 October	Establishment of the General Agreement on Tariffs and Trade (GATT) which created a set of rules governing the conduct of international trade.

1948

February	Belgium, Luxembourg and the Netherlands established the Benelux customs union.
17 March	Treaty of Brussels was signed by Belgium, France, Luxembourg, the Netherlands and the UK. It constituted a 50-year alliance against attack in Europe.
16 April	Organisation for European Economic Co-operation (OEEC) was formed to coordinate Marshall Plan assistance.
5 May	The International Committee of the Movement for European Unity held a European Congress in The Hague (Hague Congress). Winston Churchill chaired the meeting which was attended by 800 delegates.
24 June	Start of the Berlin blockade by the Soviet Union.
October	European Movement established in the wake of the May 1948 Hague Congress.

1949

28 January	France, the UK and the Benelux countries decide to establish a Council of Europe. They ask Denmark, Ireland, Italy, Norway and Switzerland to assist with the task of drawing up the statute of the Council.
4 April	Creation of the North Atlantic Treaty Organisation (NATO) by Belgium, Canada, Denmark, France, Iceland, Italy, Luxembourg, the Netherlands, Norway, Portugal, the UK and the USA.
5 May	The statute of the Council of Europe is signed in London.
30 May	The creation of the German Democratic Republic (GDR) is announced.
3 August	The statute of the Council of Europe enters into force.

1950

9 May	In a speech inspired by Jean Monnet, the French foreign minister Robert Schuman proposed to pool French and German coal and steel industries under a new supranational authority that would be open to all EU countries (Schuman Declaration).
20 June	Start of the intergovernmental conference (IGC) negotiations in Paris between the Six to implement

the Schuman Declaration, which led to the European Coal and Steel Community (ECSC).

1 July The European Payments Union (EPU) was established, providing multilateral payments among the Organisation for European Economic Cooperation (OEEC) countries and their associated territories.

24 October Pléven Plan for a European Defence Community (EDC). It envisaged the creation of a supranational army of initially 100,000 men, including West German troops, financed by a common budget and placed under the leadership of a European Minister of Defence who would be responsible to the Council of Ministers and Common Assembly.

1951

15 February Belgium, France, Italy, Luxembourg and West Germany attended a meeting in Paris with a view to creating a European Defence Community (EDC). The meeting was also attended by six observer countries: Canada, Denmark, the Netherlands, Norway, the United Kingdom, and the United States.

18 April The Treaty of Paris, which established the European Coal and Steel Community (ECSC), was signed by Belgium, Netherlands, Luxembourg, West Germany, France and Italy 'to establish, by creating an economic community, the foundation of a wider and deeper community'. The Treaty was to become operational in 1953 and established the first common European authority. The ECSC High Authority was subject to democratic control through an Assembly composed of representatives from the six national parliaments, as well as to rule of law through the Court of Justice.

1952

27 May European Defence Community (EDC) Treaty was signed by the Six in Paris. A Treaty of association was signed with the UK.

25 July European Coal and Steel Community (ECSC) came into operation. Jean Monnet was appointed President of the High Authority and Paul-Henri Spaak was appointed President of the Common Assembly.

10 August The ECSC High Authority took office.

1953

10 February	The common market in coal and iron ore came into being, with the Six abolishing customs duties and quantitative restrictions in these materials.

1954

11 May	Alcide de Gasperi was elected President of the European Parliamentary Assembly.
30 August	French National Assembly rejected the European Defence Community (EDC) Treaty.
23 October	Treaty of Brussels was amended to create the Western European Union (WEU).
29 November	Giuseppe Pella was elected President of the Common Assembly.

1955

5 May	Germany was integrated into the North Atlantic Treaty Organisation (NATO) and the Western European Union (WEU) by the Treaties of Paris.
14 May	Soviet Union created the Warsaw Pact.
20 May	Benelux countries proposed to other European Coal and Steel Community (ECSC) countries the creation of a European atomic organization and customs union.
1 June	René Meyer was elected Resident of the High Authority of the ECSC.
1–3 June	Messina conference of 'the Six' established the Spaak Committee to look at ways in which 'a fresh advance towards the building of Europe' could be achieved.
8 December	The Council of Europe adopted as its emblem a blue flag with a crown of 12 gold stars.

1956

6 May	The Belgian foreign minister, Paul-Henri Spaak, submitted a report on the draft Community Treaties establishing the European Economic Community (EEC) and the European Atomic Energy Community (Euratom).
29 May	Spaak Report was approved by foreign ministers.
26 June	Start of negotiations between the Six with the intention of forming the EEC and Euratom.

27 November	Hans Furler was elected President of the ECSC Common Assembly.

1957

7 February	UK proposal for establishment of the European Free Trade Association (EFTA).
25 March	The Treaties of Rome were signed which established the EEC and Euratom.

1958

1 January	The Treaties of Rome came into effect, thereby creating the EEC and Euratom.
7 January	Walter Hallstein was elected President of the EEC Commission, Louis Armand was elected President of the Euratom Commission, and Paul Finet was elected President of the ECSC High Authority.
19 March	Robert Schuman was elected President of the Parliamentary Assembly that replaced the ECSC Assembly.
13 May	For the first time members of the Parliamentary Assembly sat by political grouping rather than by nationality.
3–11 July	A conference in Stresa established the foundations for the Common Agricultural Policy (CAP).

1959

1 January	First tariff reductions in the common market took place.
7 January	Robert Schuman was re-elected President of the Parliamentary Assembly.
2 February	Etienne Hirsch was elected President of the Euratom Commission.
8 June	Greece requested an Association Agreement with the EEC.
20–21 July	Austria, Denmark, Norway, Portugal, Sweden, Switzerland and the UK decided to create a European Free Trade Association (EFTA).
31 July	Turkey requested an Association Agreement with the EEC.
11 September	Piero Malvestiti was elected President of the ECSC High Authority.

1960

January	Benelux Economic Union formally came into operation.
4 January	Stockholm Convention, establishing the European Free Trade Association (EFTA), was signed by Austria, Denmark, Norway, Portugal, Sweden, Switzerland and the UK.
28 March	Hans Furler was elected President of the Parliamentary Assembly.
3 May	EFTA formally came into existence.
9 June	The Six rejected early negotiations to join with EFTA.
14 December	Organisation for Economic Cooperation and Development (OECD) Treaty was signed in Paris, replacing the Organisation for European Economic Cooperation (OEEC) with the inclusion of Canada and the US.

1961

1 January	The EEC took its first action in establishing a common external tariff.
10–11 February	Paris summit of the Six on the development of the Union with regard to enlargement. The communiqué of the meeting expressed a willingness to create agreements with other European countries, especially the UK.
10 March	Hans Furler was re-elected President of the Parliamentary Assembly.
July	The EEC signed an Association Agreement with Greece.
31 July	Ireland formally applied for accession to the EEC.
9 August	The UK formally applied for accession to the EEC.
10 August	Denmark formally applied for accession to the EEC.
2 November	Publication of the Fouchet Plan for a European political community.

1962

10 January	Walter Hallstein took office as President of the Commission of the European Economic Community and Pierre Chatenet was appointed President of the Euratom Commission.

14 January	Start of the second stage of transition to a common market. The Community fixed the basic features of the CAP, as well as regulations for grains, pig meat, eggs and poultry, fruit and vegetables.
9 February	Spain formally applied for accession to the EEC.
17 April	Collapse of the Fouchet plan negotiations.
30 April	Norway formally applied for accession to the EEC.
1 July	European Agricultural Guidance and Guarantee Fund (EAGGF) began operation.
1 November	Association Agreement between Greece and the Community entered into force.

1963

14 January	French president Charles de Gaulle vetoed the UK's application to join the EEC.
22 January	Franco-German Treaty of Friendship and Cooperation (Elysée Treaty).
5 February	In the Van Gend en Loos judgment, the Court of Justice ruled that member states had accepted that their sovereign rights were limited as a result of the Community being a new legal order.
25–29 March	Gaetano Martino was re-elected President of the European Parliament.
20 July	Yaoundé Convention was signed, consisting of an association of 18 African States and Madagascar with the EEC for five years.
September	EEC signed an association agreement with Turkey.

1964

10 January	Walter Hallstein was re-appointed President of the EEC Commission.
21 March	Jean Duvieusart was elected President of the European Parliament.
1 June	Yaoundé Convention entered into force.
1 July	CAP came into effect.
15 July	European Court of Justice ruling on *Costa* v. *ENEL* which emphasized the supremacy of EC law over national law.
1 December	Association Agreement between the EEC and Turkey entered into force.

1965

8 April	Merger Treaty brought the ECSC, Euratom and the EEC into a common institutional format (the European Communities), with effect from 1 July 1967.
1 July	European Council failed to achieve agreement on the financing of the CAP. This resulted in France boycotting the Community institutions for seven months in opposition to the Commission proposal that all import duties and levies be paid in to the Community budget, and the powers of the European Parliament be increased, a period commonly referred to as the 'empty chair crisis'.
24 September	Victor Leemans was elected President of the European Parliament.

1966

29 January	The Luxembourg compromise resolved the empty chair crisis that had hampered the Community's activities for seven months.
6 March	Alain Poher was elected President of the European Parliament.
1 July	President Charles de Gaulle withdrew French troops from the command of NATO.

1967

10–11 May	Denmark, Ireland and the UK submitted formal applications for membership of EEC, ECSC and Euratom.
1 July	Community Executives (ECSC High Authority, EEC and Euratom Commissions) were merged into a one 14-member Commission.
21 July	Norway requested negotiations to be opened for its accession to the Communities.
27 November	At a press conference de Gaulle stressed the incompatibility of the EEC with the state of the UK's economy, thereby bringing to an end the UK's second application to join the EEC.

1968

1 July	Customs union was completed 18 months ahead of schedule. A common external tariff was established.

21 August	In Czechoslovakia the 'Prague Spring' reforms that had been initiated by Alexander Dubček resulted in opposition from the Soviet Union.

1969

11 March	Mario Scelba was elected President of the European Parliament.
28 April	French President, General Charles de Gaulle, resigned and was succeeded in July by Georges Pompidou.
29 July	Second Yaoundé Convention was signed.
1–2 December	At the Hague Summit the Six agreed to complete, enlarge and strengthen the Community. The Council agreed to finance CAP by giving the Community its own resources from 1978 onwards and strengthening the European Parliament's budgetary powers.

1970

22 April	Treaty of Luxembourg provided for the introduction of 'own resources' for the EC that were to be based on customs duties, agricultural levies and VAT and would replace direct contributions from the member states. The budgetary powers of the European Parliament were also extended by the Treaty.
30 June	Resumption of accession negotiations with Denmark, Ireland, Norway and the UK.
2 July	Franco Maria Malfati took office as President of the new Commission.
31 July	Davignon Report stated the need for twice-yearly ministerial meetings on political cooperation, bringing into play European Political Cooperation (EPC).
7–8 October	Werner Report provided member states with an outline for Economic and Monetary Union (EMU).
27 October	Davignon Report was approved by member states, thereby initiating the process of European Political Cooperation.
19 November	Foreign ministers of the Six met in Munich for the first time in an effort to harmonize views on foreign policy under the auspices of EPC.

1971

1 January	Second Yaoundé and Arusha Conventions came into force.
1 February	Common Fisheries Policy took effect.
12 February	Walter Behrendt was elected President of the European Parliament.
22 March	Member states agreed on a plan to achieve EMU by 1980. This was not achieved, however, because of difficulties in the international economy.
24 March	The Six took their first steps to modernize farming in accordance with the Mansholt Plan.
May	Community issued its first joint foreign policy declaration on the Middle East.

1972

22 January	Treaty of Accession was signed by Denmark, Ireland, Norway and the UK.
24 April	Basle Agreement entered into force establishing the system for the narrowing of the margins of fluctuation between the currencies of the Community (plus or minus 1.25 per cent), otherwise known as the snake in the tunnel. The participating countries were Belgium, France, the FRG, Italy, Luxembourg and the Netherlands.
22 May	Irish electorate accepted membership of the European Communities in a referendum vote.
22 July	Conclusion of special relations agreement between the Community and EFTA countries: Austria, Iceland, Portugal, Sweden and Switzerland.
24–25 September	Norway withdrew its application to join the Community after a Norwegian referendum showed a majority against entry.
2 October	Referendum in Denmark on joining the European Communities produces a majority vote in favour of membership.
19–20 October	Paris Summit of the Nine prepared a blueprint for the future development of the Community. It was the first summit meeting of the Heads of State and Government of the future enlarged Community of the Nine.

1973

1 January	First enlargement of the EEC. Denmark, Ireland and the UK officially joined the Community and the Six became the Nine.
13 March	Cornelis Berkhouwer was elected President of the European Parliament.
3–7 July	Start of the Helsinki Conference on Security and Cooperation in Europe (CSCE).
23 December	Organization of Petroleum Exporting Countries (OPEC) announced the doubling of the price of crude oil sold by the six Persian Gulf members.

1974

4 June	UK outlined details of its terms of renegotiation of EEC membership.
9–10 December	Paris meeting of Heads of State and Government resulted in the institutionalization of summit meetings through creation of the European Council.

1975

28 February	First Lomé Convention was signed, replacing the 1963 and 1969 Yaoundé Conventions and the Arusha Agreement. The Convention was between the EC and the 46 underdeveloped countries in Africa, the Caribbean and Pacific (ACP countries).
March	European Unit of Account (EUA) was created as a basket comprising fixed quantities of the currencies of the nine member states.
10–11 March	Conclusion of the UK's renegotiations at the first European Council meeting in Dublin.
11 March	Georges Spenale was elected President of the European Parliament.
18 March	European Regional Development Fund (ERDF) was established.
5 June	UK referendum on EC membership in which 17.3 million voted 'yes' to stay in the EC and 8.4 million voted 'no' to withdraw; 64.55 per cent of the electorate voted.
12 June	Greece formally applied for EC membership.
22 July	Signature of a Treaty strengthening the budgetary powers of the European Parliament and establishing the Court of Auditors.

1 August	Final Act of the Conference on Security and Cooperation in Europe (CSCE) was signed in Helsinki by the 35 nations which took part. It initiated the CSCE process which included human rights provisions and confidence-building measures, regular implementation reviews and follow-up meetings.

1976

7 January	Belgian prime minister, Leo Tindemanns, published his report on political cooperation, which had been called for at the 1974 Paris Summit.
1 April	First Lomé Convention entered into force.
20 September	Signature of the instruments on the election of the European Parliament by universal suffrage.

1977

6 January	Roy Jenkins took office as President of the new Commission.
18 January	Collective bilateral trade and aid agreements were signed with the Mashreq states of Egypt, Jordan, Lebanon and Syria.
8 March	Emilio Colombo was elected President of the European Parliament.
28 March	Portugal applied for EC membership.
April	MacDougall Report on the role of federal finance in overcoming regional differences in the Community.
3 May	Trade agreement signed between the EEC and Lebanon.
1 June	Treaty strengthening the budgetary powers of the Parliament entered into force.
1 July	Court of Auditors started operation.
28 July	Spain formally applied for EC membership.
27 October	Roy Jenkins, speaking at the European University Institute in Florence, called for EMU to be put back at the top of the EEC agenda.

1978

3 April	Trade agreement concluded between the EEC and China (entered into force on 1 June 1978).
7–8 April	At the Copenhagen European Council meeting the German Chancellor Schmidt and the French President Giscard d'Estaing discussed the issue of the

European Monetary System (EMS) as a new route to EMU in a private meeting with the other Heads of State and Government.

6–7 July	European Council Summit in Bremen approved the Franco-German plan to establish the EMS.
4–5 December	European Council meeting in Brussels adopted a resolution on the establishment of the EMS.

1979

1 January	European Currency Unit (ECU) was devised as a replacement for the European Unit of Account (EUA).
20 February	Principle of mutual recognition was established by the European Court of Justice in the *Cassis de Dijon* ruling.
13 March	EMS began operation (±2.25 per cent for all participants except the Italian lira at ±6 per cent). The four main concepts of the EMS were the ECU, an exchange and information mechanism, credit facilities and transfer payments.
28 May	Accession Treaty with Greece was signed in Athens.
7–10 June	First direct elections to the European Parliament.
31 October	Second Lomé Convention (Lomé II) was signed between the EEC and the 58 ACP states.
December	During discussions on the UK contribution to the EC budget at the Dublin European Council meeting, Prime Minister Thatcher caused a row by demanding 'our money back'.

1980

1 January	Greece entered the EC. The ECU replaced the EUA in the budget of the EC.
May	Provisional solution on UK budget problem that was intended to last for three years.
13 October	Community foreign ministers reached agreement on the London Report which strengthened and extended European Political Cooperation.

1981

1 January	Greece became the tenth member of the EC.
6 January	Gaston Thorn took office as President of the new Commission.

6–12 November   'Draft European Act' (commonly referred to as the Genscher–Colombo plan) was submitted by the German and Italian governments to further develop European Political Cooperation by creating a common foreign policy and the coordination of security policy.

1982

19 January   Piet Dankert was elected President of the European Parliament.
23 February   Referendum in Greenland resulted in a majority in favour of withdrawal from the EC.

1983

25 January   Agreement on the Common Fisheries Policy after six years of negotiation.
19 June   'Solemn Declaration on European Union' was signed in Stuttgart at the European Council meeting by Heads of State and Government and foreign ministers.
14 September   MEP Altiero Spinelli presented to the European Parliament a draft Treaty establishing the European Union.

1984

January   Establishment of EEC–EFTA free trade area.
14 February   European Parliament adopted by a large majority the Spinelli plan for the draft Treaty establishing the European Union.
12 June   Paris meeting of the seven foreign ministers of the WEU decided to reactivate the organization.
14–17 June   Second set of direct elections to the European Parliament.
25–26 June   Fontainebleau European Council reached agreement on the UK budget rebate, as well as deciding on an increase in the resources of the Community from January 1986 by raising the VAT percentage from 1 per cent to 1.4 per cent. For 1984 the UK received a compensation lump sum of 1000 million ECU and in subsequent years it was to receive two-thirds of the difference between what it paid in VAT and what it received from the Community. Member states also

decided to establish an ad hoc committee on institutional affairs to examine amendments to the Treaty of Rome, under the chairmanship of the former Irish foreign minister, Jim Dooge.

24 July Pierre Pflimlin was elected President of the European Parliament.

26–27 October WEU foreign and defence ministers published the 'Rome Declaration' which demonstrated their decision to increase cooperation within the WEU.

14 November In the first instance of its kind, the European Parliament refused to grant discharge to the European Commission for the implementation of the Community budget for the 1982 financial year.

8 December Third Lomé Convention was signed between the EC and the 65 ACP countries.

1985

7 January Jacques Delors took office as President of the new European Commission.

9 March Dooge Committee recommended the convening of an intergovernmental conference to examine the reform of the Treaty of Rome.

29–30 March Brussels European Council reached agreement on the Integrated Mediterranean Programmes.

14 June Schengen agreement. Belgium, France, Germany, Luxembourg and the Netherlands agreed on the gradual abolition of frontier controls.

28–29 June Milan European Council meeting approved the Commission's White Paper on completing the internal market. The meeting also established an intergovernmental conference to look at numerous issues as well as reform of the Treaty.

2–3 December At a meeting of Heads of Government in Luxembourg of the European Council it was agreed to complete the internal market by 1992. Proposals for institutional reform were pared down to a minimum, with only a limited extension of majority voting and only a modest extension of the powers of the European Parliament.

1986

1 January Portugal and Spain joined the EC, thereby enlarging the membership to 12 member states.

| 17–18 February | Signing of the SEA, which modified the Treaties of Rome. |
| 1 May | Third ACP–EEC Convention entered into force. |

1987

20 January	Lord Henry Plumb was elected President of the European Parliament.
14 April	Turkey applied to join the EC.
1 July	SEA came into effect.

1988

February	Delors I budget package for the years 1988–92. Agreement was reached on the guidelines for increased EC budgets, with tighter and binding controls being agreed on CAP expenditure.
29 March	European Commission publishes the results of a study 'Europe 1992 – The overall challenge' into the benefits of a single market that was based on the work of a group of independent experts chaired by Paolo Cecchini. The study was generally known as the 'the Cost of non-Europe'.
27–28 June	Hanover European Council agreed to Jacques Delors' proposal for a new study on EMU.
20 September	In a speech to the College of Europe in Bruges, Prime Minister Thatcher challenged the supranational influence of the EC.

1989

12 April	Delors Report proposed a three-stage process for EMU, namely linking the currencies together, integration between states and the creation of a European central bank.
2 May	Borders were opened between Austria and Hungary resulting in a massive influx of Germans from the GDR to the Federal Republic. This was the first move towards the fall of the Berlin Wall in November 1989.
15–18 June	Third set of direct elections to the European Parliament.
17 July	Austria applied to join the Community.
25 July	Enrique Baron Crespo was elected President of the European Parliament.

July	Poland and Hungary Assistance for Economic Restructuring programme (PHARE) was established, and was thereafter extended in 1990 to include other East European states.
September	Collapse of Communist governments in eastern Europe. Trade and cooperation agreements were concluded between the EEC and Poland.
9 November	Collapse of the Berlin Wall.
17 November	In Czechoslovakia a student demonstration marked the start of the Velvet Revolution which led to the collapse of the Communist government, with Václav Havel becoming the country's first non-communist president.
15 December	Fourth Lomé Convention was signed between the EC and 69 ACP countries.

1990

29 May	The founding charter of the EBRD was signed in Paris at the Elysée Palace by representatives of 40 countries, the EC Commission and the European Investment Bank.
8 June	Turnberry NATO foreign ministers meeting issued a 'Message from Turnberry' which noted their determination to grasp the opportunities resulting from the changes in Europe, and to extend friendship and cooperation to the Soviet Union and other European countries.
19 June	Schengen Agreement to abolish border checks was signed by Belgium, Luxembourg, the Netherlands, France and Germany.
25–26 June	Dublin European Council agreed to the establishment of a second intergovernmental conference that would concentrate on the political construction of Europe. The parallel IGCs would take place in Rome on 13–14 December 1990 to amend the Treaty of Rome in order to allow the introduction of political union and EMU by 1 January 1993.
1 July	Stage I of EMU formally began. This meant that limited monetary functions and the technical preparations for the Monetary Institute were carried out by the Committee of Central Bank Governors. The German Union Treaty also entered into force. German monetary union was established.
3 July	Cyprus applied to join the EC.

6 July	NATO Summit in London produced the London Summit Declaration on a Transformed North Atlantic Alliance. Major steps were announced to bring East–West confrontation to an end, including a fundamental review of NATO strategy and arms control initiatives.
16 July	Malta applied to join the EC.
31 August	Treaty signed between the GDR and FRG for German unification.
12 September	Two-Plus-Four Treaty on the Final Settlement with respect to the reunification of Germany.
3 October	Reunification of Germany was marked by the incorporation of the former GDR into the FRG as three separate Länder.
19–21 November	Paris Summit of Conference on Security and Cooperation in Europe at which 34 Heads of State or Government signed a Charter for a New Europe.
23 November	Transatlantic Declaration on EC–USA relations.
27 November	Italy became the sixth EC country to sign the Schengen agreement, while Portugal and Spain joined the system as observers.
15 December	Opening of intergovernmental conferences on EMU and political union which resulted in the Maastricht Treaty on European Union.

1991

15 February	Czechoslovakia, Hungary and Poland signed the Visegrad Declaration.
15 April	Inauguration of the European Bank for Reconstruction and Development.
16 May	Start of civil war in Yugoslavia due to ethnic and political tensions.
25 June	First steps towards the breakup of the Yugoslav Federation commence with the proclamation of the independence of Croatia and Slovenia.
1 July	Sweden applied for membership of the EC.
1 July	Warsaw Treaty Organization was disbanded.
19 August	President Gorbachev was overthrown in the USSR.
3 September	EC foreign ministers meeting in The Hague. Lord Carrington was appointed Chair of the Peace Conference of the former Yugoslavia.
10 October	European Parliament voted to increase the number of German MEPs from 81 to 99 in order to take account of unification.

7–8 November	Rome NATO ministerial meeting discussed the future relationship between NATO, EC and the WEU. Rome Declaration on Peace and Cooperation issued.
8 November	EC formally imposed sanctions on Yugoslavia.
9–10 December	Maastricht European Council produced agreement early on a Treaty on European Union (TEU), including the decision to establish a single currency by 1999.
16 December	Europe Agreements were signed with Czechoslovakia, Hungary and Poland.
20 December	Inaugural meeting of North Atlantic Cooperation Council. Foreign ministers and representatives from the 16 NATO countries participated, as well as six central and eastern European countries and three newly independent Baltic States.

1992

7 February	TEU was formally signed at Maastricht by the EC foreign and finance ministers.
14 January	Egon Klepsch was elected President of the European Parliament.
12 February	Delors II budget package proposed a 30 per cent increase in the EC budget between 1993 and 1997 (subsequently approved at the December 1992 Edinburgh European Council).
14 February	Agreement was reached on the altered EC–EFTA accord to establish the European Economic Area.
18 March	Finland applied for EC membership.
24 March	Month-long Helsinki CSCE Conference began as part of an attempt to resolve its role in post-Cold War Europe.
2 May	European Economic Area was signed in Portugal.
20 May	Switzerland applied for EC membership.
22 May	France and the FRG announced the creation of a joint military corps based in Strasbourg so as to provide the EC with its own military capacity. It would comprise two divisions, 35,000 strong.
2 June	Danish referendum on the Treaty on European Union resulted in a no vote by 50.7 per cent to 49.3 per cent of votes cast, a margin of only 46,269 votes. The turnout was 82.3 per cent.

18 June	Irish referendum on the Treaty on European Union produced a result of 69 per cent for and 31 per cent against.
2 July	Luxembourg ratified the Treaty on European Union.
31 July	Greece ratified the Treaty on European Union.
25 August	International Conference on the former Yugoslavia opened in London. Lord Owen was appointed chairman of the EC-sponsored peace conference after the resignation of Lord Carrington.
20 September	French referendum on the Treaty on European Union produced a result of 51 per cent for and 49 per cent against.
September	The Italian lira and the British pound left the EMS on account of exchange rate turbulence. These events were referred to as 'Black Wednesday'.
26 October	Italy ratified the Treaty on European Union.
4 November	Belgium ratified the Treaty on European Union
25 November	Norway applied to join the EC.
25 November	Spain ratified the Treaty on European Union.
6 December	In a referendum in Switzerland the electorate voted against the Agreement establishing the European Economic Area, which resulted in the suspension of its application to join the EC.
11–12 December	Edinburgh European Council meeting. Agreement was reached on several important issues, including: Danish opt-outs from the TEU; the clarification of subsidiarity and transparency; the Delors II financial package; and the opening of accession negotiations in early 1993 with Austria, Finland and Sweden, and with Norway later in 1993. The agreement reached at Edinburgh saved the process of European integration after it had been stalled since June 1992 owing to the Danish 'no' vote in a referendum.
15 December	Netherlands ratified the Treaty on European Union.
18 December	Germany ratified the Treaty on European Union.

1993

1 January	Single European Market entered into force, implementing the SEA that had originally been drawn up in 1985 and implemented in mid-1987. This meant that there would be free movement of goods,

	services, capital and people throughout all the member states of the EC.
1 January	Czechoslovakia separated into two new independent states, the Czech Republic and the Slovak Republic (or Slovakia).
21 January	Cooperation agreement signed by NATO and Franco-German Eurocorps.
1 February	Negotiations commenced on the accession of Austria, Finland and Sweden.
February	EC signed a Europe Agreement with Romania.
18 May	In a second referendum the Danish electorate voted in favour of the Treaty on European Union. Approval took place after an agreement had been reached allowing Denmark to opt out of participation in the final stages of EMU and the common defence policy.
5 April	Start of negotiations on the accession of Norway.
18 May	In a second referendum, the Danish electorate voted in favour of the Treaty on European Union (57 per cent for and 43 per cent against).
21–22 June	Copenhagen European Council instructed the European Commission to prepare a White Paper on growth, competitiveness and employment. The Council also agreed that Austria, Finland, Norway and Sweden should join the EU by 1995 at the latest, and that the associated countries in central and eastern Europe could become members as soon as they satisfied certain economic and political criteria, which would become known as the 'Copenhagen criteria'.
2 August	UK ratified the Treaty on European Union.
2 August	ERM of the EMS effectively collapsed and agreement was reached to allow currencies to fluctuate within a broad band of 15 per cent either side of their central rates, rather than the 2.25 per cent band for strong currencies or the 6 per cent for the Spanish and Portuguese currencies.
4 October	EU signed Europe Agreements with the Czech and Slovak Republics.
1 November	EC formally became the European Union (EU) because of the TEU.
8–9 November	Brussels General Affairs Council decided to rename the Council of Ministers as the Council of the EU.
5 December	European Commission adopted a White Paper entitled 'Growth, competitiveness and employment

– the challenges and ways forward into the 21st century'.

11–12 December Brussels European Council drew up a short-and medium-term action plan in response to the Commission's White Paper on growth, competitiveness and employment.

1994

1 January Stage 2 of EMU began and the European Monetary Institute was established in Frankfurt as a precursor to a European central bank. Stage 1 of EMU had come into effect in July 1990. Stage 2 was implemented according to the timetable which had been set out in the TEU. This was despite the setback suffered by the EMS when the ERM collapsed in August 1993.

1 January European Economic Area (EEA) agreement entered into force, in which the EU and the five EFTA member states were linked.

1 February Association Agreements between the EU and Poland and Hungary came into effect.

9 February NATO agreed to a United Nations (UN) request to authorize air strikes in the former Yugoslavia. A 20-km total exclusion zone was declared around Sarajevo and the Bosnian Serbs were required to withdraw their heavy weapons from the zone or place them under UN control within 10 days.

30 April Conclusion of accession negotiations with Austria, Finland, Norway and Sweden.

1 April Hungary was the first former Communist state to apply for membership of the EU.

5 April Poland applied for membership of the EU.

11 April NATO planes bombed Bosnian Serb armoured vehicles in a response to the resumption of the shelling of Gorazde.

22 April NATO authorized the use of air strikes against Bosnian Serb heavy weapons within the 20-km exclusion zone around Gorazde unless certain conditions were met. These were an immediate ceasefire; the retreat of Bosnian Serb forces by 3 km from the centre of Gorazde; and the permission of humanitarian convoys and medical evacuations. Furthermore, NATO also authorized the use of air strikes against the Bosnian Serbs in the event of attacks against any UN safe

area, or if the Bosnian Serb heavy weapons entered the 20-km exclusion zones around these areas.

26 April   First meeting of the 'Contact Group' on the former Yugoslavia was held in London. The group comprised representatives of the UK, Russia, France, Germany and the USA. The purpose of the group was to act as a vehicle to present a united front to the warring parties. It concentrated on securing an agreement on a territorial allocation as the first step to a political settlement. As part of this process it produced a map for the various parties to consider.

11 May   Vienna Agreement between Bosnians and Croats established the Bosnian/Croat Federation at 58 per cent of Bosnian territory. The agreement divided the Federation into eight cantons and determined the composition of the federal government.

13 May   Meeting in Geneva of the foreign ministers of Britain, France, Russia, the USA, the EU troika and the Vice-President of the European Commission, with regard to the situation in the former Yugoslavia. The meeting called for a four-month cessation of hostilities and requested negotiations to commence within two weeks, under the aegis of the Contact Group. The basis of the negotiations was to be a territorial division of 51 per cent for the Bosnian Federation and 49 per cent for the Bosnian Serbs.

26–27 May   The conference launching the Stability Pact for central and eastern Europe took place in Paris.

9–12 June   Fourth set of direct elections to the European Parliament.

12 June   Austrian electorate voted in favour of EU membership in a referendum vote.

24–25 June   Although the main business of the Corfu European Council were discussions relating to the European Commission's White Paper on growth, competitiveness and employment, the meeting was overshadowed by the UK's veto of the nomination of the Belgian prime minister Jean-Luc Dehaene as President of the European Commission due to his 'interventionist tendencies'. At the Council the Acts of Accession of Austria, Finland, Norway and Sweden were also signed, while partnership and cooperation agreements were signed between the EU and Russia.

12 July	Ruling by the German Constitutional Court that German forces could take part in armed missions outside the NATO area. The provision was that on each occasion the decision had to be subject to parliamentary approval.
15 July	Extraordinary meeting of the European Council in Brussels agreed on the selection of Jacques Santer to succeed Jacques Delors as President of the European Commission for a five-year term from January 1995.
28 July	Klaus Hänsch was elected President of the European Parliament.
4 August	President Milosevic announced the decision to sever political and economic ties with the Bosnian Serbs because of their rejection of the peace plan.
16 October	Finnish electorate voted in favour of EU membership in a referendum.
13 November	In a referendum the Swedish electorate voted in favour of EU membership.
29 November	European Parliament, Council and Commission adopted the 1995–99 financial perspective.
9–10 December	Essen European Council meeting established the approach for continuing and strengthening the strategy of the White Paper on growth, competitiveness and employment. Special reference was given to measures to combat unemployment and to bring the trans-European networks into operation.
22 December	Schengen Group reached agreement on the abolishment of frontier controls on 26 March 1995.

1995

1 January	Austria, Finland and Sweden joined the EU. The EU's population increased from 345 million to 368 million.
23 January	Jacques Santer takes office as President of the European Commission for a five-year term.
26 March	Schengen Agreement entered into force in Belgium, France, Germany, Luxembourg, the Netherlands, Portugal and Spain.
28 April	Austria became the tenth EU country to sign the Schengen Convention.
2 June	IGC Reflection Group was launched. The first ministerial meeting in Messina revealed that a large gulf existed between the UK and the majority of the oth-

	er member states over the extent of reform that was desired.
9 June	It was announced that the former Swedish prime minister, Carl Bildt, would succeed Lord Owen as co-chairman of the International Conference on the Former Yugoslavia.
12 June	Association Agreements were signed with Estonia, Latvia and Lithuania.
20 June	NATO requested the permission of the UN for air strikes on Banja Luka airport as a response to Bosnian Serb violations of the No Fly Zone.
22 June	Romania formally applied for EU membership.
26–27 June	At the Cannes European Council, member states confirmed 1 January 1999 as the date of the transition to the single currency. Agreement was also reached on external financing, which included the arrangements for the eighth European Development Fund for the ACP countries.
27 June	Slovakia formally applied for EU membership.
12 July	UN and EU demanded the withdrawal of Bosnian Serbs from Srebrenica.
21 July	A meeting was held in London of the EU, UN, NATO, Contact Group and other UN troop contributors to discuss a response to Serb attacks on safe areas.
25 July	International Criminal Tribunal indicted Radovan Karadzic and Ratko Mladic for genocide and Milan Martic for war crimes.
July	EU member states signed the convention establishing the European Police Office (Europol).
13 October	Latvia applied for EU membership.
24 November	Estonia applied for EU membership.
8 December	Lithuania applied for EU membership.
14 December	Signature of the Dayton Agreement on peace in the former Yugoslavia.
14 December	Bulgaria applied for EU membership.
December	EU and United States signed a new transatlantic agenda and joint action plan.
15–16 December	Madrid European Council meeting confirmed that the single European currency was to be introduced from January 1999, in the third and final phase of EMU. It was decided that the currency should be called the 'euro'. It was also agreed that the IGC to review the functioning of the European institutions would be opened on 29 March 1996.

1996

1 January	Entering into force of the customs union between Turkey and the EU.
17 January	Czech Republic applied for EC membership.
20 March	It was announced that the UK could face a major health crisis in the form of a possible link between BSE, which is found in cattle, and the fatal disease found in humans known as Creutzfeldt–Jakob disease (CJD).
29 March	IGC to review the Treaty on European Union with a view to preparing the EU for further enlargement was launched in Turin.
21 May	UK adopted a policy of non-cooperation with the EU until a timetable to lift the ban on the export of beef was settled.
24 May	UK vetoed a EU bankruptcy convention as part of its policy of non-cooperation.
4 June	European Commission announced that it would phase out the UK export ban on tallow, gelatine and semen over the following weeks if stricter health controls were imposed (commencing on 11 June). On the same day the UK government put forward to EU agriculture ministers its plans for the eradication of BSE from cattle herds, which despite some additional safety measures was the reiteration of its existing stance.
10 June	Slovenia applied for EU membership.
June	UK ended its policy of non-cooperation with the EU after agreement was reached on the conditions for the eventual lifting of the ban on British beef.
13–14 December	Dublin European Council meeting reached agreement on a single currency stability pact.
19 December	Denmark, Finland and Sweden signed the Schengen Agreement.

1997

14 January	José María Giles Robles was elected President of the European Parliament.
16–17 June	Amsterdam European Council meeting finalized the treaty which had been negotiated during the IGC, while the newly elected UK Labour government accepted the Social Chapter. However, the treaty did not resolve key institutional questions, including the

reform of voting in the Council of Ministers, the extension of majority voting and a condensing of the European Commission.

16 July   President of the European Commission, Jacques Santer, presented Agenda 2000 to the European Parliament in Strasbourg. This represented a package of plans to cover EU enlargement, the budget and the future of the CAP.

18 July   Austria, Germany and Italy agreed to implement the Schengen Convention from 1 April 1998.

2 October   Treaty of Amsterdam was signed by EU foreign ministers.

12–13 December   Luxembourg European Council meeting reached agreement on inviting six countries to start membership talks in March 1998: Czech Republic, Estonia, Hungary, Poland, Slovenia and Cyprus.

1998

1 February   Europe Agreements with Estonia, Latvia and Lithuania entered into force.

25 March   European Commission recommended that 11 member states adopt the single currency from 1 January 1999 after having examined the statistical data issued by member states on 27 February. Austria, Belgium, Finland, France, Germany, Ireland, Italy, Luxembourg, the Netherlands, Portugal and Spain were all considered by the European Commission to have met the convergence criteria. Denmark, Sweden and the UK had previously opted out of joining the euro in the first wave and Greece was not considered to have met the required criteria.

29 April   Kyoto Protocol on climate change was signed in New York.

3 May   Brussels EMU Council decided that 11 of the 15 EU member states were deemed to have qualified to adopt the single currency on 1 January 1999, namely Austria, Belgium, Finland, France, Germany, Ireland, Italy, Luxembourg, the Netherlands, Portugal and Spain. Denmark, Sweden and the UK had previously opted out of joining the euro in the first wave and Greece was not considered to have met the required criteria.

1 June   Establishment of the European Central Bank (ECB).

15–16 June	Cardiff European Council set out key aspects of the EU's strategy for economic reform to promote growth, jobs, prosperity and social inclusion.
September	Malta reactivated its application for EU membership.
December	European Parliament's refusal to approve the final accounts of the 1996 budget precipitated a crisis in the European Commission.
11–12 December	Vienna European Council reached agreement on the employment guidelines for 1999 and the arrangements for the external representation of the euro, and approved the action plan for the creation of an area of freedom, security and justice.

1999

1 January	Official launch of the euro. It was adopted as the official currency by Austria, Belgium, Finland, France, Germany, Ireland, Italy, Luxembourg, the Netherlands, Portugal and Spain.
12 March	Czech Republic, Hungary and Poland joined NATO.
16 March	European Commission collectively resigned after the publication of the report of the Committee of Independent Experts that tackled the allegations of fraud, mismanagement and nepotism within the Commission.
24–25 March	Berlin European Council reached agreement on Agenda 2000 and asked Romano Prodi to be the next President of the European Commission.
1 May	Treaty of Amsterdam entered into force.
3–4 June	Cologne European Council adopted the first European Common Strategy concerning Russia and issued declarations on Kosovo as well as on the strengthening of the Common Foreign and Security Policy. At the meeting, member states also reached agreement on Javier Solana's appointment as High Representative for CFSP and Secretary General of the Council. Finally, the Cologne meeting adopted the European Employment Pact and established the parameters of the Nice intergovernmental conference as well as setting out an EU Charter of Fundamental Rights.
10–13 June	Fifth set of European Parliament elections.
18 June	Establishment of the European Anti-Fraud Office.

20 July	Nicole Fontaine was elected President of the European Parliament.
September	Romano Prodi took over as President of the European Commission.
15–16 October	At the Tampere European Council (Finland), agreement was reached on guidelines and priorities relating to asylum, immigration, access to justice and combating crime.
10–11 December	Helsinki European Council reached agreement on the opening of accession negotiations with Bulgaria, Latvia, Lithuania, Malta, Romania and Slovakia, while Turkey was recognized as an applicant country. A decision was also taken to establish an IGC in February 2000 to revise the Treaties in advance of enlargement.

2000

14 February	Start of IGC on institutional reform which culminated in the Treaty of Nice.
23–24 March	Lisbon European Council decided on a new EU strategy to strengthen employment, economic reform and social cohesion to reflect the challenges of a knowledge-based economy.
19–20 June	Feira European Council (Portugal) adopted broad economic policy guidelines for the EU and approved Greece's participation in the single currency. The meeting also adopted a common strategy on the Mediterranean region and endorsed an action plan for the northern dimension in EU external and cross-border policies.
23 June	In Cotonou (Benin) a convention was signed between the EU and the ACP states to replace the Lomé conventions (hereafter to be known as the Cotonou convention).
28 September	Danish electorate rejected participating in the single currency in a referendum vote.
7–9 December	Nice European Council concluded the work of the intergovernmental conference on institutional reform and produced a Treaty of Nice.

2001

2 January	Greece became the twelfth member of the eurozone.

26 February	Formal signing of the Treaty of Nice.
23–24 March	Stockholm European Council reached agreement on the introduction of a European financial services market.
7 June	Irish electorate rejected the Treaty of Nice in a referendum.
15–16 June	Gothenburg European Council produced agreement on the framework for the completion of the enlargement negotiations.
11 September	Terrorist attacks in the USA led to the collapse of the World Trade Centre towers in New York.
14–15 December	Laeken European Council adopted a declaration on the future of the EU that included a convention that would prepare the groundwork for the intergovernmental conference.

2002

1 January	Euro coins and notes entered into circulation in the 12 member states of the eurozone: Austria, Belgium, Finland, France, Germany, Greece, Ireland, Italy, Luxembourg, the Netherlands, Portugal and Spain.
15 January	Pat Cox was elected President of the European Parliament.
28 February	Euro becomes the sole currency within the 12 member states of the eurozone. The opening session of the Convention on the Future of Europe took place in Brussels.
15–16 March	Barcelona European Council concentrated on economic, social and environmental matters.
31 May	EU ratified the Kyoto Protocol on climate change.
23 July	After a 50-year period of operation, the Treaty establishing the European Coal and Steel Community (ECSC) expired.
9 October	European Commission recommended that accession negotiations should be concluded by the end of 2002 with Cyprus, the Czech Republic, Estonia, Hungary, Latvia, Lithuania, Malta, Poland, Slovakia and Slovenia.
19 October	Irish electorate voted in favour of the Treaty of Nice in a second referendum.
12–13 December	Copenhagen European Council reached agreement on the accession negotiations with the 10 candidate countries and set the framework for the enlargement of the EU from 1 May 2004. Agreement was also reached that Bulgaria and Romania should join in

2007 and that negotiations regarding Turkey's membership should be decided in 2004.

2003

15 January	Launch of the first EU Police Mission in Bosnia-Herzegovina.
1 February	Entering into force of the Treaty of Nice.
February	Croatia applied for EU membership.
8 March	In a referendum, the electorate in Malta voted in favour of EU membership.
23 March	Slovenian electorate voted in favour of EU membership in a referendum vote.
1 April	Cotonou Agreement entered into force. It was signed by the EU and 77 ACP countries.
12 April	Hungarian electorate voted in favour of EU membership in a referendum vote.
16 April	Treaty of Accession signed in Athens between the EU and Cyprus, the Czech Republic, Estonia, Hungary, Latvia, Lithuania, Malta, Poland, Slovakia and Slovenia.
11 May	Referendum in Lithuania resulted in a vote in favour of joining the EU.
17 May	Slovakia accepted EU membership in a referendum.
8 June	Polish electorate accepted EU membership in a referendum.
14 June	In a referendum, the electorate in the Czech Republic accepted EU membership.
20–21 June	Thessaloniki European Council (Greece) discussed the draft EU constitution that was produced by the Convention on the Future of Europe chaired by Valéry Giscard d'Estaing and accepted it as the basis for the forthcoming IGC negotiations.
26 June	Agreement was reached on the reform of the CAP.
14 September	Swedish electorate rejected joining the single currency in a referendum vote.
20 September	In Latvia the electorate voted in favour of EU membership in a referendum.
4 October	Start of the IGC in Rome with the purpose of creating the first European Constitution.
12–13 December	At the Brussels European Council meeting there was an inability to reach agreement on the IGC negotiations concerning the draft EU constitutional as a result of a lack of agreement over the weighting of votes in the Council of Ministers.

2004

February	European Commission adopted its financial perspectives for 2007–13.
25–26 March	Brussels European Council discussed the progress of the IGC negotiations and highlighted the desire of the member states to agree on the Constitutional Treaty before the June European Council meeting. Member states also discussed the Lisbon Strategy as well as economic, environmental and social issues relating to the EU. Finally, the Council adopted a Declaration on Combating Terrorism in the wake of the terrorist train bomb attacks in Madrid on 11 March.
29 March	Bulgaria, Estonia, Latvia, Lithuania, Romania, Slovakia and Slovenia became full NATO members.
March	Former Yugoslav Republic of Macedonia applied for EU membership.
1 May	Enlargement of the EU to 25 member states with the accession of 10 countries: Cyprus, the Czech Republic, Estonia, Hungary, Latvia, Lithuania, Malta, Poland, Slovakia and Slovenia.
10–13 June	Sixth direct elections to the European Parliament were held in 25 member states.
29 June	Brussels European Council approved the draft Treaty establishing a Constitution for Europe. Agreement was also reached on the nomination of José Manuel Durão Barroso as President designate of the Commission. Agreement was reached on the appointment of Javier Solana as Secretary General of the Council and High Representative for CFSP and Pierre de Boissieu as Deputy Secretary General. Member states also agreed that Javier Solana would be appointed EU Minister for Foreign Affairs on the day of entry into force of the EU Constitution.
20 July	Josep Borrell Fontelles was elected President of the European Parliament.
29 October	Heads of State or Government and foreign ministers signed the Treaty establishing the Constitution for Europe.
4–5 November	Brussels European Council focused on three issues: the preparation of the Mid-Term Review of the Lisbon Strategy; an area of Freedom, Security and Justice, the 'Hague Programme'; and communicating Europe.

November | European Commission headed by President José Manuel Durão Barroso took over from the Commission led by Romano Prodi, with the office to be held until 2010.
16–17 December | Brussels European Council.

2005

12 January | European Parliament approved the European Constitution.
1 February | Association Agreement between the European Union and Croatia entered into force.
16 February | Kyoto Protocol on climate change entered into force.
20 February | Spanish electorate accepted the Constitutional Treaty in a referendum vote.
22–23 March | At a summit meeting agreement was reached on easing the provisions of the Stability and Growth Pact, while a decision was also taken to redefine the objectives of the Lisbon strategy.
13 April | European Parliament gave its approval for the entry of Romania and Bulgaria into the EU, with accession scheduled to take place in 2007.
29 May | France rejected the Constitutional Treaty in a referendum vote.
1 June | Netherlands electorate rejected the Constitutional Treaty in a referendum vote. The combined effect of the 'no' votes in France and the Netherlands threw the ratification of the Constitutional Treaty into doubt.
16–17 June | Brussels European Council.
10 July | Luxembourg voted yes in a referendum vote on the Constitutional Treaty.
15–16 December | Brussels European Council reached agreement on the EU Financial Perspectives for the period 2007–13. This included a deal on reducing the rebate that the UK received from the EU and at the same time increasing the percentage of contributions paid to the EU by other member states, such as France.

Further reading

Websites

There is a huge number of websites devoted to the study of the EU. The most useful is the official site of the EU, which can be consulted at http://www.europa.eu.int and contains links to all of the EU institutions and areas of policy that are dealt with at the EU level. A helpful gateway to a great deal of information is the UK-based SOSIG (http://www.sosig.ac.uk/eurostudies). The European Commission's Delegation to the United States provides an informative website that includes many useful links (http://www.eurunion.org/). Useful national government websites include the UK Foreign and Commonwealth Office (http://www.fco.gov.uk). A full list of national governments can be found on the EU official website at http://europa.eu.int/abc/governments/index_en.html. There are in addition a number of organizations that are devoted to the study of the EU. This includes the University Association for Contemporary European Studies (http://www.uaces.org/), the European Community Studies Association (http://www.ec-sanet.org/), and the Centre for European Policy Studies (http://www.ceps.be/index.php). Research papers focusing on European integration can be accessed at European Integration On-Line Papers (http://www.eiop.or.at). Other organizations that have an interest in EU affairs include the Royal Institute of International Affairs (http://www.riia.org/riia), the Federal Trust (http://www.fedtrust.co.uk), and the Institute of European Affairs (http://www/iiea.ie).

Reference

Bainbridge, Timothy (2002) *The Penguin Companion to the European Union*. London: Penguin, third edition.

Cook, Chris and Paxton, John (1998) *European Political Facts, 1900–1996*. Basingstoke: Palgrave Macmillan, fourth edition.

Dinan, Desmond (1998) *An Encyclopaedia of the European Union*. London: Macmillan.

Hill, Christopher and Smith, Karen (2000) (eds) *European Foreign Policy: Key Documents*. London: Routledge.

Leonard, Dick (2005) *The Economist Guide to the European Union*. London: Economist Books, ninth edition.

Phinnemore, David and McGowan, Lee (2002) *A Dictionary of the European Union*. London: Europa Publications.

Urwin, Derek (1996) *Dictionary of European History and Politics since 1945*. London: Longman.

Vanthoor, Wim F.V. (2002) *A Chronological History of the European Union 1946–2001*. Cheltenham: Edward Elgar.

Young, John W. (1999) *The Longman Companion to America, Russia and the Cold War, 1941–98*. London: Longman.

Introductory texts

Archer, Clive (2000) *The European Union: Structure and Process*. London: Continuum, third edition.

Bale, Tim (2005) *European Politics: A Comparative Introduction*. Basingstoke: Palgrave.

Blair, Alasdair (2005) *The European Union since 1945*. Harlow: Longman.

Bomberg, Elizabeth and Stubb, Alexander (2003) (eds) *The European Union: How Does it Work?*. Oxford: Oxford University Press.

Bromley, Simon (ed.) (2001) *Governing the European Union*. London: Sage/Open University.

Cini, Michelle (2003) (ed.) *European Union Politics*. Oxford: Oxford University Press.

Dinan, Desmond (1999) *Ever Closer Union*. Basingstoke: Palgrave, second edition.

Dinan, Desmond (2004) *Europe Recast*. Basingstoke: Palgrave.

George, S. and Bache, I. (2001) *Politics in the European Union*. Oxford: Oxford University Press.

Jones, Robert (2001) *The Politics and Economics of the European Union*. Cheltenham: Edward Elgar, second edition.

McCormick, John (2002) *Understanding the European Union*. Basingstoke: Palgrave.

Nicholl, William and Salmon, Trevor (2001) *Understanding the European Union*. London: Longman.

Nugent, Neill (2003) *The Government and Politics of the European Union*. London: Palgrave, fifth edition.

Pinder, John (2001) *The European Union: A Very Short Introduction*. Oxford: Oxford University Press.

Richardson, Jeremy (2001) (ed.) *European Union: Power and Policy-Making*. London: Routledge, second edition.

Wallace, Helen, Wallace, William and Pollack, Mark A. (2005) (eds) *Policy-Making in the European Union*. Oxford: Oxford University Press, fifth edition.

Historical survey

Armstrong, David, Lloyd, Lorna and Redmond, John (1996) *From Versailles to Maastricht*. Basingstoke: Palgrave.

Beloff, Max (1963) *The United States and the Unity of Europe*. London: Greenwood Press.

Camps, Miriam (1964) *European Unification in the Sixties: From the Veto to the Crisis*. Oxford: Oxford University Press.

De Porte, A.W. (1986) *Europe Between the Superpowers*. New Haven: Yale University Press, second edition.

Dedman, Martin (1996) *The Origins and Development of the European Union, 1945– 1995*. London: Routledge.

Dell, Edmond (1995) *The Schuman Plan and the British Abdication of Leadership in Europe*. Oxford: Oxford University Press.

Duigman, Peter and Gann, L.H. (1994) *The United States and the New Europe, 1945– 1993*. Oxford: Oxford University Press.

Fursdon, Edward (1980) *The European Defence Community: A History*. Basingstoke: Palgrave Macmillan.

Haas, Ernst (1968) *The Uniting of Europe: Political, Social and Economic Forces, 1950– 1957*. Stanford: Stanford University Press.

Henig, Stanley (2002) *The Uniting of Europe*. London: Routledge, second edition.

Hogan, Michael (1987) *The Marshall Plan: America, Britain and the Reconstruction of Western Europe, 1947–1952*. Cambridge: Cambridge University Press.

Joll, James (1983) *Europe since 1870*. Harmondsworth: Penguin, third edition.

Laqueur, Walter (1993) *Europe in Our Time*. Harmondsworth: Penguin.

Lipgens, Walter (1982) *A History of European Integration, Vol. 1, 1945–47*. Oxford: Clarendon Press.

Lipgens, Walter (1985) (ed.) *Documents on the History of European Integration: Vol. 1, Continental Plans for European Union, 1939–1945*. Berlin: Walter de Gruyter.

Lipgens, Walter (1986) (ed.) *Documents on the History of European Integration: Vol. 2, Plans for European Union in Great Britain and in Exile, 1939–1945*. Berlin: Walter de Gruyter.

Lipgens, Walter (1988) (ed.) *Documents on the History of European Integration: Vol. 3, The Struggle for European Union by Political Parties and Pressure Groups in Western European Countries, 1945–1950*. Berlin: Walter de Gruyter.

Lundestad, Geir (1998) *'Empire' by Integration*. Oxford: Oxford University Press.

Mayne, Richard (1962) *The Community of Europe*. London: Gollancz.

Mayne, Richard (1970) *The Recovery of Europe*. London: Weidenfeld & Nicolson.

Mayne, Richard (1983) *Postwar: The Dawn of Today's Europe*. London: Schocken Books.

Mayne, Richard and Pinder, John (1990) *Federal Union: The Pioneers*. Basingstoke: Palgrave Macmillan.

Milward, Alan (1984) *The Reconstruction of Western Europe 1945–51*. London: Methuen.

Milward, Alan (2000) *The European Rescue of the Nation State*. London: Routledge, second edition.

Moravcsik, Andrew (1999) *The Choice for Europe*. London: UCL Press.

Pinder, John (1998) *The Building of the European Union*. Oxford: Oxford University Press.

Stirk, Peter (1996) *A History of European Integration since 1914*. London: Pinter.

Urwin, Derek (1995) *The Community of Europe*. London: Longman, second edition.

Vaughan, Richard (1976) *Post-War Integration in Europe*. London: Edward Arnold.

Weigall, David and Stirk, Peter (1999) (eds) *The Origins and Development of European Integration*. London: Continuum.

Winand, Pascaline (1993) *Eisenhower, Kennedy and the United States of Europe*. Basingstoke: Macmillan.

Young, John W. (1984) *Britain, France and the Unity of Europe 1945–1951*. Leicester: Leicester University Press.

Young, John W. (1991) *Cold War Europe 1945–1989: A Political History*. London: Edward Arnold.

Memoirs and biographies

Acheson, Dean (1970) *Present at the Creation*. London: Hamish Hamilton.

Beloff, Max (1957) *Europe and the Europeans*. London: Chatto and Windus.

Bond, Martyn (1997) (ed.) *Eminent Europeans*. London: Greycoat Press.

Butler, Michael (1986) *Europe: More than a Continent*. London: Heinemann.

Cockfield, L. (1994) *The European Union: Creating the Single Market*. London: Wiley Chancery.

Duchene, François (1994) *Jean Monnet: The First Statesman of Interdependence*. New York: Norton and Company.

Grant, Charles (1994) *Delors: Inside the House that Jacques Built*. London: Nicholas Brealey Publishing.

Hallstein, Walter (1962) *United Europe: Challenges and Opportunity*. Oxford: Oxford University Press.

Jenkins, Roy (1989) *European Diary, 1977–1981*. London: Collins.

Loth, W., Wallace, W., and Wessels, W. (1998) (eds) *Walter Hallstein: The Forgotten European?* London: St Martin's Press.

Marjolin, Robert (1989) *Architect of European Unity: Memoirs 1911–1986*. London: Weidenfeld & Nicolson.

Monnet, Jean (1978) *Memoirs* (translated by Richard Mayne). London: Collins.

Ross, George (1995) *Jacques Delors and European Integration*. Cambridge: Polity Press.

Spaak, Paul-Henri (1971) *The Continuing Battle: Memoirs of a European 1936–1966*. London: Weidenfeld & Nicolson.

Tugendhat, Christopher (1987) *Making Sense of Europe*. Harmondsworth: Penguin.

Institutions and actors

Alter, Karen (2001) *Establishing the Supremacy of European Law*. Oxford: Oxford University Press.

Beach, Derek (2005) *Dynamics of European Integration: Why and When EU Institutions Matter*. Basingstoke: Palgrave.

Beetham, David and Lord, Christopher (1998) *Legitimacy and the European Union*. Harlow: Longman.

Brown, L. Neville and Kennedy, Tom (2000) *The Court of Justice of the European Communities*. London: Sweet and Maxwell, fifth edition.

Chryssochoou, Dimitris (2000) *Democracy in the European Union*. London: I.B. Tauris.

Cini, Michelle Cini (1996) *The European Commission*. Manchester: Manchester University Press.

Corbett, Richard, Jacobs, Francis and Shackleton, Michael (2000) *The European Parliament*. London: John Harper, fourth edition.

Dehousse, Renaud (1998) *The European Court of Justice: The Politics of Judicial Integration*. London: Macmillan.

Denza, Eileen (2002) *The Intergovernmental Pillars of the European Union*. Oxford: Oxford University Press.

Greenwood, Justin (2003) *Interest Representation in the European Union*. Basingstoke: Palgrave.

Hayes-Renshaw, Fiona and Wallace, Helen (1997) *The Council of Ministers*. Basingstoke: Macmillan.

Hix, Simon (2005) *The Political System of the European Union*. London: Palgrave, second edition.

Hix, Simon and Lord, Christopher (1997) *Political Parties in the European Union*. Basingstoke: Palgrave.

Hooghe, Liesbet (2001) *The European Commission and the Integration of Europe*. Cambridge: Cambridge University Press.

Judge, David and Earnshaw, David (2003) *The European Parliament*. Basingstoke: Palgrave.

Kreppel, Amie (2002) *The European Parliament and the Supranational Party System*. Cambridge: Cambridge University Press.

Newman, Michael (1996) *Democracy, Sovereignty and the European Union*. London: Hurst.

Nugent, Neil (1996) (ed.) *At the Heart of the Union*. Basingstoke: Macmillan.

Nugent, Neil (2001) *The European Commission*. Basingstoke: Palgrave.

Peterson, John and Bomberg, Elizabeth (1999) *Decision-Making in the European Union*. London: Palgrave.

Peterson, John and Shackleton, Michael (2002) (eds) *The Institutions of the European Union*. Oxford: Oxford University Press.

Shaw, Josephine (2000) *Law of the European Union*. London: Palgrave, third edition.

Sherrington, P. (2000) *The Council of Ministers: Political Authority in the European Union*. London: Pinter.

Smith, Julie (1999) *Europe's Elected Parliament*. Sheffield: Sheffield Academic Press.

Stevens, Anne and Stevens, Handley (2001) *Brussels Bureaucrats?* Basingstoke: Palgrave.

Usher, John (1998) *EC Institutions and Legislation*. Harlow: Longman.

Wallace, William and Wallace, Helen (2000) *Policy-Making in the European Union*. Oxford: Oxford University Press, fourth edition.

Warleigh, Alex (2002) (ed.) *Understanding European Union Institutions*. London: Routledge.

Westlake, Martin (1999) *The Council of the European Union*. London: John Harper.

Main areas of policy

Ackrill, Robert (2000) *The Common Agricultural Policy*. Sheffield: Sheffield Academic Press.

Armstrong, K. and Bulmer, S. (1998) *The Governance of the Single European Market*, Manchester: Manchester University Press.

Artis, Michael and Nixson, Frederick (2001) *The Economics of the European Union.* Oxford: Oxford University Press.

Avery, G. and Cameron, Fraser (1998) *The Enlargement of the European Union.* Sheffield: Sheffield Academic Press.

Barnes, I. and Barnes, P. (1995) *The Enlarged European Union.* Harlow: Longman.

Baun, Michael (2000) *A Wider Europe: The Process and Politics of European Union Enlargement.* Oxford: Rowman and Littlefield.

Bretherton, John and Vogler, Charlotte (1999) *The European Union as a Global Actor.* London: Routledge.

Cecchini, Paolo (1988) *The European Challenge, 1992: The Benefits of a Single Market.* Aldershot: Wildwood House.

Cini, Michelle and McGowan, Lee (1998) *Competition Policy in the European Union.* Basingstoke: Palgrave.

Crouch, Colin (1990) *The Politics of 1992: Beyond the Single European Market.* Oxford: Basil Blackwell.

Dyson, K. (1994) *Elusive Union: The Process of Economic and Monetary Union in Europe.* Harlow: Longman.

Dyson, K. (2000) *The Politics of the Eurozone: Stability or Breakdown?* Oxford: Oxford University Press.

Dyson, K. (2002) (ed.) *European States and the Euro: Europeanization, Variation, and Convergence.* Oxford: Oxford University Press.

Dyson, K. and Featherstone, K. (1999) *The Road to Maastricht: Negotiating Economic and Monetary Union.* Oxford: Oxford University Press.

Geddes, Andrew (2000) *Immigration and European Integration.* Manchester: Manchester University Press.

Ginsberg, Roy (2001) *The European Union in International Politics.* Boulder, CO: Rowman and Littlefield.

Grant, Wyn (1997) *The Common Agricultural Policy.* Basingstoke: Palgrave.

Gros, D. and Thygesen, N. (1992) *European Monetary Integration.* Harlow: Longman.

Hantrais, Linda (2000) *Social Policy in the European Union.* Basingstoke: Palgrave, second edition.

Holland, Martin (2002) *The European Union and the Third World.* Basingstoke: Palgrave.

Hooghe, Liesbet (1996) (ed.) *Cohesion Policy and European Integration.* Oxford: Oxford University Press.

Laffan, Brigid (1997) *The Finances of the European Union.* Basingstoke: Palgrave.

Levitt, Malcolm and Lord, Christopher (2000) *The Political Economy of Monetary Union.* Basingstoke: Macmillan.

McCormick, John (2001) *Environmental Policy in the European Union.* Basingstoke: Palgrave.

Marsh, Steve and Mackenstein, Hans (2004) *The International Relations of the EU.* Harlow: Longman.

Matláry, Jane Haaland (1997) *Energy Policy in the European Union.* Basingstoke: Palgrave.

Nugent, Neill (2004) (ed.) *European Union Enlargement.* Basingstoke: Palgrave.

Peterson, John and Sjursen, Helen (1998) *A Common Foreign Policy for Europe?* London: Routledge.

Smith, Hazel (2002) *European Foreign Policy.* London: Pluto Press.

Stevens, Handley (2003) *Transport Policy in the European Union*. Basingstoke: Palgrave.
White, Brian (2001) *Understanding European Foreign Policy*. Basingstoke: Palgrave.

Theoretical and conceptual works

Burgess, Michael (2000) *Federalism and the European Union*. London: Routledge, 2000.
Christiansen, Thomas, Jørgensen, Knud Erik and Wiener, Antje (2001) (eds) *The Social Construction of Europe*. London: Sage.
Chryssochoou, Dimitris (2000) *Theorizing European Integration*. London: Sage.
Hix, Simon (1999) *The Political System of the European Union*. Basingstoke: Palgrave.
Hoffman, Stanley (1995) *The European Sisyphus*. Oxford: Westview Press.
Hooghe, Liesbet and Marks, Gary (2001) *Multi-level Governance and European Integration*. Boulder, CO: Rowman and Littlefield.
Knill, Christoph (2001) *The Europeanisation of National Administrations*. Cambridge: Cambridge University Press.
Moravcsik, Andrew (1998) *The Choice for Europe*. London: University College London Press.
Nelson, Brent and Stubb, Alexander (2003) (eds) *The European Union: Readings on the Theory and Practice of European Integration*. Basingstoke: Palgrave, third edition.
O'Neill, Michael (1996) *The Politics of European Integration*. London: Routledge.
Rosamond, Ben (2000) *Theories of European Integration*. Basingstoke: Palgrave.
Schneider, Gerhard and Aspinwall, Mark (2001) (eds) *The Rules of Integration*. Manchester: Manchester University Press.

Treaty negotiations

Corbett, Richard (1993) *The Treaty of Maastricht*. Harlow: Longman.
Blair, Alasdair (1999) *Dealing with Europe*. Aldershot: Ashgate.
Feus, Kim (2001) (ed.) *The Treaty of Nice Explained*. London: Kogan Page/The Federal Trust.
Forster, Anthony (1999) *Britain and the Maastricht Negotiations*. Basingstoke: Macmillan.
Galloway, David (2001) *The Treaty of Nice and Beyond*. Sheffield: Sheffield Academic Press.
Neuwahl, Nanette, Lynch, Philip and Rees, Wyn (1999) (eds) *Reforming the European Union*. Harlow: Longman.
Westlake, Martin (1998) *The European Union beyond Amsterdam*. London: Routledge.

Index